D1433316

# TALES
## from the
# TAP END

Judy Steel

BIRLINN

First published in 2010 by
Birlinn Limited
West Newington House
10 Newington Road
Edinburgh
EH9 1QS

*www.birlinn.co.uk*

ISBN: 978 1 84158 873 5

British Library Cataloguing-in-Publication Data
A catalogue record for this book is available from the
British Library

Set in Bembo at Birlinn

Printed and bound in Great Britain by
MPG Books, Bodmin

# CONTENTS

# ILLUSTRATIONS

# ACKNOWLEDGEMENTS

I would not have persevered with writing these memoirs had it not been for the early encouragement of Julian Colton. Others who have helped me along the way by comments, criticisms and corrections have been Janice Parker, Maggi and Norman Hackett, Robin Crichton, John Carnegie, Mona Shea, Sheena Jones, Joan Duff, John Nichol, Peter Hellyer, Richard Buccleuch and Lesley Dick. I am grateful to all of them, and especially to Pat Neil who not only did this, and encouraged me as each section was completed, but also acted as an extra proofreader.

At Birlinn, my thanks go to Hugh Andrew, to Kenny Redpath and especially to my editor Tom Johnstone.

Finally, as always, my everlasting gratitude to David, not only for his help with this book, but for the life we have had together.

# DEDICATION

For my sisters,
Joan and Fay,
who were here before me

for my grandchildren
India, David, Caledonia, Hannah, Persia, James and Rio,
who will be here after me

And for all those, above all David,
who have enriched my life in between.

# Prologue

The title of this book is not in Scots: it does not, therefore, allude to the height of Aikwood Tower, nor to the rarefied social milieu in which I sometimes find myself these days.

It came about like this.

David and I, like the Romans, have always found that the bath is an excellent place for having conversations. Unfortunately, the bath we shared at Cherrydene, the home where we brought up our family, was on the small side, and I inevitably found myself in the uncomfortable position of having my back pressed up against the taps.

On one of the many occasions when I complained about this, David replied: 'A woman's place is at the tap end of the bath', and it seemed to me that did sum up our relationship.

'That's what I'll call my memoirs one day,' I warned, abandoning the working title I'd had in my mind up until then, 'Is my coffee sugared?'

This incident took place over thirty years ago, but the phrase never left my imagination. When we moved to Aikwood, and had to plan a bathroom from scratch, we installed a two-person Jacuzzi in a Roman-themed bathroom, created partly in honour of the legion which had occupied the fort on the hillside behind the tower, two millennia previously. The taps of this bath are on the side, and perhaps there is some symbolism in that.

But as I was preparing this prologue, after finishing the book, and long, long after I had named its first section, I realised that there is another meaning to the word 'tap' – and that is the tap-root, the strongest root, of a tree, while the strongest, central branch is the leader. So maybe this is also the story of how I put down my roots in the Ettrick Valley, and of how I provided the sustenance for a leader.

The book is not really an autobiography, it is about memories. Over the years I often tried to keep a diary, especially at elections, but found that I did not have the self-discipline. For the last ten years, however, I wrote a weekly column in the local newspaper: other than consulting the odd one of these, and also a partial record that I made during the restoration of Aikwood, some early family letters, and occasionally checking events in David's autobiography, *Against Goliath*, published in 1989, I have relied simply on my own powers of recall. Family and friends have been very helpful in putting me right where I have got details wrong, and have added some incidents that they have remembered. In one or two cases, I have changed names to avoid embarrassment.

I had for years talked about writing my memoirs, and many people had encouraged me to do so. Indeed, I had made tentative starts, but I am a writer who needs the discipline of a deadline. What spurred me to seek a publisher who would impose this was the parliamentary expenses scandal, and the realisation that so much had changed about the way we run our politics – and especially our elections at grass-roots level – since those heady days of the 1960s and 70s. And I think there are other parts of my life that are vignettes of a broad social history that are worth recording and celebrating.

# Part One

# THE ROOTLESS YEARS

# 1

# *The Road to Damascus*

*February, 1950*
I stand, a stocky girl a couple of months short of her tenth birthday, at a
bus queue in High Wycombe. An event is about to take place which will
influence the rest of my life.

My straight hair is scraped from a side parting into a ribbon which is
constantly coming loose; and I see life through the pair of wire-rimmed
spectacles which I have used for the last year. I wear the uniform of the
Godstowe School, a girls' prep school so posh that, like Eton, it has its
own game. The Godstowe Game is, or was, a kind of cross between
touch-rugby and netball. Do not expect me to remember its rules, which
were as obscure to me then as those of Hogwart's Quidditch in the Harry
Potter books are now. I cannot even recall the school uniform.

But that is not surprising – it is my fourth school in five years, and I
will not last long at it. In the meantime I must play the Godstowe Game,
keep a straight back in case of bad deportment marks, and exercise my
choice to have carpentry lessons rather than Greek Dancing. There are
some things about Godstowe that are bearable. Carpentry is one of them;
it is taught by the only male teacher I will encounter throughout my
entire school career.

Another very bearable school event is happening currently: a mock
election. Four senior pupils, 12 or 13 years old, are candidates: Conservative, Labour, Liberal and Communist. They make speeches, wear
rosettes in party colours. I am fascinated. It is much more interesting than
the Godstowe Game.

For February, 1950, is the time of the second post-war election. Clement Attlee's radical government has gone to the country, which will show
itself just as ungrateful for the creation of the National Health Service as
it was for Churchill's war leadership five years earlier. Attlee will return
to government with a tiny majority, and continue, among other duties,
to host meets of the South Bucks Foxhounds at nearby Chequers. We
have been *en famille* to see him carry out this function, a slight figure in

a raincoat, dull among the scarlet coats of the riders and the glossy sheen of the horses. He certainly does not exude that field of energy that will become known by future generations as charisma, and which will be seen as an essential prerequisite for a leading politician – especially a Prime Minister. Attlee is not surrounded by this aura, nor by security officers.

To the mortification of my family, I burrow through those standing around him till I reach the front. I stare hard at the insignificant looking man who is Britain's Prime Minister, and shout in their direction, 'I've got a great view of him!'

Worse is to come. I sidle up and poke a finger at the shabby raincoat. 'I touched him!'

In 1950, you could get that near to a prime minister. And a Labour Prime Minister saw nothing wrong in huntsmen sipping cherry brandy in front of Chequers before moving off to chase foxes.

Perhaps that was it. Perhaps politics is contagious. Perhaps the course of my life has all been determined by touching a prime minister at a hunt meet.

That's fanciful, and also incorrect. It's the episode at the bus-stop that does it. My bus is approaching, and so is someone sporting a yellow rosette and holding a bundle of leaflets. I sense for the first time the atmosphere of an election, the excitement and the buzz that will be an integral part of my adult life. Even now, I respond to it.

The Liberal election worker – for I recognise his party affiliation by the colour of his rosette – is distributing leaflets to the people in the bus queue. I stretch out my hand for one. To the credit of the party worker, he does not withhold it from me, although it is obvious it will be several elections before I reach the voting age of twenty-one. I take it from him, literally as I board the bus, and settle down to read it.

One policy, positioned in the right-hand column of the front page, jumps out: 'The Liberals are in favour of parliaments for Scotland and Wales.'

'What an excellent idea,' I think, and become immediately committed both to the cause of a Scottish Parliament, and through it, to the Liberal Party.

The bus made its way through the chalky, bosomy Chilterns. I had never lived away from the hills. First, it was the grey Ochils that crowd down behind the hillfoot towns near Stirling, including Dollar, the one where I was born. Then a mixture – the volcanic mass of Arthur's Seat and the politely tamed Blackford Hill which help to give Edinburgh its enviable skyline. For a school year, there were the triple-headed Eildons, landmark of the Borders, blazing broom-gold in the summer and with heather in the autumn, touched always with the magic from legends of the Queen of Elfland, and of Michael Scott the Border wizard.

For the last two years before my parents and their four daughters, of whom I was the youngest by nearly seven years, moved here to rural Buckinghamshire, there was Deeside, with dark forests of Scots pine and the towering Grampians. Now there were the more domesticated shapes of the Chilterns, with their prehistoric designs scored into the chalk and their wide-boled beeches that gave High Wycombe its furniture industry.

All these hills in my short life already, and there were still the mountains of Perthshire to come into it before I would find the hills of home in the Ettrick Valley.

It was an eleven mile journey home through the Chilterns on the top of the double decker bus, plenty of time to read the leaflet. We stopped mainly at pubs with names like the Rose and Crown, the Black Prince, the Fox and Hounds etc. If I managed to save a couple of pence, I could buy a packet of Smith's crisps for the journey home. I would crush them inside the bag, and mete the pieces out to myself at each pub sign.

The sign I disembarked at was the Nag's Head, in Monks Risborough, a picture postcard village of thatched cottages and a twelfth century church. In the mornings, my sister Alison, seven years my senior, was also on the bus, on her way to the equally posh senior school, Wycombe Abbey, where she continued the starry scholastic triumphs that had marked her school career. But in the afternoons, I came home alone. Me, my homework, my bag of crisps, and, on this occasion, a political tract.

I didn't have to cross a road to reach our house, a two-storey extended double cottage which boasted, bizarrely, a covered-over well in the sitting room. My mother did not feel it necessary to come and meet me, because the bus stop was on our side of the road. Getting run over seemed a more likely hazard than being abducted, although I do remember an incident being discussed in hushed tones by my parents, and warnings not to take sweeties from, nor get into a car with, a stranger. 'Why not?' never brought a satisfactory answer. The *something terrible* that might happen was never spelled out. Meantime, I must just avoid sweets, and lifts, from strangers.

(My sister Joan told me, nearly sixty years later, that our mother had an obsessive worry about one or other of us being abducted into the White Slave Trade.)

My parents had no problem, however, about my visits to the village bakery where Mr Eggleton reigned. It was half way along the short road to my home. As my bus reached the Nag's Head, he would be starting to tip flour from the chute in the loft into the ancient mixing bowl, four feet at least in diameter, which was positioned underneath it. He added water, salt and yeast and pressed the switch which rotated both the bowl and its great mechanical arm. Almost every evening, I called in to see the ritual as the dough turned from its separate components into a smooth, sweet-smelling mass; and to help – or, more likely hinder – Mr Eggleton as he carried it to the deep troughs where it would lie swelling over-night. Each evening, he presented me with a roll made from left-overs of yesterday's dough mix, baked that morning, which I ate by the fireside for my tea along with a boiled fresh egg from my mother's hens, and a tomato, before Alison and my father came home.

In the holidays I went in the mornings to watch the team of bakers knead and prove and shape the dough. Mr Eggleton, always patient, gave me elementary lessons in bread-making, including how to plait a roll. I also visited his pigs, which lived beside the bakery. I kept away on the day when their throats were to be cut, but their dying squeals resounded through the quiet village for what seemed a good half hour. All my life I would be able to conjure up that sound.

Mr Eggleton made only white bread, in one-pound square loaves, and they remained uncontaminated by the pigs. At certain times of the day, during the holidays, if I had a commission from my mother to run along to the bakery for one, I had to take a dish towel to wrap the loaf in, or it would be too hot to handle. The crusts were crisp, and at each end, where the loaf had lain up against its neighbour in the oven, the bread was soft and steaming. I peeled off layers on my way home, so that by the time I delivered it, the loaf had a large dip in it at each end.

But on that February night I did not stop to watch the alchemy of the dough. Tonight, I was in a hurry. I had important news for my parents: I have discovered politics. I have discovered the Liberal Party. I have discovered the concept of a parliament for Scotland.

I had only lived in this strange country, England, for less than a year. I was an uneasy transplant, and I yearned for my original soil. There was much I enjoyed about Monks Risborough – Mr Eggleton's bakery, of course, and also an elderly Welsh cob called Johnnie, who lived in the field next to the church and would allow me to clamber on to his broad bare back. But my heart remained in Scotland. At my previous school, in Aberdeen, we wore kilts and we were taught about the wars of Scottish independence. Not just Bannockburn and Stirling Bridge, Robert the Bruce and the spider and William Wallace's betrayal and terrible death, but a host of colourful stories, well told by a teacher, the forgetting of whose name I genuinely regret.

Robert the Bruce and William Wallace were my heroes, along with Captain Robert Falcon Scott. It would be many years before the highly imaginative and historically inept interpretation of Wallace's life in the film *Braveheart* rediscovered him as a folk hero for Scotland, and spread his fame throughout the world. Scott, on the other hand, had already been given the celluloid treatment in *Scott of the Antarctic*, which had been my ninth birthday treat. After our move to England, the highlight of a visit to London with my father had been boarding Scott's ship, the *Discovery*, then moored on the embankment. On a school trip to the British Museum I ignored the Elgin Marbles and the Egyptian mummies and, in a state of high emotion, pressed my nose up against the glass of the case containing Scott's diary, opened at its last, iconic entry.

Alas, in my fifties, I would read and become totally convinced by Ronald Huntford's debunking of the Scott myth *The Last Place on Earth*, and would transfer my Antarctic admiration to those other great men of southern exploration, Roald Amundsen and Ernest Shackleton. But at ten my hero-worship was unabated, and the great ambition of my life was to be the first woman at the South Pole.

But now polar exploration paled beside the immediacy of politics, as I decided that I would campaign, in the spirit of Bruce and Wallace, to establish a parliament for Scotland. Perhaps, instead of going to the South Pole, I would become Scotland's first woman Prime Minister. I did not expect such an obviously sensible policy to take another fifty years to come to fruition: it seemed certain the Liberals were bound to sweep to power with such policies.

And that, I told my parents, was what I had become. They could hardly have been surprised. In a letter just after we had moved south, Alison questioned them, a note of challenge in her writing: 'Does it really matter if (a) Judith meets lots of boys, and (b) is a Scots nationalist?'

Political issues were a part of family conversation, although my parents kept their own voting intentions close to their chests, and they encouraged my enthusiasm.

'Why don't you write a letter to *The Times*,' suggested my father. Maybe it was a joke, but I took up the idea. They provided the stamp. After I had written the letter, urging readers to cast their votes for the Liberals on the grounds that 'After all, why should Scotland and Wales not have their own parliaments?' I decided to add my age – 9 years and 10 months. That, surely, should guarantee publication.

For days after it had disappeared into the maw of the postbox beside the Monks Risborough Rectory, I scanned the letter page of *The Times*. They did not publish it.

I was downcast that their readership was deprived of my words of wisdom, but there were other things I could do for the election effort. I made a yellow rosette, I made a placard, stuck leaflets all over it and marched up and down the quiet street of Monks Risborough (there was only one street), shouting, 'Vote For Brian Law.'

It is an extraordinary feature of my memory that I cannot recall the name of a single person who taught me before the age of twelve; but I can remember the name of the Liberal candidate in the Buckinghamshire South constituency in the 1950 election.

Unlike most of his fellow Liberal candidates in that disastrous election, Brian Law did not lose his deposit. Overall the party gained under ten per cent of the popular vote. Half of their existing twelve seats were lost, and there were only three gains, two of them in Scotland. One was Orkney and Shetland, where a Major Jo Grimond became the MP. The other was in the Scottish Borders, where Archie MacDonald scraped home in Roxburgh and Selkirk, defeating the younger brother of the Duke of Buccleuch. They were all names that would become a part of my adult life.

If the Liberal party's performance in the 1950 election was a disaster, so was my progress at Godstowe School, where I was absorbed neither by its poshness nor its Englishness. Somehow I was always the person actually caught in any piece of childish wickedness. My end-of-term report – the only one I still possess from all my years of education – placed me 24th out of 24. It was, my mother told me, the greatest disgrace that had ever befallen our family. My tenth birthday party was cancelled and an air of gloom hung about the house, to be rivalled only by the atmosphere when my sister Joan's degree from Oxford turned out be third class.

The summer term brought cricket instead of the Godstowe Game. I had a physical fear of the cricket ball, always afraid that it would shatter my spectacles, and if I ventured onto the field without them I could not see the ball, the wickets or even figures on the outskirts of the field. Unlike my classmates, I did not know the rules of the game and had to pick them up as I went along, just as I had to do, equally unsuccessfully, with classroom subjects and the whole different culture of the English Home Counties.

I did not always play. I was frequently banned from the pitch for some misdemeanour, and had to march up and down a strip of concrete instead. I found this mindless occupation preferable to playing cricket, and the misdemeanours proliferated.

There was one good thing about cricket. You had to wear these shoes with reinforced toes. They were very good for kicking – people, not cricket balls. Especially the High Wycombe Grammar School boys, who waited for the same bus as me and who knew by now how to wind me up, by making anti-Scottish remarks or imitating my accent. Now I could kick them with my cricket shoes. This was very satisfactory, for, as they were big boys, they could not kick little girls back. Instead they reported me to their headmaster, who complained to the headmistress of the incredibly posh Godstowe School.

Shortly after this I found myself sitting the entrance exam for another school. I had lasted till the end of term at Godstowe, and had not realised it was also my last day there. A mystery has always hung over my abrupt departure: the most my parents would say, decades later, was that they had been told I might do better at another school.

The other school, my new school, was Berkhamstead Girls School. It was further away than Godstowe and so I was a boarder. For the first time, I flowered academically, but the counterbalance to this was the hell of the boarding house. In the junior house, our heads were inspected monthly with a fine comb for nits. Each Friday we lined up before the matron. 'Syrup of Figs or Milk of Magnesia?' she asked and each Friday I could not decide which was less disgusting.

Then there was the twice-weekly porridge, not smooth and seasoned like my mother's, but lumpy and unsalted. The other girls sugared theirs, but 'Only Sassenachs take sugar on their porridge,' – or so I had been taught by my sisters, so I sprinkled salt over mine, never achieving the right result.

Oh, the dreadful memories of school meals, at Godstowe, at Berkhamstead, and later on! How I hated them – the fatty, gristley stews, the mince from the cheapest cuts with an inch of grease floating over it, the rubbery meatballs that were raw inside, the squares of what was called omelette made with egg powder, which left a wersh taste on the tongue, the cold, solid custard with ribbons of skin, accompanied by coarse, bitter rhubarb. Then there was the pudding I called 'fishes' eyes and glue' that was actually tapioca. Even now I find it difficult to make or enjoy mince or rhubarb – they conjure up for me the misery of school meals. Sometimes I think my passion for cooking and eating fine food is in defiance of them.

But across the road from the boarding houses, in the school itself, there were brilliant teachers who sparked something in me and I raced away, making up for the time before my short-sightedness was discovered when I couldn't read the blackboard, and for that horrible year at Godstowe. I stopped clowning and soaked up knowledge. The teachers were patient, inspiring and encouraging. I wrote and illustrated and bound little books about horses and dogs and showed them to the teachers, who praised them. At the end of the first year I was top of the class, and the family honour was restored. And, joy of joy, I was rewarded with weekly riding lessons all the following year.

Even if I was in trouble in the boarding house – the senior one by this time – riding could not be taken away from me because my parents had paid for it as an extra. We went by car on Saturday mornings to the stables, which were some miles away. Oh, the joy of putting on jodhpurs and not school uniform! The rides were hacks rather than lessons, mainly on a redundant airfield. The horses lived in deserted Nissen huts, and so did the sad-looking, shabby people that we saw on our rides. 'Displaced Persons', they were called, refugees from Eastern Europe: there was no question, in those days, of refusing asylum.

I learned much at Berkhamstead. Apart from lessons, I learned some great hymns. We got plenty of practice at them – weekly church services, morning assembly, and evening prayers in the boarding house. I was no singer, but I enjoyed thundering out such classics as:

> I vow to thee my country, all earthly things above,
> Entire and whole and perfect the service of my love.

or:

> And did those feet, in ancient times,
> Walk upon England's mountains green?

Sixty years later, in New Zealand, two of my old schoolfriends from those days, Sheena Dowling and Moyna Martin, reminisced. Because Sheena and I were to go on a jaunt to France once she returned, I formed part of their conversation. Moyna recalled how I always substituted 'Scotland' for 'England' in Blake's *Jerusalem*. 'And what's more, she belted it out, even though she could never sing in tune,' she added.

Every Saturday and Sunday afternoon our personal sweetie tins were handed to us. Sweets were still rationed, but our parents managed to send a half-term's supply with us. In the boarding houses we were allocated three sweets on weekends only – a fruit gum counted as a half, and a dolly mixture as a quarter. No wonder our teeth were so good. Then we would go for walks. If it was raining we still went, in a long crocodile of black umbrellas. I learned to hate the walks as much as school meals. I had loved exploring the Deeside forests and the Chiltern beechwoods with my father, as he patiently taught me how to recognise trees by their leaves, fruits and bark. Once, deep in the shadow of the summer leaves, we found a colony of bodgers – the disappearing craftsmen of the Buckinghamshire woods who worked chair-legs with unmechanised lathes. My father knew the names of wild flowers and insects, and I soaked up the knowledge he handed on to me.

But school walks seemed to have only one purpose: to get us through Saturday and Sunday afternoons. We walked in the Ashridge woods and on Berkhamstead Common, and I hated it. As with my aversion to mince, I have never re-learned to love walking.

One thing helped to pass the time as we marched along in crocodiles – we educated each other, often with wild inaccuracy, in the facts of life.

'They rub each other,' said one girl, who had managed to observe her mother and stepfather *in flagrante*. 'That's what people do when they are in love. They rub each other and suck each other.' Just what they rubbed and sucked was not very clear to us; nor did we relate such activities to the birth of babies, which I insisted made their entrance into the world via the mother's navel.

For a few, menstruation was beginning. The status of a girl called Angela in my dormitory shot up when her first period came. We, the uninitiates, pooled our sweetie rations to bribe her to let us see her in a sanitary towel. Angela agreed. She knelt on the bed and pulled her pyjama bottoms down and then up in a flash. The sight was certainly not worth the sweeties. I had seen such things before, but at least this time I knew what I was looking at.

Towards the end of 1951 there was another general election, and Berkhamstead too had its school mock election. Here, it was eighteen-year-olds who were the candidates, who made the speeches. Rosettes were sold, and I bought a Liberal one for threepence. Then realisation dawned on me that no-one else in the boarding house, but no-one, was a Liberal. I tucked my rosette between the pages of a book, and when it was discovered, I behaved like St Peter and disowned it. My vote in the mock election was a very secret one indeed.

The whole house listened to the election results on the radio in the senior common room. The whole house cheered at each Tory gain. Why was it so one-sided? I could not understand. My parents had not explained the class-based nature of British politics to me last time round – the conversations in our family were about issues, Scottish self-government and the morality of the war in Korea.

There was certainly nothing for a Liberal to cheer about in the 1951 election. Deposits were scattered to the wind like autumn leaves, and the nationwide vote slid to 2.5%. Among the three seats that were lost was Roxburgh and Selkirk.

# 2

# *Isles of My Ancestors*

*October 1988*

I am with my husband by a roofless cottage on Stronsay, one of the outer isles of Orkney. It looks out over one of the island's three bays, where there is a fine beach of white sand, and the grassy banks include lovage and grass of Parnassus, and where the seals bask in the shallows. We are on Stronsay to look for traces of my ancestors.

We have come to the Orkneys to celebrate the silver wedding of our friends from Edinburgh University, Bill and Sue MacArthur. On my very first day of lectures, I had sat next to Bill in the English Literature class. Full of the excitement and enthusiasm of freshers' week, we had introduced ourselves, and then found we shared the same tutorial group. Bill laughed at my efforts to read from Robert Burns in the group, so anglicised was my voice, and I vowed never to speak the lines of Scotland's national bard again. But our friendship endured.

Many years later, over our dining table, Bill announced to Sue that he had sold his successful printing business in Edinburgh to invest in a fishing boat, and that they would be moving to Orkney. 'You've done what?' she said, appalled. 'You've sold the business?'

He had indeed done so, and they did indeed move, to the island of Sanday, another of the outer isles with a population of three hundred. There they had lived ever since, bringing up their five children and knitting themselves into the fabric of the island community. When Bill's mother, a music teacher, joined them, she set about reviving the great tradition of fiddle playing, and before long there were over thirty fiddle players on Sanday, where once there had been none. Sue taught at the island's tiny secondary school as well as working for the Open University: Bill had latterly started to combine his fishing with his old craft of political cartoons, notably for *The Herald*. I have always admired the MacArthurs and their way of life greatly, although I do not envy it.

The previous day, the day after the joyful celebration in the community hall, eleven of us, bound together from our days as students, had walked along a beach in the north of the island. Bill talked to us of searching it for the drowned body of a neighbour's son: he himself had survived the sinking of two fishing boats. Again I thought, their lives were so different to those of us who lived on the mainland, so much more visceral. Beside us, one seal after another raised its head above the waves and accompanied us, until there were also eleven of them. Then and now, is all too easy to believe the island myths of the silkies, the young women who are drawn away into the waters by their sexual love of the seals. There is something about these animals that sets them apart from the commonplace of the animal kingdom.

The cottage, Grindlay – or, to be precise, the rickle of stone walls – that was before us was where my great-great-grandparents lived. The knowledge had not been handed down to me – I had found it out in the record of the 1851 census at the Kirkwall Registrar's four days earlier.

'Why do you want to know about your ancestors?' asked Jo Grimond, our host in Kirkwall. I was comfortable with him now; in my youth he had been a distant hero.

In the mid–1950s, he had taken over the leadership of a Liberal Party that was all but extinct. He had restored it to credibility by the force of his personality, his original thinking and his ability to inspire – especially young people. He was tall, handsome in a patrician way and charismatic. When David and I were students, he had been Rector of the university, and had unwittingly played a part in bringing us together. Now, it was over twenty years since he had retired as leader, and he spent most of his time in his beloved Orkney with Laura, his formidable wife. She was the grand-daughter of a Prime Minister, Asquith, and had been brought up in sophisticated London society. Throughout Jo's career, she had been at his side. Now she was happy to put her considerable energies into being an Orkney councillor, and it was a long time since I had been over-awed by either of them.

'People like you, from posh families, know all about your ancestors,' I replied. 'People from ordinary backgrounds like mine don't go any further back than our grandparents.' And so I went off to the Kirkwall Registrar, where the records are wonderfully easy to investigate because of the small populations of the island parishes.

The census record of 1851 told me that in that year, my great-grandmother, Annie Fotheringhame, was still 'a scholar' at fourteen, while her brother James, three years her junior, was a cowherd on a neighbouring farm.

Was Annie raised on tales of the silkies? Why was she still at school in her teens? What ambitions, if any, did she harbour? Did she dream, as she looked out onto the cold northern seas, of a life beyond them? Within a year or so of the census, she would have had no time for ambitions or dreams. Her parents died of typhus in this cottage, and she was left as the eldest of five siblings. It was a tailor, not a silkie, who later spirited Annie away from the island of her birth, where she had entered domestic service. Peter Stevenson, journeyman tailor, from the neighbouring and even smaller island of Eday, married her one Christmas Eve when they were both twenty-two.

I took a stone away from the ruins of Grindlay, the nearest I have come to an ancestral home, and kept it carefully. Later I would arrange for it to be built into the garden wall at Aikwood Tower, along with relics picked up on our travels from beside Hadrian's Wall and the Great Wall of China, and a chunk of the Berlin Wall, bought at a party fundraising event. It would remind me of my origins among agricultural labourers in the unforgiving Orcadian soil, if I got above myself, or *au dessus de ma gare,* as we used to say in family parlance.

Meantime there was plenty to explore. Three churchyards, for example. None of them yielded a tombstone inscribed to any of my ancestors. We toured the island in a rickety hired car: vehicles on the Outer Isles require no MOT. We called at places named on birth and marriage certificates and census records: Grindlay, Gutterhole, Holland, Clayquoy.

The roads were quiet, the fields peaceful, even more so than in our own Border countryside. At the roadside, at farm road ends, bicycles were propped up against fences. We pondered this phenomenon, and then realised that the children on the island pedalled down the farm track, left their bikes by the road, and took the school bus. At the end of the day they retrieved the bikes. If we had stopped to examine them, I expect we would have found they were not even padlocked. I wonder where else in Britain, outside the smaller Scottish islands, children could be brought up with such confidence in the honesty of their neighbours.

We trudged over fields to the Stronsay blowhole, where the incoming tide explodes up in a fountain through the earth several yards in from the cliff. Years later, we would visit a similar phenomenon of nature advertised as a tourist attraction in Tahiti, look at each other and compare it unfavourably with this one. We pottered around the main village, Whitehall, named after a house built there in Charles II's reign by the privateer Patrick Fea. My mother, allegedly inspired by Walter

15

Scott's novel of Shetland and Orkney, *The Pirate*, as well as by my father's romantic Orcadian ancestry, decided, during her second pregnancy, to call their baby Patrick Fea if it was a boy. Instead, their second daughter was christened Ann Patricia Fay, and was always known by the last of these names. Some years later, she, Joan and I would come here, and also to Eday.

Our day in Stronsay was magical. The sky was blue, the sea was calm and the sun had a residual warmth. As we called at unlocked front doors in our quest, we were greeted at each one with the same relaxed Orcadian courtesy. No-one seemed to find what we were doing strange, and the bush telegraph worked so well that by the end of the day our arrival at a farm or cottage seemed to have been forewarned. At night, in the pub where we were staying, the bar filled up with Stronsay natives who claimed to have some connection with the almost defunct Fotheringhame surname.

I was the first of Annie's descendants to set foot in the isle of her birth.

Peter and Annie Stevenson lived in Eday for the first few years of their married life. Peter, who had been a journeyman tailor at the time of their marriage, now combined this with crofting, and here their first two children, James and Maria, were born. But the island was too small for Peter, and around 1867 he and his young family set off for mainland Scotland. The boat docked at Leith, and the young family walked from there to Edinburgh, where Peter set up his own business in Dundas Street in the New Town, and they produced another eight children.

Their granddaughter Gladys, my Auntie G, left a description:

> My uncle James and his brother George tailored for their father. I remember a back room in his premises, four or five men sitting cross legged on the floor, sewing or pressing with a heavy goose [tailoring iron] in perpetual gloom reeking of steam and dampness . . . the salon to the front was lined with shelves filled with gentlemen's suitings. He tailored for the legal 'gentry' – advocates, lawyers etc who lived in the New Town and walked each morning about 10 a.m. to the Courts – up the Mound to Parliament House – morning suits, striped trousers and bowler hats, walking sticks and briefcases. In the early evenings a horse drawn cab would come round to collect and deliver their briefs – far too large and important to be delivered by post . . .

Most of Maria's generation followed in their father's footsteps. She herself was apprenticed to a 'court' dressmaker in Moray Place. Models for the dresses would be brought in from Paris twice a year, taken apart and a 'toile' made for a customer. The style would be adapted for the latter's special requirements and the finished dress would be sent to her home by cab. Even in those days, the handmade lace would cost £30-40 a yard. Later, Maria and her sister Barbara set up their own successful business.

Because I am the family scavenger, I fell heir to some old cards of lace that had belonged to Granny MacGregor. Over the years, I have used them all up: the last fragment went to tie my daughter-in-law Lynne's wedding flowers.

# 3

# South African Family Folklore

When my grandmother Maria Stevenson married my grandfather William MacGregor, she was twenty-nine and he was five years her junior. Both my grandfathers died before I was born, and my grandmothers before I was ten, so that when in years to come I too became a grandmother, I had little first-hand experience of the relationship. My recollection of Maria is that of a stout, rather bronchial old lady, still with considerable presence and authority. She had had to show much fortitude in her life. As a young woman, she had been jilted by her sweetheart in favour of her best friend, and apparently she came to William on the rebound. I wonder how long it took her to realise her mistake, for her marriage brought her little happiness and forced her to depend on her own resources in an heroic way.

By the end of the nineteenth century, William and Maria had two living children, Gladys and Ian. It was the time of the Boer War, and two of William's brothers served in South Africa, sending enthusiastic letters about the wonderful countryside and its potential. Neither of them were able to take advantage of it – one disappeared without any record of how he met his end, and the other returned so shattered by his experiences that he spent his remaining years in an asylum. South Africa, however, was to become part of our family folklore.

Gladys – who became known to all her nieces and nephews, and those of the next generation, as 'Auntie G' – used to tell me that her first memory was of being taken along Princes Street on her father's shoulders on the night that the news of the relief of Mafeking came through. 'Have you heard? Have you heard the news?' complete strangers asked each other, cheering and waving Union Jacks. The crowd swept along to the offices of the *Scotsman* to see the great news confirmed in black and white, and, above the crowd, the small girl took in all the sights and sounds.

William was fired by the potential of South Africa. Perhaps he was bored with his work as a clerk in Register House – he had been dux of George Heriot's school – but his mother's impoverished widowhood dictated this fairly humdrum existence. Or maybe the defects of his character were already showing, and any chance of promotion had been blocked. At any rate, the young couple determined to emigrate. But as the Boer war ended, and Queen Victoria died, Maria was pregnant again. It was decided that she should stay behind until after the birth, while William went on ahead.

He wrote to her after his arrival. He told her about the marvellous job he had found, the house they would live in. But he sent no money. The baby, my father, was named after William, but always known by his second name, Douglas.

Maria was left without support. Her former business had disintegrated under the management of her incompetent sisters, who had taken it over when both she and Barbara, who had run it until then, were married, and the latter left for New Zealand with her new husband. 'I never saw my favourite sister again,' said Maria sadly, many years later. Now, left alone, she took in sewing and let out part of the flat. Eventually, to pay for their passage, she sold all the furniture and set off with her children, aged seven, four and one, for South Africa.

In Durban she found there was no house, and William had no job. They did, however, have relatives who took them in, and Maria got a job well below her capabilities, making alterations in a Durban clothes store. Eventually William found a job as a clerk on the South African Railways, and the family moved to Ladysmith. Maria loved South Africa, but William's drinking habits and general irresponsibility made life with him intolerable.

A curious episode in the folklore of my family arose out of that South African sojourn. We always called it *The Story of Marguerite*.

The MacGregors had become friendly with a family of Boer farmers, the de Jegers. There were two daughters in the family, and Annie, at eighteen the elder, had a wonderful singing voice. She took private singing lessons from a Scot, Grant Taylor, who had been introduced to them by my grandfather. It was an old, old story. He was married, they became lovers, she became pregnant. She confided in Maria, who concocted a plan with her.

Maria – and, no doubt, Grant Taylor – persuaded the de Jegers that Annie's voice deserved better training than South Africa could offer. They agreed to send her to Edinburgh in Maria's care, and to pay for the fares of all the family except for Douglas, the youngest, who would be left with them as a kind of surety, a little hostage.

De Jeger, the Boer farmer, adored the little boy, who started school on the farm, in a tin hut together with children of different races. A little 'Kaffir' girl was appointed to look after his needs. 'She was like a little slave to me,' he recalled, but not happily. The 'little slave' could not tie the bows on the laces of Douglas's shoes. She was strapped to a tree and whipped with a sjambok. Fifty years later, he would tell me the story with a sense of anger, helplessness and guilt.

My grandfather, William MacGregor, had accumulated debts; Maria had to sell everything before her return to Scotland, as she had had to for her outward voyage. Once in Edinburgh, she rented a flat and supported her family, but while they were waiting for the birth, Annie developed a condition called 'white leg'. It was a condition that was potentially fatal, and the doctor advised Maria to write and tell her father what the situation was. So the whole story was revealed in South Africa. Grant Taylor, arriving at the farm, was horsewhipped from the house. He then returned to Britain, working his way on a boat, and called at the house where Maria and Annie were living. Maria refused either to let him in or to see Annie. It seems incredible, and there might have been a different ending – of some kind – to the story if she had been kinder; but her youngest son was half a world away, in the care of the very people who must have felt that she had betrayed them.

Annie gave birth to a baby daughter, her name registered as Marguerite after the heroine of *Faust*. Then she returned to Natal on her own, leaving the baby behind. Maria loved her little charge deeply. She wanted to keep Marguerite and bring her up herself, and wrote to South Africa to say so. But the grandfather was adamant: the child, the daughter of sin, must be cast out from family life.

For a year Maria looked after the baby: she could sing, but not speak yet. Then a lawyer's letter arrived, telling her that a nurse from the orphanage would come to collect Marguerite on a certain day 'at five o'clock'.

On that winter evening, she and Gladys sat in their home in Dundas Street with the baby. Beside her was a collection of little clothes that Maria had made. They waited for the clock to strike. As it did so, the hooves of a carriage horse were heard outside, stopping at their door. The nurse knocked on the door and came in to take the baby.

'That's her little trousseau,' said Maria, pointing to the last loving task she had carried out for the little girl. But even that was rebuffed.

'She won't need those where she's going,' said the nurse, and the door closed behind her.

Maria kept those clothes for years.

There was a sequel to the story of Marguerite, though whether it is a happy, or even a satisfactory one, I cannot say.

Forty years later, as Maria was near the end of her life, weak from chronic bronchitis, she was being cared for by Gladys in the latter's home. She must have known her time was short, and at the end of a long life fraught with difficulties which she overcame with considerable fortitude, one thing haunted her. Over and over again she repeated it: 'I wonder what happened to Marguerite?'

Gladys began to make enquiries, first of all at the orphanage where the child had been placed. Eventually she tracked her down in Birmingham, and wrote to her. The reply came: Marguerite, who knew nothing of her origins, would come to Edinburgh. It was arranged that Gladys would meet her off the train: Marguerite would be wearing a blue coat.

At Waverley station the train from Birmingham pulled up. Gladys watched the passengers disembark: a smartly dressed woman in blue approached. She moved forward expectantly, but the woman swept on. It seemed that everyone had passed the ticket barrier, and then, far behind the other passengers, Gladys saw a minute, bent figure in blue, hirpling along.

'I knew,' she said later, 'I knew that was Marguerite.'

It was thus that Maria was reunited with her beloved charge.

As a child, the austerity of the orphanage had led to Marguerite contracting tuberculosis of the spine; her later life had been hard and disappointing, and her eventual marriage was miserable. Even her romantic first name had been taken from her. 'Margaret' had been deemed quite sufficient. Why then, she asked, did she have this different form of it on her birth certificate?

Marguerite's gratitude to Gladys knew no bounds. 'You have given me my identity,' she said. Somehow, she scraped together the fare to South Africa and tracked down Annie, who was now respectably married. There was no joyful reunion. At the threshold of her mother's house, she announced herself. She was told by a servant that if she had anything to say, she should get in touch with the family lawyer, and the door was shut in her face.

The unkindness from her blood family was matched on the positive scale by the goodness of Maria's. After her mother's death, Gladys kept contact with Marguerite, and each year the embittered woman would come to the city of her birth and stay in Gladys's beautiful New Town house. It was always a difficult visit, one that Gladys dreaded; but she kept it up over the years out of a sense of – what? Honour to her mother, or deep sadness and sympathy for the life that Marguerite might have led as the granddaughter of a wealthy Boer farmer, or as her own foster-sister?

Gladys, our 'Auntie G', was a remarkable woman, and so was Maria.

In due course, Douglas was taken back from the freedom of the farm and returned to Edinburgh, which he had left as a baby. He was sent back on a six week sea voyage in the care of a woman he had never met previously; at Southampton it was a forgotten uncle who, able to travel to Southampton on a railway employee's pass, met him from the boat. All my father's early memories were of South Africa. William also returned: Gladys's brief family memoir, penned after the death of both her brothers, made clear the welcome he received: 'Needless to say HE followed; he worked his passage home on some ship and arrived on the doorstep. He ultimately left for South Africa about 1912 – he had a minor clerical job in Glasgow to which he travelled daily, contributing as little as possible always, and my mother renting rooms in "a good address in a large flat" and dressmaking.'

There was a final terrible row between my grandparents when they were on holiday. Back in Edinburgh, William's sons made sure that he caught a train that would take him to Southampton and the ship to South Africa. He never featured in the family again. One day in 1936 Joan, then seven years old, asked Granny MacGregor why she was wearing black. 'I'm in mourning for your grandfather,' she said. It was the first that the young girl knew of his existence.

# 4

# *In the Service of the Empire*

My parents met, playing tennis, when they were both students at Edinburgh University in the 1920s. My father, Douglas MacGregor, had been preceded there by his sister Gladys and his brother Ian. They were the first generation of university students in their family, as was my mother, Ann Dyce. She was the eldest child of John Dyce, who worked as a compositor at the *Scotsman*, and his wife Jane Rankin, a tailoress and dressmaker. From both my grandmothers, therefore, I inherit a gene that has made me confident with shears and sewing machine, and when, in recent years, I have felt the need to credit my costume design, I have taken a name which is a combination of theirs – Maria Rankin.

Ann won scholarships to what was then known as the Edinburgh Ladies College and is now the Mary Erskine School, one of the richly-endowed Merchant Company Schools in Edinburgh. At university, she was a brilliant student of English, taking the prestigious James Elliot Prize in her final year. Like the majority of Edinburgh students of their time, both she and my father lived at home: as the children of ratepayers, they were exempt from fees at 'the Tounis College', but they had holiday jobs and would coach schoolchildren to earn a supplement. My mother lived on such a tight budget that it did not even include tram fares: she had to walk to and from the Old College and her home every day, in all weathers.

Teaching was the most usual profession for educated women in the 1920s, though jobs were scarce. My mother found one at a girls' school in Birkenhead, where she was desperately unhappy. Away from home, and from her fiancé, she was bullied by the dreadful headmistress, and found that she didn't really have the right temperament for teaching. But her ordeal was finite: on marriage, she would have to give up her job. In the 1920s, women were not allowed to continue in teaching after marriage. It was taking away employment from the veterans, widows, and perpetual spinsters created by the war. She only went back to teaching for one brief, unsuccessful period in the 1950s: but she never gave the impression that she felt her learning had been wasted in a life as a wife and mother.

My father, meantime, who had graduated in agriculture and forestry, was finding the job market in Scotland as hard then for a young graduate as it is today. A spell working in a timber-yard was all he could find, and after toying with the idea of emigration to Rhodesia, he decided to enter the Colonial Forestry Service in West Africa. It was to be his work for the next twenty years, first of all in northern Nigeria and then in Sierra Leone. It was against this background that the first half of his marriage was spent. His children grew up never setting foot in either country: West Africa was the 'white man's grave,' and no parent would think of exposing a child to the climate and risk of disease there.

Their first tour together as newly-weds, though, must have been a grand adventure. They married in June 1927, in Oxford, where Douglas was doing postgraduate studies in tropical forestry.

Researching the Orcadian side of my family, I found that none of my forebears on that side had been married in church until then. This was not unusual: Scottish marriage customs and laws were very distinctive, and different not just to what was usual south of the Border, but to what we have now. The best known difference was, of course, the fact that from the age of sixteen, young men and women could marry without parental consent, and until the age of majority in England was lowered from twenty-one to eighteen in England in the 1970s, there were many runaway couples who headed for Scotland. But that was by no means the only dissimilarity.

Another Scottish custom was that the minister frequently conducted the ceremony in a house – sometimes the manse, sometimes the bride's house, sometimes the bridegroom's, sometimes at a neutral venue – the Co-operative Hall was a typical one. In England, *places* were licensed for the conduct of marriages; in Scotland, it was always a *person*, a clergyman of some kind, and he could officiate anywhere. I have been to a Buddhist wedding service on a Berwickshire hillside, at which the couple's horses were present. The bride sang her vows through a song by Robert Burns, there was an unfurling of flags, and the celebrant joked that he was agent no. 003, licensed to perform Buddhist marriages.

Until the 1930s, a marriage could take place without even a minister at the ceremony. The bridal couple exchanged their vows *de praesenti* – in front of two witnesses. Later, the couple could go with these witnesses to the Sheriff, attest the ceremony, and be granted an official certificate. But it was the exchange of vows, not the certificate, that legitimised the marriage. It was one of Scotland's three forms of irregular marriage, and it was the one made famous by runaway couples from England at Gretna Green. The legendary blacksmith had only the legal status of a witness, but he certainly managed to achieve a semi-official one.

Another, less well-known form of irregular marriage was *promisso subsequente copula*, where a couple who had promised to marry in the future, and who then had sexual relations on the basis of that promise, were married by the sexual act itself. It was of course, a protection for women, but in the case of a young Frenchman living in Glasgow in late Victorian times, it may have been his death-knell.

The case is a famous one: Madeleine Smith, daughter of a prosperous Glasgow business man, had a passionate affair with Emile l'Angelier. They had promised to marry; however, Madeleine then found a better marital option and broke off with the young Frenchman. He pursued her, writing letters in which he described her as his wife – did he know that in Scots Law, he could claim that in fact as well as sentiment? Madeleine bought arsenic, Emile died of poisoning by the same substance, and at her trial for murder at the High Court, Madeleine received the most notorious 'not proven' verdict in Scottish legal history.

Then there was marriage 'by habit and repute', in which, if the couple lived together as man and wife, then in time they did in fact acquire this status.

My maternal uncle had been married *de praesenti,* but my parents had a church wedding. There they sit, the small wedding party of a couple of dozen, on a bank in the garden of a hotel in Oxford. My mother's bouquet is modest, and there is no veil of tulle, no billowing white dress, no frock coat adorns my father. The dresses and hats of the women are fashionable and festive – especially Granny MacGregor's and Auntie G's. Why are they here in Oxford, where my father had been taking a postgraduate degree in tropical forestry, and not in their native city?

At the beginning of that year, both my Dyce grandparents had been laid low with the flu epidemic that had swept Britain during the previous winter. Ann and her brother Willie nursed them at home, their mother being apparently the more ill of the couple. As she responded to treatment, John Dyce's condition deteriorated and he died. Jane was still so ill that they dared not tell her, but made all the arrangements for his funeral themselves.

As they fed her nourishing soup at night, she began to perk up. 'That was good,' she said. 'Is John getting some as well?' They had buried him that day. A photograph exists, which I found in an old wallet, of the grave covered over with flowers, its headstone already bearing the name of Tommy, who had died of meningitis at the age of three.

Jane Dyce was prostrated by the death of John. She wanted Ann to abandon Birkenhead, put off her approaching marriage, and return to Edinburgh to help support her little sisters. There was no question of a marriage taking place from that distressed household. When the Oxford wedding was mooted, Jane Dyce at first refused to go: she was in mourning; it was not appropriate. It was Gladys, Ann's sister-in-law to be, who broke the impasse and persuaded her to attend.

Douglas's first posting was at Olokemoji, in Northern Nigeria: he was to spend twenty years in the colonial forestry service in West Africa. The fractured family life that this dictated was one that seems unbearable now; but which was shared by thousands of others in the service of the British Empire. The pattern of their lives would be an eighteen-month 'tour' followed by a week's home leave for every month served. Travel to and from West Africa was a three-week sea voyage, stopping at Madeira or the Canaries. These islands, were, to my mother, a kind of Shangri-La.

They would, later, bring back gifts for their daughters from there: I remember the 'Madeira blouse' as an especially valued item in the dressing-up hamper; and I still have the canework, dolls–size three-piece suite from the Canaries that was Alison's. They are probably valuable antiques, or museum pieces, but I would rather my grandchildren played with them.

*January 2009*

*We are into cruises these days, David and I. We have been introduced to it by our friend Michael Shea, who at one time seemed to spend more time aboard ship than on dry land. Saga cruises are the ones we like best: the ships are smallish and stylish. David gives lectures on them on his political life and other subjects, and we do a poetry reading together and call it a working holiday This one is our longest yet – five weeks around Africa. We join the ship in Dakar, a rather unpleasant town in Senegal, where, even despite David's extensive travel experience, including Dakar, we find ourselves fleeced by locals on the make, not once but thrice. Our first port of call after that is Freetown in Sierra Leone, where my father spent the war years and where my mother joined him for those two years after it. The port buildings, on the left, long and low and pitch-roofed, look as though they have not changed since my parents left them to come back to their family for good.I am wearing the sun hat which my mother brought back sixty two years ago.*

My sister Joan was born on their first home leave. When Ann went back to West Africa, the heart-wrenching pattern of leaving her babies behind in Scotland began for her. Joan was left, as many children were, in a kind of private children's home. There, she cried so bitterly and so incessantly that she developed a squint. Auntie G had been told not to visit her for at least a month, so that she would 'settle down,' and not be distracted by the sight of a familiar face. Obviously, better arrangements had to be made.

It was the MacGregor side of the family that provided the solution. Granny MacGregor bought a house at the best address she had occupied so far, Royal Circus on the edge of Edinburgh's New Town, and her children were her tenants. It had four floors: Maria occupied the ground floor, and her three children and their families one floor each, quite independent of each other. My Uncle Ian, a doctor, was also in West Africa, in what was then the Gold Coast. His wife and children were on the top floor, then Douglas and Ann and their children. When the parents were away a nanny would be in charge of the children. Gladys, who was the official guardian to all of these children, and her daughter Sheila were in another flat. It must have been a strange, female-dominated atmosphere for Douglas when he came home in leave, accentuated by the birth of Alison. When the news arrived of a third daughter, he was busy painting a wall in the flat. Gladys, taking the phone call, relayed the news to him. He grunted and carried on painting.

Auntie G had studied maths at Edinburgh University. She was perhaps the best-dressed female undergraduate of her time in the Old College, for her clothes were always made by her mother, and she had the looks and panache to carry the most stylish of garments with distinction. She had many admirers – I once saw a poem that had been addressed to 'Glamorous Gladys', detailing her charms. She was engaged, or about to be engaged, to a divinity student when she abandoned him to marry a dashing South African officer and went out to that country with him.

I cannot visualise her as a minister's wife, but the South African husband turned out to be a grievous mistake. She found life on the family farm stultifying: she had nothing in common with the women of the 'dorp', although she did learn the niceties of table-setting from her mother in law! Her years on the farm were like the book of Exodus: first the drought decimated the crops, then the locusts. The birth of her daughter was terrible, and the young African nurse hired to help with the baby consumed the contents of the bottles. It was some time before

Gladys discovered why the child was not thriving. The farm never paid – and the irony was that, many years after she had been divorced from her first husband, diamonds were discovered on it.

She was determined to return to Scotland, and knew that another child would make such an escape impossible. How I wish her correspondence with her mother had survived! For, back in Edinburgh, Maria visited the Marie Stopes clinic in Abercromby Place, procured a contraceptive device and sent it out to her daughter.

Since the farm yielded no money, Gladys took herself and her daughter off to Johannesburg, where she found a teaching job. But there seemed to be no way of saving up her fare: her salary barely kept the two of them. Then there arrived, from my father, out of his first salary, money to pay her fare.

She came back, ostensibly for a holiday. History repeated itself: the South African husband failed to send her any money either for her upkeep or her return fare, and eventually disappeared from the farm.

Gladys's first, unsatisfactory marriage was over, although it was some time before there was a divorce, and she had to go back to South Africa to fight for it. Although the no-teaching-jobs-for-married-women rule still held, Gladys managed to enlist the help of two formidable ladies, Miss Blackstock and Miss Dougal, who ran St Oran's School in Drummond Place. Somehow, they found a way around the regulations, and Gladys taught maths. Among her pupils were Douglas's three daughters, Joan, Fay and Alison.

My sister Joan, recalling St Oran's, remembers that all the academic work was done in the mornings. Then the school, of about a hundred girls aged from 5 to 18, would use the afternoons for sports, music, art and drama. When, at the age of ten, she transferred to Dollar Academy, no slouch school for academic attainment, she was a year ahead of her age-group and won a scholarship to the prestigious St Leonard's school in St Andrews.

Just before the outbreak of war, Gladys bought her own house in Abercromby Place. In the elegant drawing room of her new home, she married for the second time, to a childhood friend, Sandy Mackenzie, our 'Uncle Sandy'. To me, he was the gentlest of souls, and as a child I did not understand what caused the redness of his nose and the whiff of something unidentifiable on his breath as he would bid me good-night with the eternal phrase 'chin-chin'. He had been a pupil at George Watson's school, had seen service in the First World War, had come home to go to Edinburgh University to read classics – and then spent the rest of his life teaching Latin and Greek to new generations at the same school that he had attended. He was a poor disciplinarian and was always given the weaker classes to teach. 'Sandy Mac' was still an institution at George Watson's when David and his brothers were at that school. In his spare time he compiled, twice a week, the *Scotsman*'s most erudite and devilish crosswords.

When she was in her late eighties, I drove Auntie G back to Edinburgh from what would be, for her, the final visit to my father, her beloved youngest brother. Both of us were consumed by grief, but perhaps hers was sharper than mine. You expect, after all, to outlive your parents, but not your younger siblings. On the dark motorway, the rain lashed the small car I drove: the wipers were faulty and the constant streams on the windscreen replicated our mood. My youngest child sat in the back as she told me the stories of her twenties and thirties, and her everlasting gratitude to my father. He was, she said, the only man in her life who had never let her down. And she repaid him, over the years, in her commitment and devotion to his family.

Auntie G was a presence in our lives almost as constant and influential as our parents. One of the many pieces of sage advice she gave me was, 'Always have friends younger than yourself.' Of course, as I canter towards the finishing post of life and contemporaries begin to fall by the wayside, this advice appears especially sound; but she said it for another reason. Not only was she never lonely throughout her old age, she kept in touch with the modern attitudes and young lives with which she always had such an accepting affinity.

# 5
# *Warbaby*

The outbreak of war in 1939 changed the lives of the young MacGregor family as it did everyone's. Douglas's war work would be the organisation of timber for the troops from Sierra Leone – Freetown, its capital, had at that time the largest deepwater port in the Empire outside the UK. The war years in Freetown are described in *The Heart of the Matter*, Graham Greene's wonderful novel informed by his own wartime experiences there. Douglas and Ann had foreseen the gathering clouds, and decided to move out of Edinburgh at least for the duration of the war, for there would be no question of Ann joining Douglas in West Africa again until it was over. The idea of being with her daughters full-time must have meant that the ill wind blowing over Europe and the world had a certain warmth in it for her.

Poor Alison, I often think, who at this time was reunited with a mother she hadn't seen for two years and separated from her beloved 'Nanny Auld', the mother figure for most of her first six years. With blue eyes and fair, curly hair, she was Nanny Auld's undisputed favourite: now she was moved away from the home and the school she had known, and about to be displaced as the family's baby. For Ann was pregnant again.

Even now I find it difficult to answer the question, 'where do you come from?' since I feel that the right answer is one's birthplace, and that it assumes a long link between family and that place. Both my parents and all my sisters were born in Edinburgh, it was the family base until just before I was born and Auntie G's house in Abercromby Place remained the family focus for different generations until her death in 1988. I was the odd one out. Dollar, which was my birthplace, is a small, pretty town, one of the 'hillfoot' towns at the base of the Ochil hills near Stirling. Its main claim to fame is an excellent school, which was what motivated my parents to buy a house there. Education there at that time was free to ratepayers in Dollar: fortunately, their house was the second one inside the town's boundary.

They may have hoped for a son with this fourth pregnancy, but another daughter duly arrived, on 29 April 1940. I made my entrance conveniently at ten in the morning, so that I was there for my sisters to admire on their return from school. Not only was my birth at home, but so was my baptism: another old Scottish custom.

My memories of Dollar are mainly of high days and holidays, and things to do with the war. I remember the iron railings of the front garden being taken away 'to build aeroplanes', the building of a cairn on the hill behind Dollar when VE Day was announced, and the appearance of unknown items such as ice creams (pale pink 'sliders' of a very watery substance that made both my cousin and myself sick), and balloons – available in only one colour, blue. And of course there is every war baby's seminal experience of The First Banana. I bit through mine, skin and all, spat it out, and refused to try any more. My sisters bore the remains off to school in triumph.

I was a naughty little girl, encouraged greatly by Fay, nine years my senior and always the most like me in appearance, with straight hair and the wide-cheeked, round-chinned face of Annie Fotheringham and Maria. It was she who taught me to hold my nose in the air, put my tongue out, stick my thumbs in my ears, and waggle my fingers, especially at her enemies. My mother, bicycling through the town with her four-year-old on the carrier seat behind her, couldn't see what I was up to, and was appalled when the victim of my rudeness came to the door to complain.

Worse was to come the first time I can remember being taken to church. Bored with the service, I stood on the pew and repeated the manoeuvre at the minister. I was unstoppable. Alison was deputed to take me out and wait with me outside the door. I was determined to get my mother out of that church, and can still recall the intensity with which I screamed and bellowed, while Alison first of all tried to calm me and then threatened me with the police. 'That's the bobby's house,' she said, pointing across the street. 'He'll come and get you.' That didn't work either, and my screams continued until my mother emerged from the church, leaving one highly embarrassed daughter behind on her own. I had a delicious feeling of triumph, of having bent the will of others to mine.

There was a hayfield behind the house, and in the summer my friends and I made houses inside the hayricks. There were the ruins of Castle Campbell a short walk up Dollar Glen, and Dollar Burn that ran through the middle of the town, and the small shops and friendly shopkeepers that existed in all towns of that size. There was even a saddler, and a great treat for me was to be lifted onto the life-size plaster model horse complete with bridle and saddle. In the summer there was a town gala, and a Sunday school picnic to which you had to take your own tin mug. In the winter there was sledging and, more memorably, skating on the frozen pond: but ski-ing as a winter sport did not really exist then.

There were no playgroups or nurseries, but there were plenty of other small girls to be friends with. My best friend was called Catriona Campbell: she was the daughter of the art teacher at Dollar Academy and became a fine artist herself in her adult life. We kept hens and rabbits. The latter were Joan's especial responsibility, and she had a pair named Romeo and Juliet. When they were surrendered to the pot, their skins were cured and she had gloves made from them. I was curious: 'Which is Romeo and which is Juliet?' Of the seven hens, six were brown and one was black: inevitably, she was the only one that was given a name: Martha. We were not told of her identity on the day she appeared on the table until after we had consumed her.

My mother grew vegetables and soft fruit. 'Digging for Victory' it was called, but she and my father went on growing them, in peacetime, all their lives. There was a row of gooseberry bushes, under which, on the advice of my sisters, I frequently looked to see if a baby brother or sister might have arrived. It was Alison, only seven years older than me, who was the firmest in promoting this theory of babies.

'Was that where I was found?' I asked.

'No – you were found on the doorstep with the milk bottles.'

'Why not under the gooseberry bushes?' I wanted to know.

'Because you were a *foundling*,' replied Alison. She taught me a song, and made me feel I was the subject of it:

> Nobody loves me,
> Everybody hates me,
> I think I'll go and eat worms,
> Big fat juicy ones,
> Wee thin squirmy ones,
> See how they wriggle and turn.
> Bite off their heads,
> Suck out their juice,
> Throw the skins away:
> Nobody knows how I can thrive
> On worms three times a day.

This was followed by a pursuit, at the end of which an especially large worm was stuffed down the neck of my jumper. Is it any wonder that I still have a phobia about them to this day?

The war in Europe ended and my father came home on leave. We went on holiday to Arran, the island in the Firth of Clyde. It was one of only two summer holidays that we took as a complete family. There, as the bombs fell on Hiroshima and the war ended in Japan, my parents planned their immediate future. My mother was heartbroken at the prospect of leaving her children again, and didn't want to go back to Africa. There were tears and rows, and even the word divorce – none of which ever were a normal part of their happy married life. They must have worked out a compromise, that they would do one more tour, and then my father would take early retirement from the service that he loved.

July, 1997

*It is the first Saturday in July: the weekend of the Braw Lads' Gathering in Galashiels. Throughout the summer months, each town in the Borders comes alive to the sound of horses' hooves, bands and singing, the sight of hundreds of riders of all ages – and often many levels of horsemanship – following a young man who carries in his hand the town's flag. This one, in Galashiels, is not one of the truly ancient ones – Selkirk and Hawick vie for pride of place in longevity – but it is full of colour, of ceremony, and of civic pride.*

*I am standing on the road bridge overlooking the Tweed, waiting for the three-hundred-strong cavalcade of horses and riders to splash their way across the ford, among them my daughter-in-law. She is a braw lass (but not The Braw Lass): in other words, she was born and brought up in the town. When the river is high, the fording of the Tweed is abandoned: there's been a tragic fatality here in the past, and that was before the compensation culture set in. Nowadays, there's no margin for error. But today, though the current's strong, the crossing, always one of the most spectacular parts of the morning's proceedings, has been cleared. A line of stewards in waist-high fishing waders stand downstream of where the horses will pass.*

*As they wait, they while away the time by skimming flat stones across the Tweed's surface, competing against each other for the highest number of bounces before their stone sinks. Their actions hurtle me almost sixty years back in time, and yet only a mile downstream, to where the riders will make their return fording.*

October, 1945

I am five years old. I am on Boleside Haugh by the Tweed, just across the river and upstream of Sir Walter Scott's Abbotsford, and below an extravagant Victorian mansion known as Glenmayne, between Galashiels and Selkirk. That is where I am at school – a boarding school, at five years old! – with my sister Alison. Our parents have taken us out for the afternoon. My father skims stones across the Tweed: I try, but cannot imitate him. There's a ferry across to the Abbotsford side of the river, and a small wooden hut on the haugh selling tea and sandwiches. Tomato sandwiches are my favourites, but the ferryman's wife, who runs the enterprise, has sold out of them. I am disappointed, and then – what luck! They find another tomato. It's rather a squashy one, but they make it into a sandwich. I do not fully understand that I will not see my parents again for two years. Alison, on the other hand, understands only too well.

This was the school, St Oran's, that my sisters had attended in Edinburgh and which had been evacuated from there to the Borders at the outset of war. (Another Edinburgh girls' school, which became more famous through Ronald Searle's cartoons, also found its wartime base in the nearby mansion of New Gala House: St Trinneans.) There were at least three girls' schools in the city with the names of obscure Celtic saints. Now Fay had joined Joan at St Leonard's in faraway St Andrews, and Alison and I were at St Oran's.

I was not traumatized or upset by my parents' disappearance. I did not really understand the implications of the clothes laid out to be packed in the flat in Royal Circus, nor that this visit would be my last sight of them for nearly two years. I must have been well-prepared for it: I have no seriously unhappy memories either of St Oran's or the school I went to the following year. So much so that, squeezing my way through wishing gates on the way back from school walks by the Tweed, I would shut my eyes and make my wishes 'to have ice cream and jelly for tea,' or 'to see a fairy', but the return of my parents was not something I remember wishing for.

My mother's letters to us, which Alison kept along with her own replies, are heartbreaking. Over and over again, Mummy asks Alison to send news of me; but my big sister is more preoccupied with details of her riding lessons, her exam results, the adventures of her friends. The last page of the Galashiels-bound air letter forms is reserved for Mummy's messages to me, typed in block capitals.

> I saw a little boy about your age on his way to school yesterday, with his school books in his hand, and carrying a bottle of ink on his head. It was just balanced on his cap. Don't try doing that . . .

In another letter, she talks of taking a girl of my age and name to the beach, 'but she was the wrong colour.' Saddest of all is the one which says, 'I wish somebody would take a snap of you and send it to me – is there anybody at St Oran's with a camera? I would like so much to see what you look like with a ribbon in your hair, and with your summer uniform . . .'

Sometimes Alison's letters covered more than her immediate concerns:

> We went to see the Selkirk Common Riding on Fri. morning. We all went in a bus. We got out at the place where they came in and scrambled up a very steep bank at the side of the road. We had to cling on to bits of grass and dig our heels in. First of all we saw the riders coming down the hill opposite. Then they jumped a gate and crossed the river. A lorry came along the road and put down cinders (not enough). Then Seagull came trotting along with the Standard Bearer holding the flag. After that the others came *galloping* along. The first horse came in riderless. We recognised most of Mrs. Rogerson's horses. One horse skidded and went thud on the road. It was only winded luckily. When they had all come in everyone went to the square where they cast the colours. About five men in turn waved flags around in time to music, standing on a kind of box. Lastly, the Standard Bearer gave the flag back to the Provost. It was all marvellous. When I get a pony I'm going to ride in it.

Alas, poor Alison never had a pony, and never rode the Common Riding. The next time I went to the Common Riding was on the back of a horse, nearly twenty years after that first time, which I had totally forgotten about. It was years later that I suddenly had a 'recovered memory' about being on the toll banking, and the horse – ridden by a woman in a riding mac – falling on the road. Alison's description, unearthed by Joan and read by us on the day of the 2010 Common Riding, confirms those memories.

The holidays, at Auntie G's house in Abercrombie Place, were wonderful, despite rationing, despite fuel shortages. She had bought her six-storied house in one of the 'best' streets in Edinburgh's New Town in the late 1930s, and her second marriage had taken place in its long drawing room. Next door to this light, elegant room with Mackintosh-style panelling was her bedroom, centred on a rattan half-tester bed swathed in pink. It resembled something out of a film of that period. She kept that same bed and bedroom furniture until the end of her life: the unchangingness of the house in Abercromby Place was one of its ongoing delights not just to our generation but to the next. (After her death, it was classified as an 'A'-listed building on account of its unspoilt interior.) Uncle Sandy's study was next door, where he composed crosswords for the *Scotsman* and studied his beloved classics. Sometimes I slept on the sofa there, sometimes I shared a room with Fay. Most of the ground floor was taken up by the huge panelled hall and curving staircase, but there was also a small kitchen, a spare bedroom, and what was called the morning room.

That was where Polly lived, a grey parrot which my father had brought back from Nigeria, and which was so uncanny at imitation that after Granny MacGregor died her voice would still echo round the rooms. It ate the tops of our eggs, and pecked my fingers if I poked them into the cage. There was also an antique cloakroom, which had a large old-fashioned lavatory seat and bowl and a pull-up handle. I never saw another one of these until I went to my first banquet at Buckingham Palace. Auntie G and Uncle Sandy lived on these two floors and let out the flats in the two storeys above and the rooms in the first of the two basements below. Like Granny MacGregor, Auntie G had learnt the value of a 'good address'.

The second basement was the realm of her weekly washerwoman, Mary Weir. Large-bosomed, red-faced and red-armed, she radiated kindness, good sense and a down-to-earth attitude to life. In the 1950s, Auntie G's elder grandson was at George Watson's school; his younger brother won a scholarship to Fettes. Mary Weir, on hearing the news, came out with the immortal phrase, 'What I always say is: 'Watson's for education and Fettes for polish.' It became a family saying, one which found its ultimate truth in the person of Tony Blair.

Over the decades, Auntie G tried to persuade Mary Weir – she was always known by both of her names – to accept an up-to-date and labour-saving washing machine, but she always refused to countenance it. In the 1970s, an architect visited the house: he was interested to see the most unspoiled interior in that whole elegant street. He came up from the second basement shaken: 'There's a woman down there with a *mangle*!'

Holidays in Edinburgh, especially for my sisters, were full of visits to other relations and trips to the cinema and theatre, and Auntie G organized parties for them to which boys from George Watson's would be invited. In the summer of 1946 she arranged a farm holiday for us:

'A farmhouse half way between St Fillans and Comrie – at first they wouldn't have us, as "four children" suggested nappies etc. I wrote explaining their ages and how helpful they were making beds etc. – and a letter today said she would let us have three rooms, terms £5 a week – she doesn't *board* people – they're to bring their emergency ration cards and get their own food and she can supply farm produce . . .'

Our arrival, described by Fay in a rare letter which survives from the many that she wrote to our parents, was a rude awakening, and reflects what family holidays were like at that time, when the motor car was still the possession of a minority:

'We got off at 1.10 in a filthy train. Judith found a crossword in a newspaper and was so persistent in her pleadings that poor Uncle Sandy had to do it! Then she kept on saying 'Haven't you done it yet Uncle Thandy? You're awfully thlow.' We changed at Stirling and got into a very packed train in which we had to stand in the corridors. However we didn't have long of that for we soon changed again at Gleneagles. We passed through Crieff and then got off at Comrie, the next stop. There we found our bikes and the trunk and a taxi waiting for us. We piled into this snazzy little Rolls little dreaming where it was going to take us. The road from Comrie to Glen Lednoch is very narrow, stony and hilly and I wondered how we were going to ride our bikes along it. Suddenly the car stopped and the driver, a young ill-mannered boy, said that the trap from the farm would pick us up from there. And he got into the car and drove off and that was our last link with civilization – so we thought. The situation was so funny that Auntie G and I just sat down and roared with laughter. Here we were, five miles from anywhere – five people, a dog, a trunk, several cases, two tennis racquets and not a house in sight. Judith turned round and said, 'But how are you going to play tennith? There'th no tennith court.' This set us off into fresh outbursts of mirth. Suddenly over the hill came a horse and a tiny little trap – our conveyance . . .'

I have three very clear memories of that farm, that possessed neither a car not a tractor – of an enormous apple dumpling baked to celebrate the fortieth birthday of one of the farmer's seventeen children; of the big horses pulling the reaper in the hayfield, while the farm boys tormented a frog which had had its legs chopped off by the machine. And of a mysterious journey, in the dark and in the rain, with the pony and trap, that involved a sack of corn and the whispered words, 'black market'. There may not have been tennis courts, but there was plenty to occupy three middle-class girls on that Perthshire farm.

The same letter of Auntie G's telling my parents about this intended holiday also gave them a sketch of the six-year-old daughter they hadn't seen for eight months, and retains the flavour of the loving atmosphere she provided for us:

> 'She's a funny wee girl – give her a matchbox or something small and trivial and it delights her for a few minutes but she soon forgets and leaves it somewhere – and never does she go out anywhere without 'Something' with her – not a doll or a toy but a 'ten pound note' made by herself or a long bit of string and a few nails in a box. I have christened her "Miss May-I-have?" She has been active these holidays! – There isn't a room or a cupboard or a box of yours that hasn't been investigated and everything taken out. She soon discovered downstairs and alas for all your beautiful tidy arrangements, Douglas – it got quite beyond me – I can't be correcting all the time. It's the house that's at fault, not Judy!! – so I'll just let things go and I'll have a day or two downstairs sorting order out of chaos. Alas I cannot pretend that the family is tidy and methodical . . .'

Austerity, and parental absence, – and the freezing winter of 1946–7 – may have pervaded those two years, but I was a confident child, optimistic and loving and a bit quirky, and knowing that I was loved by all my family, including those far-off two whose airmail letters we looked forward to so eagerly. Once, it was not a letter that came, but a coconut, with my address painted on it, and duly stamped. It was fresh enough for me to enjoy the thin-tasting coconut milk.

My parents returned from Africa for good in the summer of 1947. I was at Waverley station with Auntie G and Uncle Sandy to meet them. Smoke billowed; the train roared and clanked in and stopped at the platform. I was bursting with excitement. People descended and made their way towards the exit. I looked for my parents. 'There they are,' said Auntie

G, and I recognized my father. But where was my mother? I looked around: you can't put photos in air mail letters, so the fact that she had a new hairstyle had not registered with me. I did not know her. I was baffled and bewildered, as this stranger with the upswept hair gathered me to her. In adult life, after the birth of my own children, I relived that moment from my mother's perspective and thought how deeply sad it must have been for her, to have missed two years of my upbringing, and then to be unrecognized. And there has always been something strange, and sad, that none of us knew much about that part of their lives. The only flash we had of it was when our mother – very rarely – produced an exotic dish from West Africa.

We moved to Aberdeen, where my father had a lectureship in the University's Forestry department. Among his students was Kenneth McKellar, who later abandoned forestry for a distinguished singing career. Before that move, however, accompanied by my mother and Alison, he went to Buckingham Place to collect the CBE that he had been awarded two years earlier for his work during the war in co-ordinating timber for the troops, including involvement in the construction of the Mulberry harbours. I stayed with another auntie, and it was then that I was inconsolable at their absence. When they left for London, I was distraught, as I did not believe they would come back in a couple of days. I wept, and my tears mixed with the spilt soft yolk of my boiled egg and ran down my cardigan.

Come back they did, of course, and for two years in Aberdeen I was virtually an only child during the term time. My school, the Albyn School, was another establishment for girls run by another powerful maiden lady, Miss Oliver. If you look at today's exam league tables for Scottish private schools, you will find it at the top. We wore kilts and green jerseys and I made good friends. I cannot believe the amount of freedom that we, aged between seven and nine, and in a city setting, were allowed. We would go considerable distances between each others' houses, unaccompanied, and then range the small, wild, unclaimed bits of Aberdeen, burnsides and small scrubby woods, where we made dams and dens. They were much more exciting than our own gardens, but we were never stopped from going there – or were we never found out? Only the quarry at Rubislaw was firmly out of bounds.

Bread was delivered to the door by a horse-drawn baker's cart. I began by patting his nose, then, as I became more familiar, I asked the driver if I could go up the road on the cart. As the holidays went on the journey became longer and longer, until I went the whole route with the baker's cart, running back and forth up drives and steps to help with the deliveries, my great treat being to take the reins and actually drive. I would have just enough time to help to unharness and rub down Danny at the end before running home for lunch.

Thus began my relationship with that noble animal, the horse. I had a passionate envy, and tried to cultivate the friendship, of the two girls in my class who had ponies at home. I made hobby horses out of old socks and sticks, put on Alison's old jodhpurs, and went along the streets pretending to be on a pony. I read about horses, drew horses, wrote about them. I spent my pocket money on tin models at Woolworths, named them and made them bridles and saddles out of thin elastic and bits of chamois leather. There were Highland dancing lessons at school, skating lessons at Donald's Skating rink and swimming lessons at the Bon Accord baths (always followed by a tuppence ha'penny bag of chips as a 'chittery bit'), but there were no riding lessons.

I was the first of my family with whom my father had spent more than four and a half months concurrently. I have to say that at my age of seven, it must have been a rewarding time for him, and I hero-worshipped this unknown father. At weekends he would take me on the tram to Hazelhead Park on the outskirts of the city. Always I insisted on being on the top deck, and in the last, straight stretch before the terminus the tram would pick up speed and shoogle around in a manner that was almost, but not quite, frightening. At Hazelhead there was the putting green, where he patiently taught me golf strokes, and the maze, a never-ending source of fascination. There, and in the Deeside woods, my father taught me the names of trees, how to tell them by their leaves and barks, and encouraged me to punch the bark of a sequoia – the Canadian Redwood – to feel how cushiony it was.

One day in 1948, when sweets had come off the ration, we queued for what seemed like hours at a kiosk, only to find that the owner had had to impose his own form of control. It was a scene repeated throughout the length and breadth of Britain. In a short span of time, the government was obliged to re-ration sweets, and they were still restricted as late as 1952.

In the summer, there were beaches to go to, and I look back in admiration at my parents, so soon returned from sunbathing on the beach in Freetown, who never shirked the cold waters of the North Sea. A 1929 Morris Oxford, bought in our second year in Aberdeen, meant that picnics could be taken in the countryside further afield: there was almost always the drama of the engine overheating and the search for a burn and water to cool it down.

We hadn't been in Aberdeen for two years before our reunited family was on the move again. My father hated the quibbling and backbiting of university politics, and took a job at the Government's timber research laboratory in Princes Risborough in Buckinghamshire, buying a family house in the neighbouring village. For us girls, it was a major upheaval, a move to a strange land: England.

I crossed the railway bridge over the Tweed at Berwick in a four-berth compartment with my mother and two strangers. My first impression of the other side of the Border was of its red roofs, and after the silver granite and grey slate of Aberdeen I thought this a typical feature of England.

My legacy from the Aberdeen years was one which was to undermine my self-confidence about my appearance until my fifties: I had started wearing spectacles for short-sightedness.

I have described my schooldays in England. My memory of the holidays there is, once again, of a time of great freedom, and of a great friendship.

> When I was ten my mother said:
> *There are new folk along the road,*
> *With a girl your age.*
> And I, greedy for friendship,
> Pedalled my bike along the street
> Of picture postcard cottages
> And awaited your arrival –
> An advent urchin in an aertex shirt.
>
> There followed two years' holidays
> Teeming with the equine passion
> Of pre-pubertal girls.
> Most of all I remember –
> Riding, barelegged and bridleless, the old Welsh Cob;
> Playing at circuses with your rocking-horse,
> The contents of my dressing-up chest,
> And untrammelled imaginations;
> Listening on the radio to the Grand National
> The year it was won by a mare called Nickel Coin;
> Lessons on lead-reins round leafy Chiltern lanes;

And building foot-high jumping courses
For your patient golden Labrador.

I remember too that one wet afternoon
We decided to swear blood-sisterhood,
But quailed at the incision of the knife.

Mary Groves, who was my age, was an only child: her parents had married in their late thirties. She was adored; they were well off. She had all the things I yearned for: a dolls house, a rocking horse and a yellow Labrador. All these she shared with me during those holidays between the ages of ten and twelve.

At the end of each holiday we buried a tin in soft ground beside the churchyard (I cannot remember what we put in it) and ceremoniously disinterred it again when we were reunited at the start of the next one. We rode poor old Johnnie, the Welsh cob, without bridle or saddle or the permission of his owners, until he got so fed up that he bucked us off. And then we climbed back up. There were also official riding lessons, but they rarely coincided – Mary was a step or two ahead of me.

As well as being an only child of devoted parents, Mary was also, even then, a very beautiful child, with long plaits (something else I yearned for, but my hair seemed to get stuck at shoulder length), and the beginnings of that aristocratic English Rose beauty shared by so many of the younger mourners in Westminster Abbey at Princess Diana's funeral. For the first, but certainly not the last time, I adopted the role of the fat friend, the plain Jane, the foil for a beauty.

The idyll of Monks Risborough for my family fell apart in the summer that I was eleven, as my parents planned a house-swap in Edinburgh with Auntie G, and my excitement rose about seeing Scotland again. But before we left, there was a family crisis of shattering proportions.

Alison had sat her school certificate exams in the summer term: she achieved scholarship level in Classics, for which she would be awarded a state scholarship despite her teacher's insistence that 'Girls never get scholarships in Classics.' She was expected to return to school next term to take her Oxford Entrance, where her high-flying academic career would, no doubt, continue.

Occupied with my own eleven-year-old pursuits with Mary, hanging around Mr Eggleton's bakery, shadowing Joan who had just fallen in love with her future husband, and revelling in the freedom of home and the glory of a good report card, I did not notice anything amiss with Alison. But Auntie G, when she arrived, was appalled at the sight of the thin, white-faced seventeen-year-old cowering on the train platform to meet her.

One night, even I was made aware of the turn of events that would change the calm tenor of our family life forever.

We each had our own bedroom, but there was a connecting door between Alison's room and mine. I hear her screaming, that the devil was in her room. I huddled under the bedclothes. 'Get thee behind me, Satan!' she shrieked. I shrank under the covers, I tried to shut out her words, her voice, the sounds of coming and going in the house. Next day there was a strange, strained atmosphere and I was told not to go into Alison's room,

But she waylaid me, and led me into it. There was a force about her which was irresistible. She opened a drawer in her dressing table, and pushed me towards it: two bloodstained cottonwool objects lay there. At the age of eleven, brought up in a household of women, I still did not know what they were.

'Touch them, touch them!' she whispered to me. I stood frozen with terror. 'Touch them – they'll burn you!' She pulled my hand towards them. I was saved by the appearance of Joan, against whose comforting body I hid my eyes. In the night there were more noises, more coming and going, and in the morning Alison had gone, to the first of the many institutions where she would spend a large part of her days. From then on her life, and those of our parents, would be blighted by her mental frailty; and we, her sisters, would likewise be affected by it.

What it must have been like for my parents at this time I can hardly imagine. Education, academic achievement, counted a great deal with them, probably far too much. My sister Fay, in her mid-seventies, still burns with resentment at being dismissed as 'not University material' and being taken away from school at sixteen. And Alison was the high-flyer, the scholarship girl, their pride and delight. Now she was in a locked ward in a state hospital, the recipient of crude electrotherapy and injections of insulin.

But it was not to be talked about. We discuss, nowadays, and wonder at the cloud of shame and secrecy which in the 1950s enveloped illegitimacy and extra-marital sex. The stigma of mental illness was every bit as great, and Alison's was not, initially, manifested by quiet, desperate depression (though that too would become a part of her behavioural cycle), but by irrational, noisy and embarrassing symptoms.

My parents were very happy in Monks Risborough. My father's colleagues and his working conditions at the Government timber research laboratories were congenial; my mother threw herself into village life and the country social round and made good friends. London, where Fay was first at drama school and then a student nurse at St Thomas's Hospital, was a fairly short train journey away. The proximity to Oxford meant there had been close contact with Joan when she was there, and I expect they had foreseen the same scenario over the next few years when Alison followed in her footsteps. In retrospect, perhaps because they had spent so many years away from us, they seem to have kept a very tight leash on us into our twenties; but maybe that was normal for the times.

All in all, I am sure they expected to spend far more than three years in leafy Bucks. But this family crisis changed everything. Many years later, after he was widowed, my father said, 'We ran away. We were so ashamed.' The sadness was that they could not run away from Alison's recurring illness, nor did their sense of shame about it ever really lessen.

Early in 1952, Joan married in the beautiful little twelfth-century church in Monks Risborough. She walked on her father's arm from the house, with me trotting behind holding the train. Stewart's kilt caused something of a sensation in the Buckinghamshire village: 'The bridegroom looked just like the man on the porridge oats packet,' commented one lad who had turned out to see the bridal procession. Needless to say, my parents organised an announcement in the *Scotsman*, and when Auntie G sent them the relevant copy, they spotted an advertisement for a property of fifteen acres, over half of it woodland, on the southern edge of Perthshire, a mile and a half from Dunblane. They bought it, and lived there until they died.

And so, in July 1952, aged twelve, I returned to Scotland on the night sleeper, sharing with three unfortunate strangers who had to endure my tuneless singing of a selection of Scots songs until I fell asleep.

My three years in England had left me with a love of horses and history, with a dream of a Scottish parliament, and with a posh English voice. All of these would remain with me throughout the years ahead.

# 6
# Perthshire Teens

13 March 1996

*I am in the kitchen at Aikwood, waiting for the arrival of Lucy Pappas, a marvellous, energetic woman from Peebles with whom I am to discuss some arts initiative. She is slightly late, and I switch on the kitchen radio to get the lunchtime news. 'A gunman has shot dead fifteen children in a primary school in Scotland.' In dread, I listen to the rest of the bulletin. When the name of the school is given, and it is Dunblane, I burst into tears, and when Lucy arrives, she finds me weeping. Not just for the destruction of those young lives, but for the end of the innocence and anonymity of the small cathedral town beside which I spent my teenage years.*

The property that my parents bought was on the back road between Dunblane and Bridge of Allan, and consisted of a few small fields, a stretch of birchwood, a tiny burn which provided the water supply, and an overgrown glen. There was a somewhat eccentrically-built wooden house, a small cottage, and masses of outbuildings which had been used as boarding kennels. For the first year we were there, there was no electricity, and I did my homework by candlelight. The water supply from the burn was muddy at the best of times, and on occasion small worms would find their way via the system into my bath and, no doubt, into the water from the kitchen taps. (To this I attribute a strong stomach ever since.) In the afternoon, my mother would walk to the nearby farm with a tin can to collect our milk, and meet me as I walked or cycled home from school. There was no rubbish collection at all, and that first summer was spent, in part, digging out the heaps of rusted metal left by earlier owners.

There my parents spent the rest of their lives, my father contentedly making pasture out of some of the woodlands, making tree nurseries out of fields, growing Christmas trees, adapting and re-fashioning the buildings, and keeping a variety of animals over the following thirty years. The first animals I ever saw born were eighteen piglets, in one litter of a large pink sow. He also pursued his career as a forestry consultant, working first of all freelance and then for a consortium of private woodland owners.

Often, in the school holidays, he would take me with him when he went to inspect forests throughout Perthshire and central Scotland and further afield.

The landowners had inherited titles and estates. Some of them had also inherited arrogance, and my father had no time for them: they drove him leftwards in his politics, and he would speak of them contemptuously. But there were men with whom he had dealings for whom he also had great respect – partly related to how they curated their forests, and partly on account of their manners towards those not of their aristocratic class. And there was one landowner with whom he became close friends: Sir John Noble of Ardkinglas in Argyll, whose younger brother Michael became a Tory MP and Secretary of State for Scotland.

The elder brother, however, would have fitted perfectly into the Green Party, as would my father, if it had been active then. John Noble was a landowner who set up small and sustainable industries around his estate, including the Loch Fyne Oyster Company. He was its founding chairman, but it was and is owned by its employees. He was in the vanguard in encouraging Scottish craftworkers to make a living out of their skills. A quiet man, and a great man.

My mother joined my father enthusiastically in all his ploys, and developed her own individual enterprises. Keeping hens was one; hand-weaving was a later and more satisfying one. They were founder members of the Soil Association and such other environmental organisations as existed then.

My teens, and my attitude to where we lived, undoubtedly had two phases. The first lasted for about three years. Happiness at being away from boarding school, relish at the total freedom of the countryside and, eventually, the ownership of a kind, solid Highland pony, made my cup full.

> I travelled this way decades ago,
> A fat girl on a shaggy garron
> Trotting towards another gymkhana defeat.
> The rain blurred my spectacles,
> And the saddle squelched beneath my wet bum:
> But the sodden reins slipping through my fingers
> Reeled out on Eden.

Each year there were only two agricultural shows, with attendant gymkhanas, within hacking distance, and my parents wisely never bought a trailer. Although she was not the pony of my imagination, being rather large and lumbering, I loved Rosie passionately and confided in her more than in any human. My riding was mainly solitary, for there were only a couple of other girls in Dunblane who had ponies. I would go on my own for hours, through the dark spruce woods at the back of the house, and up to Sheriffmuir, with its gathering stone and its monument to the MacRae clan who had fallen in heavy numbers in the battle there during the Jacobite rebellion of 1715. It was a battle in which my supposed ancestor, Rob Roy MacGregor, had played a somewhat dubious part.

There is a little known poem by John Keats which begins:

There is a joy in footing slow across a silent plain
Where patriot battle has been fought, where glory had the gain,
There is a pleasure on the heath where druids old have been,
Where mantles grey have rustled by and swept the nettles green;
There is a charm in every spot made known by times of old,
New to the feet, although each tale a hundred times be told.

It sums up the feelings that I began to have then about the relation between place, the past and the present. There was not only Sheriffmuir: the iconic outlines of Stirling Castle and the Wallace monument dominated the skylines, but for me, half-ruined Doune Castle was more inspirational, allowed my imagination more free a rein. 'Lang, lang may his lady look frae the Castle Doune, ere she see the Earl o' Moray come riding through the toun.' Place: past and present: and its poetry as well. This affinity would reach its full maturity when I was to move to the Borders.

I usually bicycled the three miles to school in Bridge of Allan. Once again, the Beacon School was an all-girls private school, but it was not of the same calibre as Berkhamstead or my Aberdeen school. There was a dreadful snobbery in it, and we were encouraged to look down on children who went to state schools, or, at any rate, not to socialise with them. I have to say that this was an attitude bolstered by my mother. And so I grew up, not only in ignorance of the educational system experienced by most of my contemporaries, but also of those who underwent it. Until I went to university, I knew no-one who lived in a council house.

Television was still rare when the Coronation took place in 1953, and so we were invited with about twenty others to the home of a TV owner. The arrival of the news of the ascent of Mount Everest on the very morning of the Coronation set a seal on the day. We sat in darkness, eating chicken sandwiches and viewing the proceedings on a small flickering screen: the spectacle of the young queen, the pomp and circumstance of the ceremony, and the sight of the bereaved Queen Mother watching with her grandchildren.

*April 2002*

*It's nearly fifty years later, another century, another millennium, and I am in Westminster Abbey, watching the coffin of the Queen Mother pass in front of us. It is only a week since my youngest son burst into our bedroom in our holiday house in France with two pieces of news: 'Your handbag's been found – and the Queen Mum's dead.' In that order. The night before the funeral we had gone to see her lie in state in Westminster Hall, her grandsons standing guard at each corner of the coffin*

*For the first time, seats have had to be found for the Speakers and First Ministers of the devolved nations of Britain, and the Presiding Officer of the Scottish Parliament and his wife – me – have done well, sitting at the front of the choir stalls as the cortege passes. Other politicians and their spouses take their places. I realise that I have not understood that a Royal funeral is an excuse for a millinery parade. Cherie Blair and Pauline Prescott seem to be in a particularly keen duel for ascendancy. I rather regret my plain felt bonnet, borrowed from a friend who had got it from the Red Cross Shop in Selkirk. Maybe I am letting Scotland down.*

*If Queen Victoria's passing marked the closure of the nineteenth century, perhaps the death of the Queen Mother at the age of a hundred and two is the final goodbye to the twentieth. It was half her life ago that we watched those images of the Coronation on the flickering TV.*

If there were no TV stars to idolise in the 1950s, there were film actors – and, in my case, those on radio. On Monday evenings there was a serial called 'Journey into Space', about an imaginary spaceship landing on the moon. The captain of the spaceship, Jet Morgan, was played by a Scottish actor with a particularly rich, sexy voice: Andrew Faulds. In 1966, he was elected to Parliament as a Labour MP. Some of his boyhood had been spent in Africa, and he was an activist in the anti-apartheid movement along with David. One evening, the two of them were sharing a platform in Edinburgh: my children were small and I couldn't go. 'Please bring Andrew Faulds back to stay!' I begged. He had to be back in the south by a certain time on the Sunday, and it would be difficult. My enterprising husband persuaded the stationmaster at Hawick – it was in the days before the Waverley line closed – to have a train make an unscheduled stop at his station to accommodate the visiting MP.

'I really shouldn't do this,' he said, 'it's how the Great Train Robbery was carried out.'

I met Andrew Faulds over his many years in the House of Commons, and when I did, there was always a part of me that was my thirteen-year-old self, lying on the floor with the lights out and listening to those adventures in space. He was a huge flirt, and this trait was always a highly acceptable one as far as I was concerned. At his memorial service in the House of Commons crypt, one of the hymns was 'Praise my Soul, the King of Heaven' with its line about 'dwellers all in time and space'. I thought it hugely appropriate.

One afternoon, when I was about fifteen, I was returning from school when I found a car parked at the bottom of our drive. Picnicking in it were a young man and a small, stout, middle-aged woman dressed from head to toe in tartan, with a couple of feathers in her tammy bonnet. She was the redoubtable Wendy Wood, founder and self-appointed leader of the Scottish Patriots, a breakaway section of the Scottish National Party, an indefatigable campaigner for Scottish independence, albeit often in an eccentric way. She had come to prominence over the use of the title 'Elizabeth II' for the new Queen, asserting that since there had never been a Queen of that name in Scotland before, she was actually Elizabeth I. There was a lot of sympathy for this view, but less for the direct action that some of its proponents were to take: the blowing-up of letter boxes with the new monarch's initials, and the offending number, on them.

I fell into conversation with her, and found that she was to give a speech in the Cathedral Square in Dunblane. I begged my father to take me to it, and he agreed. This fiery, feisty woman spoke of her vision of an independent Scotland, going much further than the Liberal policy for home rule that had captured my imagination earlier, and about which I had rather forgotten since returning north of the Border. Wendy Wood was a charismatic, persuasive speaker, and at the end of the meeting I signed up as a member of the Scottish Patriots.

I did not really follow it up, although I received some enthusiastic, amateurish literature through the post. This included an exhortation to join a muster of the Scottish Republican Army and instructions on how to pack a haversack for this. At school, I spoke to my friends enthusiastically of my new commitment. It reached the ears of the headmistress, who mocked me. Her doing so had one result: I totally lost respect for her. I might be immature and naïve, I might have been mistaken; but at least I was thinking for myself, and I felt that this is not the way a headmistress should behave, that she should have shown some sympathy and encouragement and at least taken me seriously. I also knew that if I had joined the Junior Unionists, as the Young Conservatives were called then, that she would have either passed no comment, or commended me.

My passion for horses included the designing and making of four-inch high felt models of them, equipped with all the saddlery trimmings. I sold some to a craft shop and gave them as presents. I was picked to take part in a children's television programme, *All your Own*, demonstrating how I made them. It featured children with unusual hobbies, which certainly included this one. My mother and I went down to London for the live broadcast, travel expenses and two nights in a hotel all paid for.

'What would you like to see while we're down there?' she asked, and my reply was immediate. 'The House of Commons.'

She got in touch, not with the local Tory MP for Kinross and West Perthshire, but with a Labour MP, James Callaghan, who had stayed with my parents in Sierra Leone. He had been part of a cross-party delegation to the colony, and there had been some discussion among the authorities as to which Brits in the community would undertake to host a Socialist MP. A friendship sprang up between the young Callaghan and my parents that would have a political consequence thirty years later. But my hopes of visiting the House of Commons and meeting him then were dashed – it was the week that Winston Churchill was announcing his retirement as Prime Minister, and Jim Callaghan couldn't get tickets for us at short notice. It would be a decade before I would meet my mother's parliamentary friend, and before I would see the chamber of the House of Commons.

The world outside provided the next stage in my political education. There were two things that came together over a period of months.

In Africa, in North Africa in particular, the nationalist tide was rising. Colonel Nasser came to power in Egypt; distrusted by Britain, France and America, he reacted swiftly when they withdrew financial support for the important project of building a dam at Aswan. He nationalised the Suez Canal, declaring that its revenues would go towards the funding of the dam. The British Prime Minister, Anthony Eden, had an unwavering and irrational hatred of Nasser. He made a secret agreement with the French and Israeli governments, and together they launched an attack on Egypt. Nasser blocked the canal by scuttling the ships in it; international condemnation of the invasion was almost universal, and the advancing armies withdrew.

The invasion of Suez under Anthony Eden's Premiership was to my generation what Iraq is to today's young people. It was illegal, it smacked of a hidden connivance, and although the duration of hostilities was short-lived, it resulted in distrust of Britain in the Middle East amongst the Arab nations. In Britain, it was bitterly divisive, and made its own waves politically. Friends fell out, families disagreed and people left the Tory Party. Eden was broken; he went off to the Caribbean for a recuperative holiday, but his resignation was not long in coming.

My parents were strongly against the invasion, and I absorbed their views. At church, in Dunblane Cathedral, the minister preached a sermon full of support for the decision that had launched British troops into battle. Beside me, my mother quivered with indignation. Was she going to actually walk out? I rather hoped she would, and relished the thought of following her in support. She managed to contain her fury, however, throughout the offering and the last hymn, and although she continued to go to church, she never regained trust in the minister. Politically, I think that up to that time they were probably floating voters, inclined, certainly in my father's case, to the left rather than the right, but from this time on they became definitely anti-Tory. Once again I found myself in a minority of, at most, two or three at school, where Suez was the first political issue that I remember being discussed.

Hard on its heels came the tragedy of Hungary. Under its Prime Minister Imre Nagy, a government had been established that challenged Moscow's domination, and it seemed that this had been achieved successfully. Then, on 4 November 1956, Soviet troops rolled into Budapest, mowing down all opposition. I wept as I heard the final broadcast from Hungary's radio station appealing for help from the West. But the British government, at any rate, did not have any moral authority in the matter, for it had been thrown away in the Suez adventure.

There may have been marches and demonstrations elsewhere at that time, but there certainly weren't any in Stirling. My genuinely deep emotions about Hungary found their way into writing poetry, only an extract of which I remember:

> Now for this love, their love of liberty, their corpses lie,
> Strewn in the gutter, bloody, limp, inert,
> And foreign tanks roll, murdering through the town,
> And Hungary's hopes lie butchered in the dirt.

Classes at the Beacon were small, and some of the teaching was good, especially that of the young history teacher. Some, on the other hand, was rock bottom, in particular that by the science teacher who could not control a small class of middle-class girls and who would from time to time hurl pens, inkpots and pieces of laboratory equipment at us. I was not stretched, but did adequately well, regularly finding the top place in the class in the arts subjects. But by now I was beginning to be distracted by the appearance of boys on my radar.

We did not, of course, form dalliances with the boys from Stirling High School. Instead, we were corralled in a bus and taken to Strathallan, a boys school in Perthshire, to watch their school productions of Gilbert and Sullivan and attend the fifth- and sixth-year dances, where we snogged in the bushes with boys whom we had never met before that night. (If this did not occur, you felt a total failure.) In the Christmas holidays, parents arranged parties for us to meet the boys from other Scottish independent schools. I found myself invited to some of these, and thereby earned myself a place on the outer fringes of the *jeunesse dorée* of the middle classes of Stirling and Bridge of Allan.

The parties, or rather dances, were formal events in hotel ballrooms: we wore long frocks and the teenage boys were in dinner suits or the occasional kilt. Did they actually own the penguin suits, those teenage boys? Conversation was stilted, and there was certainly no alcohol to enliven proceedings. We prepared for them by learning ballroom dancing, bust to bust, as an out-of-school activity. If my memory serves me right, I think that at some of them, we actually had dance cards where the boys could book their partners throughout the evening. I would take my spectacles off on these occasions and everything looked furry, but I still found myself a wallflower.

Twice, during the spring term, we girls packed ourselves into the train from Stirling to the Caledonian Station in Edinburgh, and walked out to Murrayfield to watch rugby internationals. We would be at the turnstiles when they opened at noon, with our ten-shilling notes in one hand and our picnic lunches in the other. Then we'd make our way to the very front of the terracing and await the arrival of the boarding-school boys.

In the spring and summer, the centre of our existence was Bridge of Allan Tennis Club. For the first time in my life, I tried, really tried, to become competent at a sport other than riding. I had hated and tried to avoid, in turn, the Godstowe Game, cricket, lacrosse and hockey. I never hated tennis in the same way; for one thing, the ball was soft and so I never had the fear of a hard ball landing on my spectacles and shattering them. (The chances of this ever happening in any of the other games, were, I realise now, below minimal; nevertheless they loomed large in my imagination every time I took the field.) And we had the mid-1950s gods of Wimbledon, Lew Hoad and Ken Rosewall, on whom to fix our teenage admiration.

My two best friends, half-Swedish sisters, lived beside the tennis courts. The elder, Anne, had a more local tennis hero. 'I used to throw sweeties onto the court in the hope that he would pick them up and look at me,' she told me decades later in Tasmania. The object of her desire was called Roy Erskine, and he is the grandfather of Andy Murray.

Anne and Norah Lynne Carruthers played with me patiently, and it was at their house that we sat transfixed by the black and white images of Wimbledon. But despite lessons and practice, I never mastered the game. There is something that does not co-ordinate between my eye, my hand and the flying white orb. I was as much a wallflower on the tennis courts as in the ballroom, and, while I was supposed to be studying in my bedroom, my self-loathing was poured out into the pages of a tear-stained journal, bemoaning my straight hair, my stubby legs and my spectacles. Anne later confessed to me how, while I envied her athletic build and her crisp, curly blond hair, she flagellated herself emotionally about her plooks, and yearned for my clear skin.

There was something that the three of us did together which no-one else in the group did. We had holiday jobs. Already, they would come up to my parents' house in the Easter holidays and, with me, arrange the two-year-old spruce seedlings into notched clamps prior to planting them out in straight lines in my father's nursery. It was called 'lining out' and was necessary work, and my father must have been glad of our willing, dexterous fingers. Encouraged by him and my mother, and with the acquiescence of their parents, the three of us turned up in the summer holidays at the berryfields in Bridge of Allan to sign up to pick raspberries.

Here we were thrown into the company of the children from the Raploch. It was, and still is, a multi-deprived area of Stirling, where the archetypal 'neighbour from hell', Mags Haney, wielded a reign of terror, and where Thomas Hamilton, the murderer of the Dunblane children, had his home. And where, now, at the time of writing, Scotland's first great 'Sistema' experiment is taking place: the Venezuelan system of teaching motivation and discipline through immersing children in the playing of classical music from an early age.

The Raploch youngsters were tough and mouthy, but I have to say, as a reflection on that era, that I don't remember the use of four-letter words. They were as puzzled by us as we were fascinated by them. They prowled around us, imitated our posh accents, invented speeches in it. Above all, I can remember the comment of one girl: 'If Ah wis at the Beacon schule, Ah widna *lower* masel tae pick the berries.'

Among themselves they were competitive about the poundage they picked. The undisputed champion was a thirteen-year-old called Sadie, whose fingers flashed like those of a fast typist over her can. At meal-times, we three were segregated from the Raploch pickers and had our packed lunches with the men in charge: the manager, a Pole, a mute known as 'the Dummy' and a student from Newcastle. I was allowed to drive the lorry in the orchards, the Raploch kids piled into the back, my first experience behind the wheel of a vehicle. Where wert thou, Elfin Safety?

The end of my schooldays was looming, and I had no real idea of what I wanted to do, beyond the frantic wish to escape from Stirling and Bridge of Allan and go to university, preferably St Andrews. My father was adamant: if I was to go, I had to know what I was to do at the end of it. 'Otherwise you'll do an ordinary MA and still not know what you want to do.' Careers advice at the Beacon was useless: most girls went on to do secretarial courses or nursing. My 'skeeliness' with my hands, and a small artistic ability, brought up the suggestion of occupational therapy. A facility with words was my forte, and the only outlet that I could see for this was journalism, so I put this forward as a potential career.

'You don't need a university degree for that,' said my father, and he fixed me up with an interview with the editor of the *Stirling Observer,* and accompanied me to it.

'She doesn't need a university degree for journalism, does she?' he asked. 'Just shorthand and typing?'

As the editor assented, with the proviso that a degree was always a good thing, I could see the dreaming spires receding to give way to Miss Simpson's Secretarial School.

'Perhaps,' I suggested as we drove home, 'I shouldn't go in for journalism. Perhaps I should go in for business.' God alone knows where I plucked that idea from, or what I meant by it.

'Right,' said my father, 'you don't need a university degree for that. Marks and Spencer have a very good scheme where you start off behind the counter and work your way up.' And the whole interview process was repeated. Eventually, in desperation (and perhaps in admiration of my history teacher), I suggested teaching.

He agreed to the idea of this course being preceded by university, but there were to be two conditions. One was that I had to go to Edinburgh, where Alison was currently studying law. The other came about as a result of a theory, indeed a policy, that he had recently formed, well ahead of David Cameron's idea for a national community service.

At the time, military National Service was still in force. My father's idea was that this should be served not just by boys but by girls, and that their national service should be nursing. Since my sister Fay had abandoned drama school for the wards of St Thomas's, it was a profession he greatly admired. Of his academic daughters, he had the experience of Joan marrying almost straight from university, and of Alison's continuing mental frailty. He was therefore less enamoured of women's education than his mother had been.

I was to be the first and only guinea pig for this policy of female national service. And it was not a bad idea, a domestic forerunner of today's Gap Year: it was just that I didn't want to nurse. Nevertheless I found myself, my parents again in tow, being interviewed by the Matron of the Princess Margaret Rose Orthopaedic Hospital in Edinburgh. She purred as she looked at my Highers passes. 'So why do you want to nurse?' she asked kindly.

I bit back the words, 'I don't, I don't, the last thing I want to do is carry bedpans and mop up vomit,' and murmured instead the stock phrase, 'I'd like to help people.'

I was accepted, and looked forward to the next year with foreboding, when my mother came up with a solution. It was the only time I can remember her in opposition to my father. She had found an advertisement in the *Scotsman* for 'a pupil-teacher' in a girls' prep school near Dunkeld. If I applied for this, and got the job, she would not only prevail on my father to let me cancel the nursing place, but would be my advocate about going to university. For that intervention, as much as for my birth, I never cease to be grateful to her.

I have to say that the teaching job was pretty much a disaster. Butterstone House School was five miles from Dunkeld. The girls were a far cry from the Raploch children: they were mainly not even middle-class, they were aristocratic. Some even had titles, as did more of the parents, something I found disconcerting and had no idea how to deal with. Princess Alexandra was conducting her courtship during my first term there, while staying with the parents of three of the daygirls. Sometimes she would arrive to collect them at the end of the school day. Two of the boarders were the children of a newly-elected MP, Willie Whitelaw. I was out of my social depth in a big way, and at seventeen, I was only five years older than pupils in the top class.

The children were well behaved and biddable, and within three weeks I knew I would never make a teacher. Marooned once again in an all-female society, I had no contemporaries. Some of the teachers had been governesses in the past, and were besotted with the lineages of their past and present charges. One was quite unpleasant to me, and very contemptuous of my efforts to contribute to the ghastly conversation in the staff room. I was happier in the kitchen with the maids and the cook, who told fortunes in tea-leaves. Letters came from my school friends describing their giddy lives in Glasgow and Edinburgh, while my only social interaction was country-dancing classes in Butterstone village hall on Monday nights. On free Saturdays I would bicycle the five miles to Dunkeld, take the bus to Perth, and sit through the same film twice.

And yet I never thought of leaving. I had undertaken the job for a year, and a year it had to be. In the summer term, things improved: another girl about my age joined the staff. Jane had lived in Nigeria, where she had had a colourful career, and was good company. We did some silly things, like taking baths in potassium permanganate to achieve a fake tan, and in the summer evenings we rode the resident ponies through the hills. Some of the parents took pity on me and invited me to their houses. A pearl-fisher I had met at country dancing gave me illegal driving lessons, and the end was in sight: university – and freedom – were just over the horizon.

My choice of a degree which would have a vocational element eventually came down to one – law – although I don't know that I'd have thought of it had it not already been Alison's choice. On my eighteenth birthday the letter came offering me a place in the Faculty of Law at Edinburgh University. Jane and I bicycled down to the town to celebrate with disgustingly sweet lemonade at the Dunkeld Tearooms.

# 7
## *The Tounis College*

At the time there were still only four universities in Scotland. Edinburgh University, founded in 1583, not by an archbishop, a king or a grandee, but by Edinburgh Town Council, was the youngest of them, surely the most democratically established academic establishment of its time. Even before the heyday of grants opened up university education to all bright youngsters, before slamming the door shut on them again in recent years, it was possible for those of modest means to gain degrees – those of modest means, but of a decent academic achievement. The 'certificate of fitness' demanded three passes at Highers level and two at Lowers. Higher English was essential, and at least one Lower had to be a language or a science. One of the latter had to be History or Geography (Modern Studies did not exist as a course, and History stopped at the causes of the outbreak of the First World War), but neither of these disciplines counted as a Higher. This ensured a breadth of study at school level, and I am not alone in believing that the standards we had to achieve fifty years ago in the exams that marked the end of our schooldays were higher than they are now.

At university, for the first time, I met, mingled and made close friendships with people from very different backgrounds to my own sheltered middle-class one. Many of them were there on grants, and I felt they were mostly a lot cleverer than I was. I envied their independence of parental control, for my father was funding me, and continued to exercise as tight a rein as possible.

'There are three things I want you to remember,' said my mother over lunch at Martin's the Bakers, before I and my trunk were offloaded at the hall of residence. 'Don't drink, don't smoke and don't go up to a man's flat.'

(By the end of week two, I was in a medical student's flat with a gin and tonic in one hand. 'I think I'd better have a cigarette as well,' I said.)

So here I was, gloriously a student, and it was with a hopeful heart that I passed through the main entrance from South Bridge to the Old College.

It was the Adam brothers who designed its frontage, William Playfair who finished it, and its interior, between 1817 and 1826. The building is in the midst of a busy, grubby part of the city: there is no leafy academia here; no mediaeval, cloistered buildings. Doors lead off to semi-subterranean passages to right and left of the gateway, and the university's chief servitor, the Bedellus, hovers around. Somewhere to the right was the meeting room of a mysterious, semi-masonic, all-male debating society called the Speculative Society. It is of considerable antiquity and its members were mainly young advocates: it and its hall still exist.

Above is the resplendent dome, topped by the golden boy with his torch of learning; the college buildings surround, not grassy lawns and box hedges, but a gritty surface that was used at that time as a car park by staff and – a few – students alike. The law faculty was tucked into the corner on the right – now it is the only faculty left in the Old Quad, and spreads itself right along that side of it. Administration was, and still is, on the left. Among the rooms of the latter is one which was to become my favourite in all of Edinburgh: it is now called the Raeburn Room, and houses the best collection of portraits by Henry Raeburn anywhere in the world. They are of the academics of Raeburn's own time, the men who drove the Enlightenment, and they look so comfortably at home here. You can almost believe that when the room is empty, they carry on conversations. Upstairs is Playfair's glorious library, full of classical proportions, marble busts and dusty books.

Lecture rooms for arts subjects were either here in the Old Quad, or across Chambers Street in a building called Minto House. That same side of the street housed Heriot-Watt College and the Dental School. Odd departments were scattered around the lovely old George Square, and the medical, science and divinity faculties had their own buildings, respectively in Teviot Row, at King's Buildings out at Liberton and at New College on the Mound. But the focus of university life was the Old Quad, as we called it, and its hub, its heartbeat, was the Common Room, which extended the full length of the side of the Quad furthest from its entrance. Here, within another of Playfair's pillared interiors, we bore our trays of mediocre coffee and fried egg or pie and chips (for under two shillings) to plastic tables, sat on cheap tubular-framed chairs or sank into battered rexine sofas. Here and there, students sat all day playing bridge, in preparation for failing their degree exams, and there was almost always someone thumping out bittersweet melodies on the out-of-tune piano in the middle of the Common Room. Here we watched the lives of others and seized our own with both hands.

The usual law degree, that of LL.B., or Bachelor of *Laws*, was at that time a postgraduate degree in Scottish Universities. It was possible to truncate the years of study by including two law subjects – Civil (Roman) Law and Constitutional Law – within an ordinary arts degree, and taking the remaining courses necessary for the LL.B in two years after that. During those two years, and often for the last year of their arts degree, law students who were going to become solicitors – and that was an overwhelming majority – also began their apprenticeship with a legal firm, and so were effectively part-time students.

There was another law degree, the B.L., or Bachelor of *Law,* and my father had insisted that this was the one on which I should embark. It took only three years, and had been introduced originally in the wake of the First World War, as a short cut for returning servicemen. A couple of years after I graduated, it was phased out, and the LL.B. became an undergraduate course. 'Everyone will know my age when they see "B.L." after my name,' was a remark I made that went into an account of the degree by a junior academic years later. For the B.L., Civil Law was compulsory in the first year – from Scots Law being founded on its principles – and a nod was given to general education in the study of two arts subjects. With enthusiasm, I settled on Scottish History and English Literature, and with more trepidation took my seat at the back of the Civil Law class.

In the class of forty, there were only four women. We sat at the back: two were studious, but in Jacqueline Pirie I found a fellow spirit. She was slight, elf-like (again, I felt that I was the fat friend) and like me she had just escaped from an all-girl education. At university, we were both breaking loose. We hit on a good idea for meeting people: we sold the 'Student' newspaper on commission. I could hardly have realised that it was a good training for canvassing, for giving out leaflets; nor that we would both first meet our future husbands in the guise of newspaper sellers. We threw ourselves into a giddy social life. I was so desperate for this that when the university Tory Club had a 'hop' offering free entry to freshers, I did not hesitate to go along to it.

Jacqueline lived at home, on the very outmost edge of suburban Edinburgh at Corstorphine, but I was in a hall of residence, Masson Hall, in George Square. This lovely quadrangle had been a last attempt to develop Edinburgh on the fringes of the Old Town, before the Nor' Loch below the Castle was drained, the Mound heaped up, and the New Town created. George Square had been built in a period of twenty years from the 1760s, and its purely residential use, plus its central garden, had made it immediately popular.

Two centuries later, George Square was still a homogenous entity of Georgian and Victorian buildings around the locked central garden. Walter Scott's childhood home was marked by a plaque on its western side, and a few doors along from it there was a small convent, from which the Sisters of Charity emerged from their devotions from time to time in their elongated, shovel-like starched head-dresses. The north side was occupied by George Watson's Ladies College, but the majority of the square was owned by the university and housed small departments, as well as the two residences – one for men and one for women – that were established there in the late nineteenth century.

Masson Hall, to which I returned in the evenings through Edinburgh's twilight, and the scent of bonfires of autumn leaves on the Meadows, was run on lines that would not have disgraced an Oxbridge college. We dined formally, after a brief grace, and if we were going out in the evening, needed to sign our names in a book giving our destination. The doors were locked at 11 pm, and a key for later entry was only allowed twice a week. Male visitors had to be off the premises by 5 pm. Alison had been there before me, and so my parents were confident in Masson Hall's capacity for supervision.

But, alas for them, my application had been one of the later ones, and so I was in the overflow flat, on the third floor of 18 Buccleuch Place, behind George Square. There were three large rooms, all occupied by pairs of freshers. I was lucky, in that I shared the smallest room which had a threadbare carpet. The other two rooms, generously proportioned and high-ceilinged, were floored only with linoleum. Huge, single-glazed windows faced to the north, and draughts sneaked round their frames. The twice-weekly bucket of coal did nothing to heat the air beyond the immediate environs of the fireplace, and there were times when the Edinburgh haar penetrated the wooden shutters and thin curtains and filled the large front room. Central heating was a concept for the future. A slightly older student, in a single room, was supposed to keep an eye on us in exchange for a reduced rent. The kitchen, and a box bedroom, were occupied by a widow who was supposed to caretake the flat. Her housekeeping skills left something to be desired, and so did her care of her six-year-old son: his teeth were blackened stumps.

'Mrs F,' said one of my flatmates, 'Don't you think you should take Johnnie to the dentist to see about his teeth?'

'What does it matter? He'll get another set,' she replied nonchalantly.

Above the common entrance to 18 Buccleuch Place there was an engraved stone: 'Here lived Francis Jeffrey, (1773-1850) and here the

*Edinburgh Review* was founded.' Jacqueline, who was a frequent visitor, was delighted with the association.

'Just think,' she said, 'Walter Scott must have come to *parties* here. Bottle parties, I expect.'

Jacqueline and I researched the history of the social gatherings in Buc-cleuch Place in Georgian times, and instituted our own regular Thursday afternoon salons. They couldn't be in my room, because it was too small, and in any case my Shetland room-mate, whose dialect I could not understand at all when she was speaking to fellow Shetlanders on the phone, was a serious student and would not have tolerated such an invasion. The girls in the back bedroom, who had taught me the word 'shit' for the first time (I was eighteen, remember, and had grown up in the country), were enthusiastic, and our Thursday coffee parties of Nescafe and digestive biscuits earned a modest cachet. When the snow and ice came, we skated – if not on Duddingston Loch like Raeburn's minister, then at Craiglockhart, with its ghosts of the First World War poets Wilfred Owen and Siegfried Sassoon, who met there. At night a group of us sledged below Arthur's Seat, down a terrifying run called the Gutted Haddie.

Back in the Old Quad I joined the Law Society, whose office-bearers were the sons of judges, and would in time occupy the bench themselves: James Clyde, son and grandson of Lord Presidents of the Court of Ses-sion, and Kenny John Cameron, whose father, Lord 'Jock' Cameron, was on the University Court and a prominent Edinburgh character. Nearly forty years on, this particular fellow student would sentence my son to prison. Douglas Cullen, who would preside over the enquiries into the Piper Alpha disaster and the Dunblane shootings, and who had name-sakes who have graced the bench in earlier generations, was another. These were Alison's contemporaries, not mine, but they were definitely the aristocracy of the law faculty, trailing their degrees from Oxbridge or St Andrews behind them.

I was lucky. There was a new Professor of Civil Law that year, the charismatic T.B. Smith, a reforming genius of a man who, in due course, would publish an updated classic textbook on Scots Law and became the first head of the Scots Law Commission. He had a bent for showman-ship in his lectures that made even the tenets of Roman Law, and their influence on Scots Law, come alive. If I learned one thing in those years in Edinburgh University's Law Faculty, it was the extent to which Scots Law had been a bulwark in preserving Scotland's national identity since the Act of Union.

Of course, I joined the Nationalist Club, whose office-bearers immediately swept me on to their committee. We had worthy debates on such subjects as 'Should internationalism inter [i.e. bury] nationalism?', and earnest discussions over plates of spaghetti, two and sixpence for a large helping, in the basement of Demarco's, an Italian restaurant in Forrest Road much beloved by the students of my generation. Among my colleagues were Allan McCartney, who later stood against David in Roxburgh, Selkirk and Peebles, and who in time was to become a distinguished MEP, and Gordon Wilson, who won the SNP's second seat at Westminster in Dundee East in the 1970s and became Party Leader. I can't recall ever actually leafleting or canvassing, but there was a lot of aspirational talk. They were an intense and mainly humourless lot, the nationalist students of Edinburgh University in the late 1950s, and my enthusiasm waned over the year.

I went to debates in the Union, university services at St Giles, and at both of these I loved the ceremonial of the processionals, and the colours and varieties of the gowns. On one occasion, I actually occupied the 'public benches' at a meeting of the Students' Representative Council. The university authorities wanted to rationalise and expand their accommodation, and they proposed to pull down two sides of George Square and replace them with some brutal tower blocks. I was interested in the debate about it, and opposed to the university's plans, so when a friend said that there was to be a debate about it at the SRC, and she'd like to hear it, I went with her. The SRC met in a shabby, semi-basement room in the Old Quad, and we felt very much outsiders as we found space on the uncomfortable benches. The debate, of course, had no impact on the university's plans, and they went ahead with the worst piece of desecration and subsequent rebuilding of twentieth-century Edinburgh. The peeling 1960s architecture of the Appleton Tower stands today as an indictment of those who made the decisions when we were students.

A dark, thin-faced young man got up to make what was by far the best contribution to the evening. 'Oh, I recognise him,' I said. 'He's in the Civil Law class. I think his name is David Steel.'

Inevitably, I fell in love, though not with David at this point. The object of my affections was a chemistry student who liked to play the field and had no idea that his easy charm and skilled snogging technique as we crossed the Meadows on the way back from the Conservative Club's Freshers hop was going to evoke a dog-like devotion that would last for nearly two years. It took a long time before I realised the difference between sexual attraction and love, and I was still so naïve about sex in general that when a strange incident took place, it did not disturb me.

I was returning to Masson Hall for the evening meal, when a second year student emerged from a car parked outside the front door. 'No, I'm afraid not,' she said to the man in the driver's seat. Then she saw me. 'But here's Judy – she'll do anything for a laugh, won't you, Judy?'

With absolutely no hesitation, I got into the passenger seat beside a totally unknown man. He swore me to secrecy about what he was about to propose.

'There's nothing wrong with it, but if it got out I could get into trouble. I'm something high up in the University.'

He explained that he had taken on a bet with a female friend, a Wren, about how much pain he could withstand. Would I go with him to a gym, and walk over him, stamp on him, preferably in stiletto heels? Did the offer of a fiver cross his lips? I honestly can't remember, but I did think it was a very odd thing to take on a bet about. I tried to imagine doing what he asked, but decided that it was not really for me, and declined the gym visit. Again, he enjoined me to remain silent about the matter, and I agreed to this. I kept this promise for many years; not least because, totally undisturbed by it, I forgot all about the incident until my memory was prompted in very unlikely circumstances during my first visit to the Traverse Theatre.

The summer term of 1959 came, and with it, long days of sunshine and heat. At the start of the term was the explosion of student fund-raising and high spirits known as Charities Week. A committee organised events: the Charities Queen was crowned by the Rector, the actor James Robertson Justice, on the esplanade of Edinburgh Castle, and in a horse-drawn coach they led a torchlight procession down the High Street and up to Calton Hill for a firework display. There was a jazz band Ball in Fountainbridge Palais, at which such jazz giants as Kenny Ball and Acker Bilk played, a student revue at what is now the Edinburgh Festival Theatre, and a night-club, daringly open until 1 a.m. On the Saturday there would be another parade, along Princes Street this time, of decorated lorries bearing wildly-costumed students, while on the Thursday afternoon, similarly garbed, busloads went to pester the inhabitants of the Lothians and Borders for cash for charity: These were known as the Border Raids. The bus that I organised went, not to the towns and villages of the Border country to the south of Edinburgh, but to destinations totally lacking the romance suggested by the phrase Border Raids: Skinflats and the Carron Iron Works in the industrial middle of Scotland. Charities Week still exists, but not the parades and Border Raids, and to judge from its website it is a much less explosive and wild affair altogether.

The week ended, and after a dance at the Union, I climbed Arthur's Seat with my chemistry student in the dark, to await a daybreak service conducted by the minister of the Canongate Kirk for May morning. How fortunate we were, to be young in the time before risk assessments, health and safety regulations and trigger-happy actions for damages.

Jacqueline and I frequented the Law Library as exams approached, but our concentration was weak. Downstairs, not only the Common Room awaited, but the dusty steps of the Old Quad, occupied by students basking in the sun in that lovely summer of 1959. The time was all the more bitter-sweet, because my father had told me that, for me, there would be no re-sits. I must pass first time, or he would not continue to support me.

This would be my one and only long summer vacation, because in October – provided I passed my exams – I was due to start my legal apprenticeship. It had been arranged that I was to go abroad: not to France, which would have been my own first choice, but to Denmark. My parents had been there during the previous year, where they had visited various forests. (My father's devotion to trees followed him on holiday.) At one of these, Gribskov in northern Zealand, the largest state forest in Denmark, their hosts, Ib and Else Jelnes, asked if they could recommend a family to take one of their sons for a holiday to improve his English. My mother volunteered, and Jens Jelnes arrived soon after their return. So there was a hospitality debt, and besides, my parents felt that Denmark was a safe sort of country, not a rackety Mediterranean one. At nineteen, it was only my second foray outside Britain's shores: the first had been a girl guide trip to Austria, four years previously.

Denmark, at that time, was probably the most accessible European country from Scotland. There was a direct sailing between Reykjavik, Leith and Copenhagen, on a somewhat dilapidated pre-war Icelandic boat called after the great glacier, *Gullfoss*. There were first- and second-class cabins, and dormitory accommodation, which was how I travelled. The women's side tended to get invaded by drunk and cheerful Icelanders. After two nights at sea, the *Gullfoss* steamed past Hamlet's castle of Elsinore and right up into the middle of Copenhagen with its canals, its copper spires and steeply pitched roofs and colourful, high houses. On the quayside Jens, his small brother Rolf and his father were waiting for me with a bag of pastries – wienerbrød. My tastebuds opened to my first Danish experience, and a love affair with all things to do with that small, civilised country began.

It was fostered in the family's relaxed home in the sun-dappled beech forest, where Else Jelnes's attitude to the teenagers filling it – of whom I, at nineteen, was the eldest – was in such remarkable contrast to my parents'. When she heard us scurrying around the bedrooms in the small hours, it did not worry her: she trusted us, and indeed we were up to nothing more serious than a card school. When she found Jens smoking in the bathroom, she told him to do so in public, rather than secretly. She taught me the rudiments of some Danish cooking: frika delle (Danish pork rissoles), buttermilk soup, cucumber salad, and rødgrøde med fløde (thickened red fruit gruel with cream), which I also learned to pronounce. The word is the Danish linguistic equivalent of 'it's a braw bricht moonlicht nicht the nicht' for non-Scots. Else also instructed me in the art of smørrebrød arrangement, and, although Christmas was a long way away, how to make simple decorations. In the years to come, when I was an MP's wife, these skills would come in handy when I was asked to talk to women's organisations in the constituency, for I was able to give demonstrations on these arts, and for a few years would be in considerable demand.

### RECIPE FOR RØDGRØDE MED FLØDE

*8 oz redcurrants*
*8 oz raspberries*
*4 oz blackcurrants*
*1 pint water*
*½ lb sugar*
*Vanilla pod or a few drops of vanilla essence*
*Cornflour (1¾ oz for each pint of berry juice)*
*A glass of white wine*
*Caster sugar*
*Cream*

Clean and prepare the fruit and mash them until no berries remain whole. Add water, bring to the boil, and allow to stand for 15 minutes. Pass the juice through a fine sieve and measure it. Reserve a little of the juice and return the remainder to the heat, adding sugar and vanilla, and bring to the boil, skimming any froth from the surface.

Dissolve the cornflour in the wine and the reserved, cooled berry juice, and add this thickening mixture to the boiling berry juice, stirring all the time. As soon as the juice begins to simmer, remove it from the heat and extract the vanilla pod. Pour into wine glasses, wettened and sprinkled with caster sugar, and sprinkle a little of the latter on top of each serving – this will prevent a skin from forming. Alternatively, it can be served from one big glass bowl. Serve cold with cream. (*Serves 6–8.*)

Else would send Jens and myself off with packed lunches on day-long bicycle rides – to see the work of a remarkable Danish sculptor, J.F. Willumsen, to Elsinore and Hamlet's castle of Kronborg, and to Sweden. One day, it was a car trip, and Else said, 'We are taking you to see a Scotsman. A jarl.' It was the mummified body of the Earl of Bothwell, third husband of Mary Queen of Scots, in his glass-topped coffin in the crypt of Faarevejle Church, who died in exile as a prisoner/guest/hostage of the Danish king, chained to a post and mad, in nearby Dragsholm Castle. He looked pathetically small, and so did his still intact and notorious penis.

In Copenhagen, I was *au pair* for two little girls aged three and eighteen months. I was given enough time off to explore the city, but not much money. It didn't matter: I learned how to do things on the cheap, and that is the way to learn to love a city. Amongst the things that impressed me was the Danish design of furniture, glass and chinaware, and architecture, which was so different and so uncluttered. I learned the names and the work of Arne Jacobsen, Georg Jensen and Bjørn Winblad.

Above all, I came to know the cheerful, relaxed and friendly nature of the people there; perhaps it is from them that the once-Danish Orkney islanders derive the same traits.

'Copenhagen is my Paris,' I sometimes say, and by that I mean it was where I was young and poor; and if I was not always happy – the *au pair* job came to an abrupt end – there was the safety net of Else and her family. Fifty years later, and four generations on from the Jelnes and MacGregor parents who took tea in the beechwoods of Zealand, the bond still holds. Rolf Jenes is my 'Danish brother' and I am his 'Scottish sister'.

There had been a telegram waiting for me in Denmark along with the Jelneses and the wienerbrød. Miraculously, I had passed my degree exams. For the next three years, I would also undertake my law apprenticeship. Many of my fellow students came from legal families, and for them, these arrangements would be made on an old boys' basis. The law was a tightly closed shop. The three young men who served in the same firm as me all had fathers in country practices in the south of Scotland, who were the 'country agents' of the city firm. My own father had used contacts to get Alison placed in a prestigious firm in Charlotte Square. Since then, her employers had had to cope with at least one mental breakdown, which left my father feeling embarrassed and ashamed. He would not risk that again: I would have to make my own arrangements. So, during the previous summer term, I had walked into portals of Tods, Murray and Jamieson, asked to see a partner, and simply said, 'I'd like to be an apprentice here.'

'We've never had a female apprentice before,' said the partner, 'but I don't see why not.' And they took me on.

Like Godstowe, like Butterstone House School, the firm was very posh.

> At Tods, Murray and Jamieson,
> The Jamiesons speak to the Tods,
> The Tods speak to the Jamiesons
> But the Murrays speak only to God.

I started at the same time as another student, Bill Goodburn. Later, we were joined by Denbeigh Kirkpatrick: they came from Peebles and Jedburgh respectively, so continued to share our lives as we all raised our families after we moved to the Borders. We apprentices were paid by the firm, though only a few years earlier they were actually charged fees by some of the more prestigious solicitors. Our remuneration was £50 in the first year, £100 in the second, and £150 in the third. Since we were now officially part-time students, any grants we might have received up until then no longer applied, so that it was, at that time, quite impossible for anyone to qualify in law in Scotland without family support. A violent row with my parents in my final year's apprenticeship made me vow to free myself from this, and I thought I would have to give up before I qualified. Denbeigh's father, although he did not know it, saved me: he was so horrified by the firm's meanness that he threatened to break his connection with them as the Edinburgh agents of his thriving rural practice. Our final year's remuneration went up to six pounds a week, and I was able to live on that.

We began our day at the Old Quad, with the Scots Law Class, and after it, we walked down the Mound towards our offices, which were all in the New Town. En route, we would meet the bowler-hatted advocates walking up towards Parliament House. Some things had not changed since my great-grandfather had provided their pinstripe suits. In the afternoon, the journeys were reversed as we headed towards Constitutional Law.

During that year, I also took the optional and macabre course in Forensic Medicine, which took us into the medical faculty buildings in Teviot Row. Professor Douglas Kerr had written the authoritative book on the subject; he was another showman, but he had better material with which to show off than Professor Tom Smith had in Civil Law. 'We're studying suicide, murder, rape and abortion,' was how I described it to friends in other faculties, and I did not realise what an influence a knowledge of the last of these would have on later events in my life.

We were taken on visits – to the morgue, to see the effects of post-mortem lividity in a corpse, to see an operation at the Royal Infirmary, to Saughton Prison and other places. A small museum in the department displayed gruesome sights in jars: a limb, covered with adipocere, the fatty substance that builds up after immersion in water; a cross-section of a throat with a fatal tobacco pipe stuck down it from a cycling accident, and foetuses in various stages of gestation. It was indeed much more interesting than any of our other subjects.

At the office, my first three months were spent in a small room with the accountant, who had two main problems: he was a gambling addict, and an alcoholic. He gave me things to read that I could not really understand, and communication with him after the lunch break was more or less non-existent. The four partners lived in a rarefied atmosphere and there was a department in the firm which was referred to in hushed tones as 'the Purse-Bearer's Department'. The senior partner held this office, but I – a member of the Church of Scotland, regular in my church attendance – went through my three years there without ever really finding out what it meant. It was not until I was a manse daughter-in-law that I learned that the purse was that of the Lord High Commissioner to the General Assembly of the Church of Scotland, and that the Lord High Commissioner has been appointed by the monarch, since the days of James VI and I, not to represent the royal presence, but actually to embody it during the mid-May week of the General Assembly of the Church of Scotland, when Princes Street and the Mound are thronged with sombre-suited ministers and elders.

More publicly known was the fact that the firm acted for the notorious Margaret, Duchess of Argyll in her divorce action – and yes, during the time of my apprenticeship I did read her diaries, and see the infamous photographs, including the one of Her Grace, naked apart from a string of pearls, on her knees beside a man whose face has fortunately been missed by the Polaroid camera. But even apart from the frisson of being close up to such a case, I grew to love the setting of the Law Courts in Parliament House, and all the ritual and history associated with them: the advocates, deep in discussion, walking up and down the hammer-beamed hall built to house the old Scottish Parliament, warmed in winter by fires blazing in two gigantic fireplaces. And the dramas that unfolded in the courtrooms themselves appealed to me greatly, without my realising that it was the theatre of it, the rituals and traditions rather than the law itself, which were attracting me.

Jacqueline had switched to an Arts course, but my friendships with the other law students deepened: we were a more identifiable, coherent group now that we were also apprentices. But there was another group who came to Edinburgh University at the beginning of my second year, who were associated with student publications and with the SRC, and they formed part of that circle whose friendship has lasted now for over fifty years. Prominent amongst them was Michael Shea, who, after a career in the Diplomatic Service, would become the Queen's Press Secretary and a successful novelist and writer, and who will feature many times in these memoirs. He was remarkable in having *his own flat*, in the less-than-salubrious Rose Street, which he had purchased, using a legacy, for under a thousand pounds.

Another colourful character of that year was Robin Crichton, who would become the founder and director of Edinburgh Film Productions and who lived in a caravan out in the Pentlands; he sometimes came to university on an Icelandic pony. From my own past came a friend from Berkhamstead days, Sheena Dowling, who, as we reach our seventies, is the person in my life who has known me longest, bar my sisters and cousins. She and her room-mate, Joanna Lees, formed the same immediate bond that Jacqueline and I had as freshers: the only difference is that while Jacqueline and I have drifted apart and all but lost contact over the decades, Sheena and Joanna – despite the fact that the latter has spent the last forty years across the Atlantic – have kept up that friendship with each other, and with the rest of the 'group'.

Edinburgh pubs closed their doors at ten o'clock, and so did the coffee bars. Once, I can remember going around the streets during the Festival after that hour with a couple of Italian students, trying to find somewhere to sell us a cup of coffee. It was a useless quest, as was a similar one with a Finn who wanted a glass of wine. All I could find for him was cheap port in a Grassmarket pub – that now fashionable part of the capital being, in those days, almost totally a no-go area full of meths drinkers and winos. Off the Grassmarket, though, there was a place called Studio 3 in a condemned, toilet-less building up the steps of Castle Wynd South. It was officially a club, and you could get coffee there until the small hours, along with open sandwiches of salami or peanut butter and honey on ryebread, to the accompaniment of jazz records. How bohemian it felt! Jacqueline and I signed up for membership, and were frequently to be found there. Then all of a sudden, it closed down, and we learned for the first time that it had been used for passing drugs.

We would not have known what they were. Drug-taking may have taken place amongst students, but it was mainly Benzedrine to keep awake before exams – cannabis had not reached our conciousness. Of alcohol we consumed a considerable amount at parties in student flats after the pubs had closed at ten o'clock. The worst experience I ever had with this was when my hosts at one party had stolen neat alcohol from the science laboratories and mixed it with tins of fruit salad amongst other ingredients in large sinks and served it up as a punch.

Culturally, the Mecca for Jacqueline and me was the Cameo cinema which showed art films. We'd go there and arrange to meet our boyfriends *after* the films – we didn't want our cultural experiences interrupted by the snogging that was inevitable if you went to the cinema with a boy in those days. During that time we saw films by an inspirational trio of directors: Alain Resnais of France, Ingmar Bergman of Sweden, and Andrei Wajda of Poland. In the last few decades I have also seen wonderful theatre from the latter two: Bergman's *Miss Julie* at the Edinburgh Festival, and Wajda's *Macbeth* at the Stary Theatre in Krackow. A key, charismatic figure was Jim Haynes, a laconic American who had served in the Air Force near Edinburgh and had fallen in love with it. He returned to the city and set up, first of all, the ground-breaking Paperback Bookshop on the corner of George Square. Outside it was the head of a rhinoceros; inside was coffee on tap, and as much time as you liked to browse. On the morning of my graduation, Jim allowed me to have a breakfast party of wine and strawberries there, and after it his customers finished up the remains of cheap white wine from Valvona and Crolla's throughout the rest of the morning. As I and my fellow law graduands tottered *en masse* from George Square to the McEwan Hall, a lady in a smart outfit greeted me warmly. 'Judy,' hissed Bill Goodburn, 'It's *your mother.*'

As I went up to be 'capped' by the Principal with what is alleged to be the remodelled breeks of the sixteenth-century scholar George Buchanan, a cheer went up from the row of fledgling lawyers. My mother said afterwards, in a gratified tone, 'You seem to be very popular with the other students.'

The Paperback also played host to the most memorable Fringe show of my student summers – two actors in Georgian costume sat in a corner in candlelight, performing David Hume's *Dialogues*.

Later, Jim Haynes was to be instrumental in founding the Traverse Theatre, and even now my Edinburgh Festival is not complete if I do not see the familiar figure, stooped now and slightly frail, having blown in from his home in Paris for his annual visit. On the last such occasion, I asked him to remind me of the date the Traverse had opened.

'1963,' he said, 'but in a way it began before that – I had this evening in the Paperback, with two actors . . .'

I would never have thought, as I drank in the atmosphere of that evening, that I would in time find my own niche in theatre.

# 8

# *A Shared Love of Politics*

*October, 1960*

I am in the bowels of the Old Quad, in the room set aside for the use of the Students' Representative Council. The votes are being cast for the election to that practice ground for politics, and my name is on the ballot paper for the Law Faculty's election of one representative. The SRC President, who is the returning officer, is overseeing the count, and he is not at all pleased that my pile is growing steadily above the others. He wears a chunky fawn v-necked cardigan, obviously knitted by a loving mother. He leans over the ballot papers with a longer and longer face as he scrutinises the votes; he regards me as a lightweight, compared with the very worthy student who has served in this capacity for the previous year. The returning officer's name is David Steel: I have got to know him a bit better than on the occasion when I first heard him speak, in this very hall, but like Mistress Quigley and Sir John Falstaff, our liking for each other has grown less on acquaintance, and will continue to do so over the year. I regard him as an establishment figure; he sees me as an unruly backbencher.

I am returned with a thumping majority.

Later in the term there was another election: the triennial one for the Rector of the University, the students' representative on the University Court. The post had been held for the previous three years by the veteran actor James Robertson Justice, star of many Second World War films and of the 'Doctor in the House' series. A rotund, bearded, Edwardian figure, he used to maintain that he did not act in films – he simply appeared in them and played himself. He relished the role of Rector, and was a much more participatory figure than his predecessors, who regarded the position purely as an honorary one, and would delegate most of their functions to an Edinburgh-based 'assessor'. Not only did he attend student social functions – he even came to dinner at Masson Hall, where we fluttered around him like girls in a Muriel Spark novel – but he also chaired the meetings of the University Court. It was his right to do this, but others who had held the office and regarded it as purely honorary had left this duty to the principal. The election of the Rector was always a rowdy event, with a soot-and-flour battle in the Old Quad on election day, when the war memorial outside the Common Room would be boarded up for protection. It was good-natured nonsense, but by the time David came to stand as Rector himself, this aspect had completely disappeared, and when I made enquiries about it of the sanctimonious young man who was SRC president at the time, I was made to feel very frivolous and juvenile. 'We don't go in for that kind of nonsense now,' I was told.

Robertson Justice's successor as Rector was Jo Grimond, the leader of the Liberal Party, who had that enviable quality of being able to engage with, and inspire, young people. His rectorial address was called 'In praise of politics', and in it he urged the young men and women in his audience to take an active part in the political process. It was mainly his influence that made the University Liberal Club, of which David Steel was the immediate past president – succeeded by Michael Shea – the most popular and fashionable of the University's political clubs, easily winning the annual 'mock election' in the debates at the Men's Union. I had drifted away from the Nationalists over the last couple of years, but I had not joined the Liberals – yet.

The cusp of the 1960s was a heyday in debating for Scottish universities. The *Observer's* award for an individual went to a mature student from Edinburgh, Russell Johnston, another mainstay of the Liberal Club. Russell was older than the rest of us: he had done his National Service, and an honours degree in History, and was now at Moray House training as a teacher. He was from Skye, and wore the kilt as an everyday garment, not just for balls and weddings. The Universities' team prize had gone to Glasgow, and early in 1961 their team of two came to Edinburgh to take part in a debate. There was high expectation: they arrived late, sweeping into the debating Hall with gowns flying behind them, and treated us to a virtuoso display of argument and passion. Goodness knows what the debate was about, but their contribution to it was the most electrifying I experienced in four years of Union debates there.

> In the days when we were young
> all the snapshots were black and white
> except those caught, not on camera,
> but in the memory.

One such I remember
from a setting whose name
betrays the same time-warp
as the monochrome photographs –
The Men's Union:
women permitted only
to Saturday night dances
and – more rarely – to debates.

The latter, then: under garish lights
gowns of office, gold-embroidered,
and brylcreemed heads glinted back.
Young voices – mainly male –
spoke to the future.
Later, the future would hear them.

The sharp-lineated technicolor snapshot
holds fast and does not fade
in my middle-aged memory:
those two profiled Glaswegian Turks
– conquerors of that esoteric and *Observer*'d world
of student debates –
fencing with their verbal rapiers,
provoking, scratching, wounding at their will.

I cannot remember the subject matter,
nor any of the arguments or jokes,
only that sparkling shower
of wit and well-turned phrase
clothing remorseless logic
and the rocket-tail of laughter.
Thus, for the first time, the pairing of the names
*Dewar and Smith*.

The names of Donald Dewar and John Smith were to be carved into the history of Britain, of Scotland and of the Labour Party. But forever, to me, they were those young Turks who set us alight on that evening of oratory and wit.

The party for those and such as those after the debate was high-spirited. During it, a strange episode took place: as I sat on a table waving a drink and deep in conversation, David Steel, who had been presiding over the debate in his splendid President's robes, came over unexpectedly, kissed me, and went away again. I was amazed. I was in love with a Labour man – another chemistry student, Duncan Hallas – throughout that year, and as we walked home from the Union, I kept saying, in astonished tones, 'Steel kissed me!' But my relationship with the SRC president remained spiky, at best, and I was deeply in love with Duncan Hallas.

He was very left-wing: a mature student who was a member of far-left groups before university, he became an activist for the Socialist Workers Party after it – in fact I wonder now whether he was deliberately infiltrating the Labour movement. Bill Goodburn warned me against him: 'You'd always come second to his political fanaticism,' he told me, while my friend Joanna Lees disapproved of him on other grounds. 'He's got the worst reputation with women in the whole of the University. And what's more, he's married – he's got a wife in a mental institution somewhere in England.'

Joanna's warning was too late: my emotions were already violently engaged with this twentieth-century version of Mr Rochester. I was one of several girls whom he shuffled like a pack of cards, and he caused me dreadful unhappiness. He was what my mother would have called a 'rotter'. I can see now that she was afraid for me, but she couldn't handle the wilful, distraught twenty-year-old that I was, and later in that year we had a brief but deeply painful estrangement. At one point I thought I would be joining my sister Alison in her current stay at the Royal Edinburgh Hospital for Nervous Diseases. The rift was healed by the combined forces of my sister Joan, Auntie G, and the man who was to become my best and last love – the young man who kissed me on the February evening in the Men's Union.

Although we still locked horns with each other throughout that year, the time of Jo Grimond's installation as Rector did allow me to admire David Steel's political nous, and he in turn came to compliment me publicly for my part in some of the social arrangements to do with it. But there were deeper issues than dinners and balls. The secretary of the University, a sleekit man by the name of Charles Stewart, was on a mission to deprive students of their right to install the new Rector in the McEwan Hall. He was determined that the University authorities themselves should take over the ceremonial, rather than risk the occasion degenerating as it had on the previous occasion, when bags of flour and toilet rolls had been flung around. There was a joint committee between staff and students at which this was discussed. David turned up at a crucial meeting of it with a copy of the Universities (Scotland) Act of 1884 which enshrined the rectorship – including the installation – in law. Only towards the end of the meeting did he produce and quote from it, leaving the wily secretary quite undone. As they came away from the meeting, a young and sympathetic academic congratulated David on his tactics: 'The great thing about student politics,' he said, 'is that it teaches you how to deal with rogues and villains.' His name was John P. Mackintosh.

Mackintosh was an immensely popular lecturer in British History – I remember that, although I didn't take the class, I was persuaded to go to some of his lectures. He was also deeply involved in Labour Party politics and had fought Edinburgh Pentlands in the 1959 election. Shortly after the events I am describing, he took up an academic post in Nigeria, but came back in time to fight the 1964 election in Berwick and East Lothian, a highly marginal seat held by a Tory baronet of the old school, Sir William Anstruther Gray. He failed to win on that occasion, but over the next fifteen years was in and out of Westminster in that seat until his early death in 1978. He also continued as an academic, and wrote the standard textbook on the British Constitution, *The British Cabinet*. John Mackintosh and David could not have been closer political allies if they had been in the same party, and it was a crying shame that he never held office under either Wilson or Callaghan. His independent stance on so many issues, his brilliance that was so sharp it was threatening to lesser men, and his total lack of discretion and respect for those in the higher echelons of the Labour Party did not help his chances of promotion.

His lunch and dinner parties in Edinburgh were cross-party affairs where John would unleash more parliamentary gossip in an evening than I would garner from David in a whole term, while his wife Una would look on with a tolerant eye, occasionally reining him in when she thought he was going too far.

John Mackintosh was far ahead of the Labour Party in espousing the cause of Scottish Home Rule: and he did so from a considered, rationally-argued stance. Tam Dalyell, that arch-opponent of devolution, was to write later: 'With the departure of Mackintosh for Africa, and a number of pro-devolution academics to posts elsewhere, the positive case for devolution in the late 1950s and early sixties went by default in the Labour Party.'

I came near to joining the Labour party at that time, but two things prevented me. One was that I felt it would have been ascribed to my passion for Duncan Hallas, and indeed his political talk and his oratory were as seductive as his more obvious charms, though none of them blinded me to the fact that I didn't like his opposition to Europe, nor some of his other views. The relationship came to an end – traumatic for me, but not for him – over the summer of 1961.

The other reason I held back was Labour's policy vacuum on Scottish self-government; the Liberals were still the only British-wide party that endorsed it, and besides, I liked their internationalism.

In September of that year the Liberal Party was holding its annual conference in Edinburgh. I read the reports and the agenda, and noted that they were to debate the question of Scottish Home Rule. Finding myself free, I made my way to the Usher Hall in time for the debate. What I heard convinced me of the Liberal case for federalism, and of the Liberals' sincerity. There were two speakers in particular who inspired me. One was John Bannerman, the great champion of Gaeldom and a Scottish rugby hero. The other was Russell Johnston. By the time I left the hall, I had decided to join the Liberal party, on the basis of the same policy that had attracted me to it ten years earlier.

July, 2008

*Russell Johnston and I sit together at a Portuguese restaurant in London. After thirty-three years as MP for Inverness, he is now in the House of Lords. His two passions have always been Scotland and Europe, and in recent years it has been the latter that has taken most of his time and commitment. For a while he was an MEP, giving rise to the whisper of his political opponents in Inverness, 'Russell's in Brussels.' He still spends most of his time in mainland Europe, where he has held the prestigious post of President of the Council of Europe, and although we shared much common ground and experiences when we were young, I have not seen him for some time.*

*Some time ago he was diagnosed with cancer, and he is on a heavy dose of drugs to stabilise this. As we walk along the embankment, he has to stop from time to time, weak and giddy. We are both about to go on holiday, David and myself to a cruise in the Gulf of Bothnia, Russell to Paris, where he is to meet his son. We talk together in the warm London night, reminiscing, delving deeply into the memories of our friendship of nearly fifty years. It is a closer, more intimate conversation than we would have had if David had made up the intended threesome with us.*

*I remind Russell of the debate in the Usher Hall, and how it had spurred me to join the party. 'Ah,' he says, 'David was always a Grimond Liberal; but you and I, Judy, we are Bannerman Liberals.'*

*We go on our separate holidays. Three days later the news reaches us on the ship that he has dropped dead in the street in Paris.*

*Amidst our grief for our old friend, and for our shared history, I am comforted with the thought that you don't often round off a friendship as well as I did that evening under the harsh London lights.*

When university went back in October, I joined the Liberal Club. During the summer vacation, David Steel, no longer in the exalted position of SRC President, had been adopted as prospective Liberal candidate for the Edinburgh Pentlands seat. I met him in the Common Room.

'Now that I've joined the Liberals,' I said in a flush of enthusiasm, 'I'll go canvassing for you one night.'

Shortly after this I was greatly excited to get an invitation to a small dinner that Jo Grimond was giving for selected students, academics, and other guests. The reason I had been invited was that I had been the correspondent for the Rector's arrangements in speaking at the recent Freshers' Conference. Michael Shea, as the president of the Liberal Club, and David Steel were among those also invited. I was placed between the latter and the current Conservative Home Secretary, Henry Brooke. Much to my surprise, I found that the Home Secretary was not in the least intimidating, and that David Steel, now that we were not glaring at each other across the SRC Hall, was rather nice. Since my flat was on his way home, he gave me a lift, and invited himself in for a drink. It was Horlicks. That was what we had for late night drinks in 1961.

The following week there was a conference of the Scottish Union of Students in St Andrews; I was a delegate, and so was David. There, he met his friend George Reid, who had been president of the St Andrews SRC. Together with Donald Dewar, the future televison-presenter Donald McCormick and assorted others, they had been on the first student visit from Scotland to Soviet Russia, and their escapades there had forged a strong bond between them. Our friendship with George has kept firm over the years, strengthened when he married Daphne McColl, who had been at the Beacon School with me.

George invited David to what was called, in local student parlance, a 'thrash'; he took not just me, but another girl from the Edinburgh delegation to the party, but she was quickly abandoned. We spent the party together, and afterwards a year's antipathy was blown away in a romantic walk by the North Sea. We walked into the conference hotel with our arms wrapped around each other to be greeted with dropped jaws – our disagreements had been a well-known feature of our relationship among our contemporaries, and although it was obvious to both of us that we were getting on much better together this term, such a radical development was totally unexpected. It was to me as well.

'Well!' said my room-mate – the girl who was abandoned the night before – as we struggled out of sleep on Sunday morning. 'Well, I never would have thought it!' I relived the previous night's events with pleasure, and got out of bed. I had a date: to watch the St Andrews students parade along the harbour in their red gowns.

Back in Edinburgh we became a recognised item, and the nine-days wonder of our changed relationship died down. But David expected a visit from his friend Norman Hackett, who had left university. His graduation the previous summer had been the occasion of a grand tea-party given by his landlady, Mrs Niven, in honour of her favourite lodger. Norman sat at the head of the table, gown draped around his substantial frame, white academic hood hanging down his back, mortarboard on his head, and a cake iced with the university coat of arms before him. David whispered to his neighbour: 'All this for an ordinary MA in four years!'

Norman was one of the great characters of my student days, and of my entire life since then: a Londoner, large-framed, and with a high-domed head that was already showing signs of incipient baldness, he was one of the activists in the SRC and the student political clubs. His uncle, George Brown, was the deputy leader of the Labour Party, which gave him both the glamour of being close to a high-profile figure and the slight raffishness associated with Brown's volatile personality. He was another person with whom I had clashed frequently over the previous year: he had a unique way of winding me up, to the extent that once, speechless in response to one of his insults, I took a shoe off and hurled it at him.

David went to meet Norman at the airport, wanting to pre-empt anyone else's version of his new romantic attachment.

'Before you hear it from anyone else, I'd better let you know: I'm going out with Judy MacGregor.'

Norman did not think much of this news, and when, a few months later, we got engaged, he added a PS to a letter to David: 'I have heard that you have got engaged. I do not believe this, and am denying the rumours. If they are true, please accept my congratulations and my prayers. If they are not true, I send my heartfelt relief.'

But once he knew it was true, he blew away all his prejudices and he and Maggi, whom he married three years later, have been amongst our closest friends over the years. Norman is perhaps the core of that group of us who have remained firm friends for over fifty years, and meet in Edinburgh, in France, in Orkney and in the Borders, to celebrate birthdays and anniversaries, children's weddings, and now, as we all approach the finishing post of life, gather to grieve together.

I suppose our courtship was unusual, for a lot of it was spent going to events run by the Pentlands Liberals, and on more than one occasion I infiltrated meetings of the Pentlands Tories to bring back reports. We went to hear Hugh Gaitskell speak, and found him inspiring – this was not long before his sudden death. With David, I was finding, for the first time in a romantic relationship, a real meeting of minds and common interest; and what was also important was that we spent a lot of time doing fairly ordinary, everyday things together. We laughed at, and with, each other, and when he called me, in tones of tenderness, a silly 'pudden', I knew that he loved me.

We had more in common that we had suspected. We were both the children of relatively large families – David was the eldest of five, with two younger brothers and sisters. Both of us had moved around a lot during our childhood, and both of us had had periods of separation from our parents. David's father was the minister at St Michael's Church in Linlithgow, but before that he had been the minister of the Church of Scotland in East Africa, and the family had lived in Nairobi for eight years.

Halfway through that time, David and his brother Michael, aged 15 and 13, had gone back to Scotland to take up scholarships at George Watson's – the English public school ethos of the Prince of Wales school in Nairobi was not one under which either of them flourished. The church did not even allow the kind of home leave that my father had had, and transport was still by boat to and from the colony. It was four years before the brothers would see their father, their sisters, and their youngest brother: and a single visit from their mother over that time was only made possible by the generosity of a former parishioner.

These parental separations had been at very different stages of our lives, but it was certainly one of the many things that we found drew us together. Just as my political interest had first been fanned by living outside Scotland, so had David's – it was his experiences in East Africa that awoke him. His father was one of the few Europeans to defend the rights of the Africans, and to speak out against the British atrocities during the Mau Mau emergency. He had also sent his sons to a racially-mixed YMCA camp, an experience that was rare, indeed almost unique, at that time, and which made a deep impression on David. Back in Scotland, at George Watson's, he became increasingly interested in politics, and, looking for a political party that would reflect his own growing ideals, found it in the Liberal Party under Jo Grimond's inspiring leadership. At University, he marched against apartheid, went off to help at by-elections, became president of the Liberal Club and then a parliamentary candidate.

Before long, I was visiting the manse at Linlithgow as David's girl-friend, and within a few months we were shopping for an engagement ring, which we bought in a second-hand shop in Rose Street. Its first outing was when we went to the Stockton-on-Tees by-election on polling day. It was not so long since the glorious night of the Orpington by-election, when Eric Lubbock had won the seat for the Liberals. In Stockton we were lying third, and our hopes of moving into second place ahead of the Tories were diminished when the Prime Minister, Harold Macmillan, who had once been an MP for Stockton, made an intervention. In those days, party leaders kept away from by-elections – and certainly Macmillan's foray was regarded as something of a breach of protocol, but the excuse was that it had been his first seat.

At Stockton, I learned for the first time the intricacies of what happens on election day: standing outside polling stations and filling in lists with the numbers of promised supporters who have voted, and the chasing up by knocking on doors, at periods during the day, of those who have not done so. The system was called, after its inventor, the Shuttleworth system, and I was to come to know it well over the years.

We decided to wait until the announcement of the count, and went to see the film *Gigi* to while away the time. Then we joined the crowd of differing partisans outside the count at Stockton Town Hall. The new Labour MP was Bill Rodgers: he stood on a balcony, his wife Sylvia (in a turquoise green suit) beside him. They were in their thirties, not as ancient as most MPs, and I wondered if David and I would ever stand outside a count in similar circumstances, and how long it would take for that event to happen.

Meantime, there was the more sober business of finding work. David was very unusual for our generation in studying for a law degree without serving a concurrent apprenticeship for a professional qualification. He had planned to become an advocate, but early on had realised that such a path was a very stony one indeed without existing contacts either at the Scottish bar or among solicitors, or without family financial support. It would be possible with complete single-mindedness, but by his second year, his mind was focused on politics, not the law. Walter Scott, who continued to draw an income from the law throughout his life, once said to his friend, James Hogg, that literature was 'a good staff, but an ill crutch', and that was how politics, for a young man – or indeed woman – was regarded in our youth. After all, politics *per se* was not even a degree subject at Edinburgh then.

David was offered, and accepted, the job of assistant secretary with the Scottish Liberal Party, bringing their professional administration to two. My apprenticeship was due to end just before the wedding, and I began work as Parliament House assistant with another firm after it.

We were married by David's father, on a crisp autumn day at Dunblane Cathedral – a church which has an inordinately long aisle for a bride and her father to find their way down towards the waiting figure at the end of it. We were young and optimistic, but neither of us would have guessed at the variety, and the twists of fate, that we would share in our life together – nor that the young love that we had then would enlarge so immeasurably over the years.

In the first flush of our engagement, David planned to take me on honeymoon to one of the lovely places he'd visited on student exchanges and conferences: Klosters, in Swizerland. Reality began to bite when he looked at the prices, and we decided instead to go to Paris. Then came an intrusion by the party, and by another deep love of his life.

'We're only going to be able to go away for about five days,' he said. 'Jo Grimond is speaking at a rally in Inverness for Russell Johnston the Friday after the wedding, and I'll have to be on hand for him. Then there's a fund-raising fete in West Aberdeenshire on the Saturday. So I thought, if we went to Skye, then you could come to the rally and the fete with me . . . and I could spend the money I saved on the fares to Paris getting the car resprayed for the wedding.'

Politics I was prepared for: it was, after all, what had drawn us together. But I didn't guess, even then, as we set off for Skye in the resprayed Rover, what a part cars – old cars – were to play in our married life.

Our first home was a rented, sub-standard farm cottage on the outskirts of Edinburgh beyond Wester Hailes. This would become an area of huge tower blocks, but fifty years ago it boasted prefabs, and even smallholdings. The cottage was up a farm road, and we had spent much of the summer, with the help of friends, getting it almost fit for habitation: painting it throughout and sanding the floors. The cottage, one of a terrace of three, was about a mile from the nearest bus stop, and the railway that ran immediately behind it was sometimes used as an escape route from Saughton Prison. There was no chance of sharing a bath there: there was no bath, only a shower, constructed out of an old larder. The metal window didn't close properly, and when it snowed – as it did, a lot, during that winter of 1962–3 – the flakes drifted in through the gap. In the food cupboard, I found mice in the breadbin and the soup pan. I had rejected a proposed wedding present of an electric blanket as insulting: we came to regret that.

# 9

# Adventures in Democracy

The first year of marriage rushed past: we both had to get used to the world of work as well as being married. And after a day in the office, or at court, I would join David in campaigning in the Pentlands. There were four local authority wards in the seat, and he was anxious to field a candidate in each one at the May elections for Edinburgh City Council. One of them was Sighthill, composed almost entirely of council houses, many of them in blocks, and he was having difficulty in recruiting anyone to stand. In a rash moment, I said, 'I'll do it,' and before I knew where I was, my name was on the ballot paper.

Election day began badly: my agent had borrowed a Heinkel bubble car. He stayed with us overnight, and before he left in the morning he drove the vehicle into a fence-post beside the cottage. I had asked for a day off work on election day. 'There's no chance of my winning,' I said. Nevertheless, when I saw the boxes emptied, and my name on them, for a minute a fantasy seized me: perhaps I had won!

Fortunately, the sitting Labour councillor retained his healthy majority, and thus ended my only episode of standing for election.

It was our first wedding anniversary. We had had a wonderful holiday in Denmark, where I'd introduced David both to the Jelnes family and to their country. We travelled in another bubble car – my mother-in-law's Messerschmitt. It did eighty-five miles to the gallon, was the height of the wheel of a double-decker bus, and the passenger sat behind the driver. Under its perspex hood, my back became scorched and blistered, but despite this it was a wonderful, romantic time, and David also succumbed to Denmark's subtle spell.

Which was more than could be said about the anniversary meal. Not for us a romantic dinner in a country inn, or a smart Edinburgh restaurant. We ate high tea in the Green Tree Café in Crieff, with a medley of other election workers. October 1963 was the time of the Kinross and West Perthshire by-election.

It was also, you may recall, if you are old enough, the year of the Profumo scandal, when the Minister of War was found sharing the favours of a high-class call girl with an attaché at the Russian embassy. It was also the year of the scandalous divorce of the Duke and Duchess of Argyll (into which I had unique insights), of the resignation of Harold Macmillan as Prime Minister and of the amazing scenes that followed it. In those days there was no question of party members voting for a party leader. In the case of the Tories, not even the MPs would vote. The Leader would 'emerge'. There were no nominations, no rules: everything was conducted in smoke-filled rooms. Eventually, metaphorical white smoke would go up and the cry, 'Habemus Papam!' – or rather, 'Habemus Ducem!' – would go up.

And it was the year that the Peerages Act allowed those inheriting a title to disclaim it, and to give up their seat in the House of Lords. The origin of this had been the determination of Tony Benn to stay in the House of Commons, despite the death of his father, the Viscount Stansgate. Normally an MP accepted his fate gracefully, donned the ermine, and often helped to choose his successor. (In 1935, the Earl of Dalkeith, the MP for Roxburgh and Selkirk, knew that his father, the Duke of Buccleuch, had not long to live. His constituency party were also aware of this, and had lined up a local worthy to fight the coming election. At the AGM, however, at which the Earl was expected to announce his future retirement, they were in for a shock. He did what was expected, but there was an addendum: 'So I have arranged for my brother, Lord William Scott, to take over the seat.' And so he did.)

Not, however, Tony Benn. On the death of his father he went to court, stood in the ensuing by-election, came top of the poll and was disqualified, and then fought for the right to renounce his peerage. And as soon as the act was passed, he did just this, and served another forty eccentric, iconoclastic and distinguished years in the House of Commons.

When Harold Macmillan resigned, Lord Hailsham, formerly Quintin Hogg, who had held various appointments in Harold Macmillan's government, saw how he could enter the fray for the Conservative succession. He announced his intention to renounce the peerage which had been bestowed on his father, and set off to the Tory Party conference in Blackpool. Alas, he had enlivened a previous conference by paddling in the sea in an old-fashioned swimsuit and ringing a handbell, and this was to prove fatal to his chances. He was followed by a dark horse, the Earl of Home. He too announced that he would resign his peerage, which, since he was the fourteenth holder of it, was more of a sacrifice. By mid-September, the Tory grandees came out of their private rooms and installed the metamorphosed Sir Alec Douglas-Home as party leader and Prime Minister. The next thing on their agenda was to find him a seat in the House of Commons.

His ancestral home, the Hirsel, was in the Scottish Borders, in Berwickshire. Next door was the seat of Roxburgh, Selkirk and Peebles, which had a comfortable Tory majority of nearly 10,000. The sitting MP, Commander Donaldson, made an approach to the party to stand aside in favour of the new Prime Minister, but in fact there was a by-election due immediately in another Scottish constituency.

It so happened that the MP for Kinross and West Perthshire, Gilmour Leburn, had died in the summer. This was promising territory for us Liberals: there was some sort of organisation on the ground, and an excellent candidate, Alistair Duncan Millar, had agreed to stand. The Tories had adopted the young and energetic George Younger, whose family came from the area. Now he, and his local party, were asked to put aside his candidacy in favour of the Prime Minister's. The 'Vote Younger' posters were already printed. It was a cruel dilemma for the young politician, but he did what was required of him.

The world's press poured into Crieff to see the phenomenen of Britain's Prime Minister fighting at grass-roots, and the strain became too much for the Liberal agent. He fell victim to stress, and David was parachuted into Crieff to take over from him.

I went there at weekends, joyfully abandoning the law for politics. My father was prevailed upon to chair the Liberal meeting in Dunblane. By this time the battle had also been joined, not just by Labour and SNP candidates, but by the satirist Willie Rushton as an Independent. Meetings were held in halls and around the backs of Landrovers: they weren't just rallies of the faithful: candidates were put under the microscope by opponents and also by genuine seekers after – well, not truth, perhaps, but after the candidates' beliefs and knowledge. It must be said that Sir Alec Douglas-Home, for all the aura he brought of being Prime Minister, did not shine at the village hall hustings.

The world's press found Crieff to their liking, and in one of the town's pubs I found myself explaining abstruse points of Scots Law, history, politics and culture to some of them. On the eve of poll, the candidates held successive, and increasingly crowded, meetings in Crieff Town Hall. Willie Rushton urged his supporters to vote Liberal. It was all heady, exciting and, above all, fun.

Norman Hackett had briefly defected from Labour to the Liberals. He came up to put in a day's canvassing. The drives leading up to Crieff's substantial drives were much longer than those in the city streets he was used to, and he was never a physically fit person. At the end of one long driveway, the front door of an imposing house door swung open in response to his knock, revealing a sheepskin-coated youth. Norman explained his mission.

'I'm so sorry,' said the youth. 'I can't vote for your candidate. I'm a minor.'

In those days the voting age was twenty-one. Norman misheard 'minor' for 'miner', and his Labour pedigree resurfaced.

'Oh, I quite understand your principles,' he said, before making his way back down the tree-lined drive. It wasn't until he was on the train home that the incongruity of the exchange struck him, and the lack of coalmines in leafy Perthshire.

As expected, Alec Douglas-Home held the seat comfortably, amid apocryphal tales of estate factors patrolling the country polling stations. In the wilder stories, they carried guns. The Liberal came a respectable second, and George Younger was rewarded with the nomination for Ayr, the seat he then held throughout an illustrious parliamentary career.

The Kinross and West Perth by-election was followed by a more low-key one, in Dumfriesshire, the following month. The Tory candidate was again a government minister, but nothing like as exalted as Sir Alec Douglas-Home. He was Scotland's Solicitor General, David Anderson QC, and he was about as useless a candidate as they could have picked. But the Liberal candidate was no great shakes either, and David was sent down to deepest Dumfriesshire by the party for three weeks to act as his 'aide' – in other words, to try to prevent him making too many gaffes.

After a meeting with farmers, the poor man, lacking in confidence, anxiously asked the outspoken party chairman, and future MP and peer, George Mackie, how he had performed. George, a highly successful farmer himself, did not exactly bolster the candidate's ego.

'Your answers were all very well, Charles,' he pronounced, 'But you really must stop hopping from foot to foot as though you'd just shat your breeks.'

The candidates all appeared on a special TV programme. David Anderson had an unusual solution to Scotland's ills. Since they were all caused by the nation's distance from London, perhaps they could be solved by attaching a rope to Caithness and pulling the landmass southwards. He did get back in, but by a narrow margin, and by the time of the general election the following year had been replaced as Tory candidate by the splendid man who served Dumfriesshire as its MP for many years, Hector Munro.

The Dumfries by-election had an important legacy for us. It was the neighbouring seat to Roxburgh, Selkirk and Peebles, two-thirds of which had been held briefly by the Liberal A.J.F. MacDonald in the 1950-51 parliament. This was the only seat in Scotland where the party had never dropped to third place behind Labour, and so was regarded as 'winnable'. The Tory majority now stood at just under 10,000, due to an increase in the Labour vote in the 1959 election, when Tam Dalyell was the Labour candidate. He had nursed the seat assiduously in his holidays from teaching; unable to drive, he bicycled round the huge constituency, gaining both publicity and respect. He took votes from the usual Liberal tally, and the Tory majority increased as a result.

Since then, the local Liberal Party had adopted a scion of one of the great historical Liberal families, the Honourable James Tennant. He was the younger son of Lord Glenconner of Glen House in Peeblesshire. His aunt, Margot Tennant, had married Herbert Asquith; his grandfather, Charles Tennant, had been in the cabinets of both Campbell-Bannerman and Asquith. Glen House, in the summer recess, was a fulcrum of political networking.

Alas, James Tennant and his wife may have been well-connected, but they lacked the common touch. Canvassing around farm cottages one evening, she noticed that the hour was approaching eight o'clock.

'Don't you think we should stop?' she asked of her supporting canvassers. 'Won't the workers be sitting down to dinner now?'

As relationships deteriorated with the local party, James put on his full dignity.

'Don't you know who I am?' he asked indignantly, 'I'm a Tennant of the Glen.'

Back came the reply, 'I don't care if you're the Monarch of the Glen – you won't do!'

So here was one of the most winnable seats in Scotland, minus a candidate, and with a general election only a year away at most. Having made one mistake, the Roxburgh, Selkirk and Peebles party were not going to make another. They were extremely picky. Russell Johnston, a rising star in the party, was interviewed by them. His silver tongue was of no avail against the fact that he wore his usual kilt.

'Highland wear,' sniffed the interviewing committee. '*That* won't go down well in the Borders.' The Inverness Liberals adopted him instead.

David had gone down to speak at a meeting in the Borders, and the key people in the local party had liked him. More than that, they wanted him as their candidate. Pressure began to be applied to him to give up his prospective candidacy in Edinburgh Pentlands and to take on the Borders seat. We were both very torn, and at the outset David felt that he, very much a child of the city, was not cut out to be a candidate in a rural seat.

The two by-elections in late 1963 changed that, especially Dumfriesshire.

'What people need in an MP,' he said in a moment of realisation, 'is not necessarily someone with a rural background, but someone who can master their brief, and be their advocate.'

And there were causes enough to advocate in the Borders seat: the chief ones were depopulation, caused partly by a lack of variety of employment outside the traditional industries of textiles and farming; the impending loss of the railway line under the Beeching cuts; and the lack of a decent, central hospital building.

It was not an area that either of us knew, apart from what I remembered of my year at Glenmayne. We had absolutely no family connections. Yet it was a region which I'd always regarded as a romantic one, full of history and legends, and also – a great plus for me – I knew it was great riding country. When, as a teenager, I'd handwritten a pony story five exercise-books in length, I had set it in the Borders.

I went with David to meet the elders of the local party, a quintet of men who seemed very senior to us indeed. They were manufacturers and farmers; chief among them were Will Stewart, who had a mill in Galashiels making fine tweeds and mohair rugs and garments to his own designs, and Andrew Haddon. They became David's mentors and guides, and fed us and looked after us with generosity. Andrew was both a farmer near Hawick and a lawyer in the town: he was a man of tremendous erudition, both about the history of politics and that of the Borders. He could also be very absent-minded. One day he said to his wife, 'Dorothy, do you know where the car is? I haven't seen it for a couple of days.'

Eventually he realised that he had stopped it to put a straying sheep back into its field. Then the bus had come along, so he had got on that, and travelled to and fro on it between his office and his farm until he noticed the absence of the car.

Eventually the decision to leave Pentlands was taken, and David's distressing task of telling those who had worked so hard for him there had come and gone. Early in January 1964 we went down to the Maxwell Hotel in Galashiels to meet the rest of the constituency party, who would decide whether to adopt David as candidate. I wore the outfit I'd worn to go away after our wedding, including my big furry hat.

I was amazed by the line David took with them. He could not have sounded more reluctant. They didn't have to adopt him, he said, but if they did, he would expect to fight at least two elections. (They had had a new candidate for each of the last four elections.) And they would need to find a new chairman, one with whom he could work, because he had no faith in the current one. He did not say it like that, of course, but that was the bottom line. All this from a young man not twenty-six years old. I was gobsmacked; for I knew now that I did want to make the move. We left the room while they discussed things. 'They'll never adopt you now!' I said, 'You sounded so unenthusiastic.'

But they did, unanimously.

Many years later, we both attended the hustings meeting to select the first candidate to the Scottish Parliament for the Borders seat. Among them was an impressive young woman who was twenty-eight years old. A Liberal worker whose election ancestry went back to those far-off days muttered, 'She's far ower young.'

'Margaret – I was younger than that when you adopted me!' David reminded her gently, and we remembered how Will had coped with the problem of David's extreme youth by saying, 'If he's good enough, he's old enough', while Andrew's line was, 'It's a fault that's aye mending.'

# 10
# Roxburgh, Selkirk and Peebles

The constituency of Roxburgh, Selkirk and Peebles was the only one in the UK that encompassed three counties. Its 1,700 square miles made it, in land-mass, a couple of places behind Argyll and Inverness, but the number of its voters, at 54,000, was greater. It stretched from the douce villages of Carlops and West Linton, only about a dozen miles from Edinburgh, in the north, to the wild, debatable land of Liddesdale in the south. In the north-west of it, the Tweed rose.

> Annan, Tweed and Clyde,
> Rise a' frae the yae hillside.

The Annan flows south to Dumfries, the Clyde west to Glasgow and the Tweed eastwards to Berwick, and for most of the Tweed's journey, the constituency hugged its shores and those of its tributaries, all known as waters: Leithen, Gala, Ettrick and Yarrow. Just downstream from Kelso, where the Teviot flows into the Tweed, the constituency marched with Berwickshire. Teviotdale itself is as ghost-ridden and pregnant with the past as Liddesdale, while Jed Water, another tributary, rises on the Carter Bar, or Redeswire, on the A68. It is real frontier country.

Within those 1,700 square miles there were many valleys, villages, and eight fiercely idiosyncratic towns, or burghs. Despite the agricultural appearance of the constituency, three-quarters of the population lived not in the countryside but in the towns. I list them from north to south, because it is the most politically neutral way to do so: Peebles, Innerleithen, Galashiels, Selkirk, Melrose, Hawick, Kelso and Jedburgh. The main industry was textiles, although Melrose was principally a tourist town and Kelso a market town. Ruins of four great mediaeval abbeys lay in Jedburgh, Melrose, Kelso and in the tranquil loop of the Tweed at Dryburgh.

It was the countryside of Border reivers, of Scotland's best rugby clubs, of great fishing streams, of Sir Walter Scott, of the Border ballads.

It was as beautiful, historical and romantic a slice of Scotland as you could dream of.

To begin with, we made our acquaintance with the A7, driving up and down to the constituency in the evenings and at weekends and often staying at Will Stewart's hospitable home in Galashiels. We went to Burns suppers and to performances of the local amateur operatic societies, which were active in no fewer than five towns. There was one great Border tradition in which we never immersed ourselves – rugby. David had spent too many unhappy afternoons at his Kenyan school engaged in this sport, for which he was totally unsuited. He wasn't going to pretend an enthusiasm that didn't exist.

By this time he had sold his pre-war Rover and moved on to an even less suitable car, a fifteen-year-old Daimler Consort with a pre-selector gear box, in which he was teaching me to drive. Before the end of February, it had skidded on an icy patch off the road and into a wall. The damage was not great, but such was his capacity to turn events like this to advantage that he even managed to issue a press release about it for the local papers. He had learned from Jo Grimond his wonderful way of making comments from Orkney on any current political situation. 'Speaking to constituents at the weekend, Mr Grimond said . . .' Jo admitted later that the constituents might have been Laura and Magnus in the kitchen of the Old Manse, but no journalist was going to chase up to Orkney to find where he had been delivering his speech.

The inefficient chairman in Roxburgh, Selkirk and Peebles had been replaced by a man slightly older than ourselves, who rejoiced (or otherwise) in the name of Riddle Dumble. Since his first name was Thomas, I never understood why he didn't use that instead of his unfortunately rhyming second name. He worked as a bookkeeper for a paint firm, a job well below his abilities, and nursed a seething resentment towards students. His mother was one of the outspoken posse of Gala women mill-workers who would put their hand to anything they could for the Liberals, and who, if not actually spitting at the word Tory, were not far from doing so.

Labour had never made real inroads into the working-class Liberal vote in the Border towns. Tam Dalyell, bicycling around the constituency in the run-up to the 1959 election, came nearest to it. At the heart of the party's energy were the Liberal Clubs in Gala, Hawick and Jedburgh, which were working men's clubs. In Gala, badly served by indoor sanitation in people's homes, the club contained not only bars and billiard tables, but baths. The one thing they had in common with establishment institutions like the Liberal Club in Edinburgh and the National Liberal Club in London, were that they admitted only men as members, which made me wonder where the female workers got their baths. Women were, however, welcomed for social events such as bingo or the Saturday night dances, and we made regular visits to these.

The Borders aristocracy were not much represented in the ranks of the Liberals. Indeed, I think that Christopher Scott of Gala was the only one. An immensely tall, immensely intelligent man, the Suez invasion of 1956 had been for him the catalyst that had inspired him to join the Liberals. He lived in what was known as New Gala House, a nineteenth-century Scottish baronial mansion on the outskirts of Galashiels. The original home of the Scotts of Gala, a beautiful, modest sixteenth-century house, had been made over to the town in Victorian times. Christopher wished his nineteenth-century ancestors had continued to live there, rather than bequeathing him the grand but inconvenient house that he and his family occupied. He also owned farms, fishing and cottages around the town, and he offered us the lease of one of these, an old ferryman's cottage beside the Tweed. The prospect of changing the lease of one cottage for another was not especially daunting, and there was a general feeling that it would be a great advantage if the Liberal candidate lived in the constituency.

The Tory MP, Commander Donaldson, did not have a base there, only a rented flat in Dolphin Square in London. This was seen as not quite the thing, although many of the Tories who swelled the ranks of the local party could have done what Christopher did, and offered him a modest cottage. Donaldson must have had a naval pension of some kind, but he was almost totally dependent on his MP's salary, which in 1964 was £1,750. There was no living in London allowance, so for someone of modest means there could only be one home, and he made the choice for it to be in London.

I don't know what happened in Donaldson's early days, but by the time we came along he was staying in bed-and-breakfasts when he came up to the constituency, even during the election. His wife did not come with him: although MPs' travel was paid for to and from the constituency, there was no allowance for spouses. And these expenses were paid only up to the dissolution of parliament, not until the election.

We took up Christopher's offer eagerly. I began to explore the possibility of a job with a local firm of solicitors, but we agreed that I should probably stay where I was until the election was over. At that time we expected it to be in the spring or summer. Douglas-Home's announcement that he would go for the full five-year term came as a great boost: now David would have the whole summer to work at building up a campaign.

Then Christopher told us that the cottage would not be ready until the autumn, but there was an empty farm house and would we like to occupy that for six months? The rent would be the same as the cottage. David was taken to see Hollybush and reported that it was quite big but would do us fine. When I in turn inspected it, David would open doors saying, 'I think this is a cupboard,' and a whole servants' wing, or an attic, would open up. The only bathroom was the size of a decent bedroom. Clearly, the basic furniture for a three-roomed cottage would not go very far in it.

In those days – and right up to the 1970s – there were auction sales in Selkirk's Victoria Halls every couple of months. They were run by a splendid High Tory called Len Thomson who later became Provost of Selkirk, and were held on Thursdays, so it was David who went there and bid. I think that the total he spent was sixteen pounds, and his haul included two carpets, a couple of rexine chairs, two beds and two wardrobes, a black umbrella with a silver and agate handle ('I thought you'd like it' – and I did), a round footstool and a two-foot-square table with drop-leaves that became our kitchen table. It cost a shilling. Later, as we acquired a family, it became too small, but sentiment stopped us from disposing of it. In one of his very few DIY bursts, David made a top for it out of left-over flooring.

When we moved from Cherrydene, years and years later, the fate of the table was the cause of much heart-searching. I wanted it in the new kitchen; David wanted our dining table there. 'You can't get rid of the kitchen table,' objected Rory, our youngest son, 'it's family history.' For a few years David used it as his desk, until our daughter Catriona and her family moved to a house with a kitchen that demanded a table. So there it went, and there it remains, the one-shilling table around which another generation's history is being enacted. I can still see it, in its original incarnation, a small island in the large, dark Victorian kitchen at Hollybush.

We moved down at the beginning of April. On the days when David stayed in the Borders, I would cycle the mile or so to the station and catch the train up to Edinburgh. It was our first summer of discovery of the Borders. David would go to villages and make four calls at each one – on the minister, the schoolteacher, the shopkeeper and the postmaster – the people who had their fingers on the pulse of the community. They would – and did – tell him about local issues, and they would no doubt pass on the news of his visit.

Such an approach would not be possible now. Even where village schools still exist, the schoolhouses have been sold, and the head teacher only rarely lives in the community. The parishes have been amalgamated, and the manses too have become the homes of the middle classes. The Post Office network has shrunk, and shops are in short supply.

It was, however, a ploy that worked then. Travelling down from Edinburgh on the train one evening, I shared a compartment with two ministers. 'The new Liberal candidate called on me the other day,' said one. 'He seems a very personable young man.' Bursting with pride, I felt it necessary to identify myself. I did not do so, however, when my travelling companions were two members of the local Labour party who were discussing how they had recently got rid of their candidate.

He was replaced with an advocate I knew, Ronald King Murray, a clever man who in time became Lord Advocate and then a judge. Sometimes he would give me lifts down from Edinburgh. The quartet of candidates was completed by a bizarre, brilliant eccentric, Anthony J.C. Kerr, who stood for the SNP. A linguist in fourteen languages, who now taught at Jedburgh Grammar School, he lacked the skills to organise his life properly. 'I've never actually seen any one with dandruff in their eyebrows before,' was one comment I remember hearing about him. He wrote voluminous and rather erudite letters to the *Scotsman* on a variety of subjects, and got around the constituency on an unreliable scooter.

Meantime, there were other things to think about. While we were still in Edinburgh, I had felt my whole time was funnelled into the law and politics. I suggested to David that we should go riding together. On the basis of half a dozen lessons when he was a child, he agreed to come as well, and it became our regular Saturday outing.

In Galashiels, I identified stables and we rode regularly, either in the evenings or at weekends. It was not like any riding I had ever done before: one of the differences was the large number of men we saw in the saddle. Another was that instead of cantering sedately in single file, as I was used to, when the riders reached a field or piece of moorland where the horses could let themselves stretch, they all spread out and set off together, and there were many spills.

We began to learn about the Common Ridings, and about the rivalry between the towns. One evening, I rode beside a girl from Selkirk, and as we turned our horses back towards Gala, she said bitterly: 'They [the people of Galashiels] killed our Standard Bearer.' A few years before there had been a dreadful accident at the Galashiels Braw Lads' Gathering, when the

Selkirk Standard Bearer had fallen off his horse as the cavalcade crossed the Tweed. He was drowned and his body was not recovered for a couple of days. The tone of this remark implied that the hosting town had in some way deliberately caused the tragedy.

Andrew Haddon suggested that it would do David good in Hawick if he were to follow the Cornet on the Mosspaul ride-out. From the time the Cornet there is appointed at the beginning of May, he and his followers ride out from the town to villages or farms several miles distant twice a week. The hardest, and most prestigious, of these rides is to Mosspaul, the inn that stands on the border of Roxburghshire and Dumfriesshire. The men who complete it become members of the Ancient Order of Mosstroopers, with its own badge and tie, its annual dinner and (in those days) a ball. The return journey over the hills and the mosses is nearly thirty miles, and it is not for the novice. At the two-hour stop at Mosspaul, there is much drinking. It's said that, on the return journey, the Hawick men do not leave the saddle to urinate.

'Go on the Tuesday,' advised Andrew. 'There are fewer riders than on the Saturday. And whatever you do, don't overtake the Cornet.' He then recounted to us how, in the early years of the twentieth century, Austen Chamberlain was being considered as Tory candidate in the Borders. He too was put on a horse in similar circumstances, but, without that warning, he rode out in front of the cavalcade, ahead of the Cornet. He was smuggled out of Hawick on his return and his candidature was not pursued.

It was as well that Will Boyle, who ran the stables we frequented in Galashiels, had got a measure of David's riding capacities and hired him a sensible horse. As it was a Tuesday, I could only see the return of the riders to Hawick by taking the train there from Edinburgh after work. When David got off his horse, he was so shattered he could hardly put one foot in front of the other. He collapsed on the back seat of the ancient Daimler and I drove back to Hollybush. I am sure there is something that says that the supervising driver of a learner should be in the front seat.

In Hawick, as well as Gala and elsewhere, there were strong women on the Liberal committee. Mrs Horne was one of them. We were getting Tory defections to our ranks by this time, including a woman journalist in Hawick who was something of a local personality. She turned up at a coffee morning in Hawick Liberal Club. 'Don't speak to her,' said Mrs Horne, the political enmity of years raging in her breast, 'she's a turncoat.'

'But Mrs Horne,' I said, somewhat astonished at this lack of Liberalism, 'we need five thousand turncoats if we're going to win this seat.'

Summer passed into autumn. The election was called for 5 October. I had managed to save two weeks of my annual holidays and took them in the fortnight before polling day. But the organisation wasn't strong enough for me to use the time to actually knock on doors. I had to stay in the nerve-centre of operations, the Galashiels Liberal Club, answering the telephone and stuffing election addresses into envelopes, which in those days were all laboriously handwritten by party supporters.

As mentioned above, the main local issues were threefold: the drain of population, especially of young people; the failure to replace the wartime hospital, housed in huts, with a modern building, and the future of the Waverley railway line, under threat of closure by Dr Beeching. Donaldson had spoken against the cuts, but in parliament had voted for the implementation of the Beeching plan. It made an easy target: David used the slogan, 'a voice for the Borders', emphasising the lack of one under Donaldson's years of representation. As well as criticising the stale Tory government, he attacked Commander Donaldson for his record – or lack of it. A cruel joke went around that in one parliament, Donaldson's only entry in Hansard had been a request to open a window. Then David found a speech he had made on the future of the Forth and Clyde Canal, and ridiculed him: 'I always wondered what it was he commanded.'

In the evenings there would be three meetings – fifty-five in all, over the three weeks. Gradually a momentum built up. In Peebles, at the start of the campaign, there was an audience of fourteen; at the eve of poll meeting in the same town, there were a hundred. There were two wonderful sisters in that town, Ella and Selina Connolly. They were retired mill-workers, and lived and breathed Liberalism. Soon after David was adopted as candidate, they handed over their own fund-raising contribution: a huge collection of Victorian pennies, most of which, alas, turned out to be of face-value only. On election days, they always supplied the pies at the committee rooms. Now they, and other stalwarts like them, were joined by new people coming forward and offering to help. Chief amongst them was the Peebles dentist, 'Mac' MacDonald. At a Liberal function in Peebles Hydro a year or so later, he sighed in exasperation. 'Really, I would have thought Selina would have put her dentures in for the Hydro.'

Between some meetings the distances were considerable, the greatest stretch perhaps being between Teviothead and Newcastleton, a village of about 900 electors in remote Liddesdale. Driving the candidate between the two meetings, Andrew Haddon did not regale David with Liberal policy or local issues, but recited to him the thirty-three verses of the

ballad of Johnnie Armstrong, the notorious reiver hanged at Teviothead
by James V in 1529, after being tricked into a meeting with the king.

> To seek het water beneath cauld ice,
> Surely it is a great folie –
> I have asked grace from a graceless face,
> But there is nane for my men and me!

In West Linton, a hundred miles away at the other end of the constituency, a village about seventeen miles from Edinburgh, Norman Hackett
came to hold the fort until the candidate arrived at the meeting. I went
ahead with him. He perched himself on top of a small primary school
desk and entered into a very metropolitan debate with the audience.
Worst of all, he broke the golden rule that only the candidate should
answer questions, and invited them from those who were waiting to
hear David. They were not friendly in tone, and one questioner was
positively hostile. Norman, addressing her as 'my old darling', took her
to be a Tory on account of her accent. She was in fact a Labour stalwart,
and the atmosphere grew even chillier. By the time David arrived, the
meeting was irretrievable. At the end of the campaign, the Tory majority
matched almost exactly the population of West Linton: we pointed this
out to Norman.

This was not the only disaster with supporting speakers. In Melrose,
our arrival at the meeting was so delayed that not one, but two speakers
had filled in. The atmosphere was decidedly frosty. We discovered that
each of them had lectured the audience on the same subject, so dear to
many Liberal hearts, proportional representation. One of them had even
picked up a piece of chalk and illustrated its niceties on the blackboard.
They were undoubtedly cooler-downers rather than warmer-uppers.

It was usually Will Stewart or Andrew Haddon who drove David
between meetings. Will drove a Mercedes, which made me car-sick, and
was the cause of one or two incidents of people shouting remarks about
the fact that the car was German. After the meetings we would return to
Hollybush, change into our oldest clothes and go out fly-posting, using
a paste of flour and water, on the backs of road-signs between Galashiels
and Selkirk.

We had the feeling that the tide was flowing with us – and more
strongly than our best original hopes had been. The final meetings were
well-attended and the enthusiasm was palpable. David's aim was to halve
the Tory majority and take it down to 5,000.

We headed into the count in Jedburgh, the morning after the poll, with the knowledge that Labour, under Harold Wilson, had just edged into government, and the thirteen years of Tory rule were at an end. But the result was closer than had been anticipated. Next door, in Berwick and East Lothian, John Mackintosh had failed to match the swing and take the seat for Labour from Sir William Anstruther Grey, a Tory of the old school. Afterwards, John told us ruefully of how Anstruther Grey had come up to him and said, 'I've been reading these speeches you've been making, Mackintosh. I see you are bringing politics into this campaign. You won't win an election that way.'

'And,' added John as a punchline, 'What's more, he was quite right.'

But in Roxburgh, Selkirk and Peebles it was another matter. We were sure – despite the absence of canvassing returns – that there had been a strong swing. As we made our way into Jedburgh Town Hall, David whispered to me, 'I think we might have brought it down to under three thousand.' When the votes were counted, the majority had slumped to 1,700. We were ecstatic. In his winner's speech outside Jedburgh Town Hall, the re-elected Commander Donaldson expressed his thanks to his Labour and SNP opponents for the gentlemanly way in which they had conducted the campaign, and pointedly made no mention of the young Liberal who had run him so close.

News filtered through to us of Liberal wins in the three most northerly seats on the Scottish mainland – George Mackie in Caithness and Sutherland, the Gaelic-speaking Alasdair Mackenzie in Ross and Cromarty, and Inverness, won by our friend Russell Johnston. These were the seats of which hopes had been highest. But the result in Roxburgh, Selkirk and Peebles was a surprise, and Will Stewart whisked us down to Border Television in Carlisle. *En route*, we spotted a familiar figure pushing his broken-down scooter up a hill. It was Anthony J.C. Kerr, whose tally had been a mere thousand votes.

David was interviewed along with such heavyweights as Willie Whitelaw, a Tory grandee even then, and Labour's Fred Peart, about to be appointed Minister of Agriculture by Harold Wilson. Both of them were avuncular and kind to us on that day, and continued to be so over the years.

We settled back to everyday life. I returned to work in Edinburgh with even less enthusiasm for the law. Whenever it rained, the second-hand minivan we'd bought just before the election – a sensible car, for once – gave up the ghost at the halfway point, Middleton Moor, and I was inevitably late. David applied for, and got, a job in the BBC's current affairs department. We moved from the grandeur of Hollybush to the old ferryman's cottage at Boleside, beside the Tweed just downstream from its confluence with the Ettrick. It was the place where, nearly twenty years before, my father had skiffed stones on the Tweed before leaving for Sierra Leone. It was slightly more modern than the cottage in Edinburgh – at least there was a bath, and the lavatory didn't open directly off the kitchen. And the situation, down by the Tweed, was idyllic, with the odd freight train still puffing along the branch railway between Gala and Selkirk. In autumn, just beyond the cottage, the train driver would stop the engine and climb on to it to pick crab apples from an overhanging tree.

The wretched Donaldson was prevailed upon by the local Tory Association to declare that he would not stand at the next election. Oddly enough, he confided his woes to Alasdair Mackenzie, one of the new Highland Liberal MPs. The choice of a new Tory candidate was set in motion.

Then suddenly, six weeks after the general election, during minor surgery at St Thomas's hospital, Commander Donaldson died. It was a Friday, and David was working in the BBC studio in Glasgow on that day's programme. When the news was brought to him, he thought it was a joke in poor taste by some of his colleagues, and it wasn't until they brought him a printed news statement that he believed it, and phoned me. I took his call, sitting at the desk in the corner of the cottage living-room: I literally tipped over backwards.

# 11

# The Battle of the Borders

'If anyone phones,' said David, 'don't say anything. Just our sympathies to his widow. It's not decent to say anything else, not until after the funeral.'

But when he came home, we started planning. I would give in my notice in Edinburgh to be available full time in whatever supporting roles fell to me. 'Are you having a baby?' I was asked by acquaintances at Parliament House, when I told them I was leaving. 'No, we're having a by-election.' Thus ended my legal career, with no regrets on either side.

BBC Scotland told David that if he stood as a candidate in the election, he wouldn't be able to appear on television. His contract would end. In vain he gave them other examples, such as that of Geoffrey Johnson-Smith, presenter of *Tonight*, and Tory candidate for the East Grinstead by-election: they were adamant. To be fair to BBC Scotland, they already had a case pending in the Court of Session about equality of broadcasting time. The poet Hugh MacDiarmid had stood as a Communist in Alec Douglas-Home's seat of Kinross and West Perthshire in the general election, and was now bringing a case against the BBC complaining that the Prime Minister had had more television exposure than he had.

Then David looked closely at his six-month contract (which in no way forbade any kind of political activity) and found that, although the BBC could decide not to use him, they still had to pay him until the end of March. We laughed with relief about the help this gave our immediate financial outlook, even though we were down to one salary. In effect, the BBC would be funding David to be a full-time candidate!

We waited to see whom local Tories would choose as their new candidate. Now, of course, they had a perfect excuse for their close shave in October: 'Of course, *poor* Commander Donaldson was a *dying man*,' went the whisper.

Their selection committee then came up with what must have seemed to them a perfect choice: Robin McEwen of Marchmont. His father had been the MP for Berwickshire, and he and his family still lived there, at the large Edwardian mansion of Marchmont. They were friends and neighbours of Sir Alec Douglas-Home, now leader of the opposition. McEwen was a London barrister, and had gained some notoriety as a boyfriend of Princess Margaret. His wife, Brigid, was an aristocratic beauty, and they had four photogenic children. He had fought the safe Labour seat of East Edinburgh in the General Election, so he was no novice.

We were somewhat dismayed, but Christopher Scott, who knew him, was more sanguine. He felt that Robin McEwen did not have the temperament for politics. 'I know him,' said Christopher, 'and I tell you, he *won't do.*'

Meantime, the Labour party reappointed Ronald King Murray, and the SNP thought long and hard about Anthony J.C. Kerr's showing, and decided not to endorse him, nor to put up another candidate. He immediately declared that he would stand as an independent Nationalist.

The trouble was, he did not have the £150 required as a deposit. His problem received wide publicity, and a day before nominations closed, he found an envelope with £150 in used notes pushed through his letterbox. Naturally, the Liberal supporters all blamed a Tory sympathiser: the redistribution of the small SNP vote in October was reckoned to be most likely heavily in favour of the only UK party whose policies advocated a Scottish Parliament.

Unsurprisingly, David was reselected as Liberal candidate. Even so, A.J.F. MacDonald, the MP from 1950–51, approached the local party: 'I was thinking, this might be the right time to come back, for this by-election . . . I mean, the young chap you had last time – he is pretty green, isn't he? But he did a good job – he could be my agent.'

In 1964, we had nothing to lose: now, it was make or break time.

Once again, what surprises and even impresses me in retrospect is the extent to which David never lost control of the campaign. He was the candidate and he would run it. He would choose the political ground: only he would answer questions, and at meetings, he would always be the final speaker. The fact that he and his agent, Arthur Purdom, had worked together harmoniously for a couple of years in the party's Edinburgh office meant that, where there could have been conflict between an agent and a candidate so sure of his direction, there was a deep trust between them.

Arthur had a wonderful saying which I passed on at the busy headquarters of North Edinburgh and Leith Lib Dems during the 2010 election: 'What we need is a lot fewer brilliant seconds and a lot more mediocre firsts.' I was so certain that North Edinburgh would fall into the second category. I was wrong.

Helpers, mostly unpaid, came from all over Britain. There was a posse of employed agents from the West Country, and Christopher Scott turned over Hollybush, now empty again, to hard-up students who camped in sleeping bags on the floorboards. This lack of creature comforts did not prevent the conception of at least one child, who rejoices in the middle name of Roxburgh. Meantime, journalists came to call on our snug little cottage by the Tweed, and no doubt made comparisons with Robin McEwen's ancestral grandeur.

In Galashiels, the Douglas Hotel became the headquarters of the press. Harry Boyne of *The Times*, Paddy Travers of the *Telegraph*, Peter Preston of the *Guardian* and Llew Gardner of the *Express* – great, heavyweight political journalists all of them – were some of those who came. So did Robin Day from the BBC. Nor were they flying visits: some of the journalists were almost literally embedded. On 17 March, the proprietrix of the Douglas Hotel presented Paddy Travers with a St Patrick's day cake, iced with the legend: 'To Paddy, from the little people'.

At meetings, there was no longer any need to rely on university friends or local PR enthusiasts to do the warm-up acts. All the parliamentary party save one came: that exception was Peter Bessell, the newly elected member for Bodmin. David would not have him in the constituency. It was a question of 'I do not like thee, Doctor Fell, The reason why I cannot tell.' Bessell was a person he always instinctively mistrusted. Events a decade later proved that instinct right.

That great Scottish Liberal, John Bannerman, and his wife Ray, spent much time with us. John's rugby record made him an immediate draw; he was a respected figure in this rugby-mad part of Scotland, and his speeches always had some analogy based on the sport. Jo Grimond made a couple of visits and raised us all to new heights of inspiration with his oratory. George Mackie, by now the MP for Caithness, brought his own blend of forcefulness and humour.

The best speeches of the whole campaign were made by David's friend, John Mackay, the candidate for Argyll. 'I should have brought my bagpipes,' he told the meeting in Galashiels, 'and then I could have played "McEwen's Lament" and "Murray's Farewell to His Deposit".' David admonished him afterwards: 'We mustn't let the Labour people think they're going to lose their deposit – they might not give us the votes.' He added, 'and I don't think it's right for a supporting speaker to make such markedly better speeches than the candidate!'

John Mackay was one of that generation of Glasgow University star speakers that included Donald Dewar and John Smith. He later defected to the Tories, his final argument on the subject with David being late on the day of Russell Johnston's wedding, when David said, 'If you enter the House as a Tory, John, I shall spit on you.' I think this was one of the most aggressive things I have ever heard David say. John did represent Argyll eventually as a Tory, and I was always slightly disappointed that David didn't fulfil his spitting threat. But John Bannerman's daughter, Ray Michie, took the seat from him in 1987, and that was a better comeuppance. Like Donald Dewar and John Smith, John Mackay died young, not long after he and David had gone head to head in the House of Lords over the passage of the Scotland Bill at the end of the 1990s. It was, indeed, the Liberal Party's commitment to Scottish Home Rule that had made him break with it.

These days, I think of John Mackay whenever I attend the Borders General Hospital, for the foundation stone that he laid and which bears his name is set in the wall of the reception area. But when I pass it I think, not of the Tory careerist, but of the brilliant young speaker at the by-election, and his jokes about 'McEwen's Lament', and 'Murray's Deposit'.

There was one person from the outside who gave the most constant support. Jeremy Thorpe was in his mid-thirties at the time. He had won the West Country seat of North Devon in the 1959 election, the only gleam of light for the party at that dark time. He was thirty-six at the time of the by-election, and was witty, high spirited and ebullient. He had the confidence and smooth manners that come with an Etonian education, and his wit and turn of phrase lit up the meetings. He would travel with us between meetings, diverting David as he told stories of his own campaigns or about Liberal grandees, all with his superb gift for mimicry and personal brand of storytelling. He had an inestimable quality for a politician – he never forgot a face or a name, and was always able to recall the circumstances in which he'd met somebody previously.

Jeremy came to the Borders twice, for several days at a time. On the second occasion, he came with a girl called Charlotte in his entourage, and her minute dog, Clovis, which sported a canine jersey with a THIS TIME STEEL badge pinned to it. She seemed to be a girlfriend, but now I wonder if she was merely camouflage. We had absolutely no idea that Jeremy was involved in a relationship with a man called Norman Scott, which was starting to go sour at that particular time: we would never have guessed that anything was clouding that irrepressible spirit.

He was a brilliant campaigner, always full of energy and humour, livening up whatever situation he found himself in, but always with a constant undertow of passionate Liberalism.

'The battle of the Borders,' the journalists called it. It was fought on various fronts, in such a very different way to election campaigns nowadays that the *modus operandi* is worth recording.

I'm not sure where David picked up some of his ideas. They were very simple and very effective. One was simply the kind of paper on which the posters were printed. Having decided during the previous election that his slogan for this one would have to be THIS TIME STEEL, he had it printed on what is called Dayglo yellow. That is the frightful yellow of cheap sales posters. He did not pretend it was aesthetically pleasing, only that it stood out much more strongly than the conventional posters, and that it was (in those days) still a novelty. Another idea was the printing of tin election badges, bearing the same slogan and his photo, a vast number of which were made and distributed: again, they were a novelty. Children would beg them from party workers, and thus began the indoctrination of another generation. We kept the metal badges going – a new one for each election – until they became too expensive an item, and were changed to stick-on ones. When David retired, in 1997, there were people who had rosettes with a badge for each campaign adorning them. I, on the other hand, have mislaid most of the ones I had.

Throughout the Borders, the roadside elms and limes and oaks sprouted Tory posters. But in the housing schemes, the windows were lit up with Dayglo posters, and cars bore stickers on their back windscreens bearing the legend, THIS TIME STEEL.

There were no 'target letters' in those days. There were three pieces of election literature, the first and third delivered by hand. The first was an introductory leaflet, which in this case was mainly to remind people of the result a few months before, and to stress that it was a two-horse race. Then there was the main election address, delivered by post, but in envelopes hand-addressed by party workers. This contained details of policy, and description of the candidate (usually with a family photo) and the traditional letter from him or her, plus details of the eve-of-poll meetings. And, as late as possible in the last week, there would be a final communication.

During the day, David and the other candidates would be summoned to a few all-party meetings – for the farmers, for example, convened by the NFU at the auction marts in Hawick, Peebles and St Boswells. But his main occupation was touring the textile mills, and here he was a great hit. Most of those working on the production line were women, and he seemed to lead a charmed life with them. They would take his badges and pin them on with enthusiasm, and as the campaign wore on, he would find his election addresses already adorning the looms and knitting machines. On the odd occasion when the management refused him access, the Liberals amongst the work force would make it well known, especially if Robin McEwen was allowed a visit, and he would be at the gates as a shift changed. At each mill, some of which employed several hundred workers, he would make a point of shaking hands with every single employee at the looms, knitting machines, despatch department and offices.

I didn't come with David on these visits. I had my own programme, which consisted of rural canvassing and visits to the old peoples' homes. Since I still didn't have a full driving licence, one of the visiting volunteers would drive me. It was not a proper marked canvass, simply one to make the Liberal presence felt. I evolved some rules of my own early on. One was that I preferred to introduce myself rather than having my companion do this. Another was that as I made the introduction, I would look at the householder in the eyes. If the eyes lit up, I knew we had met a sympathiser; if a veil came down, we had not. I eschewed asking *how* people were going to vote in favour of simply hoping that they *would* give David their vote. I figured that it was awkward for them to give a true response – if it was to be a negative one – when faced with the candidate's loving spouse. My own antennae from their first reaction usually gave me their voting intentions. I even had my own cards printed: 'I am sorry you were out when I called. I hope you will vote for my husband, David Steel, on polling day', with my signature printed below the message. Since there was no election date, the cards lasted for several campaigns.

Always, there was a sense of walking with political history. In Roxburgh and Selkirk, the memory of A.J.F. MacDonald's brief tenure as MP was remembered – often in the shape of some amenity, such as a village hall or a public lavatory, that he'd been able to procure for a community. For there to be such a recent folk memory of the election of a Liberal was a rare and valuable asset.

In Peeblesshire, the memory of a Liberal MP was more distant, but more deep-seated, as old people recalled Sir Donald Maclean, who had briefly served as Liberal leader after the First World War and whose son had defected to Russia as a spy with Guy Burgess in the 1950s. They still shook their heads sadly over this, recalling the young Maclean as a lad on his holidays. Then they would remember Maclean's Tory successor as MP, Captain Maule Ramsay, who was interned during the Second World War for Nazi sympathies.

In Melrose, we met a very old man who told us with pride that he had driven the coach for the winning Liberal candidate in Roxburghshire in 1906. It was not, however, until the following election that the most amazing encounter took place. David's main supporters in the village of Walkerburn, John and Margaret Gebbie, were most insistent that he should go to the house of the village's oldest inhabitant. 'I'm very pleased to meet you, young man,' she quavered, 'The last MP I shook hands with was Mr Gladstone.' She had been a girl of 12 and had presented the G.O.M. with a bouquet when he ran his great campaign in neighbouring Midlothian.

These encounters stand out from those days of calling round farms and cottages in the constituency, but each day was full of interest and incident. I have to confess that my companions and I would usually return to base with a couple or more of Tory posters in the boot. It is a habit that I have found difficult to break. In 1997, David's successor, Michael Moore, was appalled when the Tory agent rang HQ to say that Lady Steel and her son had been identified removing a poster in Clovenfords. The agent was very honourable, and promised not to tell the press, but I was given a real dressing-down.

But it was at the meetings that the election was won and lost. What a great proving-ground they were! Supporters of rival parties would come armed with awkward questions: I can still see Lord Lambton, then the Tory MP for Berwick, sitting in a village hall in dark glasses and green wellies, harrumphing from time to time at David's speech, and taking notes.

Genuinely undecided voters would attend meetings of all of the candidates, to ask them questions on policy and on matters of conscience and to weigh up their abilities. One question came up at every meeting. It was the time when Sidney Silverman's Bill to abolish capital punishment was going through the Commons, and the views of the different candidates on the subject would be probed. After one meeting, the audience member who had posed the question came up to David. 'I don't agree with your views,' he said, 'but you've been quite clear about them, and the others dodged the question. I'll be voting for you.'

A farmer called Haig Douglas asked a question – or to be precise, harangued all the candidates –about the 'cheap food' policy of successive governments since 1945, which he saw as destructive to agriculture. He continued to do this at every single election right up until 1992. At least he made the candidates aware of his views.

The Labour Party brought in heavyweights such as George Brown, who overfilled the largest meeting halls in Peebles, Galashiels and Hawick. Alas for Ronald King Murray, this did not signify enthusiasm for his cause: people of all persuasions were not going to miss the opportunity of hearing the big beasts of politics when they were orating at a nearby venue. As it turned out, George Brown addressed more people than actually voted Labour.

As for the Tories, they wheeled out many of those who had recently lost office in the election. As the phrase 'big guns' was used to describe them, I reminded David of an episode of Scottish history that had happened in the constituency. In 1460, King James II, overseeing the siege of Roxburgh Castle, had taken too keen an interest in his artillery and been killed by a big gun backfiring. It was a wonderful analogy, and the press loved it.

Midway through the campaign, the journalist Llew Gardner of the *Express* asked if he could accompany David while canvassing. David explained that he wasn't calling door-to-door, but concentrating on getting round people at their workplaces. However John and Margaret Gebbie, his faithful supporters in the village of Walkerburn, had expressed worries about how the vote was holding up in one of the streets there. So David had agreed to do some door-knocking, and invited Llew Gardner to come with him, emphasising to the journalist that this would be atypical, and we were expecting quite a hard core of opposition.

There was none. Each door he knocked on elicited a positive, even enthusiastic response. 'Honestly,' David said to Llew Gardner, 'this is not a put-up job.' Over many elections, we were to learn that the Gebbies *always* took a pessimistic view of our chances.

Llew Gardner's subsequent story in the *Daily Express* was not only the first one to predict a Liberal victory, it was also the first time that David was given the sobriquet 'The Boy David', as Gardner tied the whole by-election to the David and Goliath story. It was a nickname that stuck to him for years.

Goliath, in the shape of Robin McEwen, was having a hard time of it, especially at meetings, and sometimes his visiting big guns did in fact misfire. Challenged about figures showing that people were leaving the constituency, one of the Tories attributed this to the decrease of domestic servants in big houses. McEwen himself lost his temper at times, and made bad jokes that fell flat.

We were incredulous. Here was this intelligent man, who had already faced the hustings, falling apart. My theory was that he had never really encountered anyone outside of the aristocratic circle in which he moved, and had always been treated with deference – as part of the Borders squirearchy, as part of the Royal social circle, as a gilded youth at Oxbridge and as a London barrister. Christopher Scott had been right all along: Robin McEwen 'wouldn't do'. He retired to bed with what was said to be flu, but which was in fact a total nervous collapse. His wife Brigid took over the mill visits and read his speeches at the meetings, and it was generally agreed that she was a better candidate than he had been.

During the last few days the momentum, to us, seemed unstoppable. It was such fun, as well as unremittingly hard work. Stories appeared in the press about Tory posters disappearing from the trees – even a banner strung from the Galashiels Tory Club across the High Street went missing. I could point out its burial place, as described to me by the future MP responsible for its removal. Each evening, Christopher and Anne Scott would lay on a cold spread at Gala House – Anne's egg mousse was especially memorable – and we and others in the team would congregate there, and swap stories of the day's campaigning. Their generosity made a perfect ending to the night. It all seemed to be going our way.

### EGG MOUSSE RECIPE

*4 hard-boiled eggs*
*1 dessertspoon of Worcester sauce*
*½ pint aspic jelly*
*¼ pint double cream*
*¼ pint single cream*
*Salt and pepper to taste*

Shell the hard-boiled eggs, cut in half, and remove the yolks. Chop the egg whites finely. Press the yolks through a sieve into a bowl, add the Worcester sauce and seasoning to taste. Stir in the chopped egg whites and 3 tablespoons of the cooled aspic jelly. Whip the double and single cream together until fairly thick, fold into the egg mixture, and turn into a 6-inch soufflé dish. Smooth the top and allow it to set – this should take about half an hour. Cover the surface with a thin layer of aspic jelly.

David's third and final print delivery was an ingenious publication that did not look like yet another party political tract. It was a four-page tabloid. With the masthead *The Border News*, it looked like a neutral free-sheet. The main story was not that he was going to romp home, but the headline was 'Neck and Neck', with a photo of McEwen as well as of himself. In the right-hand column was a secondary story: 'Labour likely to save deposit'. All along, his attempt to squeeze the Labour vote had to be balanced by a reassurance to traditional Labour supporters that if they switched votes, their party would not be badly harmed.

The local press baron, Colonel Jim Smail, was a New Zealander who owned the Tweeddale Press Group. Later, he and his son John would become our friends, and Jim would be David's colleague on the board of Border TV. The Tweeddale Press titles at that time included the *Kelso Chronicle*, the *Hawick Express* and the *Southern Reporter*. The main base of the group was in Berwick, and the Smails, who lived near the town, were not only keen Tories but knew McEwen socially. On the last issue before polling day in the three papers that covered the constituency, a leader written personally by Jim Smail, as Editor-in-Chief, urged readers to vote Conservative. There was also a whole page devoted to a composite article on the candidates' wives. Practically all of it was taken up with photographs and text about Brigid McEwen and Marchmont House, while Sheila King Murray and I were squeezed into a corner each. Mrs Kerr had declined to be interviewed.

The final meeting of the campaign took place at the Roxy cinema in Kelso, after enthusiastic rallies in Peebles and Gala earlier in the evening. It was the tradition that the Liberal eve-of-poll took place at the Roxy at 10.30 pm, after the cinema audience had departed; and the place was packed, not just with supporters but with opponents whose meetings had all finished. It says something about their enjoyment of the by-election that the press corps turned out as well, although the meeting was too late in the evening to be of any use as a story.

The supporting speakers were Jeremy Thorpe and John Bannerman. We all crowded onto the space between the cinema screen and the edge of the stage, not more than two feet in depth. At the Calcutta Cup match on the previous Saturday, England had won in injury time. John Bannerman made the most of this by using a rugby analogy: referring to the need to get as high a turn-out as possible, he roared as his peroration, 'And if you see a Tory coming to the polling station in injury time – blow your whistle!'

As David rose to speak, a strange figure appeared down one of the aisles. It had two legs, and a large cardboard box, plastered with THIS TIME STEEL posters, over its top half. When a head appeared through the top of the box, it proved to be that of a Kelso eccentric, rather the worse for drink, but not so much so as to prevent him from voicing his support of the Liberal candidate in a very individual and down to earth way.

The Roxy audience erupted in laughter, and it seemed for a while that David would either fall off the narrow platform or be unable to give his rousing, uplifting eve of poll speech for the fifth and last time. Eventually, drying his eyes as the laughter subsided, he began, and the atmosphere changed as he spoke again of the need for the Borders to have a strong voice at Westminster, of the need for domestic and overseas policies to be infused by Liberal thinking.

I can still recall the exact words of how he ended that eve of poll speech.

'To look at the trees around here, you might think that the Tories have the election in the bag. But the votes do not belong to the trees, nor are they in the pockets of local newspaper proprietors. The votes are in the hearts of the people, and the hearts of the people are with us!'

We were cheered out of the Roxy, and cheered on our way home in Will's German car.

Next morning we awoke to snow. Heading towards Newcastleton, where they were to be official polling clerks, our friends Denbeigh and Jean Kirkpatrick got stuck in a drift. It was still dark and they had trouble raising help. When they arrived at the polling station to open it up, two hours late, there was an angry crowd waiting to be let in.

We began a polling day system in 1965 that we kept to right up until David's final election in 1992. Between us, we would cover every single one of the seventy-seven polling stations, from West Linton in the north to Newcastleton in the south, from Tweedsmuir in the west to Sprouston in the east. The most remote of them all was a place called Riccarton Junction in Liddesdale, which had no public road to it. There was only the railway line, and a recent forestry commission track. As the name implies, there had been a railway junction there, and the village had been built by the railway company. Once there had been a primary school, but now younger children went to Newcastleton Primary, and the older ones to Hawick High School, by train. There were, I think, only 24 registered voters by 1965, a few of them employees of either British Rail or of the Forestry Commission, but the greater number were social misfits for whom this was an almost gulag-like dumping-ground. Only about half of the sub-standard, brick-built houses were occupied. Unlike the other Border villages, which buzzed with a vibrant community life, it was a depressing place to visit, and it must have been soul-destroying to live there. By 1970 it had been razed to the ground.

Our programme was this: David would visit all the towns, and a smaller part of the country areas, while I would take on the larger landward area. At the next election, we would swap our areas around. Why did we do it? Well, for one thing, it kept the candidate (and his wife) busy on polling day. In the bigger places, where there was some organisation, it was partly to encourage the troops. It was also to check that the opposition weren't stepping over the bounds of what was allowable under election law – more than once, we had to have Tories ejected who were sitting in the same hall as the polling clerks, or demand that cars with posters over them be removed from school playgrounds. Above all, in the small, remote polling stations, it was also a means of saying thank-you to the polling clerks during their long day.

You can often smell the result at the polling stations, never more so than on that occasion. Our yellow and green rosettes and our sticker-laden car produced smiles, handshakes and thumbs-up signs. At Cappercleuch, by St Mary's Loch, where the voters' roll has never been in more than double figures, a woman rode away from the corrugated-iron village hall on a bike, giving us a cheerful wave. Over 82% of registered electors cast their votes on that snowy day – a far cry from today's meagre showing at elections.

I love polling days. At one election, I got up in time to go to our own local polling station to see the squat metal boxes being prepared for the voting papers, the sealing wax – heated in a candle flame – dripped onto the pink fastening tape. At ten o'clock that night, in the remote polling station at Tweedsmuir, in the extreme north west of the constituency, I watched the final closure and sealing up of the boxes there.

The polls closed at 9 pm on those days. Thank goodness, there would be an overnight count this time. We repaired back to the welcoming log fire at Gala House, full of stories. Jeremy Thorpe described how the Tories had what seemed like a perfect organisation in the small Peeblesshire village of Romanno Bridge, but virtually none in Hawick, the largest town. The phrase, 'But they had Romanno Bridge sewn up,' became a byword for incompetent overall organisation in our political lexicon.

Amid the high spirits, David's were low. During the day he had been given the news of his grandfather's death. In his eighties, he had been suffering from cancer for some time, and we all knew he would not leave hospital again. But he had been taking a lively interest in the by-election, and there was an additional grief for David on top of the first family bereavement he had endured, that his grandfather had died before the result of the poll was known. Nearly forty years later, another honour, not one bestowed by the people, but one from the Queen, was tinged with regret that his father, dying a month previously, had not lived to see it. But in both cases, 'I'm sure he knows,' was a sentiment both felt and expressed.

Among the gathering at Gala House that night was John Bannerman. A lesser man might have looked back on a lifetime like his in the Liberal cause, five elections fought and two almost won. At the Inverness by-election in 1954, John was about to be declared winner by a small majority. The handshakes had been made and the platform party lined up, when an official said, 'The postal votes haven't been counted.' When they were, he had lost. In the early 1960s the party had failed to find a candidate for a by-election in Paisley. There was absolutely no Liberal organisation on the ground. It was a safe Labour seat at this time, but once it had been Asquith's, and John Bannerman, then chairman of the Scottish Liberal Party, could not bear to see it uncontested. He flung himself into the fray, and achieved one of Arthur Purdom's 'brilliant seconds'. You might have thought there would be some resentment, some envy at least for the young candidate for Roxburgh, Selkirk and Peebles, now about to achieve the electoral success that had always eluded this great campaigner. But John Bannerman was too generous-hearted for that. 'If this laddie wins tonight,' he said, 'it will all have been worthwhile.'

Will Stewart gave up his well-deserved admission ticket to the count so that John Bannerman could be there. In all that great man's years of political service, it would be the first successful count he had attended. Jeremy Thorpe managed to blag his own way in – no doubt he was able to persuade the authorities that sitting Members of Parliament had some statutory right to be present.

When – very occasionally – I go to Jedburgh Town Hall today, I can still locate where David and I sat, at the edge of the floor. We held hands quietly as the agent came to update us with figures, and I think we were praying. Not, now, for victory, because from the votes stacking up on the tables we could see that had been achieved, but to be able to live up to what was awaiting us.

As we sat there, the McEwens swept in. There is no other expression for it. Brigid, elegant as always, was in a classic dark-blue outfit. (I wore a home-made dress and jacket in a local tweed, and my grey furry hat.) It was obvious, from their demeanour and body language, that they entered that hall confident of having won, and a surge of sympathy swept through us – together with anger, on their behalf, towards the Tory machine that had not warned them of the likely outcome. Maybe they didn't realise. Maybe they had fooled themselves with the plethora of posters on the trees, and the immaculate organisation in Romanno Bridge.

When the results were declared, at first in the hall and then on the steps outside to the crowd that would, singing Hawick Common Riding songs, bear David down Jedburgh High Street on their shoulders, they announced a resounding Liberal victory.

Within fourteen months, and a week short of his twenty-seventh birthday, David had turned a Tory majority of nearly 10,000, 'the third safest Tory seat in Scotland', into a Liberal one of 4,657. He had also taken the parliamentary Liberal party, for the first time in over twenty years, into double figures.

'It's Boy David!' screamed the headlines next day, and I woke up to find myself in bed with a Member of Parliament.

# Part Two

# THE CHERRYDENE YEARS

## 12
# Riding down Ettrick

A year later I'm out pounding the countryside roads on the election trail again, my car bedecked with the slogan DAVID AGAIN. Harold Wilson, frustrated by the government's majority of only five, has judged the time right to call another election in the hope of an improved result. I am on the stump early – in fact, before Parliament has been dissolved, and while David is still in London. To be precise, I am canvassing up Ettrick and down Yarrow, and I have an ulterior motive. Denbeigh Kirkpatrick, now our lawyer as well as our friend, has told us that there is a house in Yarrow coming on to the market soon. Maybe I will be able to get a sneak preview. So I decide to start my canvassing by visiting the Ettrick and Yarrow valleys, in that order. I should complete them in a day.

In the main settlement of the two valleys, the village of Ettrick Bridge, I knock on the door of an especially pretty house. It is positioned sideways to, rather than fronting, the road, a long, low, white building with dormer windows, that has obviously once been two or even three cottages. The owner responds to my overture in a hostile way. One of my canvassing mantras is: 'Never leave in a bad atmosphere.' It makes no difference if it has not been caused by me; it just doesn't do even to give someone the chance to report to friends and family, 'I sent her off with a flea in her ear.' My usual fallback when met with hostility is the response, 'I'm really sorry to hear you say that,' accompanied by the sweetest smile I can muster, and I try to squeeze a smile from their lips if not their eyes. For some reason, however, on this occasion, I say (and mean it): 'Could I just say – what a lovely house this is: I've always admired it.'

'Oh well, we're leaving it anyway,' is her brusque response, and I do a completely mad thing, which I shall never regret.

'I wonder – I know you'll think this is rather odd – but we're looking for a house, and I wondered what you're asking for it.'

I am staggered when she tells me, 'We paid £4,000 for it and we've spent about £500 on it. As long as we get our money back, we'll be happy.'

It is within our price range, and less than we'd bid unsuccessfully for another, smaller house some months previously.

'Do you mind,' I ask, 'forgetting about the election and showing me around?'

And she does. As I follow her into the cosy rooms, for the first time I really, really feel, 'This is the house I'd like to raise my children in. This would be perfect for us.'

At night, when David phones, I say, 'I've found our house!'

'Not now,' he says, 'We can't buy a house during an election. We don't know if I'll get back, and anyway, I'm officially unemployed while the election's on. How on earth would we get a mortgage?' But when he comes home, he goes on his own to see it. We get ourselves a mortgage and put in an offer. At David's public meeting in Ettrick Bridge, where his audience crouches on child-sized chairs in the school, the owners of Cherrydene turn up and tell us that they've accepted our offer, and that they are voting Liberal. Afterwards, neither of us can remember what on earth the house looks like inside – only that we both love it.

An immediate result of the Roxburgh, Selkirk and Peebles by-election was that there was a new Tory leader. Sir Alec Douglas-Home was a Border laird: that the seat had been lost to his party very much in his own backyard – and with a friend and neighbour carrying the Tory banner – meant that the inevitable question was asked – if this seat couldn't be held, what could be? He resigned a few months later, and his successor, Edward Heath, was the first Tory leader elected by the parliamentary party rather than appointed by the grandees. Heath had been the negotiator in the first, failed attempt by Britain to join the European Common Market: the achievement of this goal of British membership became his burning ambition. But he was essentially a shy and awkward man, with little public charisma.

We had spent the intervening year getting better acquainted with the Borders constituency, and falling completely under its old spells. There was a lot of it to get to know.

There is no single town that gave the Borders a focal centre, but in those days there were eight burghs with their own town councils and their own provosts, their own traditions and loyalties, their own newspapers and rugby teams, and even, sometimes, their own accents. In Hawick, the largest town, this is especially marked, and its unique vowel pronunciation sometimes leads it to be nicknamed 'the yowe and mi town', since that is how 'you and me' sounds there. It is the most landlocked town in

Scotland – perhaps that is why the dialect has evolved. This week, the sight at the travel agent there of an advertisement for a cruise to the Norwegian fjords, 'starting from Hawick', made me wonder if the ship would sail up the Tweed and the Teviot into the town. Hawick's isolated situation has often caused me to speculate that their dialect is how most Scots spoke a long time ago, and that it was the lack of communication with the outside world until the coming of the railway that caused the dialect to linger here.

If you are born in Hawick you are called a *Teri*; the rugby team wears green, the town colours that are flaunted at the Common Riding are yellow and blue, and at the Common Riding they sing the chorus:

> Teribus y Teriodin,
> Sons of heroes slain at Flodden,
> Imitating Border Bowmen –
> Aye defend your rights and common!

The chorus follows each of twenty-two verses by the town's official singer, recounting the story of the battle of Hornshole near Hawick, the year after Flodden.

In the royal and ancient burgh of Selkirk (never forget the adjectives!), they are proud to be Souters, after the town's ancient main craft of shoemaking, and to sing at the Common Riding:

> It's up wi' the souters o' Selkirk,
> That wear the single-soled shoon [shoes],
> It's up wi' the lads o' the Forest,
> And doun wi' the Earl of Hume.

The curse on the Earl of Hume, and – in another verse – his kinsmen in the Merse (Berwickshire) was because of their alleged cowardice at the battle of Flodden.

Each town has its own song, or songs: in Hawick and Selkirk there is a veritable repertoire of them. Selkirk's songs are an eclectic mix, many of which have nothing at all to do with the burgh, including one, 'Jessie's Dream', about a young girl at the siege of Lucknow awaiting rescue by Highland regiments. In Hawick, the songs – and there are dozens of them – are all devoted to the beauties and charms of 'the auld grey toun' itself.

In Galashiels, the natives are called Braw Lads after Robert Burns's lovely song, 'The Braw Lads o' Gala Water'. (By citizens of neighbouring towns, natives of Galashiels are called 'pail-merks'. The town had an unenviable lack of inside sanitation, and the use of buckets in outside sheds led to this unkind nickname, indicating the mark of buckets on their posteriors.) The town colours are black and white, and the rugby team wears maroon. God help you if you get this wrong. At an election in the seventies, the Tory candidate turned up in Hawick in a flashy maroon suit. His reputation never recovered.

These three towns, along with the smaller burghs of Jedburgh and Innerleithen, shared the same industrial base: the textile trade. For Jedburgh, Innerleithen and Hawick, this was mainly, but not entirely, fine knitwear – the firms of Pringle of Scotland and Ballantyne's of Innerleithen were world-famous. Galashiels and Selkirk were better known for tweeds – the very name of the cloth originated in the Borders, after a clerical error substituted it for 'tweel'. Kelso was predominantly a market town, while both Melrose and Peebles (Peebles natives: gutterbluids; incomers: stooryfits; town colours: red and white) had a strong tourist element.

They have their rivalries, their rugby teams, their common ridings. We threw ourselves into the latter with enthusiasm – what better way was there to cover the Border countryside and familiarise ourselves with it? From the saddle, and in friendly, down-to-earth company, we learned its hills and haughs, forded the Tweed and her tributaries. David rode in the all-male cavalcade behind the Hawick Cornet, but missed the train north the following week, and I rode at Selkirk without him, a journey of twelve miles or more over rough terrain and at a hard pace around the marches of the burgh's common lands. David Mackie's song sums up the experience:

> When dismal dark December hems a' the burgh roond,
> Gey aften I remember the sunny days of June,
> When the sun is on the marches, the lilac blooming gay,
> And the riders of the Marches gang merry owre the brae.
>
> Yince mair I knee the leather and join the saddled throng,
> Tae speil the hill o' heather wi' laughter and wi' song.
> Yince mair wi' rapture riding, I view yon valley fair
> Where silver Tweed is gliding by Fairnilee and Yair.
>
> Wi' happy heared banter, I ride tae Nettly knoll,
> Then homeward swiftly canter frae Ettrick tae the Toll;
> And there's a happy ending when Selkirk's flags are cast,
> And the silence, thoughts transcending, salutes the sacred past.

When I these scenes remember, I feel that leafy June
Has breathed on winter's ember, and brightened a' around.
Hope spans the future's arches, and bids me aim again,
Tae ride the Selkirk Marches way up the Linglie Glen.

We followed the Braw Lad together, and the Jethart Callant, and the Kelso Laddie. I even slipped over into Berwickshire to ride behind the Lauder Cornet, and to follow the Coldstreamer to Flodden. Will Boyle always provided us with sensible kind mounts. One of the young lads who frequented his stables at the time was a teenager called Ian Stark: he was to become the thrice-silver Olympic medallist for three-day eventing. I have often thought that perhaps it was only here, the Borders, where riding is and always has been democratic rather than elitist, that a brilliant young rider from a council estate could have the opportunity to develop his full potential.

We were the same age as the young men and women who were the towns' principals, and the crowds cheered David as well as them. He rode bare-headed, rather than obscured by a riding hat, to make sure that he could be seen by his new constituents.

The mood in which we passed that summer is summed up in the words of a song by the nineteenth century songmaker – best known for the song 'Annie Laurie' – conservationist, horticulturist and eccentric, Alicia Spottiswoode, who became Lady John Scott on her marriage:

When we first rode down Ettrick,
The sun was glancing, our hearts were dancing,
Our bridles were ringing, the birds were singing,
And blithely our voices rang out together
As we brushed the dew from the blooming heather,
When we first rode down Ettrick.

In London, David lived in a bedroom in the National Liberal Club, the cheapest available. He had to pay all his London expenses out of his MP's salary, and we had no money to waste on anything more expensive. I had of course gone down in the immediate aftermath of the election, along with Andrew and Dorothy Haddon, to see him take his seat. I had never been inside the House of Commons before, and as I sat in a privileged seat in the Speaker's Gallery, I found it overwhelming. A by-election victor always has the privilege of taking his oath by himself, and not in the general melee after a general election. When the Speaker called, 'Members desirous of taking their seats, please come forward,' the slight, boyish figure of my husband made his way towards the Speaker's chair between the elegant form of Eric Lubbock, the victor of the Orpington by-election of 1961, and the burly one of George Mackie, chairman of the Scottish Liberal Party, successful farmer, and currently the MP for Caithness and Sutherland.

As they proceeded down the floor of the House of Commons towards the Speaker, there was a rumble from benches below me. I was upset: I thought it was the Tories booing. In fact, it was the Labour members adding their approval to the seven-strong voices on the Liberal benches. In the Members lobby, Alec Douglas-Home, now leader of the opposition, approached David with an outstretched hand.

'Naturally, I'm sorry to see you here,' he said, 'But now that you are here, I'd like to wish you all the very best.'

There were no free travel passes for spouses to travel to London, and I didn't manage to make a return journey to hear his maiden speech. Women were not at that time allowed beyond the portals of the National Liberal Club, so on my visits we had to throw ourselves onto the hospitality of those of our Edinburgh friends who had taken the High Road to London. In November, I won a place in the ballot to come to the State Opening of Parliament. 'You must go,' said an acquaintance, adding tactlessly, 'you might never get another chance.'

The contents of the Queen's Speech had been revealed to the Liberals the night before it was delivered. David had been admirably discreet, refusing to share any of its details with me. As I stood in the queue to go into the House of Lords beside Emlyn Hooson, the MP for Montgomery, he cheerfully revealed to me what legislation had been promised, and what parts of Labour's manifesto had been dumped.

But such forays were very rare. During the week, I learned to be on my own, in the little cottage by the Tweed that we rented from Christopher Scott. I schooled myself to remember that my mother had had to endure much longer absences by my father, and joked that it must be rather like being married to a long-distance lorry driver.

I had no success in finding a job in the legal profession locally – a part-time one was what I wanted – despite having written to several firms of solicitors. My only gainful employment was working for a couple of afternoons a week for the Social Work Department, at a centre for adults with severe learning disabilities. I was not qualified to do this any more than my co-worker, but I found I both enjoyed it and had an untapped patience for the work. The 'centre' was in an outbuilding at an old peoples' home in Galashiels. The clients (although they were certainly not called that in the 1960s) attended on only two or three afternoons a week. It was termed an adult occupational centre, and to occupy those who attended we taught them very simple, repetitive hand-sewing – the same as my efforts in lower primary school – and even simpler basketwork.

At other times I helped to organise constituency events and made many of my own clothes; I stood in for David at weekday constituency engagements. And I went to funerals. Over the years, I went to say good-bye, on David's behalf, to local worthies, to civic dignitaries, to local government officials, to loyal party workers and to village neighbours. One year I went to ten funerals: two were on the same day.

Recently I read Pauline Prescott's memoirs *Smile Though Your Heart Is Breaking*. In it she describes her early years as an MP's wife:

> Our whole week would be geared up to the moment John came home. Everything had to stop then so that he could walk though the front door and unwind . . . Friday would be the day I did my hair and make-up, put on a nice outfit, and prepared something nice for dinner . . . on Saturdays, we'd potter in the garden or go out in the car somewhere fun with the boys, and then on Sundays we'd have a lazy day with a lamb roast . . .

I showed this to Ro Kirkwood, who had shared my experience as the wife of a Border MP, and we agreed that it bore no relation at all to being married to an MP in a rural constituency. We were lucky if we had Friday nights with our husbands – they usually were at a function run by the myriads of voluntary organisations throughout the Borders.

What amazed me even more was her revelation that, 'If I was lucky, John might have some constituency matters to attend to or a local surgery to run, so I'd have him at home for a few extra days.'

I had always thought that was what politicians' weekends were for!

I rode a lot at the local stables, and developed friendships. I was hampered by the fact that I failed my driving test for the second and then the third time. Driving lessons took place regularly without much visible effect, though it has to be said David's cars were hardly suitable for a learner.

In the summer, David redeemed his promise to take me to many places he had visited on student exchanges: Berlin, Prague, Dubrovnik, Klosters. We went in his newly acquired second-hand Humber Hawk.

'Now you're an MP, you'll need a sensible car,' the owner of Adam Purves's garage in Galashiels had said, arriving on our doorstep a day or two after the election with a vehicle formerly owned by a Hawick doctor. It had a Roxburghshire registration number, JKS 900, which, over forty years later, still adorns my Citroen Berlingo.

On this journey we travelled light. We took a double tent, foam mattress and sleeping bag, all borrowed, two tin mugs and a knife. 'I'll sleep rough but not cook rough,' I insisted. So we would find a café for morning coffee, buy bread and cheese and tomatoes for lunch, and go somewhere to have a proper meal in the evening.

Taking the ferry from Hull to Rotterdam, we made our way through Holland, Belgium and Germany to the isolated and divided city of Berlin. We crossed to its eastern sector via Checkpoint Charlie and drove through East Germany. In the towns where we stopped, we were staggered by the lack of choice and quality, especially of foodstuffs, in the shops. The petrol was of such poor quality that the Humber stuttered and limped. In Dresden, the bombed buildings were unrestored, and there were almost no private vehicles on the roads. In the countryside of Czechoslovakia, things were little better, but Prague, when we came to it, proved to be an enchanting city, just as David had promised me.

He had been asked by the Foreign Office to check in at the embassy on our arrival there: travel through East Germany was still regarded as dodgy. But first we had to find somewhere to pitch our tent. The municipal camping site was full, so we settled our canvas home on a verge nearby and went off to announce our safe arrival after a journey through communist lands. We were greeted with an invitation to lunch at the embassy, so on the appointed day we packed up our tent in readiness for our onward journey to Vienna, went to the local swimming baths for a shower, and got into our least shabby clothes. 'Where have you been staying?' we were both asked. David muttered something noncommittal; I was more forthcoming about the tent on the grass verge.

It remains a surreal memory, that lunch in the garden under the walls of Prague's castle. We were waited on by maids with frilly caps and aprons, who served us with tomatoes stuffed with crabmeat and goose with prunes, and an unremembered pudding; then we retired to the dust-sheeted embassy drawing room, where a famous Czech pianist played Janacek to us: the first time I'd ever heard of him. Afterwards we set off for Vienna, where my Austrian friend from teenage days, Fredi Gratzl, and his family welcomed us to soft beds, baths, and three days of Viennese wine, music, food and friendship. We drove on south to

Venice and through Yugoslavia to Dubrovnik, and then up to Klosters. We were away for just over three weeks in all, and covered about three thousand miles. I was beginning to learn in depth about my husband's passion for driving.

Nor was the Humber Hawk given any rest on our return, for throughout the remainder of the recess, it was used to drive around the villages of the constituency, while its new MP took the pulse of life and listened to problems in the different communities. It was something they were not used to with his predecessor.

On a personal level, we had two priorities: to start a family, and to buy a house. By the time the 1966 election was called, the first of these projects had been rather more successful than the second, and I was four months pregnant. No woman ever went into maternity clothes so soon, though I had a long way to catch up with the wife of the new Tory candidate, who was blossoming with her fourth.

Andrew Haddon and Will Stewart advised us that we should find a house in a village, not a town. 'There's such rivalry between the towns,' they said. 'If you move to one, it'll be resented by people in the others. A village, or the countryside, will give you more neutrality.'

We had looked at various possibilities over the year and made a couple of unsuccessful offers. I remember that once a likely-looking one came up in the village of Ettrick Bridge, but it was 'too remote', according to David, a judgement that he discarded as soon as he saw Cherrydene. Ettrick Bridge was the village where, in the first election, we had met Andrew Haddon's aunt, Mrs. McGowan. She was in her nineties and bedridden, but her mind was as sharp as a pin. 'I'm so pleased to meet you,' she said. 'We've always been a great Liberal family. My brother Sandy won the Border Burghs for Mr Gladstone in 1886.' He had been the eldest, and she the youngest, of a large family.

Alexander Laing Brown's tenure of the Border Burghs seat was short: he became embroiled in a divorce, enough in those days to end a political career. In one of the best of all political memoirs, *Letters to Isabel*, his successor, Thomas Shaw, described him to his eponymous daughter:

> He was quite the most powerful helper of Mr Gladstone in all of Scotland – worth a dozen of platform supporters and a hundred of the hanger-on species. He was shortish of stature and spare of build. He had a fine and lofty forehead, a gleaming eye, a good modulation of voice; and he had also that true

orator's strength – a word of power from a heart of flame. This man was resigning, and so the vacancy. I always loved him; he was my friend, eloquent, assiduous, unfailing, from my first contact with the Burghs to the last.

They had long memories, the voters of Roxburgh, Selkirk and Peebles. In that election, a woman declined to give David her vote on the grounds that, 'I can never forgive the Liberals for not sending help to General Gordon in Khartoum.' John Buchan, in his splendid autobiography, *Memory Hold-The-Door*, describes his couple of years as prospective Tory candidate in the Borders in the early twentieth century. Fifty years later, he would have recognised the people and the incidents that we encountered:

> What made my work as a candidate a delight was the people I moved among . . . they had the qualities I most admired in human nature; realism coloured by poetry, a stalwart independence sweetened by courtesy, and a shrewd kindly wisdom. To the first quality, the ballads bear witness, to the second, the history of Scotland. As an example of the third, let me tell a story from my own candidature.
>
> Heckling in the Borders is carried, I think, to a higher pitch of art than anywhere else in Britain. It is pursued for the pure love of the game, and I have known a candidate heckled to a standstill by his own supporters. Mr Lloyd George's Insurance Act had just been introduced, and at a meeting at remote Ettrickhead the speaker was defending it on the ground that it was a practical application of the Sermon on the Mount. A long-legged shepherd rose to question him, and the following dialogue ensued:
>
> 'Ye believe in the Bible, sir?'
> 'With all my heart.'
> 'And ye consider that this Insurance Act is in keepin' wi' the Bible?'
> 'I do.'
> 'Is it true that under the Act there's a maternity benefit, and the woman gets the benefit whether she's married or no?'
> 'That is right.'
> 'D'ye approve of that?'
> 'With all my heart.'

'Weel, sir, how d'ye explain this? The Bible says that the wages of sin is death, and the Act says thirty shillin's.'

The Tories had picked a candidate for the 1966 election from the same broadcasting background as David; young, able and energetic, Ian MacIntyre was the most formidable opponent he ever faced. When the election came, the Liberal majority was halved from the by-election to two and a half thousand, but David was back, confounding the theory that by-election victors don't hold their seats. Throughout the country, the Labour Party under Harold Wilson had a large overall majority, so it looked as though there would be a period of calm ahead, with at least four years before the next election. The number of Liberal MPs had risen to a dozen.

Among our contemporaries, Donald Dewar, fighting what he thought was the solid Tory seat of Aberdeen South to earn his brownie points for a subsequent safe Labour nomination, did a little too well and was unexpectedly returned. Best of all, John Mackintosh had won the Berwick and East Lothian seat for Labour. In the village of Yetholm, there were three or four enthusiastic Liberal supporters who would put out leaflets for David a couple of evenings a week. On two other nights, they would drive to the Berwickshire boundary, take the STEEL stickers off their cars, put up red ones blazoning the name MACKINTOSH, and carry out the same task for Labour. They were well ahead of their time. John's win meant that David had an intelligent and like-minded neighbouring MP with whom to work on local issues. He was especially well-versed in farming policy, and when they met with delegations from the NFU, it would be John that spoke for both of them. He used to say enviously to David, 'You're so lucky – you've no coal-mines and no fishing boats in your constituency'. They were both industries with deep and perpetual problems.

The election of 1966 was on David's birthday, 31 March, and a fortnight later we moved into the Ettrick Valley, where we have lived ever since. The village proved to be a perfect base for family life. With only about thirty houses at that time, it had a church, a school, a post office, a shop and a pub, all of which served a wider rural community. In those days there was also a district nurse, a postman, and a road-keeper. A young couple was always welcomed, and we were no exception. Over the twenty-six years that followed, I was grateful both for the friendship extended to us, and to the loyalty and discretion of my fellow-villagers when, in later years, the tabloids came snooping around, hopeful of picking up some salacious detail about us or our family.

Cherrydene, with its four bedrooms and potential for another, was a house where we could expect to live for many years. My first task when we moved in was to create my kitchen, which I did from flat-packs, although when I grew larger and larger as my pregnancy progressed, the process of DIY joinery became logistically difficult. The Border provosts, I was told, watching my enlarging bump as we went around the Common Ridings (me on foot, this year, and in the official parties, while David kept to a horse), ran a sweepstake on how many babies were in there.

A fortnight after we moved in, I passed my driving test at the fourth attempt. It was just as well: the bus to Selkirk from Ettrick Bridge, which went only twice a week anyway, was withdrawn at about that time. The ability to drive meant that I could go up to the airport with David and drive the car back, and then come to collect him on a Thursday night from the flight, called 'The Moonjet', that came into Edinburgh after midnight. There was a regular trio of us, Una Mackintosh, Kathleen Dalyell and myself, who waited for our parliamentary husbands at the old terminal at Turnhouse. If for some reason the plane couldn't land on Edinburgh's single runway and was diverted to Glasgow or Prestwick, then we had a long wait until their coaches arrived in the small hours.

On one occasion Una and I greeted our husbands with the question, 'So, where were you tonight when the vote for the televising of Parliament was on?' – knowing that both had had speaking engagements. They were mortified to find that the motion had been lost by a single vote: had they both been there, it would have been carried by the same margin.

Shortly after that election, when I used my newly-found ability to drive and went to meet David off the plane, he had something to tell me.

'I'm not sure if it's good news or bad news,' he said, as we drove along Princes Street. 'I've drawn third place in the Private Members' ballot.' This is the raffle which gives backbenchers the opportunity of putting legislation into effect: Sidney Silverman's bill to abolish the death penalty had been a recent example. It is only those who draw the first half-dozen places in the ballot who have a realistic chance of actually changing the law.

There were two outstanding measures that were ripe for reform: the legalisation of homosexual relationships and the reform of the abortion laws. I have already described how David and I had both taken the class in Forensic Medicine as part of our law degrees. Among other things we

128

had learnt in theory about criminal abortion and its dreadful effects. I also knew some girls who had undergone the frightful experience.

It is salutary to be reminded of the ways of procuring an illegal abortion at that time, and the risks they involved. One was to administer a violent shock to the mother's body – a fall downstairs, for example, could trigger expulsion of the foetus. Naturally, this would involve risk to the mother, and it might not have the desired effect. Next there was the consumption of pills 'to regulate periods' – not today's morning-after pill, but a risky concoction based on the poison ergot, which could cause contractions of the womb. Even more desperate measures were the introduction of an irritant solution into the womb and, finally, the insertion of a sharp instrument into it. These last two methods were the ones usually carried out by a back-street abortionist, and while all carried a considerable risk, these were the most dangerous. Not only were there many deaths resulting from them: there were also many more infections, leading to future sterility. Above all there was fear, shame and secrecy, and there were not a few desperate girls who resorted to suicide instead.

During the election, David had responded to a questionnaire from the pressure group the Abortion Law Reform Association. To the question, 'Would you support a bill to legalise abortion?' he had answered in the affirmative. Although the questionnaire had not asked, 'Would you *introduce* such a Bill?' he felt that the reply to the one question was a kind of pledge to undertake the other, given the rare chance to do so. An important factor for him was that the General Assembly of the Church of Scotland supported reform. They were against the legalisation of homosexuality, and David, although he personally supported it, did not want to go against his church. I made a plea for a bill for Scottish self-government. 'It wouldn't get through,' he said. 'This is my chance to actually make legislation, not just to make speeches.'

Over the years, bills had been introduced in the Commons and the Lords to reform abortion law. They had failed, not through lack of a parliamentary majority, but through lack of time. No bill had ever been brought in by someone so far up the ballot. The circumstances had never been so favourable. Roy Jenkins was perhaps the greatest reforming Home Secretary of all time; John Silkin, the Labour Chief Whip, was the son of Lord Silkin, who had introduced a previous bill in the House of Lords. Kenneth Robinson at Health was the author of another earlier bill, and Douglas Houghton, whose wife Vera was one of the leading lights of the Abortion Law Reform Association, was chairman of the Parliamentary Labour Party.

Naturally, it was regarded as a matter of conscience, and support for or opposition to David's Medical Termination of Pregnancy Bill (the title was my suggestion) did not divide along party lines. One of its most staunch opponents was David's Liberal colleague, Alistair Mackenzie, the Gaelic-speaking Free Church MP for Ross and Cromarty. Public opinion was favourable, although those who opposed reform, both within and outside the Catholic Church, were implacable and sometimes vitriolic. The bill had to be fought line by line and clause by clause.

David's mail at the House of Commons contained letters that were so personally insulting – some of them contained death threats – that his secretary binned them When he found out, he was dismayed: 'These are needed for research!' At Cherrydene, I received some mail directed at me personally, which either begged me to intervene or told me I was married to Herod. There were also anonymous phone calls, and while some of the press was supportive, some other sections were hostile and critical. It was a testing time for David, and I was not left unscathed. But I suppose you could say that, though he was still under the age of thirty, it marked his coming of age as a parliamentarian, and it gained him the respect of his elders, including Roy Jenkins. Moreover, for the first time, he worked across political divisions with like-minded people in different parties for a common cause. It was an approach that was to influence the rest of his political life.

To the credit of our Catholic friends, they kept their own counsel. Christopher and Ann Scott, devout Catholics both, never wavered in their political support, no matter how much they abhorred the bill. A few Liberal stalwarts inevitably dropped out. One of them, in a subsequent election, was discussing current events with his parish priest.

'My wife and I were great Liberals,' he said, 'but of course once David Steel piloted the Abortion Act through parliament, we've not been able to support him.'

'Oh,' said the priest, 'I can't say that it's ever put me off.' Delighted to have his priest's permission, the lapsed supporter turned up again at the local committee rooms to help.

The argument about abortion has never stopped, though. This is partly because of the advance of medical science, now able to keep alive premature babies at a period of gestation that would never have been thought possible at that time. In 1967, a foetus was considered to be viable only after 28 weeks gestation – now that has decreased to somewhere between 20 and 24 weeks. The law has been amended to take account of the latter figure. The development of the 'morning after' pill is another factor.

Above all, while the Catholic position – that human life begins at the point of conception – remains a tenet of faith, the issue will continue to be debated. There are those who believe that the 1968 Act was the opening of the floodgates to a changed social morality, and there are many women who believe that it was, above all, the starting-gun that allowed them to compete with men in working life on an ever more level playing field.

What cannot be disputed is how desperate the plight of a woman with an unwanted pregnancy was before the passage of the Abortion Act. The film *Vera Drake* was a reminder of what it was like. The risk of infection was high, filling hospital wards, especially at weekends, and often leading to infertility. Some hospitals at the time had a 20- to 30-bedded septic abortion ward.

In his retiral speech to the Royal College of General Practitioners in 1992, Dr John Marks, the former General Secretary of the BMA, told his audience of Ministers, civil servants and over 300 doctors that, 'Looking back over these forty years it seems to me that the event that has had the most beneficial effect upon public health during that period was the passage of David Steel's Abortion Bill.'

Halting that traffic in women's misery was no mean achievement for a politician who was only thirty years old when the Bill was given its Royal Assent.

## 13

# New Family, New Friends

It was strange that David was putting this legislation through Parliament at the very time when our family was starting. In July, when I was seven months pregnant, there was a Royal visit to Peeblesshire and Selkirkshire. I made myself a maternity dress in orange satin, a fabric rose adorning my large front. In Peeblesshire, I was invited to all the Royal events, and in the photograph of those waiting to be presented to Her Majesty, the bump that would become Graeme stands out proudly. In Selkirkshire, the County Clerk – of whom I shall write more in later chapters – obviously decided that the sight of a pregnant woman would be offensive to royalty, and I was excluded from the elite circle.

David was part of it, and shared a vehicle with the Sheriff and his wife amongst others. The day was very hot, and air-conditioning for cars had not yet been invented, so they wound the windows down. As the cavalcade of vehicles made its way past the council scheme of Langlee in Galashiels, the sound of a robust female voice from the crowds lining the pavements was heard: 'Ach, here come a' the hingers-on.'

Graeme was born in Galashiels Hospital at the end of August after a protracted and painful labour. Shortly afterwards, I had an example of the inter-town rivalry of the Borders, when a Selkirk worthy peered into the carry-cot. 'That's a dreadful thing you've done to that child,' he said, and I turned round to see what horror had befallen my baby. He continued: '. . . letting him be born in *Gala*.'

I had deprived my first-born of the birthright of being a Souter.

Childbirth may have been dreadful, but I took to motherhood like a duck to water. It had never really occurred to me to do anything other than breastfeed, following the example of my sisters, especially Joan, who claimed that with six children, the only bottle she ever had in the house was for the lambs. I had neither difficulty in producing milk nor embarrassment about feeding in public places, and I never found hostility to this. Once, when we visited Norman Hackett's legendary former landlady in Edinburgh, she was not the least put out that I started feeding in front of her current crop of students. 'Mother Nature's dairies, that's what I like to see,' she commented, and the phrase was adopted by all of us.

Graeme slept from 10 pm till 6 am from the time he was a week old. His christening was followed at Cherrydene by the first of the many family parties that were to take place over the decades. I served up home-made elderflower champagne made to Dorothy Haddon's recipe, and the next day my infant son slept for eighteen hours.

## DOROTHY HADDON'S ELDERFLOWER CHAMPAGNE

*4 large heads of elderflower*
*1½ lbs granulated sugar*
*1 tablespoon white wine vinegar*
*Juice and rind of a lemon*
*1 gallon water*

Melt the sugar in water, and allow to cool. When just warm, add the other ingredients and leave in a container for three days, stirring night and morning. Strain and bottle, taking a day or two to screw the tops down, and completing the process only when no bubbles are still rising. Use after a fortnight. Dorothy always said that it was the effect of the pollen on the sugar that made it alcohol; but it is really very mild.

Early in 1967, we visited those islands of my ancestors, the Orkneys, for the first time. With Graeme in a carry-cot, we stayed with the Gri-monds in the old manse of Firth. David was to speak at a fundraising 'Orkney dinner' for the local Liberal Association. On the evening of our arrival, Jo took him into his study and told him that he was planning to announce his retirement as leader. He had served for ten years and had inspired a whole new generation, putting the Liberal Party back into the public political reckoning. And though he did not say it, he and his family were still reeling from the tragedy of his son Andrew's lonely death in the middle of the 1966 election campaign.

It was a bizarre weekend, though much enlivened by young Magnus Grimond and by the Orkney dinner itself, where a wartime song about 'Bloody Orkney' was sung with great gusto, and we were served with haggis, clapshot and bere-meal bannocks. I felt comfortable to be descended from such a cheerful and forthright race as the Orcadians, similar both to the Danes who are their ancestors, and to the down-to-earth Borderers.

When we arrived back at Edinburgh airport, it was to be met by the press, for the news of Jo's resignation had leaked. Of course, they read all kinds of meanings into our stay, which had been arranged for many months. Was young David Steel the favoured political son and heir of Jo Grimond? Surely there was significance in the fact that he had been summoned to the outgoing leader's island fastness at this crucial time? No journalist can ever accept the true explanation of many political events: in this case that it was coincidence and chance that a long-standing engagement was being fulfilled.

In the leadership election that followed, David had no hesitation in pledging his active support to the young West Country MP, Jeremy Thorpe, who had campaigned for him with such style and vigour in the by-election. Emlyn Hooson, the MP for Montgomery, Jeremy's opponent, was one of the most brilliant minds at the English Bar. He had defended the Moors murderer, Ian Brady, and once confessed that he had always felt tainted by the aura of evil when in the presence of his client. Gifted with the silver tongue of the Welsh and a superb intellect, he gave the growing party a real choice, and at one point it looked as though the parliamentary group might divide equally. It was the MP for West Aberdeenshire, James Davidson, who tipped the balance after an evening's hard persuasion by David.

Our summer holiday that year was a September one. Leaving Graeme with his grandparents, we visited Michael Shea, who was then second secretary at the embassy in Bonn, and, despite the fact that I was pregnant again, we sampled the local wine festivals on the Rhine and the Moselle with enthusiasm. True to form, Michael had rented a glamorous flat in a castle overlooking the Rhine. The baron to whom it belonged was an apparatchik of the Free Democrats, the Liberals' German allies, but he had not always been inclined that way. In the grounds was a grotto with a swastika of decorative shells embedded into its walls.

Michael's romantic history while we were students and just afterwards had caused us all some gentle hilarity. Throughout their time at Edinburgh, he and my school friend Sheena Dowling had been 'an item', but when she spent a year in France as part of her honours French degree, he took other girls out. As Sheena's return approached, he prepared to ditch the current girlfriend, Trish Dorrell, a first-year archaeology student. Like Sheena, under her gentle and self-effacing exterior there was a resilient and steadfast core. Michael said to Robin Crichton, one of his closest friends, 'Trish will be dreadfully unhappy when Sheena comes back and we take up again. Could you – sort of – look after her?'

Within three weeks, Trish and Robin had moved in together, and when Trish graduated, they were married. Theirs was a joyful partnership, spent building up the film business together and raising three daughters, and Trish coped serenely with all of Robin's eccentricities. These took many forms. Once, four or five sheep strayed into his property at Ninemileburn. He penned them in carefully and phoned round the local farmers to enquire about their ownership. No-one claimed them. After a few days, Robin became fed up with looking after someone else's sheep, so he shooed them down the drive, keeping one as a kind of payment for their grazing. He shot it, skinned it and butchered it, and the next day a butcher he did not know turned up, asking if he had seen his missing sheep. 'Sheep?' replied Robin, trying to look innocent, but dreadfully conscious of the sheepskin stretched out to cure on the back of the door. 'Sorry, I can't help you there . . .'

Michael's relationship with Sheena did not survive graduation, and she married another of his best friends, Michael Jones. His eccentricities were even more extreme than Robin's, and included going off for 20 months to look after deer and goats on the island of Gometra, just off the coast of Mull, only returning to visit his family once during that time, after settling them in a remote house a mile up a rocky track outside the village of Carlops in Peeblesshire. 'How does Sheena stand it?' we all asked each other, and when her family grew up and she left her husband to embark on a life of her own, we all sympathised.

In Germany, Michael Shea told us that he was greatly taken with the Norwegian ambassador's secretary, and wanted to ask her out, but that so far she had rejected his offer of dates. Now, perhaps thinking that there was safety in numbers, she agreed, and it was a foursome that made up Michael and Mona's first date, at the Weinhaus St. Peter on the Ahr (for the first time, I ate snails). We weren't surprised when they were engaged by Christmas and married in Norway the following year, and liked to imagine that we had been a good advertisement for married life. Mona, when she came to Scotland to meet her future mother-in-law, also had to face Michael's old University clique.

My daughter Catriona was born in the four-bedded maternity unit at Selkirk a week before Christmas. Maggi Hackett was also pregnant: she was due a week or so after me, but when we had spoken on the phone the previous evening, she had just returned from hospital with what seemed like a false alarm. 'My contractions are coming every fifteen minutes now,' I told her before we left for Selkirk. David and Norman had a bet on which child would make its way into the world first: we felt we were on a winner.

This time, we hoped to do what was now becoming, if not customary, at least not rare: David would be at my side for the birth.

'Oh,' said the matron, 'We don't usually have the daddies there.'

'This daddy wants to be there,' he told her, and stayed with me late into the night. I extracted a promise that they would send for him when I went into the second stage of labour. Whether by design or accident, the message did not get passed on when the shift changed, and so David was not, after all, the first father at Selkirk Cottage Hospital to be at his wife's bedside as she gave birth.

'We didn't like to wake him,' they explained.

David phoned Norman. 'You owe me a bottle of whisky: we've got a daughter.'

'When was she born?'

'Eleven o'clock this morning,' boasted the proud father.

'In that case, you owe me one – our son was born at seven,' responded the equally proud Norman, and to this day David says that the first thing Catriona ever did was cost him a bottle of whisky.

I was learning to outwit the nurses. When my daughter was due for her first feed, they brought her to me along with a bottle.

'But I'm breastfeeding,' I said.

'Your milk isn't in yet,' replied the nurse.

'But what's there,' I said, 'is what nature intended her to have.'

The next morning, I realised that I had slept through the night.

'We just gave her a bottle, so you could have a good night's rest.'

'But I didn't want a good night's rest, I wanted to feed my daughter.' Each time feeding time came round, the nurses would draw the curtains around my bed to shield the decent bottle-wielding mothers from the disgraceful sight. Each time they did, I got out of bed and pulled them back. Eventually, they got the point, and they never found out that the small bottles of lemonade that David brought on his evening visits contained a measure of gin.

I got back home on Christmas Eve, and the Scottish Office minister, Norman Buchan, and his inspirational wife Janey, dropped in during a ministerial visit to the Borders. I was appalled that the chauffeur stayed out in the car and tried to invite him in, but all he would accept was a cup of tea in the car. Norman and Janey enlivened my homecoming with much spicy political gossip; and on Christmas Day the newly enlarged Steel family had the most scratch and most contented Christmas dinner ever: roast duck and potato crisps (David had forgotten to buy potatoes, and had to rush across the road to the Cross Keys for a couple of packets of crisps instead) at our one-shilling kitchen table with our toddler son and baby daughter.

So we entered a settled period of family life, interrupted by my first visit to Kenya. David had been so keen to show me the country he had loved so much, but its charms palled on me. Catriona was only eight months old and I was still feeding her, so that leaving her with her grandparents and the mother's help distressed me greatly. I came home early and in tears, and despite subsequent visits, have never really managed to take to my husband's beloved Kenya.

David's living conditions in London improved greatly when the Sheas were posted back there. They bought a house in Vauxhall and took him in as a weekly lodger. Michael was working at the Foreign Office during the day; when he came home, with great self discipline, he would sit down at his typewriter each night and pound out the novel on which he was working.

But my own visits to London were rare. Not only were they expensive, but my entire focus of interest was in the Borders. I deputised for David at official constituency functions that fell mid-week, and was involved with the local party at various levels. Weekends passed in a blur of Liberal fundraisers, coffee mornings and wine-and-cheese evenings: there were even such events as the Liberal Ball, and a Miss Young Liberal contest, with local heats. David overheard a mother preparing her daughter for one of these with the admonition, 'Now, mind and speak proper.' The prize for the lucky winner was a rail fare to London and a night in a hotel, plus a visit to the House of Commons and an evening night out with the MP. At one bazaar there was a bonny baby competition, which we refused to judge on the grounds that you could make only one friend but many enemies. Anne Scott undertook the task: like me, a fierce proponent of Mother Nature's dairies, she asked all the mothers if they were breastfeeding. Only one was, so Anne judged her baby the bonniest.

I became involved in the playgroup movement, as so many *Guardian*-reading mothers did. This started up as a do-it-yourself response to the lack of nursery provision. Mothers banded together, hired church halls, raised money for equipment, and looked after their own and other people's pre-school children in a rota. It was not done to release time for going to work: most playgroups only ran for two or three mornings in a week. But it did give young mothers a few hours on their own, while the days on rota duty gave a chance to form friendships. I started up a playgroup for the valleys, first in Cherrydene and then across the road in the village hall. It was the first community-run one in the Borders and still exists, although principally as a mother-and-toddler group.

Childcare was always a problem, for although I had abandoned thoughts of a career, our lives were unpredictable, and I both went with David to many events, and represented him at others. Once Catriona was born, we solved the problem by employing a school-leaver as mother's help. The first was straightforward: a nearby shepherd's daughter who had already been my babysitter. When she left to go and train as a nurse in the Hospital for Sick Children in Edinburgh, I was telephoned by the Children's Officer for Selkirkshire. Would I take on a fifteen-year-old girl who was just about to leave school, and who had spent the last thirteen years in the Priory, the children's home in Selkirk? She and her brother had been abandoned by their mother when she was two and her brother a month old. Their father had tried to feed the baby on chips and brown sauce, it had been admitted to hospital and then both children were taken into care. Now that Patsy's school days were almost over – fifteen was the leaving age then – she had nowhere to go.

Thus started what Catriona later called 'my mother's lame ducks.' Patsy was a sweet, gentle girl, a raven-haired beauty, who should have spent her childhood in a loving family. I learned so much from her about deprivation: she never described incidents with resentment, but matter-of-factly, or with some sadness. For my part, I realised that never in her life had she actually had to make choices: even her clothes were bought for her, or were hand-me-downs from well-meaning families in Selkirk. I enjoyed having a teenager to make clothes for, taking her with me to choose patterns and fabrics.

Unlike her predecessor, she had no home to go to on her time off, and sometimes it did get claustrophobic. She even came on holiday to Denmark with us. There were the normal teenage moods and there was The Boyfriend.

We encouraged her to extend herself and to look for work with some future to it. At that time, Dingleton Hospital for psychiatric illnesses in Melrose was run by the charismatic Maxwell Jones. In the late 1940s, Dingleton, under Max Jones's predecessor George Bell, had been the first psychiatric hospital in Britain to unlock its wards. It was a beacon of progress in the sad world of people like my sister Alison. Max Jones pioneered the concept of the therapeutic community and tried to run

Dingleton in that way. It seemed a good and supportive environment, and they had jobs for unqualified school leavers: activity assistants, they were called, and they could lead to nurse training. And of course they had staff accommodation. After Patsy had been with us for about a year, we encouraged her to go to Dingleton to train and kept her room for her, relying meantime on local girls as babysitters.

Within a short time, she became pregnant and married: she did so from our house. I made the dress for her and gave the party, and David took her up the aisle of Yarrow Kirk. When, many years later, the marriage broke up, she landed back on the doorstep of Cherrydene with two young children and stayed for a few weeks while she sorted things out. Now she lives happily in Spain with her second husband: we still exchange Christmas cards.

Needless to say, David and I kept in touch with the old Edinburgh circle both in Edinburgh and in London, and, sometimes, in other places in the world. Each time any of the group returned to Edinburgh, we would gather together. Throughout the decades, they have remained the most loyal of friends, bound together by 'bonds of mutual malice', and embracing partners from outside the original circle, such as Mona Shea and Astrid Silins' partner Andre Tammes. He was a theatre lighting designer, and in time we would have much in common. Above all, as David's political career advanced, they were the ones who kept his feet firmly on the ground. At the same time we developed another circle of friends in the Borders, mostly young professional couples with children like ourselves. There was still a continuing closeness with my two old fellow legal apprentices, Bill Goodburn in Peebles and Denbeigh Kirkpatrick in Jedburgh. Some of our Border friends, but not all of them, were also involved in the local party: the wives were, on the whole, full-time mothers, at any rate while their children were under school age.

We also made friends with a few of the younger textile manufacturers around Galashiels, including the design revolutionary Bernat Klein. A Yugoslav by origin, Bernat brought dazzling, unthought-of colour-mixes to the Border textile industry. He broke the existing conventions. Pinks, puces and purples or other startling mixtures vied with each other on the same fabric – and that itself was woven in a very non-traditional way. Sturdy tweeds didn't roll out from Bernat's mill in Galashiels, but confections of mohair and velvet ribbon. Princess Margaret wore a coat in his fabric, thus granting him the seal of fashion approval; but one of his workers was less impressed: 'Ach, it's a load of rubbish,' she said, furtively, in response to a remark by David praising the concoction on her loom.

I still have a Bernat Klein dress, a full-length flowing jersey gown of green, blue and purple. It stayed in my wardrobe for twenty years; then a couple of years ago I took it out and started wearing it again, and I think I like it even better as a vintage piece.

The Klein house, set in woodland outside Selkirk, was a classic of the 60s, designed by the architect Peter Womersley who also lived in the Borders. How exciting the Kleins' home seemed to us, with its sunken floor, its floor-to-ceiling windows, minimal brick and its open-plan living. Even now, when the typically brutal designs of that decade are derided and hands wrung over them, it remains an example of how good 60s architecture could be. Bernat and David were part of a group gathered together by Maxwell Jones under the name 'The Borders Forum'. Again, it was very 60s – its aim was to establish a 'therapeutic community' in the locality, outside of Dingleton Hospital itself. I never did quite grasp what this meant in concrete terms.

A flurry of excitement was caused when the writer and broadcaster Ludovic Kennedy moved to the Borders with his wife Moira Shearer, the ballet dancer and star of the classic film *The Red Shoes*. A fearless exposer of wrongful convictions – most famously, his book *10 Rillington Place* firmly put the blame for the murders for which Timothy John Evans was convicted on his lodger Reginald Christie – Ludo, as he was known, was a member of the Liberal Party. He had been a by-election candidate in Rochdale in the late 1950s, when Moira's appearances on the campaign trail added greatly to the interest from both press and public. We looked forward to the Kennedys playing a part locally. I invited them to dinner with Christopher and Anne Scott, Bernat and Margaret Klein and Maxwell and Kirstin Jones. Right from the start, there was a frigid atmosphere that we couldn't understand, until we discovered later that the artist Dawyck Haig had had the same idea the week previously, and the same sextet had been around the dinner table at his house. Max Jones, ever provocative, had announced casually to Moira, 'Personally, I always preferred Beryl Grey's dancing to yours,' and although the generous-hearted Moira might have forgiven him, Ludo never did – and certainly hadn't within the week.

Unfortunately, Ludo's move back to Scotland was tied to his growing interest in the very policy that had drawn me into the party: Scottish self-government. Soon after his move, there was a by-election in Hamilton, a seat where the Liberals had no hopes, but where the SNP had an outside chance of making their first win. Should the Liberals field a candidate or not? After all, the SNP hadn't done so in Roxburgh, Selkirk and

Peebles. But there was no reciprocal ceding, and at a local party meeting, a letter from Ludo was read out, resigning from the party and giving his support to Winnie Ewing, the SNP candidate in Hamilton. She won the by-election, and although she lost it in the next general election, she had made the SNP a force to be reckoned with from then on. Ludo never did more than give his personal support to her at that time, and eventually returned to his original loyalties; and the episode, though it saddened us at the time, did not interfere with our growing friendship. Moira, despite her essential modesty and naturalness, always rather overawed me: this was the actress whose death in *The Red Shoes* had haunted my nine-year-old dreams.

Winnie Ewing was invited down to Selkirk by one of the most ardent local SNP supporters, Walter Elliot. Walter, who has become a dear friend to me over the years, is a local historian who has made many important discoveries about the prehistoric and Roman periods in the Borders. He is a fount of information, which comes from his knowledge of the land, and he is a poet as well. His invitation to Winnie Ewing was to attend Selkirk Common Riding, and she was so taken with it that she determined to ride the following year. Alas, she only saw the mounted procession in the town, and not the hard, fast riding of the marches on the hills around it. She must have thought it would be like pony-trekking. She came back into the town with tell-tale mud all over her jacket and jodhpurs, and on a leading rein, a tiny saltire fluttering from the back of her riding-hat. 'Ach,' said one souter, 'yon woman doesnae ken her airse frae her elbow.' But she was game enough to turn up at the Common Riding Ball at night, despite her bruises.

Politics have never driven a wedge between Walter and me: we have too much in common in our shared love of history and poetry. He spent most of his working life as a fencer and woodcutter, and as well as more conventional scholarship, his knowledge is informed by the country-man's ability to read the land, and to listen to the people who work it. It was he who brought Selkirk's rare collection of mediaeval manuscripts, the Walter Mason papers, to light; he was involved with the archaelogical digs at the Roman military settlement of Trimontium in Melrose and in the setting up of the Roman exhibition. A few years ago he published *A New Minstrelsy of the Borders*. He is both dreamer and doer.

Christopher and Anne Scott introduced us to their friends among the Border gentry and lairdocracy, but we never felt comfortable with them. Conversation tended to be about things of which we had no experience, or indeed interest, and if we had not been present at any of these meetings, no doubt the state of the local Tory party would have been discussed as well. Horses might have formed a bridge, but these were hunting folk. I tried hunting twice: the first time, slightly pregnant with Catriona, I fell off, and on the second occasion, my stolid cob changed personality at the sound of horn and hound and raced away, unstoppable, over rough moorland and deep chasms. I had not enough nerve and too much imagination for hunting, and was much happier following the flag than chasing the fox. But there was a decided snobbery among many of those in the second category to those in the first, so attempts to find common ground through equestrianism simply created more divisions.

There were exceptions, of course, and foremost among them were Peter and Flora Maxwell Stuart of Traquair. Flora's background was London socialist intellectual, and Peter had worked in industry before inheriting Traquair. They were decidedly unsnobby, and near us in age. We admired tremendously the way they opened up Traquair to the public and made it work as a business. Peter got the old brewery working again; they rented out redundant buildings to craft workers, and they instituted the Traquair Fair, a very alternative event which has now become a traditional part of the Borders year. Flora's interest in and encouragement of the arts in the Borders was an oasis in what was at the time a fairly deserted cultural landscape. In her own memoir, *A Gift of Time*, she describes a mirror-image of our experiences of social life among the Borders gentry in the 1960s – with the exception that the Maxwell Stuarts were insiders in that circle, and we certainly weren't.

The most senior of all the Border aristocracy, however, treated us with great courtesy and friendship. Moving to Ettrick Bridge meant that we were only a few miles from Bowhill, home of the Dukes of Buccleuch; indeed, our children's friends at playgroup and primary school were mostly from families of the Bowhill estate workers, or tenant farmers.

We were invited to tea at Bowhill by the eighth Duke and Duchess when our children were small. Moving out of the entrance hall into the picture gallery, I looked, amazed, at the portraits of the Buccleuch family and the royalty to whom they were related. I heard the Duchess say the name, 'Van Dyck', and, tremendously impressed, asked, 'Which is the Van Dyck?'

Back came the reply, 'They're all Van Dycks in here.'

Duke Walter's heir, Johnnie, was the MP for Edinburgh North. As the Earl of Dalkeith, he had been one of the hardest campaigners in the Tory cause at the by-election. When David won, he had some harsh things to say: 'He will do as much good for the Borders as the Man in the Moon' was one comment from him, which I reminded him about in later years as he presided at a dinner in David's honour towards the end of the latter's House of Commons career. But even at the start of their relationship, the two men worked together to try to stop the closure of the Waverley line, the railway that ran through the Borders, and from that time their friendship grew. When Johnnie Dalkeith broke his back in a hunting accident he became a powerful advocate for the disabled, as well as for his beloved countryside. Once he succeeded to the dukedom and spent more time at Bowhill, his favourite of all the Buccleuch stately homes, I too got to know Johnnie and Jane Buccleuch as neighbours, and also as true and dear friends.

> The rank is but the guinea stamp,
> The man's the gowd for all that,

wrote Robert Burns, meaning that people should not be judged by their *lack* of position. But it is a two-edged saying, for – especially in a Scotland that is inversely snobbish – a title can blind others to the true metal of the person who wears it.

Among the artistic community, to whom I felt more and more drawn, were Ann Carrick and Donald Scott, who at that time lived in a beautiful, eccentric old house with a studio, the Penstead, in Melrose. Ann had been a great friend, at art school, with Auntie G's daughter. She is exactly twenty years my senior, and even now that she is ninety, I always think, 'That's what I want to be like in twenty years' time. She took me under her wing when we first moved to the Borders, and became one of my role models. She had gone into theatre design, specialising in costumes, on leaving art college, and worked for several years at Perth Theatre. When she was joined by her husband Donald, she realised that he was unhappy with the large-scale work that theatre demands. They left Perth and settled in Melrose: both were painters, but each had another speciality. Donald's was tapestry-weaving; Ann's was the creation of miniature costume figures, each one making a dramatic statement of its own. It was an art form I fell for immediately, drawn as I always have been to the small-scale world.

A few years ago, I took Ann to an exhibition in Kirkcudbright of Scottish painters. 'I first came here with my parents, when I was four: they took a house with the Peploes,' she said casually, and as we stopped at a painting by Joan Eardley, she commented, 'Ah! Now I can see what Joan was getting at with this – I couldn't get it at all when she was painting it.' I was experiencing a living history of twentieth-century Scottish art – a rich reward for taking an elderly friend out for the day.

So it was an eclectic mixture of friendships that we developed, but in those early days the majority of our friends, and those we mixed with the most, were young parents like ourselves, professionals and small business people, and the occasional farmers.

It was a time when young couples of our age entertained each other in their own homes (greatly aided by the weekly publication of a cookery magazine called *Cordon Bleu*). We ate and drank merrily with no thought of breathalysers, and careered home under the stars over miles of twisty Border roads.

Among the friends we made was a couple whom I shall call Karen and Charlie Thomson. They were the first people we knew to undertake the restoration of an old property, a dilapidated steading. Charlie had set up his own company selling agricultural chemicals. He was a great one for finding bargains and I sometimes went with him on his forays. It was the time when the old prefab houses were being pulled down, and these made a happy hunting ground. The prefab designers had an especially neat way with drawers and cupboards that could be opened either from the kitchen or the living room: these were recycled to the Thomsons' new home.

Karen had had a chaotic upbringing in the Indian subcontinent during Partition, as a result of which she had no birth certificate. She also had a chronic health problem – to do with her kidneys – and after the birth of two boys, and two miscarriages, was told that another pregnancy would be life-threatening. But her desire for a daughter was such that she went ahead with another, successful try for one, and when their daughter was born, the Thomsons seemed a complete and happy family. They had the children they wanted, in a lovely house they had restored largely with their own labour, and Charlie was running his own business.

Karen, like me, was deeply involved in the playgroup movement, and was due to come and give a talk at one of our regular mothers' meetings. Charlie phoned on the day of the talk to say that Karen had a bad stomach, and had to cry off. Not for one moment could I have guessed the awful secret that lay behind her illness.

Did I see them again after that phone call? I can't remember whether the last, hilarious dinner party at their house was before or after it. Karen served pigeons full of lead shot, and conversation and jokes flew thick and fast. David was in particularly witty and scurrilous form at the expense of a couple of Tory fellow-guests.

Then, one June day, a mutual friend phoned: 'Did you see Karen Thomson's death in today's *Scotsman?*'

No, I hadn't. There was the announcement: Beloved wife of Charlie and mother of their children. We spoke sadly, but with the knowledge that Karen's medical condition was always going to mean a short lifespan for her. Poor Charlie, we said to each other, having to bring up those children on his own. There was no mention of a funeral.

A couple of days later the *Southern Reporter* ran a paragraph to the effect that there were suspicious circumstances surrounding the death of a woman at the Thomsons' address, and that the police were making enquiries. That night, I was at the Bussing concert at Hawick Common Riding, representing David. The Chief Constable was there.

'Tom,' I asked him, 'Is there something odd about this death?'

'There most certainly is,' he said. 'The husband's unconscious and under guard after a suicide attempt, and we're waiting for him to recover to charge him with murder.'

I cannot begin to describe the impact this had on all of us who were friends with the Thomsons. It was not as though it had been my first brush with murder that year: the sister of my across-the-road neighbour in the village had died a sordid death in Galashiels a few months previously. But I didn't know that victim. This death was much closer to us, and as the circumstances came out, they were shattering. Charlie, it seemed, had been having an affair with a local farmer's wife. Although this had finished after they had been found together *in flagrante* by the farmer, he had begun to fantasise about having relations with other women if and when he was widowed. Then, suddenly, Karen was given an all-clear on her medical condition. Charlie told her that this was a great disappointment, and from then on he began another fantasy – that of killing her with the chemicals to which he had such easy access.

He went to the doctor to tell him about these fantasies and was referred to Dingleton. At the same time, Karen consulted her own GP and disclosed fears that her husband was poisoning her. I have always thought, since, that her failure to come to my playgroup meeting was one of these instances of poisoning. On the weekend of her death, the children were staying with their grandparents. Charlie and Karen went to a society wedding in the Borders, and when they came home Charlie made her a drugged cup of Horlicks. When she was unconscious, he injected her with a phosphate that leaves no post–mortem traces. If it had not been for Karen's GP, his crime might well have remained undetected. When he knew that the police were on his track, he fled to friends and then made a suicide attempt.

He never stood trial for murder. His lawyers managed to plea-bargain, and he pled guilty to culpable homicide on the grounds of diminished responsibility; his sessions at Dingleton stood him in good stead for this. He was sentenced to only seven years, which he spent in Saughton, and David used to go and visit him sometimes. Charlie took an interest in the internal politics of the Scottish prison system, which governors were on the way up and which were on the way out, and passed on much useful background material to David.

But the lesson that I learnt from the Thomsons' tragedy was this: that you never, ever, know what is happening behind a front door after it is closed on you after a good dinner party. Life in the Borders may seem tranquil, but neither in the past nor the present is that always the case.

## 14

# Narrow Margins

In David's early days in the House of Commons, the first issue with international implications in which he was involved was the plight of the East African Asian community. In 1968 the Ugandan tyrant Idi Amin blamed his country's woes on these successful entrepreneurs, most of whom also held British passports. In an act of misguided populism, Amin told them to pack their bags and head for Britain. Harold Wilson's government panicked and brought in a quota system, which applied not only to the Ugandan Asians but those throughout East Africa. The Tories, needless to say, concurred, with the honourable exception of the former colonial secretary, Iain Macleod. He, and others, were impressed by the knowledgeable advocacy of the East African Asians' cause by the young MP from Roxburgh, Selkirk and Peebles, and David later wrote his first book about the situation: *No Entry*.

The stance he took at the time had various results. One was that it gave him a reputation in the House of Commons which was then enhanced by his piloting through of the Abortion Act. The second was that it laid the foundation stones for some deep and lasting friendships with the Asian communities both in Kenya and in Britain. The most significant of these were with Fitz de Souza, who had been Deputy Speaker of the Kenyan Parliament, and Nadir Dinshaw, a prosperous and generous Harrow-educated Parsee who had converted to Christianity. Nadir loved Britain, especially London, and lived mainly in Jersey with his wife Hille and his daughter Nali, in a beautiful old rambling house by the sea at St Brelade's Bay. Nali became one of David's secretaries, and her daughter his god-daughter. Another Kenyan Asian, who worked first of all as a volunteer assistant to David and who in time would become his closest friend in London, and his landlord, was Atul Vadher.

A third result was that when David Ennals, the president of the Anti-Apartheid Movement in Britain, was appointed a minister in the Wilson government and so had to resign his position, David was approached by the Anti-Apartheid campaigners to succeed him.

'Why me?' he asked the emissaries.

'Well – Barbara Castle had to resign when she became a cabinet minister; now we've lost David Ennals. We are looking for someone who is not likely to become a minister, so we can expect a decent period of service from you.'

At this time the movement was trying to apply pressure on sports organisations to boycott matches with South Africa, whose national teams, as with every other aspect of the apartheid state, were racially selected. The main sports involved were rugby and cricket. In the autumn of 1969, the Springboks rugby team from South Africa was due to tour the UK. The matches included one against the South of Scotland at the Netherdale ground in Galashiels. Already a young Liberal by the name of Peter Hain was spearheading protests, as well as direct action which involved the digging up of pitches. Peter's family had come to Britain as political refugees from their homeland in South Africa. He was a passionate young man, and even in those young days had charisma. And he knew what apartheid meant. Another Peter, surnamed Hellyer, was also involved in the turf-digging. He also had been one of David's part-time assistants for about a year, and they had worked together on South African issues since 1968.

Anyone who knows the Scottish Borders will know that rugby holds the same semi-religious status as it does in Wales. At that time it was the only sport available to boys in secondary schools other than cross-country running. The Scottish team regularly included between a third and a half of Borderers. On the Monday after a match they would go back to their day jobs as mill-workers or tradesmen or vets, and be faced with criticism or praise of their play by friends and colleagues. Employers would be generous with time off that was devoted to the needs of the god rugby, and would bask in the reflected glory of their employees. During the 1966 election, we decided to go to an international at Murrayfield rather than stay in the Borders, as we reckoned we'd meet more constituents that way, on the walk from Princes Street and back.

There was absolutely no doubt that the protests at the rugby grounds during the South Africa tour were very unpopular in the Borders. David was faced with a dilemma. Should he join, or even lead, a protest at Netherdale, knowing that it would damage him in the constituency? Peter Hellyer persuaded Anti-Apartheid not to send their shock troops to Netherdale, but to leave David to handle the protest there himself. As a first step, he called a public meeting to explain his opposition to the tour. He invited the legendary Scots churchman and founder of the

Iona Community, the Rev. Dr George MacLeod, to share the platform with him, and also a rising young advocate, who was becoming a force in the Liberal party and who had been an Olympic athlete: his name was Menzies Campbell. In the run-up to the meeting, David kept a discreet silence about what else he might do to oppose the match, and with it, the South African regime.

I had no doubt that the right course of action for David was to be part of the demonstration. 'Even if you don't go, I will,' I threatened. But he would have gone anyway, and at the public meeting announced that he would be outside the gates of Netherdale before the match, protesting peacefully. When questions from the public were called for, a man in the audience stood up: his name was Laurence Morrison, and he had been the Labour candidate in the constituency twice in the 1950s.

'You know you'll lose a lot of votes over this,' he said. 'But you'll also gain a few, and mine will be one of them.'

There was only a handful of us outside the rugby ground to start off with, holding our placards and trying to hand leaflets to rugby supporters. The Episcopal rector from Melrose came through the gates, trying to hide from one of his parishioners in our small group. We were sworn at and even spat at, and I loved it – until the busload of Socialist Workers Party comrades from Paisley arrived. They shouted abuse at the rugby supporters, and the rest of our time before the match started was given over to trying to get them to shut up, and apologising for their behaviour.

The 1970 General Election was called in June. The Tories had sacked their excellent candidate from the previous election, Ian MacIntyre, and adopted Russell Fairgrieve, the owner of a Galashiels mill, a man with a strong rugby record and a previous constituency chairman. Unfortunately they had not done their homework very well: he was not a popular boss. He had never made a habit of connecting with the men and women who worked for him: now, when he attempted to do so, his workforce were not fooled. The word went around the town, and beyond it. The choice had been made from other candidates in the Conservative cause, including a young Edinburgh advocate, Malcolm Rifkind. Years later, he told us the remark of one of the interviewers at the selection meeting: 'I believe you're of the Jewish faith, Mr Rifkind. I'm afraid you won't find many co-religionists here.'

It was going to be a tight race. There was a national swing to the Tories, who were led by Edward Heath. The SNP, buoyed up by Winnie Ewing's victory in Hamilton, had re-entered the fray with a credible candidate. David had an additional opponent, standing on an anti-legal abortion ticket. And on one of the issues that he had championed at the last two elections, all his battling had been in vain. The Waverley railway line from Edinburgh to Carlisle, through the heart of the Borders, had been closed, with remarkable insensitivity, by the Labour Minister of Transport. But the rugby demonstration caused the most furore and emotion.

Peter Hellyer came for three weeks to show his gratitude for David's stance. Two things struck him: the friendliness of the police, and the fact that on polling day, in the village of Yetholm, the Tory and Liberal election workers shared a table in the playground of the school which served as the polling station, and gave each other information, coffee and sandwiches. Peter fell for the Borders, and, despite moving to Abu Dhabi, was to spend two or three weeks in the constituency at every election David fought from then on. On almost every occasion he went to look at tempting properties currently on the market, but never quite fulfilled his fantasy of owning a remote Borders cottage.★

On two occasions during that election, we abandoned our party rosettes and rode both at Hawick and Selkirk Common Ridings – well, only David rode at the first. The day of Hawick Common Riding I remember for another reason, which still stands out as one of the most magical experiences of my life.

Despite the tight contest ahead in Roxburgh, Selkirk and Peebles, David had agreed to give a day in support of other candidates in the south of Scotland and the north of England. The only way to do this was by helicopter. So the party hired the cheapest one available: a crop-sprayer with three seats. We took off from Hawick Moor, far enough away from the horses not to frighten them, and landed first of all at Berwick-upon-Tweed to speak for the candidate there, Alan Beith. As we looked down, we saw a small crowd gathered, but they were all wearing blue rosettes. Had the Tories effected a coup and taken over our meeting? We didn't know what the candidate looked like. Nor did we know that, in Berwick, blue was the traditional colour for the Liberals. It was our first meeting with Alan Beith, who is now the longest-serving Liberal MP in the House of Commons.

The next stop was Newcastle racecourse, and after that we headed for Galloway, where Christopher Scott was the candidate. The pilot pointed

★Early in 2010, I had an email from Peter Hellyer. 'I can't bear the thought of a Steel standing in a General Election and my not being there.' So he came and gave valuable support to our daughter Catriona at the start of her campaign in Dumfriesshire, Clydesdale and Tweeddale.

out Hadrian's Wall to us. We asked him to fly lower, and he dropped to below the legal height for flying. Then he abandoned his flight plan and used the wall as his guide. It was an unbelievable day at the beginning of June, and the Roman forts stood out below us, one after the other. After we left them behind, we came to the vast sands of the Solway at low tide, sparkling against the setting sun. I remembered Walter Scott's description, in *Redgauntlet*, of Darsie Latimer's escape from the incoming tide:

'He turned his horse and rode off, while I began to walk back towards the Scottish shore, a little alarmed at what I had heard; for the tide advances with such rapidity upon these fatal sands . . . These recollections grew more agitating, and instead of walking deliberately, I began a race as fast as I could, thinking I felt each pool of salt water through which I splashed grow deeper and deeper. At length the surface of the sand did seem more intersected with pools and channels full of water − either that or the tide really was beginning to influence the bed of the estuary. Either way, it was rather an unpromising state of affairs, for the sands at the time turned softer, and my footsteps, as soon as I had passed, filled with water. I began to have recollections concerning . . . the secure footing afforded by the pavement of Brown's Square and Scot's Close, when my better genius, the tall fisherman, appeared once more close to my side, he and his sable horse looming gigantic in the now darkening twilight.

"Are you mad? Or are you weary of your life? − you will be presently among the quicksands."

I professed my ignorance of the way, to which he only replied, "there is no time for prattling − get up behind me."'

The twilight was darkening on the last leg of our adventures of that day, as we flew over Liddesdale and the outline of the deserted railway village of Riccarton Junction, now razed to the ground. But we landed safely in the field beside Cherrydene, and did not stir out of the constituency again. Later in the campaign, Jeremy Thorpe flew into the Borders with his wife, and Catriona carried out her first political duty, presenting Caroline Thorpe with a posy. She says it is her earliest memory.

It was the last time we would see Caroline.

The following week we both rode at Selkirk Common Riding. The Standard Bearer that year was a young joiner with the enviable name of

Falconer Grieve, who was to play a large part in our lives twenty years later. Among the throng as we followed the Standard Bearer into the Market Place to watch the Casting of the Colours, we spotted David's opponent, Russell Fairgrieve. He was sitting in state on the balcony of the (supposedly independent) County Council offices, in the company of the (supposedly non-political) County Clerk, a man of massive pomposity. A Union Jack draped the balustrade. We giggled at the sight.

By polling day we weren't laughing. It was nip and tuck. Russell Fairgrieve's eve-of-poll leaflet consisted of an image of rugby posts with a ball sailing over between them and the slogan, 'Convert to Conservatism'. David's election address had blazoned him as 'Man of Action' and had an image of him, hatless, galloping up the A7 at the conclusion of Selkirk Common Riding. Once again the meetings were well-attended, although, for the first time, there was hostility at them, not from Tory plants, but from electors who were genuinely angry, mostly on the rugby issue.

Our secret weapon was the brainchild of Vincent Taylor, a clever PR man who was a party activist and who had the additional benefit of looking enough like David to be mistaken for him. Vince's idea would not work now, because it depended on the existence of old-fashioned milk bottles and an equally old-fashioned doorstep milk delivery. An early-rising team of supporters followed the milkmen, and slipped over the neck of the bottles a cardboard collar which had David's smiling face on it, and the message; 'Good morning! Vote today for David Steel.' It was reckoned afterwards to have saved the election.

At the count, though, we didn't think it had been enough. As Russell Fairgrieve made the most of the Returning Officer's liquid hospitality, and the odd snatch of news from the radio told us of lost Liberal seats amid the general Tory surge, the votes piled up and the running tally showed the Tories ahead. David was about to go off in to a corner to write his speech ceding the election. John Gebbie, always his most pessimistic party worker, came up to him, but this time he spoke optimistically. 'It's not all over,' he said: 'The Gala boxes are still to be counted.' Galashiels was always the staunchest of the burghs in the Liberal cause, but this time they had a son of their own standing for the Tories. What difference would that make?

The Galashiels boxes turned the tide, saved David's skin and his political future. The Sheriff disengaged himself from the stunned Fairgrieves and conferred with the agents. There was a Liberal majority of 770. The Tory agent demanded a recount, which was necessary as much to give the candidate time to pull himself together as to confirm the vote. At the end of the recount there was a Liberal majority of 1770, and a thousand votes unaccounted for. A third recount was called and when this gave a majority of 570, no-one was going to quibble. We were all done in.

As we drove back up the Ettrick Valley, the sun had risen behind us. A deer jumped out of a cornfield and scampered into the woods on the other side of the road. We held hands and smiled.

Of all the elections that David fought, this was perhaps the one when I was most proud of him. He had stuck to his guns, his back had been against the wall, and although it had been a close call, he had come through. Nearly forty years later, Catriona said, in the midst of a local political controversy of her own, 'If I learnt one thing being brought up in a political household, it's to do what you think is right, and then face your electors.' This was never more true than of her father in 1970.

The Europhile Edward Heath was Prime Minister, and the Liberal Party was back to where it was in 1959, with six seats. It could have been even worse: two other seats, apart from David's, were held by majorities of three figures: a few hundred votes cast another way, and the Liberal presence in parliament would have been annihilated.

Among those who had lost was Eric Lubbock, the party whip. Jeremy Thorpe immediately appointed David in his place. That was just before tragedy struck. As they were having a meeting in the House of Commons, a policeman came to the office to tell Jeremy the ghastly news: Caroline had been killed in a head-on smash on the way up from his constituency. Their son, Rupert, had come to London by train earlier with Jeremy and the nanny: now David was detailed to go and tell the latter. 'It was heartbreaking – that little boy, sitting in his high chair, with no idea what had happened to his mother – and he won't have any memories of her.' A shattered party and a twice-shattered leader groped their way forward.

Our summer holiday that year was therapeutic. I had booked a holiday in a horse-drawn caravan in County Roscommon, and we set off to Ireland via the Stranraer ferry. We were introduced to our horse, Johnnie, and given a quick lesson in harnessing him and unharnessing him, although how we would have managed without my limited experience on the Aberdeen baker's cart, I'm not sure. We slowed down to a daily mileage of ten to twelve miles, and the primitive conditions in the caravan were more than made up for by the farmhouses and pubs that provided us with grazing and evening meals along the way. We came back refreshed: for me as well as David there was a new challenge ahead.

I had followed with some interest the passage of the Social Work (Scotland) Act 1968, which reformed the social services in Scotland. The probation and children's services, those for the elderly and for the disabled and the socially inadequate, were to be amalgamated into one department where there would be, in the expression not yet coined, joined-up thinking about their 'clients'. The way of dealing with children and young people considered at risk would also be reformed. It was recognised that children who had committed offences, who had been on the receiving end of abuse or neglect at the hands of their parents, who were truanting or who were beyond parental control, were almost certainly experiencing similar underlying problems, that manifested themselves in these various symptoms. It was proposed that children under the age of sixteen who might be in need of 'compulsory measures of care' should be removed from the court system and brought before a lay tribunal, to be known as the Children's Hearing, and there would be one for each local authority that had responsibility for social work.

The volunteers who manned the hearings were to be known collectively as the Children's Panel, and they would be serviced by a paid official with the boring title of the Reporter. From what I could see, it was a job that might suit me in terms of my legal qualification and my family commitments – including the fact that, not only would I be very part-time in a small authority like Selkirkshire, I would also be responsible for organising that time. Patsy's experiences had made me realise that vulnerable children were badly served locally and probably nationally: maybe this was a chance to do something positive. And as well as my legal qualification and court experience, I had even been employed previously by the Social Work Department when I ran the handwork classes for mentally-handicapped adults. I didn't realise at the time that being involved in the setting up of a totally new system was an unusual opportunity for being creative in the law; and that I had a deep vein of creativity in me.

I applied for the job when it was advertised and was interviewed by a councillor and by the County Clerk who had played host to Russell Fairgrieve at the Common Riding during the election. He asked me if I could do my own typing and what my childcare arrangements would be. I was angrier about the first than the second question, neither of which he would have put to a male applicant, and there was an unseasonable length of time between my interview and my appointment, even though I had learned on the grapevine that my qualifications were way ahead of any other applicant. The excuse was that all the appointments of Reporters had to be vetted by the Secretary of State for Scotland. No doubt the County Clerk hoped I'd fail that hurdle. But eventually the job was offered to me, and I spent my wedding anniversary that year on a training course for a new breed of administrator, the Reporters to the Children's Hearings. Among our number was Donald Dewar, who had lost South Aberdeen at the election and whose wife had deserted him for his best man, Derry Irvine, the future Lord Chancellor. My friend Denbeigh Kirkpatrick was appointed for next door Roxburghshire, working the job, as several did, within his legal practice.

We were told to expect that the majority of cases that would be reported to us would be from the police, and that they would concern young people who had committed offences. The training which I lined up for my panel was based on that premise, and the Social Work Department supplied us with mock cases based on real ones. One of the aims of the lay panels was that they would be 'the community dealing with the community's problems', but in reality most panels were composed of middle-class professionals like myself, and the majority of members were women. The Selkirkshire panel did in fact contain a broad range of economic backgrounds, ranging from the widow of a local laird, to a couple of mill workers. This really was the community: so much so that often the panel members would know more about the families coming before the hearings than the social workers, and would spot in the background reports where those compiling them had been totally misled by their interviewees.

The training may have concentrated on young offenders as making up the bulk of our 'clients', but the Act had been in operation for less than twenty-four hours when the local RSSPCC officer applied for a Place of Safety order for a baby of six months old, who had been admitted to hospital for the third time in his young life. I was thrown into emergency hearings and a contested case before the Sheriff. I was concerned that the application might not stand up to the rigorous standards of evidence that are demanded in Scotland to prove a criminal case, so I prefaced proceedings with a request that the Sheriff give a ruling that this was not a criminal proceeding but a civil one, and that I only needed to prove on a balance of probabilities that an offence had been committed against the baby. There was no evidence as to whether the mother or the father had assaulted the baby, though the RSSPCC inspector had no doubt that it was the father. Even so, it was the Devil's own job to get the medical people to confirm that the injuries must have been directly inflicted, while the social worker was so concerned about 'gaining the trust' of the parents, so that she could work with them, that she was almost in denial about what had happened to their son.

A supervision order was made, putting the baby into the care of what was a rare resource in the area, foster parents, with visits from the parents. A few months later the social work department applied to the hearings for a variation: everything was now hunky-dory with the father and mother, they were proving admirable parents on their visits, and would the panel now please let the baby go home to them? The RSSPCC inspector opposed the move, but the panel members were moved by the social worker's plea on behalf of her 'clients', and followed her recommendation. Through gritted teeth, I said, 'So you want me to vary the supervision order?'

A further intervention from the social worker indicated that she would find her work with the parents more productive if this were totally rescinded. 'They need to feel they are trusted.' Once again, the panel went along with her and when, within the month, the baby landed back in hospital, I had to start the whole process again from the beginning. I made sure that the same individuals attended the second lot of hearings. At the first of these, the father exploded and pinned me up against a wall with his hands round my throat, his eyes full of the aggression he had turned on his helpless son, and the words, 'I'll break your fucking neck, you bitch.'

The wrongdoings of the children and teenagers of Selkirkshire came almost as light relief after the few such cases as this that I handled. Even amongst the most deprived, there was nothing like the feral condition of families that exists today in broken communities. Child sexual abuse must have happened, but only once did the hint of it come up, and in that case it was unprovable. It was the lack of communication in families, and the tragedies, that struck me the most. One boy, referred to a hearing for a minor offence, turned out to have been present some time before when his younger brother had been run over by a car and killed. Since that day, the family had never, ever, discussed their loss. It was hard to imagine that unit of adults and children each locked up in their own grief and guilt day after day and month after month.

I had discretion over whether or not to refer the young offenders to a hearing at all, and there was one category of crime whose perpetrators never got further than my desk: poachers. I regarded them as being very far from needing compulsory measures of care, but simply as having an adventurous boyhood. There was a common feature in all the police reports of poaching: they all ended with the words, 'Since the fish was diseased, the evidence had to be destroyed.' Was it simply a strange coincidence that all these lads were totally incapable of catching a healthy salmon – or was the evidence a perk of the job at the police station? I favoured the latter explanation.

The 1970–74 election brought about big changes in our personal circumstances. For the first time, MPs from constituencies away from the capital were awarded a 'living-in London' allowance instead of having to pay for their accommodation during the week out of their own salaries. David managed to get the lease of a one-bedroomed flat (some years later upgraded to two bedrooms) in Dolphin Square, that block of flats along the embankment from the House of Commons which, at the time, was the largest single gathering of flats under one roof in Europe. It had been built in the 1930s by a trust, with the express aim of providing accommodation for people working in the City of Westminster, and the rents were reasonable rather than commercial. There was a priority system for MPs, and many made Dolphin Square their London base. There were pleasant central gardens, a swimming pool and other sports facilities in the basement, and a restaurant. Dolphin Square remained our London pied-à-terre for over thirty years. Both Catriona and Rory shared it with David, rent-free, during their years as students or young workers in London. In the recent expenses scandal, this is an arrangement that has brought opprobrium on MPs by the media: we simply regarded it as the natural thing to do. When, later, MPs were able to use their allowance towards the interest on mortgages, we were never tempted to leave Dolphin Square and buy a flat. I simply did not want to own property in London: it would be too much like putting down some kind of roots. With hindsight, in view of the furore that has arisen over the use of allowances, perhaps I was right.

Nevertheless I enjoyed my visits to London much more now that we had a place of our own. Also, travel passes for spouses were now introduced: 'Three conjugal visits a year,' we used to joke. In time this number was increased to such an extent that I never used them all up; and they were also available for the children. It meant I could go down for great events. Some of these were rituals, such as the State Opening of Parliament. I took the children to that, so that their first sight of the Queen was of her arriving in a golden coach to Westminster. Later, as I stood with them in the central lobby, and the doors between the Commons and the Lords were flung open, a policeman lifted Catriona up so that she could see the sight of the Queen on the throne. Even if she has no memory of it, I do, and when I remember it I offer thanks to that kindly policeman.

For me, though, a more exciting event was the second reading of the European Communities Bill, which Edward Heath had introduced. The Labour Party was bitterly split over the question of joining the Common Market. Wilson had put out a three-line whip, but sixty of the parliamentary party, led by Roy Jenkins, defied this and marched through the 'Yes' lobby. Until the vote itself, there was no way of knowing what the number would be. Feelings and tempers ran high: respected politicians of the same persuasion were at war with each other. From the door of David's office beside the Members' Lobby, I watched the verbal fratricide between the members of Her Majesty's opposition with fascination.

Above all it was now possible for the children to share and to understand their father's London life. It was he who, while on the House of Commons services committee, first proposed a families' room for members, and we made much use of this facility. As Graeme and Catriona grew older, we would take them down singly to London (their siblings usually left on Joan's family farm), in the company of a favoured school friend. I would take Catriona to the Bethnal Green Museum, with its wonderful collection of doll's houses – as much for me as for her – or on the river to Hampton Court or to the Royal Mews. Once, when she was about eleven or twelve, there was an exhibition in Westminster Hall marking fifty years since universal suffrage was won for women. At the end of it was a suggestions box: 'How do you think women's interests can be improved in the next fifty years?'

Catriona and her friend eagerly filled up their slips in identical fashion: 'We think women should be allowed to ride at Hawick Common Riding.'

I often wondered what the organisers thought, and, when the issue of women at Hawick Common Riding became a national and international media craze, whether they remembered those aspirations of twenty years before.

For Graeme and his friends, it was usually the London Dungeon or the Natural History Museum. A visit to the British Museum was a total failure, with the boys' interest only being sparked by the discovery, across the street from it, of the London Joke Shop. The highlight of one visit was when I agreed to book seats for *No Sex Please, We're British*. And climbing the stairs to the top of the Big Ben tower was always a sure-fire success.

Another innovation which helped David enormously also came in the wake of the 1970 election. The Joseph Rowntree Trust made funding available to opposition parties to employ political assistants. They became known as the Chocolate Soldiers, because of their connection with the confectionery fortune, and also as a reference to the operetta by Strauss based on George Bernard Shaw's play. As Liberal Whip, David was one of those to benefit, and his advertisement brought in a flurry of 140 replies, which we read through together. Then a late entrant came, not from a Liberal, but from a Labour Party member, whose letter David liked for its self-deprecating and dry humour. He was a young pharmacist in Edinburgh, and his name was Archy Kirkwood; he was to become one of the staunchest and most loyal of those who were associated with David through the decades.

Archy was the first of a succession of bright young graduates who became his assistants. When it came to appointing his successor, I berated David because his shortlist did not have any women on it, and he added a couple. He returned from the interviews full of the virtues of one of these candidates.

'You'd really like her,' he enthused. 'She's a graduate of Glasgow University, and she had white thigh boots and a mini skirt, and her name is Caroline Bosomworth.'

I burst into tears. 'I don't really want you to have a female assistant,' I sobbed, 'and especially not one with white thigh boots and a name like Caroline Bosomworth!'

Years later, the BBC set up their local radio station, Radio Tweed, under the leadership of a bright young producer, Caroline Adam. I gave a lunch for her to meet various locals. At one point, David followed me into the kitchen.

'You never told me that Caroline Adam was Caroline Bosomworth!' he exclaimed.

'Is she? I didn't know. You were right, I do like her.'

Caroline rose to the top echelons of BBC Scotland, and then went into arts administration. Now she is back in the Borders, running the vibrant Eastgate Arts Centre in Peebles. We have been friends for many years, but it was only while writing this book that I confessed to her why she did not get that job with David thirty-five years ago. 'That was very nameist of you,' she commented drily. 'But it was such a *sexy* name,' I countered, and felt lightened by the confession.

So Archy was followed by Andrew Gifford, Stuart Mole, Jeremy Joseph, Graham Watson, Michael Duncan, Atul Vadher and Jeremy

Purvis. Archy, Graham and Jeremy Purvis went on to serve respectively in the House of Commons and the House of Lords, the European Parliament and the Scottish Parliament. Andrew became a millionaire. They all worked with David and travelled with him at home and abroad. Together with his long-serving (and long-suffering) secretaries Ann Dawson, Tessa Horton and Nali Dinshaw, they were his confidants and have remained our friends. But when he came home, he usually wanted a rest from politics – and my own political role felt diminished.

On the home front, I was casting around for a new mother's help. The experience with Patsy had worked well, and I had felt that I was doing something useful for her into the bargain. Having an au pair or a mother's help seemed such a luxury when I compared myself with the other young mothers of the playgroup, that I felt guilty about it. This was not so much because I was leaving my children in their care, but because I had the option to do so. I turned again to the Social Work Department to see if there were any other girls in Patsy's situation who might fit into our household.

Pauline was also in the Priory, but had only gone there recently. She and her sister had been in a List D (approved) school, after being referred there for persistent truancy. Hers was a much unhappier story than Patsy's, and she was a more troubled personality. I think she stayed with us for about a year, and during that time she would have visits from girls who had been at the List D school with her. There was always a plausible explanation given for their sudden appearances, and their need to stay for a few days – but their departure was usually followed by phone calls from the schools or visits from the police, for the girls were, inevitably, absconders. When we went to stay with the Hackett family in London, Pauline disappeared all night, taking the Hacketts' stolid Greek au pair with her, and causing all four adults left at home a completely sleepless night.

After all this we decided that we, and our children, needed a bit more stability in the form of a surrogate parent, and the immensely competent Margot came and organised Cherrydene and its inhabitants for a few years. How David loved her regime of tidiness. I found it slightly maddening that all traces of my creative jumble would be cleared up when I was out of the room for ten minutes. But she gave the children a competent care and consistency that they welcomed and I could go away, even overnight, knowing they were in safe hands.

## 15
# New Beginnings

*June, 1973*

The flags are up for Selkirk Common Riding. There must be almost as many horse droppings in the streets as there were in the days before cars, the shop-fronts are spruced up and the statue of Sir Walter Scott in the Market Place has had its annual coat of paint. We have our own horse now, as well as a small Shetland for the children. David had hired him for Selkirk the previous year from our usual stables, a fifteen-hand black cob not long off the boat from Ireland. They had parted company in the first mad gallop once the horses had crossed the Ettrick on the outward journey, and the horse obligingly stopped to await his rider's return to the saddle. 'This is the horse for me,' said David, and that was how Hamlet came into our lives, where he stayed for nineteen years.

But there is no way I'll be in the saddle this year. I'm in the maternity wing of Selkirk Cottage Hospital, or Viewfield as it is also known. The scholar and writer Andrew Lang, author of the *Red Fairy Book of Stories* and many others of that genre, lived here when it was home to the Selkirk legal dynasty of which he was a scion. The maternity wing has four beds, and though there's GP cover, most births are attended only by the midwife. There is not equipment for emergencies, so that there is a sadly high rate of infant mortality; and quite a few mothers, racing up to Edinburgh in an ambulance to the Eastern General, give birth at Lauder on the A68. Nevertheless, Selkirk folk like to have their babies here, so that they will be true souters, and, if they are boys, thus become eligible to be Royal Burgh Standard Bearer in thirty years time.

The other three mothers have already given birth, two of them to boys – indeed one of them has twins. There are no scans in these days, and the presence of two babies was not discovered in pregnancy. The mothers of all three potential standard bearers both smoke, despite the presence of the babies in the ward beside us. The third mother and I are too polite to point out that we dislike the smell of cigarettes, and that we don't think it can be good for the babies. The hospital authorities don't raise any objection.

As before, my labour is long, and at about two o'clock in the morning David goes home. We are both blissfully unconcerned which sex this one is, although we have only decided on a boy's name this time. The children are desperate for a brother.

'I shouted to the owl in Kirkhope Tower for a baby brother,' says Catriona whimsically, while Graeme avers that if I come home with a girl he will flush her down the toilet. At about four o'clock I can bear David's absence no longer: I think things are beginning to change. I ask that he be summoned back.

'Oh, poor man,' says the matron, 'he's had a hard night. Let him have a rest.'

'Have a rest!' I roar. 'Have a rest! What the hell do you think I'm having! Get him back here!' So, at last, he is here for the birth, and it is he who tells me, 'We've got another little boy,' and he who holds our new son first.

Rory made an early appearance in the public eye. When he was a few days old he came with me to a Children's Hearing in a Moses basket. I had not asked for any time off. The County Clerk, I had heard, had assumed that, once I was pregnant again, I would give up my job. I simply never mentioned that I was pregnant to him, ballooning week by week: in our infrequent encounters he could hardly keep his eyes off my stomach. But he never alluded to to my pregnancy, and neither did I. When I went into hospital, I took some files with me, and within five days was at a hearing with my baby.

A week after Rory's birth was the day of the Common Riding, and I took him down to the Market Place as I watched the casting of the colours. Afterwards we joined David at the Provost's reception, and Rory was photographed in the arms of both the Standard Bearer and the Provost.

We were much more confident parents this time, and the older children were enthusiastic helpers. And now I had Margot, who provided such stable care, and this meant that we could travel more, leaving the older children at Cherrydene.

Not long after his birth, the MP in the neighbouring constituency of Berwick-upon-Tweed, Lord Lambton, had to resign after being caught three in a bed with prostitutes of differing hues. I remembered him well from the by-election, sitting at the front of a meeting in a corrugated-iron village hall, green wellies on his feet, dark sunglasses on his nose and a trick question up his sleeve. The Liberal candidate at the last election had been Alan Beith, who was a lecturer at Newcastle University. He had just been offered an academic post in Norway. David went over the Border to a transport café on the A68 to persuade him not to take up this appointment, and to contest the by-election instead. Although Alan had been in third place in 1970, the Liberals had had a series of by-election successes, and it was felt that he had a chance of winning where another candidate might not. I went with David on his embassy to Alan.

As the two politicians engaged in conversation on strategy, I contentedly fed my baby from my left breast. Suddenly, without warning, a jet of milk spurted from the right one, hitting Alan's tie. I had seen medieval representations of the Madonna feeding the infant Christ while the other breast flows like a fountain: I'd just never experienced it in real life. Despite this disconcerting experience, Alan agreed to fight again, and David meantime pulled a sneaky and subtle trick on the Tories, who had delayed moving the writ for the by-election. He declared that, as the neighbouring MP, he would hold constituency surgeries in Berwick until a new MP was elected. The march between the two constituencies actually only covered a short part of the Roxburghshire-Northumberland border, and so this ruse infuriated the Tories splendidly.

When Rory was six weeks old we went on one of our family motor caravan holidays, this time in a very uncomfortable Land Rover model, to Denmark, Sweden and Norway. When he was four months he came with us to the Council of Europe in Strasbourg. He travelled in what looked like a basket for holding caught salmon, and indeed once a fellow passenger on a plane asked if that was what I was carrying. At other times, I often carried him on my back. At that time you could only get baby carriers at mountaineering shops, and in Strasbourg several envious French mothers stopped me to ask about this eccentric but very practical piece of equipment. Once, we went to an evening reception where the cloakroom attendants offered to look after the baby. At the end of it, I picked up my coat and swanned into the street. As David hailed a taxi, I suddenly blanched. 'Oh my God! I've left the baby behind in the cloakroom!'

The Council of Europe met three times a year, and I tried to go with David at least once, to the autumn one. It was very social, and delegates were encouraged to bring their spouses, although of course they had to pay their loved ones' expenses. I remember above all the gastronomic delights on offer – eating frogs' legs for the first time with Fred Peart, now a Lord, at a restaurant called the *Ours Blanc*; the arrival of the MP Dickson Mabon, hot-foot from the Labour conference and, as we sat in the *Orangerie* of the public gardens with a plate of *crêpes de fruits de mer* in front of us, full of semi-malicious gossip about the goings on there. Nor will I forget the bus tour which the City of Strasbourg sent us on, through the gold- and crimson-leafed trees, arriving eventually at a hostelry that went by the name of *La Grange du Paysan*. The tables groaned with pâtés and terrines, *saucissons* and *jambons*, *crudités* and bread. We sat with some of the Labour delegation – I think we were the only Liberals – and, thinking that this was the entire repast, cleared the plates of everything on them. It was the first course of five, which included a wafer-thin *quiche lorraine* and a *sorbet à l'eau de vie de framboises*. A small oompah band played, and one of the House of Commons clerks who was with the delegation insisted on conducting it. Unfortunately he, or they, decided to play *Tannenbaum*, and our table burst raucously into the words of *The Red Flag*. Dame Joan Vickers, a frosty-haired Tory grandee with a sense of humour to match, complained afterwards about the behaviour of the clerk – she was prevented by protocol from complaining about her boisterous Lib-Lab colleagues.

The time of the Berwick by-election was drawing close. The Tories were putting up a stiff fight, and pouring money into the seat. David was there a lot, and I went too from time to time, with the baby of course. On polling day, we got up at 5 am in the home of kindly Liberals and went out to deliver early morning leaflets. Then I took off in the Land Rover caravanette to be at the polling station in the tiny village of Mindrum, remote and high in the Cheviots, when polling opened. It was a day of dreadful weather, and I welcomed the warmth and cooking facilities of the motor caravan. Rory cheerfully threw Farex rice around it. I shared my facilities with an exit-poll worker as the voters trickled in and out during the long day.

Alan Beith scraped in with a majority of 74 votes. We were now on the run-in to a general election, as Heath's battered government provoked a miners' strike and in the ensuing electricity shortages was forced to bring in the three-day working week to reduce demand. At Lochcarron Mill in Galashiels, the enterprising management resuscitated the old water-wheel and kept production going for a full week. Eventually, Heath went to the country with the slogan: 'Who governs Britain?'

I recall more about the immediate aftermath of the February 1974 election than the campaign itself. David's majority jumped from three figures to over 9,000: nationally, the result was a cliff-hanger. The Tories had – just – won more of the popular vote than Labour; the latter had won more seats, but there was no overall majority. The Liberal vote, after a sparkling campaign led by Jeremy Thorpe, had risen to an all-time post-war high of nearly 20% – over six million votes, yielding a tally of only fourteen seats. The desperate unfairness of the first-past-the-post system was rearing its ugly head, and this would continue to haunt the Liberals through successive elections. In the wake of each one, there would be an outcry about the skewed results: then it would die down until the next election, as successive Tory and Labour governments buried their heads in the sands of their unearned superiority.

The SNP, which had run a clever campaign with the slogan 'It's Scotland's Oil', had seven MPs, including our friend George Reid who won the seat of Clackmannan. It was a finely balanced parliament.

Throughout the Friday and Saturday morning following the election it proved impossible for David to contact Jeremy Thorpe, and he grew increasingly frustrated. On the Saturday after an election it had become our custom to drive round the various burghs in the constituency with a motorcade and a loudspeaker, through which David would thank the voters for returning him, and stop to make short speeches in each town centre. As we came into Jedburgh, with the children in the back and the radio on, we listened avidly to the news and post-election programmes, for that was our only way of knowing what was happening. We heard that Jeremy was in London and that 'it is believed that the Liberal Whip, David Steel, is on his way there.'

'I suppose I'd better go there,' said David. 'I hope he's not going to do anything silly.'

We spotted Margot, whose home town was Jedburgh and who had the weekend off, in the crowd. We hailed her, asked if she'd take the two elder children, and passed them over into her capable hands in Jedburgh High Street there and then. Then we raced up the A68 with Rory in his carry-cot and took a plane to London.

David was very disturbed that Jeremy had not kept him in the picture about what was happening, and when we arrived in London we went straight to the house in Bayswater where he lived with his second wife, Marion. My impression was that the Liberal leader was so enthralled by the drama of what was happening, as he went secretly to and from 10 Downing Street by backdoor entrances, that he had lost all sense of what the issues were. He seemed thrilled by the cloak and dagger atmosphere of everything, and was not looking at hard realities. The bottom line was that, even with Liberal support, Heath would still be two short of an overall majority. He had gone to the country for a renewed mandate, and he hadn't got it.

It was all surreal, and when the news came in of a dreadful crash of an aircraft carrying English rugby supporters home from an international match in Paris, killing everyone on board, what was happening on the political front became inextricably mixed up for me with TV images of the broken plane in the forest near Paris, and grieving relatives waiting at London airport for news.

David steadied Jeremy and, with Jo Grimond and the Liberal leader in the Lords, Frank Byers, managed to talk him out of any damaging association with the defeated Tories. Edward Heath moved out of No. 10 and Harold Wilson moved back in. We passed the summer waiting for Wilson to call a second election, which he did in October. For the second time that year, I met with my fellow Children's Reporters for Berwickshire and Roxburghshire at a central pub, and handed over my files to them for three weeks. I made and froze casseroles and bought what became a regular part of our catering at this time: the Election Stilton. Our older children were by now thoroughly enjoying the elections and I was teaching them technique. As Catriona and I walked back down a path in the village of Newstead, I said to her, 'Put that last woman down in the Tory column.'

'But she was really nice to us,' Catriona demurred.

'You need to look into their eyes when you announce yourself,' I explained. 'Either they light up, in which case they're one of ours, or a shutter comes down over them, in which case they're the enemy. It's that first reaction that tells you.'

I drove the Land Rover caravanette around, while Archy Kirkwood chauffeured David in a powerful, new-to-us, Rover. One day, canvassing on the outskirts of Peebles, I returned to the Land Rover to get the lunchtime news. Radio 4 was still on its five minutes' worth of Scottish news as I switched it on, in the middle of an item. ' . . . The accident happened near Melrose. His assistant, Archy Kirkwood, who was driving, was not seriously injured either.'

Thank goodness for that word 'either'. With wobbly legs, I drove into Peebles and went to buy a cup of coffee and phone headquarters. A stranger came up to me. 'Mrs Steel – I think I should tell you – your husband's been in a wee accident.' Fortified by the coffee, I drove back to Galashiels to find out what had happened. In heavy rain, they had smashed head-on into a lorry on a bend of the road, but David's only injuries had been bruising to his ribs from the seat belt. Archy was unscathed. But hearing about it in that way was horrible, and David and Archy were badly shocked. The car was a much-photographed write-off.

The Tory troops this time were led, for the first time in the Borders, by a woman candidate. She was a keen anti-legal abortion campaigner, a member of SPUC: the Society for the Protection of Unborn Children. We had another name for it: the Society for the Production of Unwanted Children. She laid great stress on her devotion to family life and fought under the slogan, 'For your family's sake, Vote Christine Anderson.' She was re-adopted by the Tories after the election, and then suddenly resigned 'for family reasons'. She had run off with the Tory chairman. They lived together in great happiness for thirty years, 'and he died in my arms,' she told me when we met recently. Under her new married name as Chrissie Richards, she was for many years a prominent Edinburgh councillor and a lone voice in her party in favour of Scottish devolution. When the parliament came into being, she was punished by them for this misdemeanour by being left out in the cold when it came to seat allocations. 'We can't let it look as though we thought you were right after all,' she was told. Eventually, she left the Tories and joined Labour.

In the October 1974 election, the Liberals fought under the dreadful slogan 'One More Heave'. It was a miracle that we lost only one per cent of the vote and one seat. Harold Wilson's government had a majority of two, and the SNP were now fielding a team of eleven. Labour and Tories alike woke up to the growing demand for some kind of Scottish self-government, and put in train machinery to formulate new and more positive – if rather weak – policies for this. Edward Heath, in particular, became a convinced devolutionist, but his leadership of the Tory party had only a short course to run.

Harold Wilson's government was deeply divided on the European question. Because of this, and as a piece of populism during the election, he had promised a referendum on Europe. Since Britain was already signed up to the Common Market, it was a bit after the fact, but with his usual skill he managed to cobble together a scenario for the plebiscite, with a question on the ballot paper as to whether the government should renegotiate the terms that had been obtained by Edward Heath.

The argument was very much presented as an economic issue: in fact Britain was being asked to say yes or no to the concept of a united Europe. The Liberals, with their honourable track record of supporting the European concept right from the start, were the only party that was not badly split on the question, and so umbrella organisations were formed on both sides of the argument. Ours was Britain in Europe, with the simple slogan, 'Say Yes to Europe'.

David loved the European campaign. For the first time he was experiencing campaigning which was unfettered by the constant lack of financial resources. It had access to the sort of money which during normal election campaigns would find its way into the Tory coffers. 'It makes you realise just how easy they have it,' he said, comparing it to our constant round of fundraising coffee mornings, bazaars and cheese-and-wine evenings, the weekly raffles run in the textile mills and the penny-pinching when it came to ordering leaflets, posters and advertising space during elections. He was amazed as money was found for administrative help, offices, typewriters, private planes and helicopters.

More than that, it gave him the chance to share platforms with senior politicians, those almost of another generation, such as Edward Heath, Willie Whitelaw and Roy Jenkins. Of these he had an especial admiration for Roy Jenkins, and he in turn treated his young colleague in an avuncular way. They had come to know each other during the passage of the Abortion Act, when Roy was Home Secretary – as he was again at this particular time, after a period when he had been Chancellor of the Exchequer. His first period at the Home Office had been marked by the most progressive social legislation. As well as the passing of the Abortion Act, Sidney Silverman had steered through the act for the abolition of capital punishment, and Leo Abse had done the same for the legalisation of homosexuality. None of these would have happened without the support of the Home Secretary, Roy Jenkins.

I wonder, also, if he saw some parallel in their early political lives. Like David, Roy had been elected at a by-election at an age which made him the 'baby of the House'; like him, he had piloted through a Private Member's Bill, the Obscene Publications Bill in his case, that was closely-fought and aroused deep passions. He was a man of great political courage, which had been shown both when he led the rebel Labour members through the lobbies to vote in favour of Heath's European Communities Bill, and when he later resigned as deputy leader of his party in protest at its hostility to Europe. It would be only a few more years before he broke with it completely, and set in train the events that would lead him and David into the same party.

Already, however, they were comfortable with each other; although I cannot say that I ever was. Despite coming from a humble background, Roy Jenkins was as much of a grandee as Willie Whitelaw or Jo Grimond. He seemed to invite homage, and always to be a few levels above such a lowly person as me. My first encounter with him was during the referendum campaign, after a rally in Edinburgh's Usher Hall – there was a dinner for the speakers and their spouses at the lovely Prestonfield House Hotel, a seventeenth-century house and park situated in the middle of a housing scheme on the south of the city. It was yet another example of the comfortable funding of the Britain in Europe campaign. Roy Jenkins ordered gulls' eggs, which I'd never seen before or since,★ and which I thought wonderfully Edwardian and grand – just like Roy himself.

It was more difficult for me to do my bit for Europe at constituency level, where I was having to work alongside those with whom I was used to locking horns at elections, including Christine Anderson. As I walked into the hotel room in Galashiels booked for the 'Yes' campaign, I thought I'd stepped into a meeting of the local Tory party. The small local Labour party and the SNP were totally unrepresented – maybe they were all busy saying 'No'. The Tories seemed to expect to take charge, giving the impression that Europe was theirs and we Liberals were mere hangers-on – despite the long Liberal advocacy of European unity. I felt very uncomfortable in this company, and got none of the satisfaction that David did from the campaign. The best time was when we organised a dinner for the movement in Melrose, at which George Brown was the star speaker. David consulted Norman Hackett, Brown's nephew, on how to host him.

'For God's sake, don't let him drink before the dinner,' warned Norman.

The Browns arrived at Cherrydene and George demanded a gin and tonic as soon as he arrived. Mindful of Norman's warning, David poured him one that was mainly tonic. We gave up our bedroom to them. 'Good God!' exclaimed George. 'A double bed! I haven't shared one with Sophie for years!'

When we arrived at the dinner, he demanded another gin and tonic from the chairman, with the instructions, 'And put some gin in it – your MP's unbelievably stingy with it.' He drank steadily throughout the dinner, but when he rose to his feet after it, he delivered a clear, uplifting speech; the Tories, who had been very unenthusiastic about the principal speaker, were totally won over by his eloquence.

The Borders was very pro-European, as the interests of the textile industry were obviously served by the opportunities of the European market; but in my view both the local and national campaigns centred far too much on the economic benefits, and tried to dodge the inevitability of closer political unity. The Liberal voices, including David's, were

★In May 2010 I again ate gulls' eggs, at the Duke of Buccleuch's Northamptonshire home, Boughton. It was an occasion Roy Jenkins would have enjoyed!

almost the only ones which trumpeted the vision of a new, better Europe and Britain's place in it.

The European referendum of 1975 remains, so far, the only example of a Britain-wide ballot on a constitutional matter. I cast my vote on Rory's second birthday, and believed that I was giving him a present of a good future.

# 16

# *Annus Mirabilis, Annus Horribilis*

*May, 2009*

*We are bowling along narrow Devon lanes in David's 1965 Jaguar Mark Two, towards a classic car rally. To me, it's the black Jaguar as opposed to the red Jaguar. Two Jags, Steel, I call him, but that's a very modest Jaguar count compared with most of the members of the Jaguar Drivers' Club, of which he is president. That's why we are here today: it's their day out, and I wish they'd have it nearer to Scotland. The journey down, on the M4, was a revelation in out-of-city traffic congestion to me, so used to the quiet roads of the Borders.*

*Now we're here, though, we find Devon enchanting – Exmoor itself is a ringer for Lauder Common, though with more bent and less heather. And of course, we see the herds of Exmoor ponies I fantasised about in my youth. Obliging the tourists, a mare suckles a golden foal near the roadside. Our daughter learnt to call tourists by the local name of grockles when she worked here for a year after leaving school, a term that she brought back with her. We pass the hotel where she was employed.*

*In the narrow lanes, the towering hedges are as thick as the walls of Aikwood, and the earth bankings which they top are bright with cow parsley and wild hyacinth. On the inadequate signposts, charming Devonian place names appear, strange to our eyes and ears and tongue, and to our culture. But there is one name that crops up from time to time which neither of us will forget.*

*'I can't see the name Minehead without thinking of Minehead Magistrates' Court,' I say. David has been thinking just the same. 'I drove Nadir down to here to give evidence,' he remembers. And we are both back in the fateful year 1976, the year of Jeremy Thorpe and Norman Scott and Rinka the dog that died, and of so many other life-changing events.*

To say the year 1976 began badly would be an understatement. On New Year's Day there was a phone call from my sister Joan, who was at my parents' house. My mother had had a third stroke, more serious than the last two. She, and we, always knew this time would come. Joan thought she was also suffering from heart failure and was summoning her sisters.

Once again, my father was resisting Mummy's hospitalisation: he had managed to pull her through the previous strokes at home, and thought, rightly, that she had recovered sooner and better because of this. He was also resisting my coming to her bedside. 'I think something might happen if you are all here,' he said.

They were both now in their seventies, still living in great contentment in Dunblane. My father was a disciple, not just of Schumacher's *Small is Beautiful*, but of John Seymour's theories and book on *Self Sufficiency*. Their freezer was packed with home-grown lamb and vegetables, and a Jersey cow occupied the place where my pony used to stand. My mother went on weaving courses, set up a hand-loom, and produced bales of tweed. Later she bought a spinning wheel and learnt that craft as well. My father made butter and cheeses, bringing back memories of his boyhood holidays on a farm in West Lothian. And as my mother became less able, he took over much of her work in the house. 'But never the kitchen,' he said; 'I knew she'd notice that.' And when this final blow came, her cake tins were stocked with scones, meringues, shortbread and black bun.

My father's superstition proved correct. She died just as we turned into the drive. Fay had been by her side at the end, and had summoned up her reserves to carry out the final rites of washing and dressing her. I didn't go to say goodbye to her body. We'd been up just before Christmas, with the children, to exchange presents and to collect our tree, and I wanted that to be my last memory of her, smiling and waving us off. I knew, from the time I'd seen David's grandmother after her death, that the image of a still, empty corpse would superimpose itself on those of the living, loving, irascible woman.

For twenty-five years, she and my father had lived with the anxiety of Alison. At the time of her death, Alison was married, and my mother thought that this would end her problems, that all was resolved. Of course it wasn't, and from then on my sister was never well again for any length of time. Her hospitalisation became permanent rather than intermittent, but I am always grateful to the gentle man who was my brother-in-law at that time. He gave our mother peace of mind during her last years, and even after he and Alison parted, he continued to support her at family occasions.

I learnt much about the closeness that can come to a family at a time of mourning, of the sweetness and solidarity that can be found at the heart of grief. I recall the feeling amongst the four of us at that time as one of the best we ever shared: gladness in each other's company and the sharing of memories was a powerful counterweight to sorrow. She had not had to endure what she dreaded – months or maybe years of incapacity. It was a death as it should be: in her own home, and with her family at hand.

I was sad that she didn't live to see her friend from Freetown days, Jim Callaghan, become Prime Minister about three months later. It happened when I was down in London with Graeme in the Easter holidays. I took him to Downing Street to see Callaghan emerge from his car, wave, and enter No. 10. I went for her memory as much as for us, though I'm glad that Graeme caught the occasion. It seems unbelievable now, that we, with no passes, no identification, were able simply to go into that famous cul-de-sac and see Britain's new Prime Minister and Labour Party Leader standing before that iconic door. Not for one moment could I have dreamed that by the end of the year, there would also be a new leader for the Liberal Party.

In Devon, thirty-three years later, we are thinking of the later events of 1976, and trying to pinpoint when the Thorpe affair began for us. It was five years before the whole affair burst on the public, during the Whitsun recess. We were in my parents' caravan with the children in Fife. David was distracted and unhappy, and kept stopping at phone-boxes to make mysterious calls. At last, when the children were either asleep or occupied on the campsite playground, and we were alone, he said:

'I've got something to tell you, and it's pretty unpleasant.'

And he recounted a meeting he had had in the House of Commons, with a strange young man called Norman Scott, who claimed, not only to have had a homosexual relationship with Jeremy Thorpe during the early 1960s, but to have been 'supported' by him. Scott was undoubtedly an unstable and unreliable young man, and the tale he had to tell smacked of fantasy. There was a missing National Insurance book and other details, but the most damning part of Scott's story was that he produced letters from the former MP for Bodmin, Peter Bessell, who was a close confidant of Jeremy's. They had been written to Scott enclosing small sums of money.

'I never trusted Bessell,' said David, 'even before I met him. Do you remember that I wouldn't have him to speak at the by-election? It must have been a sixth sense.'

This meeting with Norman Scott was just before the recess; David confided in Emlyn Hooson, trusting his forensic skills. Emlyn also saw the young man, and managed to speak to Peter Bessell – now living in America, but visiting Cornwall at the time – on the phone. Bessell gave different explanations to his two former colleagues about the purpose of the payments: to Emlyn, from whom the queries came completely unexpectedly, he said that they had been to stop Scott from causing trouble. To David, of whose approach he had warning, he said that they were in connection with the missing National Insurance contributions.

Of course Norman Scott might have been lying or fantasising, and David hoped, and persuaded himself to believe, that he was. He did not want to think ill of Jeremy, although he could believe almost anything of Peter Bessell. We owed a great debt of gratitude to Jeremy, for his encouragement and irrepressible insouciance during the by-election. David supported him as leader when Jo Grimond resigned, and was at his side during the dark days when Caroline died. Since the 1970 election, until fairly recently, he had been Whip to the sadly truncated party, and had rejoiced with Jeremy in the by-election victories since then. He had shared Jeremy's confidences about the romance leading up to his second marriage to Marion.

And David always, always, wants to believe the best of people, even although his confidence in Jeremy had become dented by the events following the February 1974 election. But Emlyn was more cynical, or perhaps more realistic. He had never been a fan of Jeremy's, and found the bizarre situation more credible. When the recess ended, and they went back to London, the two of them went to see Jeremy, who completely denied all of Scott's allegations. Later, with Lord Byers, the leader of the Liberal peers, they interviewed Scott again. This resulted in Scott running away from the meeting in tears, declaring that he still loved Jeremy.

In these days of mobile phones and emails, of 24-hour news, the whole thing would no doubt have unravelled differently. What I recall of that first weekend of the Thorpe affair was the amount of time David spent looking for small change, and standing in red telephone boxes on the line to Emlyn, like a precursor of the scenes in *Local Hero*. But this was no gentle film comedy, and David's distress was considerable. His Presbyterian soul found it all unpleasant and distasteful; he felt sullied by it and also betrayed. He hoped there would be an explanation, that Jeremy would be vindicated, and indeed after he and Emlyn had seen both players in the story they had no real option but to accept Jeremy's version of events. But I think in his heart he knew that there might be some truth – if not the whole truth – in the weird young man's story. It was an unhappy weekend, and worse was to come.

However, like the kraken of legend, the matter slumbered for five years. Scott tried to hawk his story to the press, but there was no evidence to support it, and they dared not publish. It was not until 1976 that the kraken awoke.

Two court cases came up almost side by side in the West Country. One was against Norman Scott, for defrauding the Post Office of a minor sum of money. Under the privilege of a court appearance, he repeated all the old allegations, and in these circumstances the press was free to report them. At the same time, a case was coming up against a former airline pilot, Andrew Newton, who had been charged with illegal possession of a firearm to endanger life. On Exmoor, late at night, he had shot Scott's dog, Rinka, dead, and frightened Scott himself. His story, when he came to court, was that Scott was blackmailing him over a nude photo. Norman Scott, as the chief prosecution witness, had a field day in putting his side of the story: that the shooting had been a plot, the carrying out of a contract to rid Jeremy of this embarrassing figure. The story ran and ran in the newspapers. Who could blame them?

This went on for three months. The Liberal party was imploding, both in the country and in Parliament. Members of the parliamentary party gave interviews or made statements which were not so much hostile to their leader as indicative of their compete bafflement. David tried to persuade Jeremy to resign before more damage was done, but he refused to do so. From across the Atlantic, Peter Bessell muddied the waters with contradictory statements, and the local election results at the beginning of May were a complete disaster. It was not until after this that Jeremy resigned as leader, after a crucial meeting with David and Clement Freud at the latter's London home.

One of the most unpleasant aspects of what came out was Jeremy's treatment of his friend and ours, Nadir Dinshaw. This good man had been duped by Jeremy into being the innocent channel of funds from a party donor: he was asked to pass them on to a close associate of Jeremy's, David Holmes. After everything came to light, he realised that the money was not being used for its original purpose, but for more shady ones connected with Andrew Newton and Norman Scott. The betrayal of his good faith hit him hard, and so did the subsequent suggestion that he should mislead the police over it.

At last Jeremy resigned. To everyone's relief, Jo Grimond agreed to come back as interim leader. This gave three months' grace, and allowed the party time, not just to lick the wounds inflicted by the Thorpe affair, but also to hammer out a new manner of electing a leader, with a vote for every party member – the first UK party to adopt this method. For a party with thousands of members it was no longer defensible that the leader should be chosen by a handful of MPs. It seemed inevitable that David would stand, but in the meantime this respite allowed us to go to America – my first visit – during the bicentennial celebrations of the American Declaration of Independence.

David had now been in Parliament for eleven years, and he had had his fair share of overseas visits. On some occasions – especially on our trips to the Council of Europe in Strasbourg – I was allowed to go with him, at our own expense. Sometimes, overseas trips specifically excluded spouses. On this occasion, however, the British parliamentarians, and their spouses, were not only invited, but paid for, by the American government.

What an introduction to America! It was called, in one American newspaper headline, 'The Magna Carta Boondoggle', a wonderful word that found its way immediately into our own family lexicon. There were about a dozen parliamentarians from each side of the Atlantic, and from every party and legislative element: from the Commons, the House of Representatives, the Senate and the Lords. It had been decided that, to honour the anniversary, the House of Commons would lend Congress their priceless copy of the Magna Carta for a year. At a solemn ceremony in Westminster Hall it was handed over, and then we flew out to Washington for its reception in Congress. The beautifully stage-managed ceremony moved me to tears, and I was awestruck by the sheer beauty of Washington, with its parks and avenues of Japanese cherry in full flower.

Our American hosts did us proud. I was bemused by the signs for 'rest rooms', and kept looking for daybeds to lie down on. The journalist Antonia Lothian was there as the wife of the hereditary peer from the Borders, the Marquess of Lothian. She wore a permanent black eye-patch; so did another peer, Lord Mowbray and Stourton, though on the opposite eye. For some reason the Americans (and indeed some of the delegates from the House of Commons) got it into their heads that they were a married couple.

We dined in the famous Library where inauguration balls are held. (No ban on smoking even there in those days, even amongst those priceless volumes, and I remember puffing at a Balkan Sobranie.) We went to Arlington Cemetery, to pay our respects at the graves of John and Bobby Kennedy, and watched a ceremony at the Iwo Jima memorial. We were driven everywhere in a noisy motorcade with outriders on motorbikes fore and aft. The leaders of our delegation – Mr Speaker George Thomas and Lord Chancellor Elwyn Jones – were never off their feet giving speeches. And here comes the embarrassing part of the Magna Carta Boondoggle: these two Welsh wizards of oratory made speeches so fluent, so eloquent, so perfectly pitched in nuance, in tone, in construction and allusion, that they outdid every American. It was as though they had turned up in immaculately cut formal dress and our hosts were in everyday, crumpled suits. And it wasn't as if they were trying to trump our hosts: they made such speeches effortlessly. The words slid off their magical Welsh tongues in their silvery Welsh accents: it's how they do things there in Wales.

The most embarrassing part, did I say? No, perhaps it wasn't. At the last minute, a visit to the White House was shoehorned in. I could wish that there had been a more charismatic President in office then – or, indeed, even an elected one – but it was Gerald Ford, the bland Republican who stepped first of all into the vice-presidency when Spiro Agnew was forced from office, and then took over as leader of the free world from Richard Nixon when the Watergate conspiracy brought 'Tricky Dicky' down in turn. We were to go straight from the White House to the airport, for we were flying on to New York to spend a day with Mona and Michael Shea, currently head of British Information Services in the USA, before we returned to Britain.

*En route* to the White House with our noisy posse of cars and motorbikes, a sudden horrified thought struck me. I had not emptied the hotel drawers of my dirty underwear. There was no time to return for it. We confessed my plight to one of the American officials in charge of us, and a couple of cars, blue lights flashing and sirens wailing, returned to the hotel and escorted my unwashed smalls to the White House, where I was reunited with them, in time to catch the plane and put them through the wash at the Sheas' thirty-seventh-floor New York flat.

We came back to the contest for the party leadership. Although there was talk of other MPs putting their hats in the ring, the contest, when it came, was between David and John Pardoe, the MP for North Cornwall. Emlyn Hooson put aside his own ambitions to support David; Russell Johnston would have liked to have thrown his hat in the ring, but could not gather the necessary support from his fellow MPs.

This was a matter of some disappointment to those in the party who were particularly passionate about electoral reform, for without at least three candidates, it meant that there would not be a chance to use the alternative vote, or some such voting method. The contrast between David and John was more one of strategy and presentation, for you could not put a leaf between them on policy matters. Pardoe seemed much more the buccaneer; David, at thirty-eight, the young but steadier hand. Maybe he began the fashion for young party leaders, but he had been in Parliament for over a decade, and he had piloted a significant piece of legislation through to the statute book. And as Whip, he knew all the ins and outs of Commons procedure as few parliamentarians of his age did.

There was no precedent for such a leadership campaign. They went around the country to events organised by local constituency parties, making speeches and pressing the flesh. I don't remember any all-candidate hustings that are the norm nowadays. Given the circumstances under which the election had arisen, it proved quite a process of regeneration.

But, goodness, he was mischievous, my husband! There was the little trivial matter of whether or not John Pardoe had had some treatment applied to his thinning hair. David's casual musings on the subject were taken up by a reporter, who made enquiries on the matter to the owner of the hair. John exploded with rage when the question was put to him: it kept the journalists and the cartoonists occupied for days.

There was no army of speechwriters for David and John; they made up their own. As frequently happened, I was deputed to find an apt quotation to round off an important speech. 'I need a literary or historic simile for John,' David said. I thought long and hard and came up with Tigger from A A Milne's *The House at Pooh Corner*, and in particular, the incident when the cuddly tiger gets into a fight with a tablecloth:

> With one worraworraworra he jumped to the end of the table-
> cloth, pulled it to the ground, wrapped himself up in it three
> times, rolled to the other end of the room and, after a terrible
> struggle, got his head into the daylight again, and said cheer-
> fully, 'Have I won?'

It did seem to sum up John Pardoe's approach (he liked to call himself 'an effective bastard'), and when David used it, the meeting convulsed with laughter. It says a lot for their underlying friendship, and for John Pardoe's big-heartedness, that he remained a loyal colleague after that, not just in the Commons, but feeding David from time to time in his Hampstead home.

The count was to be held at Poplar Town Hall at the beginning of July. I left the children in safe hands and, in a new frock costing under £10 from Ferguson's of Selkirk (it had a floppy bow at the neck which kept going squint, and looked like its purchase price; and, gods of fashion forgive me, I think it was made of Crimplene), I headed south. It was hot, and, remembering my awful foot-cramping experience when David took his seat, I wore a comfy pair of Scholls wooden-soled sandals. Both sandals and frock were mistakes. I took my place beside David feeling frumpy as we faced the cameras.

David won this first truly democratic election of a party leader by a comfortable majority. The system, even with only two candidates, was as complicated as only the Liberal Party could make it, with quotas for each constituency depending on membership. After the declaration, we went to Emlyn Hooson's chambers, where he had laid on champagne. We went with the flow, and the next day I returned home. My life was changing, and would do so in more ways that that of being a party leader's wife. Another lame duckling was about to come under my wing.

A few days later, there was a knock at the door of Cherrydene. A troubled teenager, Billy, stood there; he had come to tell me of his predicament. I'd known him and his brothers for some years; they had made frequent appearances before the Children's Panel. My own job as Reporter had disappeared during the previous year when Scottish local government was reorganised, and the three part-time Reporters in the Borders were replaced by one full-time one.

Billy had been in foster care in our village. But his foster mother had had a recurrence of cancer, and was unable to continue to look after him. The local authority had no other suitable foster homes, and a temporary arrangement which kept Billy in the valley had broken down.

We talked gravely about his future. The current alternatives were grim: the children's home was certainly not geared to teenage boys, and much as he loved his mother, he knew that, back home, he would drift back to petty thieving and vandalism. Here, he rode ponies, helped with swimming for the disabled and had the freedom that the countryside gives to children. At the high school, where there were some sympathetic teachers, he played the violin, sang in the school choir and performed in school musicals. He dreamed of being an actor; in the meantime he wanted to find another foster home.

He faced a very real crisis. The Children's Panel was to discuss his case again. I told him that he was entitled to a representative to speak for him, and offered to be that person. He accepted gratefully, and a few days later I found myself back at a children's hearing, in a very different capacity to my old role there.

179

The panel members were sympathetic to him. But at the end of the day, there were still only the two alternatives, the children's home or his own home. I heard my voice saying: 'In that case, he can come to us for the summer holidays; and surely, during that time, the social work department can find a foster home.'

They all breathed a sigh of relief, and committed him to my care for three months.

There's a book by Barbara Vine called *A Fatal Inversion*. It's about a group of young people who live a hippy lifestyle in a house left to one of them during the summer of 1976. You could say that one of the characters was the summer itself, a lovely, languorous procession of sunny days and warm nights. Sometimes I think that the events of my own summer of 1976 were fashioned by that same weather. If it had been the usual wet, cold Scottish summer, if the children had been trapped inside our small rooms at Cherrydene, and outings to gymkhanas had been miserable, and hacks over the hills had been an enforced discipline; I might have been glad to pack our extra family member off to somewhere else by the end of it.

But instead it was the best summer I could remember since that transforming one in Denmark in 1959. There was a succession of days by the Ettrick, swimming and diving off rocks, of picnics and impromptu barbecues, of rides over the hills, and at night a full moon filtered through the leaves of the cherry tree as I sat round a small bonfire with the children, while Billy's perfectly pitched voice sang a little song that was new to me:

> When I first came to this land,
> I was not a wealthy man,
> But I got myself a hen,
> I did what I could.
> And I called my hen
> 'Now and then.'
> All the land was sweet and good,
> I did what I could.

The summer ended in Normandy, where the Hacketts had a holiday house for their visits back to Europe from Pakistan, where they were currently posted. They had with them their three boys, and their new daughter, Alex, whom they had adopted in the land of her origins, Pakistan.

'Can't I just stay on at Cherrydene?' Billy asked me, and I had been thinking the same. I thought of the uncertainties of his life so far, of how blessed my own life had been, and those of my children, and felt that there should be room in my family for another child.

When I articulated the idea, first of all to David, he was unhappy. Above all, he worried about the effect on Graeme, what would virtually be his displacement as the eldest child. My sister Joan voiced opposition on the same grounds. They were both members of the union of eldest children, and it wasn't something I understood. But the social workers did, and they also worried about my ability to cope on my own during David's absences which, with the party leadership, would become much more frequent. This honeymoon period with Billy, after all, had been over the summer holidays, the summer recess of Parliament. As a family, we were moving into uncharted waters with David's higher public profile and the greater demands of the party. Some people said we were brave while thinking we were daft; others were more outspoken.

In the end, what was supposed to be a summer holiday arrangement lasted for a decade. Billy took our name, and became regarded as an adopted child, although he always remained close to his own family. Through them, I was never far away from a kind of life that was very different from our own comfortable middle-class existence, and it was through him also that I became increasingly drawn to the world of theatre.

But everyone was right who foresaw the effect it would have on Graeme. It is something for which I cannot forgive myself, my insensitivity to the needs of my firstborn son, and it was to cause much estrangement between us over the years before the wounds were healed.

# 17

# Bumpy Road

In September 1976, I went with David to his first party conference as leader. It was held in the seaside town of Llandudno, and he was nervous and tense before he made his leader's speech. It would not be bland: he intended to sound a warning that he wanted the party to be more than a talking shop, more than an influence: he wanted it to exercise power. To this end, he intended to grasp the nettles of coalition and compromise, and confront the party with the concept of sharing power. He knew that, in doing this, he would not be allowed a smooth ride, a rapturously compliant reception. Some of his closest colleagues thought that he was going too far in what he was proposing to say, and the Young Liberals warned him that they would protest against any talk of coalition.

A couple of hours before he was due to deliver the speech, Clement Freud took him away from party officials, from delegates and from me, and walked with him by the sea, talking of nothing in particular – about anything but politics.

*April, 2010*

*It is the eve of the first televised party leaders' debate. I think of the three men, Gordon Brown, Nick Clegg, and David Cameron, being groomed and rehearsed by their aides in the run-up. I remember Clement Freud's walk with David, and if there was a way of contacting Nick Clegg's staff, I'd email them and say, 'For goodness sake, let the man go off on his own for a bit.' It would have been an unnecessary suggestion. I find out later that he has prepared for the debate by moving himself and his entourage out of the town, where the TV studio is situated, into the countryside, and on the day of the debate has gone, at his own insistence, for a walk throughout the afternoon. On TV screens that night, he bursts, gloriously invigorated, into people's consciousness, and fires up the whole campaign.*

Clement Freud understood that need for peace before a time of trial. Known to his friends as Clay (and woe betide anyone who used the abbreviation without permission), he had been elected as MP for the Isle of Wight at a by-election in 1973. I had first met him before that, when he was donating his formidable culinary skills at a party fundraising barbecue in London, and I upset him by cutting off a slice of the ham before it was, in his eyes, ready. At the time of his election, he was famous as the lugubrious face and voice of TV adverts for dog-food; it was a legacy that he hated once he became a politician. He took his political career very seriously, and he had a tremendous amount of knowledge and experience to contribute both to the party and to Parliament.

He was a man of great loyalty. Throughout the Jeremy Thorpe drama, he was the person who stayed closest to the embroiled leader, and it was he who, in the end, persuaded him to go. He was not afraid to be seen supporting Jeremy during the trial, and years later, at the celebrations of the golden wedding of Clay and Jill Freud, the frail former leader, shaky and almost incomprehensible with Parkinson's disease, was among the guests. In later years, Clay would invite himself to stay with us for a few days, and we would cook together quite amicably, which I regarded as something of a triumph. He was reputed to be a difficult man, particularly in the kitchen: I have known another MP's wife driven in tears from her domain, unable to handle him as he prepared a meal for her guests at a fundraising supper.

He would come up to Scotland, where he was rector, first of Dundee and then of St Andrews University, and cook or speak at fundraisers over the years. These would be for the Liberals and also for the Traverse Theatre, at a time when I was on its board and it was still in cramped premises in the Grassmarket. We roped in the catering students of Napier College to assist him with the Traverse fundraiser. The meal was prepared at the college and transported to the Grassmarket for its final cooking. Alas, the oven in the Traverse's very basic kitchen would not hold all of the meal, and I was deputed to go up and down Victoria Street in search of a kindly restaurant owner whose business was slack enough to accommodate a baking tray of stuffed tomatoes.

As a quid pro quo, David and I would go to his constituency events in East Anglia, always rather more exotic than ours, with such attractions as demonstrations from his friend Uri Geller, the spoon-bender; and we would usually go to see a show at the summer theatre that Jill Freud ran there.

In later years he would come to the Edinburgh Fringe each summer to record that wonderful programme, 'Just a Minute', making sure that we were invited, and if I had a show on the Fringe myself that year, he would always work the title of it into an answer. He died on the eve of his eighty-fifth birthday: the menu was already chosen for his celebratory meal with a dozen friends, including David. Instead, they attended his funeral.

All that lay ahead: but I never forgot that wise and sensitive act of kindness at Llandudno. David was calm as he went into the hall to make his first speech as party leader; during it, he stood up to the malcontents and set out his own agenda. By the end, the young Liberals were cheering him as wholeheartedly as anyone.

It was the first time that a Liberal leader – and perhaps any party leader – led a life where his family base was not in London but in the constituency. The basic tenor of my life went on as before: looking after children and ponies, attending to things in the constituency, involving myself with local organisations, and – more than ever now – fielding telephone calls.

My penchant for spending as little as possible on clothes, or making them myself, was taken in hand by our friends Nadir Dinshaw and his wife Hille. Their daughter Nali was now one of David's secretaries, as well as a good friend, and David became in time an unofficial godfather to her daughter Kitty. Each February Nadir would whisk us off to their home in Jersey, and Hille would take me on an expedition to dress shops much more stylish than any I would have entered on my own. I learned not to look at the price tags, as she gently encouraged me towards fashions far more sophisticated than I would have dared to try out on my own. If only I'd been a couple of sizes smaller! Nevertheless, I built up a wardrobe that would see me through most occasions in this new role. But although invitations poured in thick and fast to great and glamorous events in London – and indeed elsewhere – it was only rarely that I was able to go to them.

There were some, however, that could not be resisted – Wimbledon, and a seat in the Royal box; the Queen's Jubilee events of 1977, and the wedding of Prince Charles and Lady Diana Spencer at St Paul's a couple of years later. David's stylish but unreliable Alvis, chauffeured by Billy, stuttered and boiled its way along the streets lined with cheering crowds. 'It's like coming in at the Toll at Selkirk Common Riding!' I exclaimed. We were delivered to St Paul's – just – and then the Alvis had to be pushed round the corner, much to Billy's chagrin.

Then there was the unveiling of the Madame Tussaud's waxwork – so unlike its subject that Catriona did not recognise it as her father.

And who, in the late 1970s, would have denied themselves a seat at a televised and star-studded audience with Dame Edna Everage? I dressed carefully for it, in one of my favourite dresses from those that had been showered on me by the generous Dinshaws. It was by Jean Varon, of black billowy chiffon printed with tiny autumn leaves and sewn with occasional sequins.

Ominously, we were shown to the front row. Dame Edna breezed in, delivered her outrageous introduction, selected her first victim, and then, looking around for another, invited the audience to ask her questions. David, rashly, was first there, requesting her advice to politicians.

'Well, David,' came the Australian drawl, 'I've noticed that you've got a very bad habit of chewing your cuticles. So my advice to you is, every time you're going to do that, just think that you've dipped them in your little jobs, and I assure you that will cure the habit.'

Beneath the wildly winged diamante spectacles, her eyes slid manically along to me.

'And here's your lovely wife, Judy MacGregor. How are you, Judy?' She came and kissed me on the cheek, her smell and touch feminine, then stood back. 'My, that's a lovely dress you're wearing. I bet you made it yourself out of some old curtains.'

Through my laughter, I wanted to protest; 'Excuse me, it's by Jean Varon.' But I stopped short, for two reasons. One was that I didn't know whether the designer's name had a French or English pronunciation, and I was bound to get it wrong. The other was that, like a chess player, I could see a move ahead to what her response would be: 'Well, darling, on you it just looks like old curtains.' I decided that discretion was the better part of valour, it was wiser simply to take it in good part, and resorted to giggling in order to avoid speaking. Although I've never seen it myself, I'm told that my moment with Dame Edna pops up from time to time, even now, on 'TV's best comedy moments', and every time this is reported to me, I reflect that the brilliant Barry Humphries is earning a repeat fee.

Formal dressing up in London reaches its ultimate platform at grand and glittering banquets in Buckingham Palace or Windsor Castle, when there is a state visit from the president or monarch of another country, and the leader of the Liberal Party was always on the guest list. Here, all is rigid etiquette; gold plate, exquisitely-painted china, banked flowers and candles on the table, a line-up of silver cutlery and crystal glasses at each place. Liveried footmen serve food and wine much as they would have done a hundred years ago; in the minstrels' gallery, army musicians play a selection of popular tunes. Here I would, with a sense of relief, catch sight of the familiar faces of Michael and Mona Shea, there as part of the Royal household, and would wish I had been placed next to one of them rather than whoever my grand neighbour was for the evening.

Once we had been presented to our royal hosts and their presidential or monarchic guests, we would take up our places in the dining room. In would come the procession for the top table; we would bow or curtsey as they passed, and the Queen would take her place at the head of the U-shaped table against a background of rich swagged curtains, a tiara sparkling on her head, and previous monarchs looking down on us, more than life-size, from their portraits. Who could not savour such occasions? They were events that could not be imagined, only experienced.

Lord Minto was the convener of the Borders Council at that time. He was a brave man, who had battled alcoholism in the days when it was regarded as a vice rather than an illness, and who, having come through it, was strong enough to become Chairman of the Scottish Council on Alcohol and President of Alcoholics Anonymous. Gibbie, as he was known to his friends, had been greatly supported in this struggle by his second wife Mary, and was devastated when she died.

The Minto family had played a part in the history of the British Raj, and in the early part of the twentieth century Gibbie's grandparents had been the Viceroy and Vicereine of India. This meant exactly what it does in translation: for the period of their appointment, they enjoyed semi-regal status, the highest honour in the Empire. And they had acquired the trappings to go with it, including the Minto tiara. Gibbie took it into his head that Mary would have wanted to lend me this to go to a Buckingham House banquet, and insisted on lending it to me. The Queen (or, as he called her, the Commander-in-Chief), he assured me, would recognise it.

We took out overnight insurance for a vast sum, collected the Minto tiara from Garrard's, the Court jewellers, and slept with it under the bed in Dolphin Square. My hair was coiffeured to receive it; it was affixed, and off we set for Buckingham Palace. As we were presented that night, was it my imagination that the Queen's eyebrows shot up slightly to see this lowly subject beneath the weight of vice-regal dia-monds? I sat down to the banquet with the thought, 'I've got the second-best tiara here.'

Alas, as the night wore on, the tiara dug deeper and deeper into my skull: my fine hair was no protection. I could think of neither food, nor wine, nor ambience, nor conversation. My fingers kept straying to my head, trying to shift the damned thing slightly and relieve the pressure.

And at the end of the evening, there was a deep groove in my scalp. Obviously, I was not bred to wear a tiara.

I don't want to give the impression that I didn't value the experience of attending these events, or enjoy them. But I never quite felt at home at them, and I would always think of the chorus of a song which is often sung at the Common Ridings:

> What though in the halls of the great we may meet,
> With men o' high rank and braw order,
> The heart sighs for hame, and nae music sae sweet,
> As the soft Lowland tongue of the Border.

David went abroad a lot; sometimes I was included. There were two particularly memorable visits, each with an especially strong individual memory. The first was to China, in those days very untouched by the West, with Lord and Lady Tanlaw – Simon and Rina. Rina is Malay-Chinese herself, so we were at a great advantage when it came to catching nuances within official explanations. They were also hilariously good fun as fellow-travellers, and we laughed our way through much of the visit.

All the Chinese – men and women – wore identical khaki 'Mao' suits. Our limousine was one of very few cars on the roads, and in the fields that we passed on the train between cities, agriculture seemed almost entirely un-mechanised. Before we flew out there, the Chinese ambassador in London had invited the Tanlaws and ourselves to dinner at the embassy to plan the schedule of the visit.

'And what would Madame Steel like to see?' he asked, after Rina had expressed her wish to see a school and a birth control clinic. In a fit of ridiculous romanticism, I replied, 'I would like to see little white horses galloping across the Mongolian plains.'

'I am afraid there will not be enough time to do that,' replied the ambassador, totally unruffled; but a visit to a collective farm was shoehorned into our itinerary, and five magnificent heavy stallions lined up for my inspection.

We were in Beijing over Easter, and having been informed that the churches in China were now 'liberated', asked if we could go to a church service on Easter Sunday. It had to be in the evening, to fit in with the plans to go to the Great Wall that had already been made for us, and our host from the Chinese foreign office told us in delight that he had found a 'music service' for us to attend.

'Is it a Protestant service or a Catholic one?' enquired by husband. Our host was puzzled.

'It is a *Clistian* service,' he replied; and I wished that the Christian Church was as simple as he saw it.

The congregation had only been free to worship publicly for about six months; and in February, a scratch choir had been got together. We sang hymns to traditional British tunes, most of the congregation singing in Chinese and ourselves in English, and then the choir started on excerpts from Handel's *Messiah*. When it came to the Hallelujah Chorus, we all rose and joined in as one, tears streaming down many cheeks including ours. These were not Christians for whom religion, and Sunday worship, was the conventional, respectable thing to do: they had risked persecution to keep their faith alive. As well as the old people who had done this, there were youngsters there who were celebrating Easter as a congregation for the first time in their lives.

After mainland China, with its massive problems, the regimentation and low expectations of its people, I took a scunner to the brash materialism of Hong Kong.

On another occasion we went to Russia in a party of about half a dozen Liberals, including Russell Johnston, and in a private plane belonging to a wealthy party member, Anthony Jacobs. This seemed preferable to accepting Aeroflot tickets from the Soviet government – nowadays, I suppose, it would all have to be declared in the register of Members' interests, and no doubt a shock-horror story created from it. In Moscow we stayed at the British Embassy, and were due to go on to Leningrad, as St Petersburg was then called, also by the private plane. Russell and Colin Brown, the *Guardian* journalist who was covering the visit, decided to go on the overnight train instead, and I opted to join them.

We arrived at dawn. It was January, and we drove through frosty, almost deserted streets past the Winter Palace, where I literally gasped at its sheer beauty. It was the anniversary of the lifting of the siege of Leningrad, and throughout the city eternal flames glowed, and red flags fluttered at half mast. We visited the cemetery where countless bodies of the siege victims lie in mass graves with no more identification than the year in which they died. An old woman, supported by her children, cried in front of the memorial. The sight of bridal couples surprised us. We learned that it is a custom for newly-weds to pay their respects at the siege cemetery.

These were the occasional, glittering occasions; the privileged travel opportunities that came to me as the wife of the Liberal leader, and I am fortunate to have experienced them. Real, everyday concerns occupied my life in Ettrick Bridge, looking after the children, keeping up with their school progress – or lack of it – and their interests, especially the equestrian ones. Keeping horses is both expensive and time-consuming, and over this period we usually had two, and sometimes three, ponies, in addition to the faithful Hamlet. Then there was the business of transporting them. We had, first of all, a single-axle trailer with which to transport them to Common Ridings and Pony Club events. I pulled it with an Austin Maxi, which was not really up to the task. I was never able to reverse it properly, and on one terrifying occasion the whole apparatus, with ponies on board, slid backwards down an icy hill. In time the trailer gave way to a lorry, but it was a vintage one (David's choice, of course!), with no power-steering and double-declutching, and on hot days the petrol would evaporate en route from the tank to the engine, and the lorry would splutter and die on us.

Catriona was the keenest on riding of the children, but Billy had an innate ability for it. The Pony Club, recognising that such few boys as were members tended to drop out in their teens, brought in the tetrathlon competitions for them, which consisted of four disciplines: cross-country riding over fences, cross-country running, swimming and pistol-shooting. It was the last discipline that often kept them interested in the competition. Billy was good at all of them, and Anne Scott gave us the long-term loan of a superb pony for him which had been outgrown by her own five boys.

We were very much newcomers on the Pony Club scene, and at one event another mother said to me: 'See that man over there – doesn't he look just like David Steel?'

'Yes, that's my husband.'

'He really does look like David Steel. It's an amazing likeness. Don't people often say so?'

'He *is* David Steel.'

She had thought that I was Billy's real mother, and that I had the same surname as he had.

The tetrathlon team made it to the finals at Stoneleigh, where Billy fell off a borrowed pony that he wasn't used to at the last jump, injured himself, and was unable to run. I had become such a competitive Pony Club mum that, rather than show sympathy, I was furious with him.

One mother watched her son's progress round the cross-country course with a mixture of pride, concern and suppressed fury. 'You know, I look after that horse. I feed it, water it, muck it out, groom it and clean its tack. I even exercise it when he's at school. I do everything except actually get on its back and ride round the cross-country course.'

The Yarrow and Ettrick Show, held in one or other of the valleys on the second Saturday of September, would mark the end of an exhausting horsey summer. Soaked through all my waterproof clothing and watching the tail-end of the gymkhana there on a day that was extraordinarily wet even by Yarrow Show standards, I turned to another mother and said, 'Why do we do this?'

'I'll tell you why we do it,' she replied. 'We do it because we know who they're with and where they are.'

I had to give another rationale to Catriona, heartbroken at her failure to win a single rosette at another Yarrow Show (even Graeme and the dog won a second), and seething about a judgment that deprived her of her coveted bit of ribbon.

'Gymkhanas are teaching you two things in life, dear,' I comforted her. 'Life's unfair, and grown-ups cheat.'

We were never backward about involving our children in the political life. We saw their integration into it as like the way that a farm child will grow up, his or her parents' livelihood being their entire life as well. Robin and Trish Crichton's daughters grew up in the same way: Edinburgh Film productions involved all of them from an early age. Our children had been born into politics, been carted around conferences and meetings in Moses baskets, spent their Saturdays at constituency coffee mornings and bazaars. During the Christmas recesses, they would come with us on our visits to old peoples' homes and to hospitals. Once we took Rory with us to a home near Melrose run by the Brothers of Charity for men with special needs: it was an institution with which David had a particularly close connection over the years. A huge image of the crucified Christ dominated one room. Rory tugged at David's jacket: 'Look, Daddy,' he said excitedly, 'Tarzan!' Fortunately, the Brothers didn't hear.

The children had had their photos taken time and again for the local papers when they had come to events with us; now they exhibited great patience with the national press. We never thought of leaving them out of things.

Justin Cartwright, today a highly successful novelist but then a film-maker, arrived to make the first party political broadcast under David's leadership. The idea was to introduce him to the public by making the film in and around Cherrydene and featuring his family. The making of that party political film was a highlight in their young lives: they trooped down to the river with fishing rods, and I brought forward the making of the Christmas pudding by three months. 'The Hovis Kitchen Scene', Justin and others called it, and the end result, framed by music by Tchaikovsky, set a template for a new kind of party political broadcast.

The years since David had taken over the leadership had been eventful, and not easy. In that first speech to that first party conference in Llandudno, he had warned his audience that 'the road I intend to travel will be a bumpy one.'

Within a year he had the opportunity to provide the party members with their first bump. A couple of Scottish Labour MPs had defected to set up their own more left-wing splinter party, and the government had been steadily losing by-elections, in which our own vote had been disastrous. As well as a Liberal group larger than there had been for many years, there were the Ulster Unionists and the Scottish and Welsh Nationalists to be put into the balance. The election of these had forced Labour's hand on moves towards devolution, and they had brought forward a bill to establish what they called 'assemblies' in both Scotland and Wales. But the idea was still new to them; they had sought no co-operation with other parties, and the bill was deeply flawed.

Callaghan faced many problems, of which one of the greatest was inflation, and another was unemployment. The government had borrowed heavily; Jim Callaghan admitted that they could not spend their way out of inflation, the need for public expenditure cuts had been accepted and the International Monetary Fund were ready to step in with a loan. Then the Callaghan government was defeated on a procedural motion connected to the Bill to set up the assemblies in Scotland and Wales.

Mrs Thatcher put down a vote of no confidence in the government, and it was at this point that the Labour government approached David for support. They found, however, that the young Liberal leader was no pushover, and was not prepared simply to give it his MPs' support for a one-off vote. He wanted an agreement that would be much more substantial. There was a good personal rapport between David and James Callaghan, as there never had been with Harold Wilson; Callaghan, partly on the basis of his old friendship with my parents, had always adopted a somewhat avuncular attitude towards David, but the bottom line was that they liked and trusted each other. A lot of history is forged by personal chemistry.

The time was not right for a coalition – that is something that needs, usually, to be created in the aftermath of an election, and in any case such a relationship between one of the two monster parties at Westminster and one which, thanks to the electoral system, still had fewer than twenty MPs, was not really a runner. The agreement that they hammered out was that the Liberals would give support to the government over a period of a year, in what became known as the 'Lib–Lab pact'. It was a completely new concept in British politics, and it gave rise to much suspicion and misunderstanding, although it was an arrangement that had been tested often in Europe. Callaghan survived that vote, and Mrs Thatcher never forgave David for denying her an election in 1977. She always treated him with disdain, and when, years later, he rose to ask his last question to her as party leader at Prime Minister's Questions, she totally ignored the significance of the event.

The Lib–Lab pact lasted for eighteen months, and it gave the country the political stability that it needed at that time. Among the legislation that was saved by the Lib–Lab pact was the bill to set up a Scottish Assembly, which was piloted through the Commons by the young Scottish minister and rising political star John Smith. It has to be said that the assembly that was proposed was a pallid affair, and those who supported Home Rule found it difficult to enthuse about it. As it progressed, an extraordinary clause was added by George Cunningham, a Labour MP who was hostile to the bill itself. This was the condition that, in the ensuing referendum, a simple majority would not be enough. Those voting 'yes' had to constitute 40% of the entire electorate. It is worth considering how many governments have come to power with votes well below that figure.

Yet there was such optimism and confidence about the outcome that the government purchased the old Royal High School in Edinburgh as a home for the Assembly, and people were beginning to consider putting their names forward to serve in it. If I had ever dreamed of such a candidature myself, and in fact I did think about it very seriously, it was the wrong time for me. In the Borders, Archy Kirkwood, who had come to love the area, saw it as an opening and hoped to stand in the local seat. He and his wife Rosemary bought a house near us in the village; Andrew Haddon took him on as a legal apprentice in Hawick and he set to with great application to qualify as a solicitor. Their presence near us over the years was to be a great support, and in time Archy became the MP for the redistributed seat of Roxburgh and Berwick – but at Westminster, not in Edinburgh.

There were many in the Labour Party who were still hostile to the whole concept of Scottish self-government: of these Tam Dalyell remained the most outspoken over the years, posing his classic 'West Lothian' question, which, in truth, cannot be solved unless by a federal constitution or total independence. And in 1978, the devolutionists in the party lost their most intelligent and convinced advocate when John Mackintosh died. We stood at his grave in the quiet churchyard of Yester Kirk in Gifford in East Lothian, mourning the best of colleagues and the most entertaining of companions. It was a grievous loss to Scottish politics and to all his friends. Over thirty years later, we still miss him.

The Lib-Lab pact ended, as had been arranged at its inception, in July 1978; but Callaghan did not, as was expected, call an autumn election. The referendum campaign in February 1979 was a lack-lustre affair, and there were many valid objections to the assembly as it had been enacted. The Labour Party had been driven by motives of expediency that were more to do with 'stopping the nationalist tide' than with principle, and they had not listened to any voices outside their own party grouping. Added to this, the referendum came after the 'winter of discontent', when strikes and industrial unrest were at a new high, and the government seemed unable to control events. Worst of all was the strike of gravediggers, with the effect on public morale of seeing bodies lie unburied.

The 'No' campaign built on this anti-Labour feeling. In the closing stages came an intervention from Sir Alec Douglas-Home, who had retired from politics. He was, he said, in favour of devolution, but not this shape of it. 'Vote "No",' he said, 'and the Conservatives will deliver a much better scheme for you.' His voice was authoritative, and swayed some votes. In the end, the slim majority in favour of the Act was not enough to reach the 40% threshold, with most of the rural areas, including the Borders, voting 'No'. The Act fell, and with it, the SNP's support for Callaghan's government.

Within a month, Mrs Thatcher put down another vote of no confidence. A big political occasion was always more of a draw for me than a social one, and this was going to be a major event. If James Callaghan's government lost, it would fall, and for the first time since Ramsay MacDonald's government was forced out of office in 1924, a ruling party would be driven to the polls, not at a time of its own choosing, but immediately, as a result of that vote. The numbers were finely balanced; it would be an historic occasion, and I had no intention of missing it. I made hasty childcare arrangements and snatched the time to go down to London on the day of the debate, getting to the House of Commons just before the vote was called. I had missed Michael Foot's speech, one of the great treats of parliamentary oratory, but the sense of drama through-out the Palace of Westminster was palpable.

'Can you squeeze me in?' I asked the attendant, for it was obvious that there was now standing room only. He recognised me, and the electricity of the occasion loosened his usual correctness. 'I can squeeze you anywhere, Mrs Steel,' he said cheekily, and I found floor space to stand on in the gallery, in an atmosphere more charged and tense than I had ever known, amid a rising crescendo of noise and excitement.

Above the hubbub, the Speaker called the vote and gave the command for the lobbies to be cleared. 'Ayes to the right, Noes to the left!' The MPs trooped out, and observers craned their necks to see where the Liberals, the maverick MPs, the Ulster Unionists, and the Scottish and Welsh Nationalists were heading.

They came back from the lobbies, filling the chamber to bursting point. The four tellers took up their position before the mace and announced the result to the Speaker – and the racket that had been raised at the end of the debate increased fourfold.

'Ayes three hundred and eleven, Noes three hundred and ten,' reported the tellers, and the noise went through the great roof of the Commons chamber.

The vote of no confidence had been carried by a single vote.

'Mr Speaker,' shouted Callaghan above the tumult, 'We shall take our case to the country.'

The election battlebus is now a familiar – probably over-familiar – sight at British elections. I don't think it is often remembered that it was David who pioneered it, in that first election as leader. Jeremy Thorpe in his time had flown between key points in a helicopter, but that was expensive, taking a disproportionate amount of the party's hard-earned budget, and complicated arrangements had to be made for it. And a helicopter is not exactly the kind of vehicle to which the man or woman in the street can relate. A coach, on the other hand, is universal transport; it does not need landing-pads or airports or stations to get into town centres; it does not need auxiliary transport to ferry its passengers to other destinations; and it could accommodate the press. David borrowed the idea from the use of coaches by pop-stars; it was one such that was adapted by Parks of Hamilton for his use, amid great secrecy. With him would travel his team of two secretaries, his assistant and his press officer, and journalists would be able to purchase seats on the bus to help defray its costs.

It turned out, also, to be ideal for four unexpected additions to the entourage. Right at the start of the campaign, the appalling news came that Mrs Thatcher's Northern Irish spokesman, Airey Neave, had been assassinated by the IRA. His car had been blown up at the entrance to the underground car park of the House of Commons itself. Immediately, all party leaders were assigned protection officers. David's first train journey with one of them showed how quickly they could react: as they rumbled northwards, a slightly inebriated passenger approached, held out his hand – and stumbled. The security officer's hand went immediately inside his jacket – he was, of course, fully armed.

On the home front, they wanted a sketch plan of Cherrydene, to use in the event of a hostage-taking situation. I was phoned from Hawick by the local police superintendent: could he come and carry this task out on such and such a morning? 'Yes, that's fine,' I replied blithely. 'I'll be out, but I never lock the door anyway.' He never came, no doubt put off by such low-security personal precautions.

At one election, we were sleeping peacefully when we were wakened at four o'clock in the morning by two of the protection officers coming into our bedroom. 'It's all right, go to sleep,' one said, as they went towards the window. If we had looked out as well, we would have seen a tent on the hillside across the Ettrick. The police left our bedroom and made their way to the tent. Beside it was an elderly car with a Liverpool registration mark. They checked, and found that it belonged to someone who had been identified as being at an IRA rally in the city. Reinforcements were summoned from Hawick, and the unfortunate couple who had gone away for a quiet weekend with a borrowed car awoke to found themselves surrounded by the might of the law.

But security was not always so tight. During another election, my friend John Nichol parked his car outside the gates of Cherrydene, and strolled through them, carrying David's shotgun which he had borrowed to rehearse with. The place was, as he described it, crawling with politicians and security police and the general entourage, so he simply went into the kitchen, left the gun on the table, and went away again.

On the battlebus, the protection officers merged easily into the team, so much so that at more than one election, a fleeting relationship sprang up between one of the security personnel and one of the secretarial team. Dedicated crews from the BBC and ITV were also part of the entourage. The presenter Alistair Stewart was the link man in the ITV team, which was always onto a story well ahead of their rivals. They invented a chorus about their BBC rival, Michael Cole, whenever he went AWOL from a scoop. One of them would shout, 'Where's Dexter?' (Cole's middle name.)

And the rest would reply: 'Don't know! Don't care! Don't like him anyway!'

Thus the Liberal leader would tour Britain, and at weekends the bus would trundle into the Borders where he caught up with the local campaign, and did some of his meetings in the towns and larger villages. I covered the smaller communities during the week, writing my own speeches rather than reading from ones prepared by David, and answering questions as though I was actually the candidate. No-one took it amiss. It would never have occurred to us that we should both desert the constituency.

When the circus rolled back into the Borders, there was something of a carnival atmosphere. On one occasion, the travelling hacks were astonished to find David and myself being hugged warmly by a group of men and women of varying special needs, among whom we had made many friends over the years. Sometimes, as they were pushed aside in the melee, the local press pack was less than enamoured of their invading media colleagues.

One of them grabbed me: 'This is just not right, Judy, we're not standing for this. We've been photographing him for years, and we'll still be here after all this lot have gone. He ought to remember that. You'd better make sure we're treated better than this.' My sympathies were all with the locals, and I relayed their feelings in no uncertain terms.

David loved coming back to the Borders after the week trundling round Britain. He would never have missed his meetings at Yetholm, where the questioning would go on for hours, searching and erudite, or at the Roxy Cinema in Kelso. At each election, as we drove towards the latter, after meetings earlier in the evening at Peebles and Galashiels (the farmer Haig Douglas always turning up at the latter to ask his perennial question about the Cheap Food Policy), we would listen to the news-reader on the radio: 'The election campaign is over; the last leaflet has been delivered; the last meeting has been held,' and we would chorus joyfully together, 'Not at the Roxy, it hasn't!'

Sometimes, after the meetings, during those elections when he was party leader, we would summon the energy to go round some of the nightshifts in the mills and the new electronics companies, usually in Selkirk, when we were on the way home. Unlike daytime visits, these were not fixed up beforehand, but were impromptu – and the welcome was all the warmer.

During the week, I had been taking on some of what David usually did. As well as making speeches at the village hall meetings, I toured workplaces, showing an interest in what everyone was doing, asking them to vote for David and doling out badges. And although I had always felt confident when canvassing for him around the farms and villages and the retirement homes, I felt I was a poor substitute among the mill-girls who had always enjoyed his visits, and who gave him such loyalty. But they would look up from the intricacies of their looms and knitting machines, usually indicate their approval, and only occasionally make a caustic comment about his absence. At the end of the day, it was that loyalty that came through, both from them and from the Border electorate at large: they gave him what he had always secretly hankered after: a majority of over 10,000.

He had taken over a party that was unbelievably demoralised, whose former leader was still awaiting trial for conspiracy to murder, and which he had led into an arrangement with the sitting government that was totally unprecedented in British politics, a pact that was controversial and not by any means universally popular, and whose significance and worth would not be recognised for another couple of decades. Yet the vote held up reasonably well, and the number of Liberal seats was still in double figures.

And for the country, there was a Tory government, led by Britain's first woman Prime Minister. On the steps of 10 Downing Street, she uttered the words of St Francis of Assisi: 'Where there is discord, let me bring harmony.'

As the years passed, both during and since her 'reign', nothing could have turned out to be more inappropriate.

By the time she left office, most of those looms and knitting machines, whose operators we canvassed so enthusiastically, were stilled, like so much of Britain's manufacturing industry, and a culture of greed and selfishness had grown up whose harvest we have been reaping in the twenty-first century.

# 18
# Different Stages

March, 2002

*I am in the village hall at Westruther in Berwickshire, with the young stage manager of Rowan Tree Theatre Company, Matthew Burgess. The tour is of a play of my own,* The Four Horsemen, *about the previous year's plague of Foot and Mouth Disease. Matthew has been in this hall before, on another tour with another company, and has warned me about coming to it.*

*'But we've always had good audiences in Westruther, in their old hall,' I say. 'And I promised them, when David and I came to open the new one, that we'd come back.'*

*But Matthew is right. The hall which looked so superb at its opening, and which in due course I will see come into its own as a wedding reception venue, is not suitable for our purpose. The acoustics are terrible. There is no stage and no natural focal point. There is no-one on hand to help us from the hall committee, and I was taught long ago, by my first stage manager, not to ask actors to help with a 'get-in', otherwise they will be here for hours. Worst of all, there are huge windows letting in the early summer sunshine and rendering the lighting totally ineffectual. For that problem, there is a remedy, and it's one that I can administer. I climb onto the narrow windowsill and begin sticking black bin bags over the windows with gaffer tape.*

*As I do so, I take stock. What am I doing, at the age of sixty-two, touring round halls bringing professional theatre to remote communities? Why do I have to be so hands-on? Why is there always so little funding that I always have to be hands-on? How did I get myself on this window sill?*

There was certainly nothing in my background to have foretold it. Nothing at school encouraged such an interest: the only plays we studied were Shakespeare's, which I loved for their poetry rather than their drama. We had never lived near a theatre, and as a young teenager and a student, it was the cinema to which I went with friends, and to which I was taken regularly by my parents. Once a year, however, they would take me to the Edinburgh Festival, and there, in the Assembly Hall, I saw the fine actors Paul Rogers and Ann Todd in a rather lugubrious production of *Macbeth*. The following year in the same venue was a production of Sydney Goodsir Smith's *The Wallace*, with Ian Cuthbertson in the title role. It was well suited to my nationalist tendencies, and had as much effect on me as Mel Gibson's *Braveheart* did on younger generations forty years later.

Apart from pantomime, I can remember only one play that I saw when I was young, and it is strange that it remains in my memory, for *The World's Wonder*, by Alexander Reid, was about the Scottish wizard Michael Scott, and it starred the great Scottish comic actor Duncan Mac-Rae in the title role. I would write a play myself about this legendary figure in time, and live in the tower associated with him.

Then, in the years before and after I was forty, a few things all came together. One was that, through Billy, I had become familiar with the Scottish Youth Theatre which had been set up in the late 1970s. He went to two of their summer schools in Edinburgh and Glasgow. I was interested and inspired by the work they did, which was so much more challenging and emotionally true than anything I had seen by way of school or amateur productions – and, sometimes, professional ones.

Also at about that time, I made my first visit to the Traverse Theatre. It seems surprising that I hadn't been before then, but it had been founded about the time we were leaving Edinburgh for the Borders, and it also had at that time, to get round some of the planning problems, the status of a club. So it seemed rather a 'closed shop', and it wasn't until an invitation went out to all the Scottish MPs to see a particular play that we went along. The play was one in which we had an interest, because it featured a voice from our own political past.

*The Case of David Anderson, QC* was by a playwright called John Hale. Anderson had been the solicitor-general in Douglas-Home's government, and the Tory candidate at the Dumfriesshire by-election at the time when David became convinced that he could represent a rural seat, and agreed to move his candidacy to Roxburgh, Selkirk and Peebles. Anderson had not fought the following general election, but he had been appointed as a reporter for public enquiries at the Scottish Office after he had stepped down. During one of these enquiries, in Ayr, he was accused of breach of the peace for approaching two teenage girls and asking them to carry out a sadistic act for his own gratification. When the case came to trial, there was a real fault in the evidence of identification, but he was found guilty by the Sheriff. He appealed, and lost. From then on, he took every opportunity to proclaim his innocence, and to put the blame for the whole incident on some mystifying plot by MI5. He deluged MPs with duplicated pages of increasingly obsessive arguments in his defence. David had had many missives from him over the years; however, Anderson's great coup was persuading John Hale, who took up the story with some enthusiasm, to write the play.

Anderson – who went to see the play almost every night of its run at the Traverse – was played by Corin Redgrave. 'He is much more convincing than David Anderson himself,' I remarked. He had only been on stage for a short time when I realised that the lines I was hearing were familiar to me: requests to the girls to walk over him, excuses about a bet with a friend who was a Wren – I had heard them all before, in a car on a winter evening in George Square. I had completely forgotten the incident – now it was unfolding again in front of me.

What could I remember about that man in the car? My mind kept veering towards this, and then, in a flash, I recalled that he had been wearing an old school tie from Glenalmond. It so happened that the programme had CVs, not just of the actors, but of the main protagonists as they had appeared in *Who's Who*. I looked at Anderson's: it said, 'Educated at Trinity College, Glenalmond.' It brought home the realisation that I was one of a string of young women to whom he had made this suggestion.

It certainly made for an interesting baptism at the Traverse, and when we had supper afterwards with their Press Officer, Pat Lovett, I had to tell her that far from convincing me of Anderson's innocence, it confirmed his guilt.

Before long, Lesley Carstairs, a young friend originally of my nieces but also of Joan and myself, went to work at the Traverse, and persuaded me to come more often. It opened up a whole new concept of theatre to me, in its new writing, the intimacy of the small theatre itself, and the high standard of acting and production values. I was often, through Lesley, the recipient of requests to supply items needed by the stage management for productions, such as horse harness and a decent-sized tree from one of our fields. Graeme's pet lamb, destined for the pot, was conscripted for a publicity call for *Accounts*, Michael Wilcox's play about sheep farming and gay relationships in the village of Yethom. Before long I found myself asked to go onto the board, and during my years as a board member I saw early performances by Gerda Stevenson, Ken Stott and Tilda Swinton amongst others, and revelled in the first plays of Liz Lochhead, John (now Jo) Clifford, Chris Hannan and Rona Munro.

Both the Traverse and the Scottish Youth Theatre were completely new theatre experiences that opened up my mind to what was possible. Meantime, back in Ettrick Bridge, I was building up some hands-on experience. It began as a kind of therapy.

I was going through one of my dark times. The first had happened just before I started going out with David, and I had climbed out of it. Now I was finding that coping with a family mainly on my own was dreadfully stressful. I had the feeling that I was neither an adequate mother nor an adequate partner to David. I spiralled downwards, feeling more and more impotent.

There were good friends who supported me through that time: my neighbour, Alison MacKerchar, who had come to take over the village pub with her husband, was key among them. Her younger daughter Claire and Rory were best friends, totally inseparable. Rory at four even went to ballet classes with Claire. It was at a time when Billy was also taking ballet classes – in Edinburgh, so that no-one at Selkirk High would know about it – and Catriona was going to football practice in the village. I enjoyed the unpredictability of their preferences. Through Alison McKerchar, I learned how unremittingly demanding the life of a publican is, and any romantic illusions about the Steels retiring from politics and running a pub were banished by the cold water of reality. Alison was a true friend to me during difficult and distraught times, and when she and her family moved to Girvan in Ayrshire, I missed her dreadfully.

A somewhat hippy couple, Maggie and Thom McCarthy. moved to live just outside the village with their two sons. They had built up retail businesses in Edinburgh's Cockburn Street, and made enough money to move to rural bliss while still in their thirties. Thom was a Vietnam veteran, and had developed agoraphobia while in Edinburgh. He felt that he could cope better with this in a country setting. He bought the old joiner's workshop in the village and set up a pottery, grew his own vegetables and herbs, shot rabbits and caught fish. The McCarthys' boys became friendly with my family, and Maggie was the confidante of many of my negative thoughts during that time. The two of them were adherents of an alternative sect beloved of the Beatles, that of Guru Maharishi, and Maggie was determined that he would be my salvation. She took me up to a meeting of his followers in Edinburgh, and I watched films about his teachings; but I could not find anything in it for me.

Thom's crops included cannabis, though I didn't know that at the time, and it was at a Fourth of July party there that I was first offered a joint. 'No thanks!' I said sharply, and continued to drink far too much Martini. Fortunately, I had come by pony and trap and one of the children drove me home.

In time the McCarthys separated. Maggie moved away and died young, of breast cancer. Thom remained where he was for a few years, carrying on a fairly colourful love-life, and then moved to Samye Ling Tibetan Monastery at Eskdalemuir. Here, first of all, he masterminded the project to set up the meditation cells there, and then oversaw the purchase of the Holy Isle off Arran for the Tibetan community. In the nineties he moved back to Edinburgh and opened up more shops. With impeccable timing he sold up just before the credit crunch and retired to a cottage next to Samye Ling. He has remained a staunch friend over the decades.

Archy Kirkwood had fallen for the Borders during his time as David's assistant, and was determined to pursue his own political career from the base. He especially loved Ettrick Bridge, and some time after he married Rosemary Chester – an active Liberal in her own right – the former postmaster's house came on the market. They bought it, and are now among the most senior of the village's residents. Archy spent a lot of time away, so Ro and I were in the same situation – but also, she was someone who understood, and with whom I could share, the political niceties of what was happening nationwide.

In Selkirk, an old acquaintance from Edinburgh University, Lindsay Neil, moved to the town as one of its doctors, with his wife Pat and their young daughter, who was a week older than Rory. Pat and I became immediate friends, and she and Lindsay had two sons after they moved to Selkirk. Both professionally and as a friend, Lindsay saw me through various crises at that bad time. Then their own tragedy knocked my concerns into perspective: their elder son, Ruairidh, was killed in a car accident. A young driver showing off to his two nephews and their friend as he took them to Kelso for a swimming lesson in the school holidays, in the era before compulsory rear seat-belts, a skid on a badly cambered corner, and a young life ended at the age of twelve. By an appalling coincidence, Lindsay was the doctor on duty who was called to the scene of the accident.

When I look at the people I admire most in my life – and role models, I think, need to be of your own gender – the one I admire most outside my own family is not a consummate and loved political figure like Shirley Williams, nor an inspirational playwright like Liz Lochhead, much as I revere both of them. It is Pat Neil.

I have learned so much from Pat. First and foremost, I have learnt that the death of a child is something from which you never fully recover: the best you can do is turn your grief into a positive force. Some parents do this by setting up small trusts in their child's name which will help research, or alleviate conditions, for fellow-sufferers from the illness which caused their child's death. Pat and Lindsay received tremendous support from an organisation called Compassionate Friends, which is a banding together of bereaved parents to support others in their situation. She went on to work – on a voluntary basis, as all the Compassionate Friends are – for them over ten years, in particular editing a moving regular booklet to which parents contributed their own grief writing.

Pat herself had found solace in a series of moving poems about her own loss, her darkness, and the return of light. She says, 'The one most powerful grip I had on life at that time, indeed for years, was the mantra that "I have to Do the Day". So each Day was Done as best I could, and only much later did I realise what a feeble effort it was. A pretty animal existence really, just survival, minute by minute, stretching to hour by hour, then day by day and so on, till about four years on I seemed to be able to look properly outwards again.'

When she had left school, Pat had gone to Spain to do a diploma course at Madrid University, and stayed there for seven years. When she returned to the UK, she became a librarian in my old haunt of the Edinburgh University Law Library, and it was in Edinburgh that she met Lindsay. He was an army doctor, and they spent their early married life in Singapore. But Pat was not a typical army wife: she learned Chinese and Chinese cookery, while she and Lindsay browsed the streets of Singapore when he was off duty, educating themselves about Chinese porcelain and art.

Pat's life in Selkirk has been that of a home-maker. Within that role, she has developed other interests to the point of professionalism: giving demonstrations of Chinese cookery and running a catering business with another doctor's wife. Immersion in these kept her sane in the first terrible months of grief. She has gone in for furniture painting, and now, like me, is a quilter. The next generation come to her home in Selkirk with love and for comfort, just as we MacGregors did with Auntie G.

Lindsay meantime takes up causes in his adopted town with vigour and effectiveness. The signs bearing Selkirk's old street names, the Selkirk Silver Arrow returned from the Royal Company of Archers to be placed on display in Selkirk after a gap of a couple of hundred years, the formation of the Ettrick Forest Archers – all these and more are Lindsay Neil's legacy to Selkirk. And his quiet companionship of David on Fridays on Bowhill Loch as they cast their flies, often uselessly, and talk men's talk, has been an oasis that the latter looks forward to each week throughout the fishing season.

The Neils know the real values of life.

All these – and others in Ettrick Bridge – helped me to cope when the stresses and strains of our lifestyle took its toll, but it was my wise father who gave me the best advice: 'Find something to do with your hands,' he said, and, making an effort, I did. First of all, I refurbished the dolls' house I had made for Catriona's fifth birthday, and then embarked on making costumes for a village production of *Joseph and the Amazing Technicolor Dreamcoat*.

And doing these things, I found myself very much at home, and recovered some of my equilibrium. Before long, I took the lead in a frenzy of community theatre-making in Ettrick Bridge that lasted for about four years, with two annual productions – one performed entirely by teenagers and children, the other integrating them with adults. I brought in expertise from outside wherever I could, including regular workshops for the village children by the Scottish Youth Theatre: I think we must have satisfied their target for rural involvement. With total brass neck, I phoned up Kedzie Penfield, an American choreographer who was living in the next valley, and asked her to choreograph *Joseph*. She found herself crossing over to our valley for the next few years to help on various projects. At one time, she was choreographing Scottish Opera's production of *My Fair Lady* in Glasgow during the week, and the Kirkhope Creativity Company's production of *Alice in Wonderland* at the weekends – the latter, needless to say, on a purely voluntary basis. I had never been the least interested in performing: but the putting together of a production, the meshing of all the elements, began to take hold of me, and when I began writing, and heard my own words spoken, or when I saw what I had visualised coming into its own reality, I experienced a satisfaction that was completely new to me.

I had fantasised about a particular project for some years. A medieval feast was an event which involved many different skills – mime, juggling, costume and mask-making, music and dance and acting, winemaking and cooking. It was when Elspeth Smellie, a young art school graduate, came to live in Ettrick Bridge as Thom McCarthy's assistant at the pottery, that I started to bring it to fruition. I knew that she played the clarsach – the small Scottish harp, an instrument I had only heard once, at a medieval feast run by George Foulkes during an Edinburgh University Charities week. Elspeth was due to finish her stint at the pottery, and I thought, 'If I don't get a medieval feast organised before Elspeth leaves the village, I'll never forgive myself.' We based it on a bowdlerised version of Chaucer's *Canterbury Tales*, and it was amazing how even non-academic teenagers took to it.

Thus the feast came about, and for the first time I fell under the spell of the clarsach. It was to be the first of many, many collaborations with Elspeth, as well as the start of a good friendship – I am now godmother to her daughter Morgan. She did not leave the village, but married a young man who also came to live there at about that time. Although he has gone on his way, Elspeth remains loyal to her adopted countryside of the Borders. She now gives clarsach lessons in the Great Hall at Aikwood once a week, and it is a lovely thought that the skill of playing Scotland's original national instrument is being passed on here.

David, despite all the other calls on his time, took part in a couple of the early productions with great forbearance. He enjoyed it particularly when I co-wrote a Christmas show based on the life and stories of Hans Anderson, and he was cast as Prime Minister in *The Emperor's New Clothes*. He played it in drag, in an electric blue evening dress and matching wig, and managed a passable imitation of Margaret Thatcher's pretentious tones. The *Sunday Times* got to hear about it and sent a photographer up from London for the last night, which was on Hogmanay. There arose a conspiracy among the company to protect him from being photographed in his blue frock. First of all, the photographer was threatened that if he took a picture during the performance, the camera would be removed ('smashed to the ground,' I think the actual threat was). We did not know enough to threaten him with breach of copyright, but he must have been aware of the possibility. After the performance, when the Liberal leader was in a less outrageous costume, photographs were allowed, 'But only of the whole cast', who obligingly made him almost invisible in their midst.

The photographer pleaded. 'You know what I want,' he said, to which he got the dusty reply, 'Yes, and you're not going to get it.' Poor man: I wonder where he spent that New Year, without the photograph he'd been commissioned to take.

These productions, and learning from what I saw and digested at the Traverse, were my apprenticeship, and what I was doing caught the attention of those running the Scottish Arts Council at the time. I was asked to go onto its drama committee, and my five years of service on this proved another valuable part of my education.

Meantime, on the political stage, things were moving in an exciting way. The initial euphoria at the thought of a woman leading one of Britain's political parties soon wore thin. I was at Westminster the night that the result of the Tory MPs' ballot was announced, when Margaret Thatcher defeated Edward Heath, and can recall the atmosphere of promise that there would be a new Britain where women would stand shoulder to shoulder with male politicians. Any expectations I had of Mrs Thatcher as a proponent for the advance of women in politics were quickly dispelled on our first meeting, at a reception in the Speaker's rooms. I was with Catriona Stewart, wife of the SNP leader Donald Stewart, who worked as his secretary in London. We were introduced to the new leader of the opposition. She preened herself at us. 'Oh,' she said, in that irritating, patronising voice, 'how nice to meet you. And may I just say, how lovely your hair looks.' She patted her own immaculate coiffure. 'You ladies of leisure are so lucky – we working women never have the time to get it done!'

Such was the longest conversation I ever held with the woman who became Britain's first woman Prime Minister.

As Mrs Thatcher forged ahead with her 'conviction politics' of the right, the Labour party found itself increasingly in the hands of the left-wingers and eurosceptics. The social democrat wing became more and more dissatisfied, and their leadership was scattered. Shirley Williams had lost her seat, Roy Jenkins had gone to Brussels as President of the European Commission, John Mackintosh had died. But Roy Jenkins was keeping his lines of communication open, and as well as those in the Labour Party, David was among his contacts.

They met regularly from the time just after 1979 election, discussing how best to move things forward. Roy Jenkins made a major speech, the annual Dimbleby lecture, in which he set out a clear call for the realignment of the political centre, and called for electoral reform – after all, through his new role he saw the results of proportional representation throughout Europe, and was not afraid of it. Events continued to develop during 1980, and then Shirley Williams, along with David Owen and Bill Rodgers, signalled their intention to leave the Labour Party if it committed itself to withdrawal from the EEC. The party conference of that year called for just that, and for unilateral disarmament. Not long afterwards Michael Foot was elected party leader. Throughout all this time, David had been in contact not just with Roy, but with other unhappy Labour politicians. There was one, however, now of that number, who was disdainful of the

Liberals right from the start, and that was David Owen. Along with Roy, Shirley and Bill, he formed what became known as the Gang of Four, and from the Owens' London home they issued what became known as the Limehouse Declaration, setting up a Council for Social Democracy.

The SDP was officially launched in March 1981, and in June the Alliance between it and the Liberal Party was announced, with a photo-opportunity of David and Shirley sitting on the grass 'looking like a pair of superannuated student lovers' as one commentator unkindly put it. It was more than an electoral pact: it was an agreement between the parties to campaign together on a joint programme, with the definite aim of a coalition government.

They were heady days. The Alliance soared in the opinion polls, for a time leading the other parties. When David concluded his now notorious conference speech with the phrase 'go back to your constituencies and prepare for government!' it was, within the context of the time, a perfectly credible scenario, arguing that the next government could not be formed without them.

Within a short time Shirley was back in the House of Commons having won a by-election in Crosby. In Roy's case, it was in Glasgow Hillhead, and I was dubious as to how this urbane Londoner would go down there, especially after his answer to the question whether he would live in Glasgow was, 'One would have a wesidence'. The Tory candidate was Gerald Malone, who had stood against David in the Borders in 1979; Labour's standard was carried by a young Glasgow councillor, Vincent Cable. An opinion poll during the campaign put Roy in third place, and with my usual pessimism I feared the worst. But I need not have worried: he squeaked home, and the day after he won Hillhead, Roy came to the Scottish Liberal Party conference in St Andrews. It was perhaps the high point of the Alliance, as he and David marched down the aisle of the conference hall together in happy unity, to a standing ovation and ringing cheers.

Then, within weeks, as so often, the British political scene was changed utterly by events far away. Those relics of the outposts of empire, the Falklands Islands in the South Atlantic, were occupied by Argentinian troops. Mrs Thatcher embarked on the Falklands War which blew aside all the criticisms of the Tories' domestic policies and made her position unassailable. It was a justifiable war; but the nation, whipped up by the tabloids, indulged in a frenzy of unpleasant jingoism, and Margaret Thatcher became Boadicea, Elizabeth Tudor and Winston Churchill rolled into one.

A year later, she called the election. The Alliance was still in a strong position, though not as high in the polls as it had been. Michael Foot, that great orator and politician of principle, did not make a credible alternative Prime Minister, and the Labour Party was saddled with left-wing policies. The prospect of a 'hung parliament' (I tried, unsuccessfully, to encourage the use of the word 'balanced' as a substitute) was a very real one, and I still think it might have happened but for the respect, bordering on reverence, that both David and Shirley Williams had for Roy Jenkins. This meant that Shirley gave up her chance to become leader of the new party, and when it came to the election an uneasy compromise was reached about the nominal figureheads of the Alliance. David would 'lead the campaign', Roy would be the putative prime minister in the event of an Alliance majority.

And yet David was much the more popular figure with the public. One poll gave him a lead over Roy of 38% as the preferred person to lead the Alliance. I, and others, thought he was wrong in agreeing to the 'prime minister designate' label that was landed on Roy Jenkins by David Marquand – but he took the view that, given Roy's vast experience in government, this was the right thing to do, and would give the Alliance more credibility. In any event, during the election, the label encouraged the press to see not a joint leadership, but a single one, and although the television crews, in particular, followed both men, it was the images of Roy Jenkins that were broadcast at night. He was fighting hard to retain Glasgow Hillhead, and was mostly based there: David, on the other hand, was rattling around the whole of Britain in the battlebus, drawing huge and enthusiastic crowds.

Peter Hellyer made his usual foray to the Borders from Abu Dhabi. I cannot begin to describe how important his support was to me. When, at the weekend, David and his entourage would roll back into the Borders, still largely preoccupied with what was happening in the national campaign, I often felt very excluded. But Peter was there for me, working shoulder to shoulder throughout the whole three weeks.

In the same way I felt this sense of isolation at party conferences – not the Scottish ones, where I would encounter so many friends from the past – but the federal ones in places such as Brighton and Bournemouth were always a trial for me. I would go, not for the whole conference, but in the run-up to David's speech, when he was most preoccupied, and had to undergo the hated ritual of The Photocall of the Leader with His Wife. Once in the conference hall, I would enjoy the debates and speeches, and David's often moved me to tears with pride. But at the end of it, as he took the applause, I again had to come away from being an engaged Liberal and be The Adoring Wife Kissing Her Husband after the Speech. Once again, though, I had my own mini support system, although on this occasion it came to me from the Ettrick Valley and not from the Middle East.

Vicky Davidson comes from generations of farmers in the Borders on her father's side, and from Hawick butchers and cornets on her mother's. She was at Kirkhope Primary School, Selkirk High School and the Pony Club with Catriona, and she became a friend of both of us. Inspired by David, especially by his stance over apartheid, she read politics at Edinburgh University and, like him, became president of the Liberal Club there. On several occasions she came to the conferences with me as an informal aide, usually sleeping on the sofa of our suite. As Peter Hellyer was my rock during the stressful times of general elections, Vicky fulfilled the same role at conference. They were my political supports during those times, just as my friends and my sisters were my domestic buttresses.

During the 1983 election, David would phone home every night, full of the adrenalin of a successful day. Peter Hellyer and I, after a day of canvassing and meetings in the Borders, would watch the election reports on television giving another chunk of coverage to rather ill-at-ease appearances by Roy. The opinion polls were stuck fast, and David was under pressure from his closest advisers, Richard Holme, Stuart Mole and Ming Campbell, to 'do something'.

It was against this background that David called what became known as the Ettrick Bridge Summit, when the Gang of Four were summoned to Cherrydene and the media followed them. What went on around my dining table I do not know, for although Peter and I kept our ears to the door, we were not able to make anything out, but the atmosphere was not a happy one. And David, after it, did not want to talk – only to rest.

In the Borders, the boundaries had been changed and the new seat of Tweeddale, Ettrick and Lauderdale was smaller without the rolling acres of Roxburghshire. The Midlothian villages of Stow and Heriot had been added, and the Berwickshire burgh of Lauder. I always felt a sense of personal triumph about delivering the vote in these communities while David was touring the nation. The new seat of Roxburgh and Berwick, where Archy Kirkwood was the candidate, had been calculated, notionally, as a Tory one. Gerry Malone had expected to be reappointed as Tory candidate, but was pipped at the post by a junior Scottish minister, Ian Sproat. He was expecting to lose his seat in South Aberdeen: Gerry Malone went there to fight it in his place.

When polling day came, we watched the start of the overnight results in a more despairing mood than ever before, even though it turned out to be more successful than any election had been for the Liberals since before the war. The Alliance had garnered 25% of the votes, but these had not translated into seats. There were only 23. Among them was Archy Kirkwood's win in Roxburgh and Berwick. In Aberdeen, Gerry Malone held the seat for the Tories, and when the Roxburgh result came through, was reported to be 'whooping with grief' at Ian Sproat's fate.

Ettrick Bridge now had two Liberal MPs. (My friend Walter Elliot wrote a witty poem bemoaning the fact that they now outnumbered dykers in the village.) We all came back to Cherrydene in the dawn and drank champagne to toast Archy's victory. Then he went off, without having slept, to change into his riding gear to follow the Cornet at Hawick Common Riding. What a way to celebrate an election!

Later in the day I barbecued a whole lamb for the press corps who had followed David the length and breadth of Britain, and before they all departed, ITV hosted a 'wrap party' at the Philipburn Hotel in Selkirk, which ended with most of the guests in the swimming pool. Nobody had thought to bring swimsuits.

David had spent the last part of the campaign with an appalling, fluey cold. In this condition, as we were making a stately progress around Galashiels on top of the battlebus, neither of us noticed a rope strung across the road. David's neck came up against it, and it snapped. He was lucky – it could quite easily have been a fatality. It shook us both.

Still suffering from the after-effects of flu, shock and the strain of the election, he went down to London to meet up with his new band of MPs. Already he knew that Roy Jenkins was resigning as leader of the SDP. David Owen, the least enthusiastic of all the original 'Gang of Four' as regards closer cooperation, and eventual merger, between the SDP and the Liberals, was his obvious successor, since Shirley Williams had lost her by-election seat. David came under attack about the campaign from some of his closest colleagues, and came back home in the most hurt and despondent of moods, determined to resign as leader.

Ro Kirkwood typed up his letter of resignation, and David gave it to Archy to deliver in London. I was appalled by David's intention to step down after coming so close to success with the strategy that he believed in. I felt that if he abandoned it now, leaving the party to the warfare of a leadership contest, with the whip hand of the Alliance held very firmly by the divisive Owen, the dream of a strong third force in British politics would never come to reality, and David would blame himself in the future for throwing it away at this point. I rang Archy and he came up the road from his house to Cherrydene. We discussed it with each other in the kitchen, united in purpose, and then we both talked to David into the small hours, until he agreed not to go through with his resignation. In retrospect, I am surprised at the line I took, because it would certainly have given us an easier life over the next few years.

Nevertheless, he was adamant that he must take a break of at least two months – not just because he physically needed it, but to make a point with his colleagues in parliament and the party at large. To be honest, I can't remember what that point was; but it was of consuming importance to him. I could see that he was going to need a lot of love and support from me at this time.

He was made a lovely offer when his crisis went public by Stephen Winyard, a Peeblesshire business man. The Winyard family – Stephen and his parents Bob and the formidable Gaynor – had asked David to help them, as the local MP, when they planned to take on the derelict shell of Stobo Castle 'and turn it into a health spa'. David looked at the decaying building, thought, 'These people are mad,' and did all he could to help them. Today, Stobo Castle is Peeblesshire's second biggest employer. Then, when it was still in its infancy, Stephen offered us several days of privacy and luxury: it was the kind of thoughtful gesture that we have come to know, over the years, is so typical of him.

During his time off, David made three visits to the by-election in nearby Penrith for Michael Young, our candidate, and, as Rector of Edinburgh University, he had duties to carry out for the celebrations of its 400th anniversary. This would be his first public appearance since the announcement of his 'sabbatical', and we knew that the press would follow him. He didn't feel up to staying with anyone, and certainly not to commuting up and down the A7 all week. I hit on an idea: as Rector, he had an office in my old stamping-ground of Buccleuch Place. We brought up a mattress and bedding, and stayed there on the office floor. It turned out to be wonderfully private, and more than a touch mysterious. Many of our own University contemporaries came back to Edinburgh for the tercentenary: unlike us, they had not seen the changes to the University over the years. 'I went to the Common Room, and it wasn't there!' mourned Joanna Lees, back from the USA. The Rector's private party for his friends was not a sophisticated event in the Raeburn Room, but a student-like 'thrash' in Buccleuch Place.

My father and Auntie G, as former graduates sixty years and more ago, came to one of the events. It would be their last outing together. In September, my father was diagnosed with cancer of the oesophagus, and he died a few weeks later. He managed to come home from hospital, which was what he wanted, and we sisters went to and fro in relays to help him, while our stepmother fluttered around uselessly and complained about the doctor. At the end, it was I who was with him holding his hand as he made that final journey into the unknown, one of the greatest privileges of my life.

Coming out of Dunblane Cathedral at his funeral, one of his forestry colleagues said, 'He left a lot of good trees behind.' Whether it was the trees he'd planted that he meant, or the dozen grandchildren standing in the front pews with their parents, I wasn't sure. But it seemed a good epitaph.

*Maria Stevenson, who married my grandfather William MacGregor and became our Granny MacGregor.*

*My Orcadian grandparents Peter Stevenson and Annie Fotheringhame, with their youngest son Tommy, who 'took a train to Glasgow one day and never came back'.*

*Gladys MacGregor, our 'Auntie G', on her graduation from Edinburgh University.*

*Left: My Mother, Anne Dyce, in the 1920s, with her newly bobbed hair.*
*Right: My father, Douglas MacGregor, in his twenties*

*My parents' wedding, Oxford, June 1927. My parents are on the right of the front row;*
*Granny MacGregor is on the left in the third row, my Dyce grandmother and Auntie G*
*are on the left in the second row.*

*My parents in Nigeria during the 1930s.*

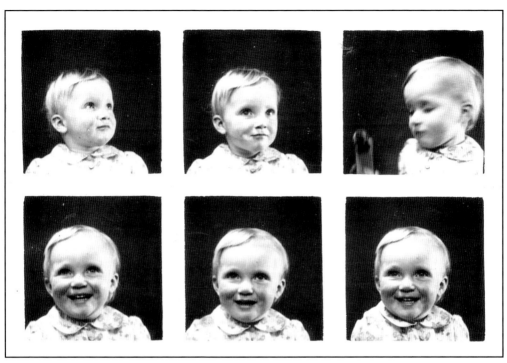

*Me as a baby.*

*Left: Family group in Dollar, 1944. Alison (holding Ginger the dog), Fay, Mummy, self, Joan. Right: Me, aged about three.*

*The MacGregor girls, 1946. Left to right, Alison, Fay, self, Joan.*

*Aged six, outside Abercromby Place Garden opposite Auntie G's house.*

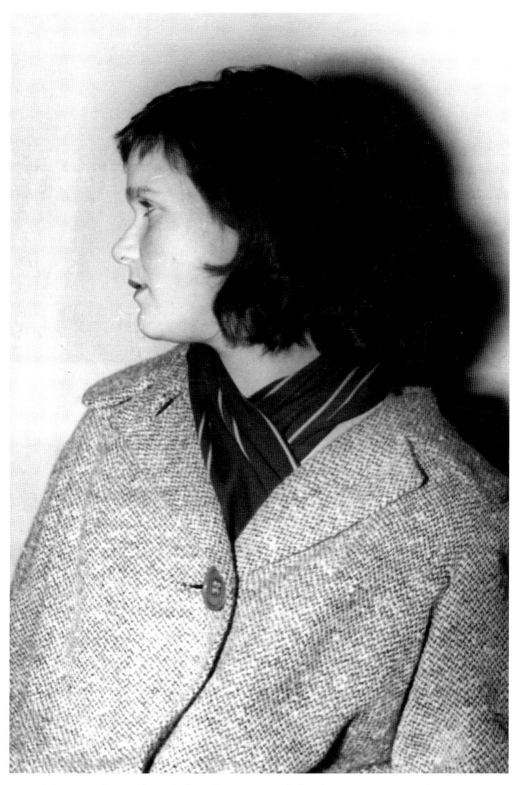

*This was taken at the end of my first term at Edinburgh University, December 1958.*

*Our wedding at Dunblane Cathedral. Right to left: David's parents, Michael Shea, Jacqueline Pirie, my niece Mary Duff, the happy couple, David's brother Michael, Norah Lynne Carruthers, my parents.*

*Making our way down Jedburgh High Street after David's by-election victory, March 1965.*

*Outside Jedburgh Town Hall after the October 1974 General Election.*

*Our young family: Graeme, Catriona and Rory as a newborn, June 1973.*

*June 1976. This photo of us in Ettrick Bridge was taken during David's campaign for the Liberal Leadership. Our lives would change radically.*

*I made the dolls' house, a model of Cherrydene, for Catriona's fifth birthday.*

*The Leader's wife, campaigning in his constituency during the 1979 election.*
*(Photo credit: Jane Bowen)*

*The cork wall and the one-shilling table in the kitchen at Cherrydene, late 1970s.*

*Fording the Ettrick at Selkirk Common Riding, 1978. Rory, at five, was the youngest rider.*

*(mrs) Gladys Prickle preparing a meal in the Aikwood kitchen while Graeme acts as butler.*

*The Rowan Tree Company touring van – complete with rowan tree! – in autumn 1987.*

*A production shot from Rowan Tree's award-winning* The Lasses, O, *2009. From left:*
*Seylan Baxter, Lilias Kinsman Blake, Gerda Stevenson and Rachel Newton.*
*(Photo credit: Andrew Wilson.)*

*Catriona's Hindu wedding to Rajiv Bhatia, December 1992. They had already been married in the church in Ettrick Bridge that June.*

*Getting in the mood of 'Scott's Selkirk', Christmas 2001 (Photo credit: Rob Gray)*

*Making the Christmas pudding with the grandchildren, 2002. Left to right: Persia, Hannah, India, Catriona, self, Caledonia and David. Not in photo: James. Not yet born: Rio. (Photo credit: Bertrand Rieger.)*

*The Granny with the Jaguar Tattoo, 2010. (Picture credit: Brendan McNeill.)*

# 19

# *The Ettrick Shepherd*

On the tenth anniversary of David's election, the committee of the Hawick Liberal Club asked me to suggest a present for him. 'I saw two volumes of the *Collected Works of the Ettrick Shepherd* in the antique shop along the road recently,' I said, 'that might be nice, if they've not been sold.' And so they bought them, and presented them, but it was me on whom they made the most impact.

For those who know little about the Ettrick Shepherd, as the writer James Hogg liked to be known, I should give a brief biography, for he was to play a major part in my life from the mid-eighties onwards.

James Hogg was born at the head of the Ettrick Valley, about sixteen miles from Selkirk, of a farming family that had fallen on hard times. The date of his birth is unknown. Hogg himself believed it to have been on 25 January 1772 – thus sharing a birthday with Robert Burns. Late in life, he saw the entry for his baptism in the parish records: it was 9 January 1771, so that he had been born either within that year, or at the end of the previous one.

At the age of six he enrolled at the parish school in Ettrick, which, to the credit of the Scottish Borders Council, still exists despite a puny roll. It is a good dozen miles from Ettrick Bridge, and many of the farms from which its pupils are drawn are more remote still. Hogg's attendance there was brief: within a year, family circumstances forced him to leave and start work as a cowherd – the lowliest rung of the farming ladder. His wages were five shillings (25p) a year, and a pair of boots.

But despite his lack of formal learning, he was the inheritor of a different kind of knowledge. His mother, Margaret Laidlaw, was reckoned to be the best teller of ballads in the valley, and his uncle too was a renowned storyteller, both of history – especially the dark times of the Covenanters – and of the legends of the countryside. And his grandfather was the 'far-famed' Will of Phaup, who, as his tombstone relates, in the words of his grandson, 'for feats of frolic, agility and strength had no equal in his day.' He also claimed to be the last man to have seen the fairies in the Ettrick Valley – at Carterhaugh, near Bowhill, scene of one of the greatest of the Border Ballads, *Tamlane*.

As well as this inheritance, there was the religious legacy of Ettrick Parish. Throughout the eighteenth century it had been served by the Rev. Thomas Boston and his son. Boston Senior was an evangelical preacher who could draw congregations of several hundred to his sermons – an amazing phenomenon in such a remote place. His *Sermons* were published, and the rigid Calvinist doctrines they preached became influential both in Holland and in the United States. His parishioners may have worn his views more lightly, as they held them alongside their concurrent beliefs in fairies and brownies; but it meant that the adults among whom Hogg grew up had listened to sermons imbued with theology of the most rigorously intellectual kind.

The progress of Hogg's farming career drew him down the valley, to Singlie Farm, where he learned to read and write under the tutelage of a fellow herd, and to play the fiddle. In his late teens he became shepherd at the remote Yarrow farm of Blackhouse. There, the Laidlaw family who farmed it encouraged his literary aspirations, opened their library to him, and their sons, William and Alexander Laidlaw, became his lifelong friends.

At social gatherings on the valley farms, Hogg became known as 'Jamie the Poeter' because he made songs and verses for the young men and women there, who were themselves steeped in a tradition of music and song. His first printed piece appeared, anonymously, in the *Scots Magazine*. *The Mistakes of a Night* recounts the sexual adventures of a local lothario who finishes up being forced to marry the mother of his inamorata. Then, on a hillside in Yarrow, another farm servant recited to Hogg the whole of Robert Burns' great poem, *Tam o' Shanter*. It is an amazing demonstration of the isolation of the valleys that Hogg had never heard of Burns, and by his own account, when he learned that the poet had died the previous year, he wept. Nevertheless, he determined that, 'If a ploughman could be a poet, so could a shepherd.' He now had ambitions beyond his native valleys.

There was another young man, the same age as James Hogg, with another ambition – to collect the old Border ballads and thus, so he believed, save them from extinction. He was Walter Scott, the newly appointed Sheriff of Selkirkshire. It was almost inevitable that he should hear of Hogg and of his mother, and he set out to meet them. The paths of the two young men were to run side by side until the end of their lives. It is a relationship in which Scott is always portrayed as the patron, and Hogg as the recipient of patronage, but at the time of their first meeting, Scott was not the Wizard of the North, the best-selling poet and novelist, the Great Unknown, the most eminent Scotsman of his day. He was simply a young lawyer and antiquarian enthusiast, who was seeking to collect the oral traditions inherited by Hogg. In that situation, Hogg was the giver and Scott the beneficiary.

Nevertheless, the acquaintance and then friendship with Scott was of great benefit to Hogg. It widened his world immeasurably, and when Scott's third volume of the *Minstrelsy of the Scottish Border* contained several original ballads by its editor, Hogg was spurred into print himself. During the first decade of the nineteenth century he tried to find a balance between his writing and farming careers, in Ettrick and in Dumfriesshire. The farming ventures met with as many failures as his father's had before him, and when I first became interested in Hogg, there were still many in the Ettrick Valley who talked about this, rather than his writing.

In 1810, Hogg took himself off to Edinburgh to try to make a living as a writer, despite Scott's dictum that 'literature is a good staff, but an ill crutch'. He threw himself into producing a magazine, *The Spy* (it was the era of *Blackwood's Magazine* and *The Edinburgh Review*). His robust countryman's writing style was too much for the sensitivities of potential subscribers in Edinburgh's drawing rooms, and *The Spy* failed. But with the publication of his long poem, *The Queen's Wake*, in 1813, the recognition as a poet for which he longed was assured.

Its structure may have been borrowed slightly from Scott's *Lay of the Last Minstrel*, in which the eponymous bard entertains Anne, the first Duchess of Buccleuch, with a long ballad about the exploits of her ancestors. In *The Queen's Wake*, Hogg imagined Mary, Queen of Scots, summoning the bards of Scotland to a ballad-making competition at Holyrood Palace.

Although the whole poem with its various ballads was highly praised, it was in particular the thirteenth bard's song that lifted Hogg to pre-eminence. *Kilmeny* is the story of a young girl who goes missing, and, like Thomas the Rhymer, returns after seven years with the gift of prophecy. There was a time when nearly all Border schoolchildren, and many in other parts of Scotland, had to learn at any rate part of it:

> Bonny Kilmeny gaed up the glen,
> But it wasnae to meet Duneira's men,
> Nor the rosy monk of the isle to see,
> For Kilmeny was pure as pure could be.

It was only to hear the yorlin sing,
And pull the cress-flower round the spring,
The scarlet hip and the hindberry,
And the nut that hung from the hazel tree,
For Kilmeny was pure as pure could be.
But lang may her minny look owre the wa',
And lang may she seek the greenwood shaw,
Lang, the laird o' Duneira blame,
And lang, lang greet or Kilmeny cam hame.

It was his greatest success during his lifetime. Writing never made him enough of an income to marry, but in 1820 his situation was improved by the grant to him by the young Duke of Buccleuch, rent-free, of the farm of Altreive in the Yarrow Valley. He married his long-time sweetheart Margaret Phillips, daughter of a prosperous Dumfriesshire farmer, and they settled down to happy family life, combining farming and writing.

Alas, farming misadventures followed him like the most faithful of sheepdogs. This time it was not his farm that failed, but that of his parents-in-law. He handed Altreive over to them while he took on the much less profitable neighbouring farm of Mountbenger at a lease he could not afford. But it was during this time that he wrote the work for which he later became best remembered: *The Private Memoirs and Confessions of a Justified Sinner*, a dark psychological novel of Calvinist predestination and divided personality. In any modern list of the most important Scottish novels of all time, you will find it near the top. And the central belief of its anti-hero, Robert Wringham, that faith justifies any act and that God will save his elect, has an especially appropriate resonance to it in today's world of religious extremism.

The high reputation of this novel began, not in Hogg's own time, but in the following century. And its importance was pointed out, not by a fellow Scot, but by a Frenchman, André Gide, who was asked to write a foreword for an edition of it in the 1940s. This renowned novelist, recognising its essentially Scottish provenance, regarded the book as amongst the finest and the most troubling of any he had encountered.

Hogg died in 1835, a charismatic and idiosyncratic figure who in some ways outlived his time, the time of oral traditions and beliefs in a supernatural world, and yet in some ways was ahead of the time when his writing would be properly valued. His last published work was a series of essays, *Lay Sermons*, which could not have been further from Thomas Boston's fire-and-brimstone approach to life. This is a slightly adapted extract which I put into verse as part of the libretto for a short opera, and which we have subsequently given several times to friends for a reading at either weddings or funerals:

> Take a prospect of human life
> Through a vista of reason,
> And you will see
> It is a voyage to an undiscovered country.
> As we advance,
> Provisions wear out
> And the vessel turns crazy.
> But the voyage has begun
> And we should try to make its conclusion
> As happy and prosperous as we can.
> What better can we do
> Than choose true and honest companions
> And with all our skill
> Steer clear of the quicksands that would swallow us,
> Steer clear of the rocks that would dash us to pieces.
> Thus shall we enter the harbour with hope,
> And look back on the dangers we've escaped
> With pleasure and with exultation.

The *Collected Works* that were presented to David had been published to mark the centenary of Hogg's birth in 1770. Edited by a Victorian clergyman, they had been heavily cut to remove anything considered offensive at the time. When I suggested them as a gift from the Hawick Club, my knowledge of Hogg was scanty. I knew his statue at St Mary's Loch, the monument at his birthplace up the valley, and his grave in Ettrick kirkyard. I had learned his poem, 'A Boy's Song', at school in Aberdeen, and I understood its evocation of a country childhood.

> Where the pools are bright and deep,
> Where the grey trout lies asleep,
> Up the river and o'er the lea,
> That's the way for Billy and me.

Over the years I dipped into the Victorian volumes, with their tissue-thin pages, their double columns and their minuscule font. Despite these drawbacks, I found a lot to enjoy and admire, even though the scalpel of

Victorian respectability had sliced out much of the liveliest work. Not much from *The Spy* found its way into those pages, and *Confessions* was toned down: even the words 'Justified Sinner' were changed to 'Fanatic'. Hogg's romping novel *The Three Perils of Man* (they were war, women and witchcraft, the latter taking place at Aikwood Tower) fared as badly as *The Siege of Roxburgh*. All allusions to witchcraft and sex were obliterated by the Rev. Thomson's literary – or rather moral – red pen.

Gide's championing of Hogg's genius was the beginning of a resurgence of interest in his writings. But it was the work of a more recent generation of scholars, led by the late Douglas Mack of Stirling University, who, from the 1980s onwards, worked tirelessly to bring this novel and Hogg's other works the attention that they deserved. Among those influenced was the playwright Stuart Paterson.

In 1983, I read in the *Scotsman* that the Glasgow theatre company, TAG, was touring Paterson's adaptation of *Confessions of a Justified Sinner* to schools and communities around Glasgow and the Lothians. I phoned their office. 'Why aren't you bringing it to the Borders? To James Hogg's own countryside?' I asked.

'Because we haven't been asked to.'

'I'm asking you.'

'There's such a thing as a fee . . .'

They gave me a contact at the Scottish Arts Council, and thus I began to learn about theatre funding. Since there was no interest from any of the local authorities, and there were no theatres, the Arts Council offered, as a complete one-off, to give me and a like-minded friend near Kelso personal guarantees against loss to promote two performances of the play in halls in Kelso and Selkirk. This took me further into Hogg's world, and into the world of theatre.

TAG carried out an audience survey and sent me the Selkirk results. To the question 'Why did you decide to come to the play?' by far the majority ringed the answer, 'The subject matter'. I realised that there was an interest in Hogg ready to be tapped, and by this time I was beginning to discover the many sides to his writing and to his character. It was approaching the 150th anniversary of his death, and I found myself among a group of people in the village hall called together to plan how to mark this.

'A Hogg Supper,' 'An exhibition,' 'A concert,' were some of the suggestions. Tentatively, I put forward the idea of a festival.

'But who would come to it? Who would be interested? Nobody has heard of him outside the valley,' was the general response, but I got the go-ahead to pursue the idea. Key to my plans was the support of the newly-appointed director of sports and leisure for Ettrick and Lauderdale District Council, Ian Yates. I was entering, seriously, the world of the arts, and some of my ideas were both idiosyncratic and innovative, although I didn't think of them as that. Ian Yates, newly arrived from an English local authority, backed them all to the hilt. 'We can do a Hogg Festival as a one-off,' we agreed. 'If it doesn't work, we leave it as a one-off. If it does, we can look at having an arts festival in the Borders on a regular basis.'

By now I had done enough research on Hogg to realise how multi-faceted was his genius. Unlike Scott, he was also a musician, playing both the fiddle and the flute, and a composer of song tunes as well as verses. Unlike Burns, he was a prose writer as well as a poet. He had even tried his hand as a playwright, although none of his *Dramatic Tales* had ever been performed. Surely, some of his stories, like *Confessions,* could be turned into theatre, and surely his own life story could be the subject for a solo play?

At the Traverse, I had seen a solo play about the life of James Miranda Barry, the nineteenth century army surgeon who, on death, was discovered to be a woman – thus being the first female medical graduate from Edinburgh University. The playwright, Frederic Mohr, had used the possibility that she was the illegitimate daughter of an Irish adventuress who had come to London and moved in enlightened circles, and that, in her determination to become a doctor, Barry had given up both her Catholic religion and her womanhood, both of which barred students from English universities. I was transfixed, not just by the subject and by the performance of the brilliant young actress, Gerda Stevenson, but by the intimacy and immediacy of the form. I ran a fund-raising function for the Traverse, a one-off performance of *Barry*, at Surgeons' Hall, with a Victorian buffet – an early example of the now fashionable site-specific theatre in its own way. The interval ice-cream was served – on saucers – among the grisly exhibits in the Surgeons' museum.

Some years before, David and I had gone to the vast Victoria Hall in Selkirk, where 400 chairs were laid out for the audience to watch the wonderful Scottish actor Russell Hunter perform *Cocky,* his award-winning show about the nineteenth-century judge, Lord Cockburn. We were two of fourteen in that hall, which is filled night after night every February for performances of the local Amateur Operatic Society. We felt ashamed that so few had turned out, but also realised how much the size of the venue detracted from the production. Now I could see how a tiny space could add to the audience experience. Always attracted to the small-scale – the dolls' house was the supreme example of this – I had found a theatre form that appealed greatly to me.

I discussed with Peter Lichtenfels, the artistic director of the Traverse, the possibility of commissioning Frederic Mohr to give Hogg the same treatment. Mohr's first essay into writing had been *Bozzy*, based on the life of James Boswell, whom he had played himself under his actor's name of David McKail. Directed by the young director John Carnegie, it was a huge success. Later, the same writing and directing team also produced similar gems about John Paul Jones, the Dumfriesshire-born founder of the American Navy, and the eighteenth-century actress, Charlotte Sharke.

But Traverse productions were very firmly based in the old Grass-market, and since a festival based around Hogg would need to be in the Borders, the play would need to be toured there. At the time, the Scottish Arts Council would not countenance funding a tour of less than three weeks. With a mixture of boldness and ignorance, I made arrange-ments for *Hogg* to be seen, not only in village halls, but in such places as Tibbie Shiels Inn, James Hogg's own favourite hostelry at the head of St Mary's Loch; in Walter Scott's courtroom; and in the dining room of the Tontine Hotel in Peebles where Hogg had addressed a dinner in his honour.

I scratched around for sponsorship as well as public funding. Much of it was small-scale, firms agreeing to put up a few hundred pounds to sup-port a performance in their own community. From Buccleuch Estates, I was loaned a couple of holiday cottages for accommodation; from a garage in Broughton, a vehicle was lent. The telephone and petrol bills at Cherrydene shot up. I didn't really know what I was getting myself into, and I was learning on the hoof.

From New Zealand, Hogg's great-granddaughter, Norah Parr, announced her intention to come across to the academic conference on her ancestor that Douglas Mack was organising, and to stay on for the opening events of the Festival. 'My father donated Hogg's fiddle to Edinburgh University,' she wrote to me. 'Why not see if you can get it put back into playing condition?'

I approached the curator of the university's collection of historic instruments about it. He told me firmly that the fiddle, although a good one, had no real value in terms of the collection, which was intended to chart the development of different musical instruments: it was of curios-ity value only. And while he was willing to lend it for the exhibition that was to take place in Selkirk over the summer, he certainly had no budget to make it fit to play.

So I turned to the public relations department, which we had got to know well over David's period as rector. 'Wouldn't it be good publicity for the University,' I suggested to their PR director, 'if the fiddle was restored?'

He jumped at the idea, had it paid for out of his own budget, and in due course the restored fiddle was featured prominently in the *Scotsman* with its restorer Gordon Stevenson, Norah Parr, and the violinist, Leonard Friedman, who was to play it at a couple of concerts.

Readings of Hogg's poems and stories took place at various pubs around the valleys, and at the Gordon Arms in Yarrow, Gerda Stevenson and the actor Paul Young read the letters between him and Margaret Hogg. There was a concert in Yarrow Kirk where he'd been an elder, and I roped a couple of galleries into running Hogg-related art exhibitions. I also asked Kedzie Penfield to create a dance piece based on the words of Hogg's *Kilmeny*, with clarsach music by Elspeth Smellie and a heavily edited version of the poem read by the young actor/director, Lloyd Quinan, and danced by the actress Leigh Biagi. The publishing house Canongate agreed to my editing an introductory selection of Hogg's works, including poetry, fiction, letters and even some journalism.

In the midst of all this, I also had my baptism as a playwright, with my treatment of a short story of Hogg's, *The Witches of Traquair*. It had a professional cast, creative and technical teams, and groups of local children were trained up as well. Like the solo play, it toured throughout the Borders. I have to say that in retrospect it was not a good piece of work: I knew too little of the craft, and I stuck too slavishly to the original story. But I learned about production and touring on my feet, greatly aided by a superb stage manager, Scott Anderson, who is now director of the drama programme at Queen Margaret University. I have had lasting and profound respect for the profession of stage management ever since. We had some city/country misunderstandings. When Scottie said he was going to B&Q to buy some timber, I thought that he was heading for the sawmill at Bowhill, part of the Buccleuch and Queensberry estates.

With the benefit of hindsight I can see it was a wildly over-ambitious festival, running over the entire month of October and throughout the whole of the Borders. Yet somehow it held together, and gave me belief in my capabilities – and that I could realise some kind of vision. And it left me with alliances and friendships that have lasted since that time, especially with Scottie Anderson, with the actor, Donald Douglas, who played the Ettrick Shepherd in the Traverse production, with a young schoolteacher from Selkirk, John Nichol, cast as an autobiographical character in an amateur production of a short sketch by Hogg, and with Janice Parker, who had recently been appointed dance therapist at Dingleton Hospital, and shortly afterwards came to live in Ettrick Bridge.

## 20

# Myths, Ballads and Rowan Trees

The twentieth anniversary of David's election came and went. It was marked, first of all, by our collaboration on a book, *David Steel's Border Country*. The collaboration meant that I did all of the research and most of the writing, while David did some of the writing and all of the marketing. There was also a frightful celebratory dinner organised by David's constituency agent. It was held in the cheerless surroundings of Galashiels Academy's assembly hall, and the meal might have been prepared and served by the school dinner service, pre-Jamie Oliver. The speeches started late and there were far too many of them. Peter Hellyer, who was driving Jo Grimond, managed to crash the car loaned by our friendly local garage. They weren't hurt, but the chief guest arrived late, and not in the best humour. I vowed that in five years' time I would take over the running of the next significant anniversary dinner.

The dual leadership with David Owen had its strains over the course of the parliament: the 1987 election was to test their relationship to its frail limits. Where, with Roy Jenkins, there had been mutual trust and respect, and minds working together, Owen from the start had made no effort to disguise his disdain for Liberals. Socially we got on well with the Owens, particularly at a weekend in their country house near Hungerford with their children and Rory.

As well as their strategic differences, how the two Davids were respectively portrayed by the media did not make things easy. Owen was their darling; Steel was definitely on the wane as far as they were concerned. It was his third election as a party leader, and I learned that this is one too many for an opposition party leader's shelf-life.

In that relationship, David was almost fatally wounded as a political figure by the representation of him week after week on the satirical TV programme *Spitting Image* as the puppet in Owen's pocket. The caricature was well short of the truth, but it was what people saw, and what they believed. I could hardly bear to watch it, and often left the room:

David always sat through it. I suppose he needed to know what they were saying, and his marvellous, resilient humour even allowed him to see the funny side. But for me, loving him, and knowing his political toughness and determination, it was deeply wounding to see him so ridiculed. However, when I too was given a puppet, I rather liked it: she had a strong Scots accent and spent all her time knitting and soothing.

The print press, cartoonists and commentators alike, followed where *Spitting Image* had led, and comparisons, not just between the two Davids, but between the Steel family and the glamorous Owens appeared in them. I was especially unfavourably contrasted with Debbie, the slim metropolitan wife who was a successful literary agent, while I was a frowsy careerless bumpkin. As my self esteem shrank – and, at the same time, my figure ballooned – I found that interviews, especially by women journalists, which I used to be able to take in my stride, became more than I could handle. 'Never let a journalist over your doorstep,' said Ro Kirkwood, and she never did so. Maybe she was right. They commented negatively on my kitchen, my house, my appearance, my mothering capacity, my lack of a career. I never told them about the arts work that I was doing: they would have dismissed it as 'amateur dramatics', and not understood its subtleties or what it was all about.

Some strange incidents relating to the press coverage had occurred over the years. One night, David phoned me in a state of some distress and confusion. 'I think I've been set up,' he said. He had been at a reception, and a voluptuous would-be starlet had made her way towards him, grabbed him, and then tripped him up. As they fell to the floor, she held on to him, and, worse still, her bosoms popped out of their scanty moorings. 'There were photographers there,' he said, ' and I got the feeling that they had been tipped off that something like this was going to happen. I'm afraid it'll be all over the papers tomorrow.' It was, and it portrayed him as both undignified and lecherous. But who would want to set up such a scenario, and why? In the end we decided that he had simply been the victim of a self-publicity stunt by the woman involved – but the fact that he was on his own in London made him an easy target.

On another occasion I came to the front door at Cherrydene to find a reporter from the *Daily Mail*. 'You'll probably guess what I've come about,' he said, by way of introduction.

I cast my mind around. 'No, I'm sorry. What is it?'

He shifted his feet uncomfortably. Eventually he said, 'It's been reported that your marriage is in trouble.'

I was flummoxed, and horrified. He continued. 'At the opening of the dolls' houses exhibition in Edinburgh you had a violent row. And then you went into the Canongate Kirk for a reconciliation.'

I remembered the incident. I had been asked to lend my model of Cherrydene for an exhibition of dolls' houses. With my own reproductions of our furniture, and the tiny figures of the family made by Ann Carrick, it proved the hit of the exhibition right from the beginning, despite much more intricate and priceless models being on show. The children who came to the museum over the weeks that it was there nearly all voted Cherrydene their favourite, mostly because 'it really looked like a home'. David had come to the opening, and had been photographed with the dolls' house. I put on a show of offence that he, and not I, the maker of the house, had been singled out for attention. 'Well,' I said, 'I did make a fuss, but it was all really a bit of a joke.'

'And the Canongate Kirk?'

'We went there for *a cup of tea*. It was the nearest place we could get one. You said there was another incident?'

'Yes, you were invited to a lunch party in the Borders and you didn't turn up.'

I racked my brains. 'That's awful. I can't even remember it! Let me get my diary.'

I fetched it and flicked through the pages. None of them gave me a clue as to where, and with whom, we had committed this social solecism, and to this day it remains unsolved. But the reporter was satisfied that the incidents that had been fed to him did not add up to another failed political marriage, and he departed apologising.

But someone had been watching us, had made mountains out of these trivial happenings in our lives – and tried to weave together a story from them. I never found out who it was, but was sure that it came from Edinburgh, not the Borders. It was in stark contrast to the loyalty and reticence of our neighbours in the village. On another occasion, a journalist went into the Cross Keys, then owned by a couple who had not been there long, and whom we did not know well, chasing a story about one of the boys.

As he pressed his enquiries with the publican, the latter said, 'I'm afraid I'll have to ask you to leave my pub.'

His visitor reached into his pocket. 'Would it make any difference if I showed you my cheque book?'

'Yes, it would make one – the difference is that you can leave my pub *right now*.'

And when Graeme was hitting headlines for a misdemeanour that had landed him in court, a reporter from the *Sun* managed to track down an old school friend of his. This young man was unemployed and had just moved in with a new partner who had a couple of children by a previous relationship. The financial inducement offered by the tabloid journalist would have made a real difference to his circumstances at the time. As he steadfastly refused it, the journalist admitted that he simply could not understand the Borderers, and their concepts of loyalty and honour.

On the eve of the 1987 election, David phoned me from London. The press were in full cry: there was a story going around that he was having an affair with a friend of ours, Ming's wife, Elspeth Campbell. The rumour had, apparently, started at the Scottish Tory conference. I was to fend off any press representatives who arrived on the doorstep, and to warn Rory, who was at school in Edinburgh, about what might appear in tomorrow's papers. When I told him, he burst into laughter at the idea.

Needless to say, the rumours appeared, along with a photograph of David and our friend, side by side at 'a social function'. It had been Ming's constituency dinner, and both he and I had been in the original photo, which had been cropped to make the story more convincing. In the original, the supposedly errant couple had been flanked by their respective spouses: now they were made to look like an item. An especially unflattering photo of me looking like a fish out of water at a London event went side by side with it.

It was obvious that the story had been timed for the start of the election campaign, to cause maximum disruption, and dealing with it had the effect of diverting David's attention from the campaign for several precious days, as he instructed lawyers to issue injunctions and then prepare libel cases. Meantime, I went to the meeting launching Ming's campaign in East Fife, and spoke for him, presenting him with a rosette and ending with the customary Border Common Riding salutation of 'Safe oot, Safe in'.

It was an unhappy start to the campaign. In the Borders, I felt badly cut off from David, more than ever before, and Peter Hellyer's companionship and support was crucial to keep me going.

Another phone call came from David, far away in the South West of England, which caused a bit of disharmony on the matrimonial front. 'The North Cornwall Liberals are presenting me with a Labrador puppy tomorrow,' he said excitedly. Our old Labrador, Jill, was beginning to fail. We had not discussed what would happen after she died, but David had been thinking of a replacement for her in due course, both as a house pet and as a shooting partner. In contrast I felt that the chapter of our lives that was filled with children, ponies and a dog was drawing to a close, and fond as I was of Jill, I wanted to be free of the ties that a dog imposes when, in the foreseeable future, she died.

'But I don't want another dog! We've never discussed it!' I protested.

'It's all set up,' said David. 'The hand-over is taking place tomorrow, and it's almost guaranteed to make a top slot on the one o'clock news.'

In vain I continued to protest. I felt as though I was having an unwanted pregnancy, and I threatened, if the press asked me what the dog was to be called, I would say 'Rinka', in memory of Norman Scott's dog that was shot in the scandal that brought down Jeremy Thorpe.

'Just see how you get on with it over the summer,' pleaded David. He was, I knew, convinced that I would fall for the puppy – which turned out not to be a Labrador, but a Flat-coat Retriever, and was named Lucy after Catriona's best friend. I remained immovable, and eventually we came to an arrangement that Graeme and his partner Lynne looked after her while David was away, and he would pick her up from their cottage in the hills when he came home at weekends or recesses. Only when Lucy in turn was old and getting incontinent did I soften – mainly because it was hard on Lynne to have a soiling dog among three children – and I agreed to take her full time.

The campaign of 1987 stuttered on. Each day the media nitpicked their way through the utterances of the two Davids to find contradictions. Unlike Roy Jenkins and David Owen, David went through two elections with the system of the dual leadership. It was severely tested in different ways on both occasions – and in between – and he could see that it was not possible for the two parties to go on as they were.

The election was not nearly as successful as 1983: seats were lost, and in particular those of Roy Jenkins and Bill Rodgers. The SDP were down to only five MPs; the Liberals dropped from nineteen to seventeen. Even election day itself had a couple of unpropitious moments. When David looked out of the bedroom window, he saw our old horse, Hamlet, lying on the grass, his legs stuck out beside him. 'Oh, no,' he thought, 'the horse has died – what a field day the press will have.' Then, to his relief, he saw the horse clamber to his feet. And as we went into the count – this time in the austere, characterless surroundings of Galashiels Academy – I slipped on a wet floor and went down flat on my face. I was shaken, but relieved that the fall had taken place just outside the public arena of the hall, and not inside it.

Once again, we returned to Cherrydene in the light early hours of June. But this time it was raining, and there was no impromptu champagne to celebrate David and Archy's local victories. On ITV, Alistair Stewart, as linkman, said: 'And now it's over to Michael MacMillan at Ettrick Bridge, of which I have so many happy memories. Michael, how is it there?' And the picture switched to a bad-tempered-looking MacMillan, standing on the Cherrydene porch with his umbrella up, in the pouring rain.

Some time later the phone went. It was my sister Fay, from East Fife. 'Isn't it a wonderful night?' she asked exultantly. For her and for the Liberals of East Fife, who had laboured so long to achieve Ming Campbell's election, it certainly was. For us, clustered around the leader, looking at the national picture, it was difficult to feel the same. When the last result came in, there was another little fillip: Ray Michie, nee Ray Bannerman, had won Argyll and Bute from the Tories. The great-hearted John Bannerman's daughter had made it to the House of Commons.

As usual, we returned from the count with the dawn. A couple of hours later, at six o'clock, with none of us having slept, Catriona and Rory changed into their riding clothes and we went down to Selkirk, where they picked up hired horses and set off behind the Standard Bearer for Selkirk Common Riding. The ITV team were mesmerised by the glorious sights and sounds, and their coverage of the Liberal leader on the day after the 1987 election was interspersed with images of happy crowds, of bands and flags, and of a magnificent procession of men and women on horseback.

This time there was no hesitation and no doubt in David's mind as to the right course to take for the future of the Alliance, and he acted decisively and quickly. In a conversation with David Owen as the results came in, he stressed the need to get the two parties together – and by that he meant a merger. Owen went public opposing such a move; and within a few days David had issued a well-argued statement setting out his own reasons for believing that a merger of the two parties was the correct course. He was articulating the will of both sets of supporters.

The rest of the year was taken up with political infighting, positioning and manoeuvring. At their respective conferences, both parties voted for merger – the SDP by a handsome margin, the Liberals by an overwhelming one. David Owen had totally misjudged the mood of his party members, and resigned as SDP leader.

Meantime, I turned my attention to cultural matters.

Once the Hogg Festival was over, Ian Yates and I had met to see where we could go from there. He was enthusiastic about holding a regular arts festival; I was keen that we should exploit the rich seam of ballads, legends, history and literature of the Borders in programming this. We agreed that it should be on a biennial basis; that so far as possible projects should be home-grown, but the main elements should be professional, not amateur. We agreed, also, that the Borders-wide format had worked well, and that we should repeat this. The idea of going round the village halls was in part founded on my experience of going round the different villages and towns during elections, and recognised that the Borders was the sum of small parts, not an area with a natural centre to it. It was, perhaps, the first example of the shape of an arts festival being influenced by a political campaign.

Ian Yates and I set up a company with a proper board and constitution this time: it was called the Borders Festival of Ballads and Legends. We approached various people to come on the board. John Smail, editor of the *Southern Reporter*, agreed to be chairman, and also on the board were Walter Elliot and Flora Maxwell Stuart. In planning the programme, among the items I brought in were three or four performances by a company called Theatre Alba, of a play by Edward Stiven based on the old Border ballad, *Tamlane*. It was the only company working exclusively in Scots, albeit of a rather contrived kind. The ballad tells how a feisty girl, Janet, defies advice and goes to meet the mysterious Tamlane at Carterhaugh, near Selkirk in the Ettrick Valley. When she becomes pregnant as a result of this encounter, she goes back to find him, but he tells her that he is under the power of the Queen of Elfland, and to win him back to the land of mortals, she must undergo various tests. He warns her:

> They'll turn me in your arms, Janet,
> An adder and a snake;
> But haud me fast, let me not pass,
> Gin ye wad by me maik.

> They'll turn me in your arms, Janet,
> An adder and an ask;
> They'll turn me in your arms, Janet,
> A bale that burns fast.

> They'll turn me in your arms, Janet,
> A red-hot gad o' airn;

But haud me fast, let not me pass,
For I'll do you no harm.

First dip me in a stand o' milk
And then in a stand o' water;
But haud me fast, let me not pass –
I'll be your bairn's father.

And next, they'll shape me in your arms,
A tod, but, and an eel;
But haud me fast, nor let me gang,
As you do love me weel.

They'll shape me in your arms, Janet,
A dove, but, and a swan;
And, last, they'll shape me in your arms
A mother-naked man;
Cast your green mantle over me –
I'll be myself again.

Janet is resolute, and wins her man, and the Queen of Elfland is left cursing them. It is a great ballad, and Janet's steadfastness throughout Tamlane's metamorphoses can be likened to the changes that partners in a marriage go through during its course. The play was to open the festival with an outdoor performance at Melrose Abbey, and I have to say that it was spectacular. A troop of local schoolchildren had been rehearsed to follow the Queen down the aisle of the Abbey: as they ran behind her, a flock of crows flew up from the ruins as though choreographed. Alas, the audience was not great. I had managed to time the event to coincide with a presentation by the community to the hugely popular head-teacher of Melrose Primary School on his retiral.

Once again, I planned to write a play myself. The year was the four hundredth anniversary of the execution of Mary, Queen of Scots. As David and I had cast around for an idea to follow up *Border Country*, someone had said, 'Why don't you do one on Mary Queen of Scots? After all, you've got the connection with Linlithgow, where she was born, and Jedburgh, where she nearly died.' We put the idea to our publisher, Weidenfeld, that we should write about the places – in Scotland only – associated with the ill-fated queen. The publishers liked it, I had done most of the research for it during 1986, and *Mary Stuart's Scotland* made its appearance in due course. But in the making of it, I lost most of my sympathy for Mary herself. When she had arrived in Scotland, the eighteen-year-old widowed queen of France as well as the Queen of Scots, it was her adopted country and not her native one that she knew and understood. Wisely, at first she leaned heavily on her elder, extremely capable half-brother James Stewart, who had led the Protestant Lords of the Congregation and overthrown Mary's mother, Mary of Guise, as Regent a few years earlier. So long as she worked alongside him, her reign was a success; it was when, infatuated, she threw his advice aside in order marry Darnley that her troubles began. From then on it was a downhill journey to Darnley's murder, another ill-judged marriage to the Earl of Bothwell, through her enforced abdication on Loch Leven, her flight to England and her eventual execution.

And yet, when you look at her times, what is always astonishing is the extreme youth of all the main players in her story. She herself was only twenty-five when she abdicated.

I warmed to the romantic figure of her third husband, the philandering but politically loyal Borderer, James Hepburn, Earl of Bothwell. I always had been taken with him, ever since reading two highly romantic novels about him. One of them, banned by my mother during my teens because of a mild account of Bothwell's rape of the Queen, was *The Gay Galliard* by Margaret Irwin. The adjective certainly was not descriptive of its subject's sexuality, and I recently saw it republished without the 'gay' in the title.

I had had the idea of writing a play about the other women in Bothwell's life: his early lovers and his wife. They were well-documented and all of them were resourceful women. But when I started researching, I never got beyond the first of his lovers, Janet Beaton, immortalised in Walter Scott's epic *The Lay of the Last Minstrel* as the Wizard Lady of Buccleuch.

In the standard biography of Bothwell, written in the 1930s, Janet is credited with having had five husbands and 'numerous lovers'. This gobbet of information has been repeated in every subsequent reference to Bothwell, including Lady Antonia Fraser's biography of Mary Queen of Scots. As I sat in the library of the Borders Council, going through a history of the family of Buccleuch, I found that Janet had had only three husbands, and the only recorded lovers were Bothwell and the man who became her third husband, Walter Scott of Buccleuch. And that she loved him greatly was beyond doubt. When he was murdered in an ongoing feud with the Kerr family, she pursued his murderers ('at the head of 200 Scotts, armed in war-like fashion' said the complaint against her) to the remote church on the hillside above St Mary's Loch, where she broke into the sanctified building and then burnt it.

So I wrote my play, *The Wizard Lady of Buccleuch*, about her, and the young red-haired actor/director Lloyd Quinan, whom I'd met during the Hogg festival, came to direct it. He was patient with me, and both constructive and respectful towards me as a writer. If I had sat in on all the rehearsals I would have learned a lot, but I was too busy with all the other elements of this over-ambitious festival that I'd conceived. There were several outdoor performances at historic sites of *Tamlane*, and a first ever production of James Hogg's gothic play, *All Hallow Eve*. And I had booked a very small show for very small village halls: a cycle of traditional stories called *The Bothy*, and performed by the actress Anne Lacey. It was to have five performances in all. I went to the village hall committees concerned, urging them to support the event when it came to them

But I was not the only person to have seen the theatrical potential of the anniversary of Mary Queen of Scots' execution. The most exciting theatre company in Scotland at that time was Communicado – and now, nearly thirty years on, it still has that same vigour and imagination. Its passionate and visionary director, Gerry Mulgrew, was not the product of any drama school. He was a French teacher, and then one day a touring production came to the school where he taught, and he knew: 'this is what I want to do'. He came through the ranks of community theatre and was not bound by conventions. His productions fused physicality and musicality with the spoken word, and he made magical images out of human bodies and simple props. In 1987, he commissioned the rising playwright Liz Lochhead to write a play about Mary. The result was *Mary Queen of Scots Had Her Head Chopped Off*, and it became a late twentieth-century classic.

Gerry Mulgrew cast Anne Lacey in the title part, which meant that the five performances of *The Bothy* in the Borders were now off her radar. At the time I learned this, I had in my hands the printer's proof of the programme, and I had made a commitment to the hall committees about the kind of show they could expect: a storytelling evening. There was nothing for it: I would have to put something similar together myself, there was no budget to do anything else. But I needed a name for it. Where, apart from a bothy, was a good setting for telling stories? Into my mind came the painting by Robert Herdman which had been on the cover of my Hogg anthology. *The Rowan Tree*, that was it. I altered the name on the programme proof and sent the corrections back to the printer. But what was The Rowan Tree going to consist of?

Also at the back of my mind was the popular Scottish song of the same title, sentimental perhaps, but with a lovely cycle to it, about the seasons of life as well as of the tree itself. That gave me my structure: childhood, courtship, maturity, old age, and I found stories and songs to fit this theme. But who would perform it, and who would help me on the production?

I found an actor and actress in Selkirk: one trained, one untrained. Carol Wightman, who had been to drama school, was now working in local radio; John Nichol was the young teacher who had caught my attention during the Hogg Festival. He was a 'natural', especially for this intimate style of performance, and his use of Scots was genuine and natural – unlike, alas, too many professional Scots actors. He brought with him a traditional musician, Ian Hardie, who was shortly to give up a legal career for full-time music. The stage management I found even closer to home: Janice Parker, who now lived in Ettrick Bridge, had technical experience from the Edinburgh Fringe. I designed the set myself, around Herdman's painting. It was complete with a live rowan tree, berries and all, and the company toured around the halls in our family Landliner caravanette.

The festival ended just before our silver wedding anniversary. We celebrated it with a jazz evening in the village hall, and a more staid lunch the following day for older friends and relatives. Then we took off to New England and Yale, where David had been booked to give the Chubb Fellowship lecture. It was a few days of relaxation and companionship, well away from the culture of the Borders and the internal politics of the Alliance. David would come back to more testing times as he steered the Liberal Party towards its merger with the SDP, and we were heading towards new chapters in our life together in more ways than one.

# 21
# New Challenges

*January, 1988*
The phone rings, and it is David, speaking from London where the final stages of the merger are being hammered out. He speaks in a voice I have never heard before; one of defeat, of despair. 'I don't think I'll still be leader by the end of the day,' he says. 'I don't think the merger's going to go ahead. I'll have to resign.'

After David Owen had resigned as their leader, Robert Maclennan had taken over. Although he was a Scottish MP, he was not one that I knew well. He had defeated George Mackie in 1966 in Caithness and Sutherland, where there were Maclennan family connections: it was an unlikely seat for Labour, but he had held it throughout six elections. And he was also an unusual figure in the Scottish Labour party – for a start, he was a barrister at the English bar, rather than an advocate at the Scottish one, let alone a former industrial worker or Trade Union official. He had a rather diffident manner in conversation, but could speak eloquently in public, and there was no mistaking his intellectual force. His brother David and his sister Elizabeth were both founding members of the great left-wing Scottish theatre company 7:84, and took part in the tour of John McGrath's iconic play which saw the company's birth, *The Cheviot, the Stag and the Black, Black Oil*. Bob had a wide cultural hinterland himself. In the future, he would start up the Northlands Festival in Caithness, which was very much based on the Borders example, and would write the libretto for an opera about Thomas Muir, the Scottish radical of the nineteenth century.

He had been one of only three Scottish MPs to break away from Labour to join the SDP. Both he and Charles Kennedy had held their seats comfortably in the 1987 election. Charles had always been in favour of merger; Bob had been more reluctant, but had accepted the decision of party members, and as by far the most senior of the SDP quintet remaining in the Commons, was the party's obvious leader.

The negotiations over the autumn had been cumbersome and tortuous, and often ill-tempered. Once the constitutional framework had been agreed, there was a demand from the SDP for a 'policy prospectus' for the new party, to be put to the special conferences to be called by both parties early in the New Year. Bob Maclennan, and the two young assistants who were to be charged with drafting it, came to Cherrydene for a discussion with David. Sandwiched among the political talk, Bob and I found time to discuss James Hogg, and *Confessions of a Justified Sinner.*

Christmas came and went. Bob went to spend New Year with relatives in America, and in early January David flew to Africa on a charity project with his friend Atul Vadher. It involved much travel, and as Atul couldn't drive, David had to do it all. He came back exhausted, rather than refreshed, in no shape to be thrown into the final stages of the negotiations. It was the policy document that caused the crisis, and it looked as though it was a breakdown that would throw away all the work and dedication and vision that had brought everyone so far. It was no wonder that David's voice held those tones of despair and utter tiredness.

'Do you want me to come down?' I said.

'Yes, please do.'

So, blessing spouse travel warrants, and abandoning a meeting of the Scottish Arts Council in Edinburgh and preparations for a Burns Night in the village hall, I flew to London. At Westminster, the first person I saw was Robert Maclennan. I bristled, and was filled with resentment at the sight of this decent man whose company I had always found so enjoyable. I passed a bitter remark to him and went in search of my husband. I found that the other Liberal MPs would not allow him to resign – 'You got us into this, you'd better see us through it,' – and the worst of the crisis had passed. But the policy document, although abandoned, found its way into the public domain. 'It's a dead parrot,' said David to the press, echoing a line from a Monty Python sketch, but the attempt at humour earned him no respite.

It had been a terrible week, and David felt humiliated and bruised. He could not even come home to lick his wounds: he had promised to propose the toast to the 'Immortal Memory' at a large and prestigious Burns Supper in Glasgow, sponsored by the radio station West Sound. It was the kind of Burns Supper I hate: a lot of formality, including full kilt outfits and long frocks, a far cry from the down to earth celebrations of the Bard that I had become used to in the Borders. We advanced like zombies into the tartan throng.

Among them was the Labour MP, George Foulkes, whose constituency was served by West Sound. George's time at Edinburgh University had overlapped slightly with ours, but we did not know him well. After that night, though, I will never forget the tact and understanding that he and his wife Liz showed towards us. George did not refrain from alluding to the political situation – I don't think anyone else there mentioned it, they just awkwardly skirted around it – but used words of sympathy and kindness, and made it his job to look after us throughout the long evening.

Early on the following Saturday morning I was on my way to Blackpool, to the conference at which the old Liberal Party would vote itself out of existence and into a permanent merger with the flashy Social Democrats. I was not with David, who had travelled from London, but in a bus with others from the constituency. It was a snowy, slushy journey, and Blackpool, when we arrived, looked especially tawdry and uninviting. Riddle Dumble, David's constituency agent, fussed around the passengers, and me especially, like an anxious hen.

In the hall, the atmosphere was electric, and the speeches rose to the occasion. The veteran Nancy Seear, leader of the party in the House of Lords, thundered out an especially trenchant contribution, making the opponents of the merger look naïve and ill-informed. The conference voted itself into the new age of the Social and Liberal Democrats by 2,099 votes to 385. But who would lead the party? Some felt that David, having been both its progenitor and midwife, should have the reward of being its first leader. We passed the first few months of the year in a state of uncertainty.

I found myself lunching with two of his closest parliamentary colleagues, David Alton and Archy Kirkwood. Alton was passionate in his support of David as leader of the new party. But Archy was very equivocal. He was always a canny operator, but on this occasion there was more than his habitual caution. I got the feeling that he had perhaps already pledged himself to Paddy Ashdown. I didn't mention this to David, however, when he asked my advice, as he always does at such moments, and usually I give it robustly. But this time I simply didn't know what he should do. He had earned the leadership of the new party, but thirteen years of driving towards this goal already had taken their toll, especially the later ones. He was still only 50, but he was tired.

David's birthday, on the last day of March, was two days after that of Maggi Hackett, and in 1988, their joint half-century, we went to celebrate with her and our respective families at the Hackett house in Wavre, in Belgium. Shortly after we returned, I had agreed to go with David to a State Banquet at Windsor Castle in honour of King Olav of Norway. David came to meet me at Heathrow and we went to the Windsor Liberal Club, where I changed into my posh frock in the toilets. Then David said, 'Before we go to the Castle, there's something I want to tell you.' He drove us down to the bank of the Thames. It was a lovely April evening: there were swans on the river, and even that great waterway seemed as much at peace as when Wordsworth had viewed it in the early morning from Westminster Bridge. It would have been a romantic setting for a proposal of marriage.

'I've decided,' he said, 'that I'm not going on. Someone else can take on the leadership, someone fresh and energetic.' A wave of relief and happiness swept through me. I think by now I had more than half-expected that this would be his decision, but I did not expect it to have that effect. I had thought myself more ambivalent, that I would have regrets. Instead, it felt like a renewal, an opening for new possibilities, whatever they might be – and already he had articulated one of them.

As I gazed down the long, lovely, candle-lit banqueting table at Windsor later that night, with its abundant flowers, its gleaming surface, its golden cutlery and crystal glasses holding the finest of wines, I looked at the faces of the crowned heads and the holders of high office. I thought that this would probably be the last of such occasions that I attended, and I was not really sorry. I would be seeing much more of David in the future.

We were, undoubtedly, middle-aged now, but it was not too late to embark on a totally new adventure – indeed, it was a good time to do it. That we were able to undertake the one we did, and fulfil a dream, was partly due to the steps that David had taken at the beginning of the 1987 election, when the story about his supposed adultery filled the tabloids. He had issued libel writs as well as injunctions: the newspapers involved, with the exception of the *Sun* and the *News of the World*, rapidly withdrew their allegations and apologised, but actions were still outstanding against those unrepentant two.

Then a libel action against the *News of the World* by Koo Stark, a former girlfriend of Prince Andrew's, came to court, and she was awarded swingeing damages by the jury. The newspapers' lawyers promptly decided to settle all outstanding cases against them: David's was one of them. For the first time in our lives, we were in possession of a substantial sum of money. There was also David's six-figure advance from Weidenfeld for his autobiography to look forward to. Up until now, Cherrydene had been our only asset.

David's idea was that we should now move from it. Not to a bungalow, which, as Rory unkindly put it, was what we should have been thinking of, but to take on the restoration of a derelict Border tower, and live in it. And not just any tower, but a specific one: Oakwood Tower, which lay a couple of miles from the village towards Selkirk.

I too had had my fantasies about such a project. Indeed, I had fuelled or possibly kindled David's enthusiasm, many years before, by giving him, as a Christmas present, a book by the sculptor Gerald Laing about his own very hands-on restoration of Kinkell Castle in the Black Isle. But the difference between us was that I really did see it as a fantasy – the same kind of dream that conjures up images of renovated farmhouses in Tuscany or castles in Seville.

Perhaps that is not quite honest. For projects like those, if we ever did dream of them, were no more than holiday conversations on sunlit days far from home, when the air is heavy with heat-haze and rosemary. Gold-walled, red-roofed, shuttered buildings set among vineyards might have caught the summer imagination, but they had no more substance than snapshots. Border towers, on the other hand, were present in our everyday lives. They do indeed have substance: their thick greywhacke walls, topped by a slate roof in similar hues – or, more often, a roofless void and a rowan tree growing from a decaying gable – were a part of the countryside where we had put down our roots.

All over the south of Scotland there were once such towers: simple, mainly rectangular, fortified houses of four or five storeys in height. They are as typical and specific to the area as the Martello towers along England's southern coastline, so much so that their outline features in many a logo of companies or organisations based in the Borders.

They were not grandiose, not castles, although there are many castles here as well. The latter, all along the Tweed and its tributaries, have names well-known in legend, song and history. Neidpath Castle on the Tweed just above Peebles is one. The seat of the Earls of March, it was only captured once – by Oliver Cromwell's troops – in its six centuries of existence. Like so many places in the Borders, it has poetry associated with it, such as Thomas Campbell's tragic *The Maid of Neidpath*:

> Earl March looked on his dying child,
> And struck with grief to view her:
> 'The youth,' he cried, 'whom I exiled,
> Shall be restored to woo her.'

At Hermitage Castle, a grim thirteenth-century frontier fortress in Liddesdale, the vassals of Lord Soulis were so enraged by his cruelty that

> They wrapped him up in a sheet of lead,
> A sheet of lead for a funeral pall:
> They plunged him into a pot of oil –
> And boiled him, lead and bones and all.

Hermitage holds a place, too, in the imagination of many a romantic novelist. It was the destination of Mary, Queen of Scots when she rode from Jedburgh to visit the wounded Earl of Bothwell on a wet October day – and on her return to the town she came near to death of a fever. 'Would that I had died at Jeddart!' she would repeat in later years, for it was then that her fortunes began to run downhill.

But the tower houses, the peel towers, were not inhabited or visited by royalty or earls. They had existed as a simple architectural form for some couple of centuries until the time the building of them by land-owners worth more than £100 was made compulsory by James V in 1535. They were ordered to erect:

> A sufficient barmkin [palisade], upon his heritage and lands, of stone and lime, covering three square feet of the square, one ell thick, and six ells high, for the reset of him and his tenants in troublous time, with a tower in the same for himself if he thinks it expedient . . . all strengths, barmkins and peels to be built and completed within two years.

It is difficult to gauge how many landowners did erect them, for many did not last the century or even the decade. The 'rough wooing' of the infant Mary, Queen of Scots by Henry VIII's troops in the south of Scotland wreaked terrible devastation on abbey, steading, town and tower alike. Later centuries saw many old buildings used as quarries for new ones.

The Selkirkshire volume of the *Report of the Commission for Ancient Monuments* lists the sites of over a dozen towers, four of them in the Ettrick Valley. Some had been incorporated into more capacious houses, from modest farmhouses to the graceful Bemersyde House at Dryburgh. In the 1970s, the enterprising Kedzie Penfield and her husband Steve Fox rebuilt Salenside Tower in the Ale valley, using modern building methods and materials. To do so, they had to do battle with the local planning authority, who deemed the height of such a structure 'out of keeping' with the local environment.

In the whole of Selkirkshire, there were only a few towers that still had their walls intact, including Kirkhope and Oakwood in the Ettrick Valley.

It was Kirkhope that we had fantasised about first. South-facing, on a hill above the village, it had been the focus of family walks and rides many a time, and we had scrambled among its stones, despite warning notices. It was here that five-year-old Catriona had 'called to the owl' to bring her a baby brother.

'It would be wonderful to restore Kirkhope Tower,' we would say to each other; and so, probably, did half the people who knew it. But it was roofless; the stairs had crumbled and so had the floors, and its gable end was splitting. Moreover, it had contained only one room on each floor, and there were neither road nor services to it.

Oakwood, halfway to Selkirk, was screened by trees and formed part of a farm steading. Like Kirkhope, and indeed like most of the Ettrick Valley, it belonged to the Duke of Buccleuch. One day in the early 1970s, as many others did before and after us, we had borrowed the massive key from the estate office, driven up the farm road, and explored the tower.

What struck us both at once was its warm atmosphere and lack of a sense of desolation. It felt entrancingly like a home waiting for people to come back to it, although it can only have been what was called the Great Hall that created that atmosphere. Above were rotting floorboards, pigeon droppings, and the skeletal carcasses of birds and rodents. The barrel-vaulted ground floor was piled high with calcified lime that had lain there since before the war.

But the Hall itself, with its friendly, modest proportions, with a remnant of plaster on its walls, with its wonderful 'joggled' fireplace and its rough flagged floor – that was a real room. It required little imagination to see it filled with furniture, with people, to hear laughter and conversation around a blazing log fire. We were distressed to see that there were cracks in the front wall of the tower and broken windows. David wrote to its owner, the 8th Duke of Buccleuch, to report on them, and ended his letter with the thought that it would be nice if someone were to restore it as a home. At this time he was not thinking of it as a project for us, it was just the concept in principle. The handwritten ducal reply came, thanking him for pointing out the things that needed attention, but ending with the opinion that it could not be made into a home, as it was too close to the farmhouse, and it was not a good thing for people to live so near to each other.

Some years later, David raised the question of Oakwood again with Johnnie, the 9th Duke, who by this time had become a friend, and was to prove an even greater one throughout the years. By now, inspired by Gerald Laing, David was wanting to undertake the task himself, and when we began the reverie about restoring a tower, it was Oakwood that we had in mind. When the farm was re-let, Johnnie Buccleuch kept the tower and its surroundings out of the tenancy agreement.

As for me, I was prepared to go so far as to admit that it was the only house I'd think of moving to from Cherrydene. I was prepared to humour David, in turn ironic, enthusiastic, reluctant and always totally sceptical. We had never in all our marriage amassed any capital, and this project would need plenty.

'It's a wonderful idea, darling, and I'm sure you'll live there some time, but it will have to be with your second wife – make sure she's rich,' I would say.

'We'll do it together – you'll see,' would come his reply, although he would never explain how this might come about.

'We certainly won't do it while you're leader of the Liberal Party,' I would say. 'It would definitely be one thing more than I could cope with.' At this point, I think I had some vision of us being like Gerald Laing, and labouring away on the construction work ourselves.

'All right – we'll talk about it seriously when I'm not leader.'

David went public with his decision to stand down as leader at a constituency meeting the following month. A few days later, I was at Bowhill for a lunch given by the Buccleuchs in connection with a school open day for the estate. I said to Johnnie: 'I think David may be in touch with you shortly.' I didn't say what it was about, but the next day there arrived at Cherrydene a hand-delivered tube with our names in ducal script. Inside there was no note, just the photograph of a frontispiece illustration of the published plays of James Hogg: it was of Aikwood Tower.

# Part Three

# THE AIKWOOD YEARS

## 22
# A Comparatively Good State of Repair

*November, 1988*

It is raining steadily when we arrive at the tower to meet Niall Campbell, the factor of Buccleuch Estates, and Dr Richard Fawcett of Historic Scotland. The tower is a Grade A listed building, and, because it is uninhabited, a Schedule I monument. We would have to work very closely with Historic Scotland: it seemed that every step we would take would need their approval. They are also the grant-making body.

The tower has never looked so uninviting. Dr Fawcett is not really interested in our plans to turn it into a family home: his priority is simply the preservation of it as it stands now, a testament to previous centuries. Our inspection begins on the ground floor, where we enter the larger of the two barrel-vaulted rooms through large double doors. They were part of the previous century's transformation of the tower into a farm building. Will we have to reinstate the solid wall? 'No, no,' says Dr Fawcett, gazing up at the archway they occupy. 'That's a classic example of nineteenth century industrial brickwork. You must keep it.'

At the back of the tower is a single-storey building, now used as a cattle court but once an elegant small two-storey farmhouse of unknown period. The nineteenth century had seen it reduced in height, originally to serve as a substantial stable, and now as a stripped-out cattle court. With beasts hock-deep in straw and glaur, and chunks missing from the masonry, it looks in worse shape than the tower itself.

We go into the latter through the ancient front door, which gives access to the stairs and to a small barrel-vaulted chamber. Here, bizarrely, four lines of wire straggle from curved wall to curved wall. A long time later, before the work gets started, two old men, who had lived in the cottages as boys, explained it. 'That was auld Mrs Linton's washing line. Wull Linton [the tenant farmer in the 1920s] was aye awfae guid tae tramps. He'd let them stay in a shed, but there was yin, whae had a wudden leg, and was an eddicated sort of man. And when he came, Wull wad let him stay in the tower itssel, and we used tae get a tip for making up a bed of straw for him.' And they fell to disputing whether they had earned a penny or sixpence.

Above this, what had been the laird's room seems cramped and inhospitable, but has signs of recent habitation. Well, not really recent, but not sixteenth-century. It is earlier, perhaps, than the washing line. There is some rough and ready brick repair work, and an extraordinarily ugly wooden surround to the old fireplace, which Dr Fawcett says he hopes we'll keep. There is also an alcove in the wall which we are told by Dr Fawcett will have been a 'dry closet' – an early earth-filled inside lavatory. Over the winter, when we are ploughing through our researches on the tower's past in Register House, we find that Will Linton's father had moved into the tower about a hundred years previously, but that one winter of the experiment had been enough.

We move on to the Great Hall, austere and dark on this sodden day, but full of potential. Here, as on the floors above, the plasterwork is scrawled with the names of those who have been inside its walls during its unlived-in centuries. David's mentor, Andrew Haddon, has regaled us with stories about a party there in his youthful days in the 1930s, when some of the young farmers of the area had gathered with a wind-up gramophone, and sausages that they cooked in the huge fireplace. It is this feature which now seizes Dr Fawcett's attention.

'A joggled lintel!' he cries ecstatically. They are, apparently, rare, and this one, with its three huge stones fitting into each other like a giant jig-saw is a classic of its kind. Once again, David and I visualise a blazing log fire in it, friends and family drinking claret in the glow. We proceed up the left-turning stairs with their wide freestone newel post – yet another rare classic – to what will be our bedrooms. At the top level, I don't follow the rest of the party across the floorboards: they are rotting, and I suffer from vertigo, another reason why this whole enterprise commends itself to me less than a hundred per cent at this time. The roof is in worse condition than we had thought, and even to our ignorant eyes, the huge chimney stacks will certainly need attention. (Once the scaffolding was up, and the masons were working, we found that we had caught the tower just in time, before the big lum collapsed through the roof and real dereliction set in.) No-one has made the tower their home for centuries, and yet it still has a feeling of life, an absence of real neglect. Landlords and tenant farmers alike have shown it some respect and care.

Dr Fawcett is very clear with us about what we will be allowed to do. We can reinstate old openings, but not create new ones. Every detail of the plans will have to be scrutinised. Grants from Historic Scotland can only be for restoration work – replacement of rafters, roof and windows, but not for water and electricity, and certainly not bathrooms. Stone repairs outside and inside are eligible, but not drains.

'What will you do about bathrooms?' he asks, adding hopefully, 'I suppose there's no chance of you being totally true to history, and simply having a dry closet?'

It was a far cry from the exquisite chateaux of the Loire among which we travelled on that summer's caravanette holiday. Our trip was not without incident: I trapped a muscle in my back, and was in great pain. As I stretched out in the back of the camper-van, my head on a white pillow, I looked through half-closed eyes out of the window. A passer-by looked in, crossed himself reverently, and moved on, obviously mistaking our vehicle for a hearse.

My back improved, and we managed to continue through the chateaux. Loveliest of all was Azay-le-Rideau on the Cher, a tributary of the Loire, where we saw a *son et lumière* unlike any we had witnessed before: a promenade performance, with live musicians and dancers and boats outlined in small lights rowed across the moat. We made our way to the Loire's source, stood at the watershed between the Atlantic and the Mediterranean, and followed the deep-ravined Ardèche to the Rhone. At the Mediterranean, we turned east to Italy, where our university friends George and Helen Inglis had converted another derelict farm building into a home. The scale we were aiming at was huge by comparison, but their conversion gave us heart.

At Pisa, the annual conference of Liberal International awaited us. We parked the caravanette and registered as delegates, to find that there was a security flap on: where was the former leader staying? No trace of him could be found in any of the hotel registers. The truth must have confirmed any ideas that the Italian authorities may have held about the strangeness of the British: he was staying in a *car park*! On the last night, there was a reception in a beautiful old monastery in the hills outside Pisa. When everyone else departed back to town in the conference buses, we snuggled down in our home on wheels in the monastery orchard. We were awakened by the sound of the opening shots in the Italian small bird shooting season and, when we turned on the BBC World Service, the unmistakable sound of the voice of Donald Dewar.

The year that heralded so many changes in our lives was coming to a close. Catriona was at college in London now, and Graeme had moved in to live with Lynne Turnbull in Galashiels. Billy had married and moved away. As he receded in our lives, the chasm between ourselves and Graeme was gradually bridged. But Cherrydene's walls were sheltering another teenager besides Rory. This time it was a Tibetan girl, who had come to Britain to be a maid in a ducal castle in the Highlands. I suspected that her visa might not stand close examination. Desperately unhappy and lonely, and treated with dreadful insensitivity, she was helped to find her way to Samye Ling, the Tibetan monastery over the hill from us, at Eskdalemuir in Dumfriesshire. My American friend Thom McCarthy was living there at the time, and he set himself the task of finding a home for her among his friends and former neighbours in Ettrick Bridge. I agreed that she could come to us, as an emergency, for a fortnight: she stayed for four years. 'Why was it,' I said to myself later, 'That when I knew that Thom was, metaphorically, coming towards me with a parcel clearly bearing the label "problem", I have to run and seize it from him with both hands?'

Perhaps it was no wonder that my children would regale their friends with tales of their mother's procession of 'lame ducks'. 'I swear,' I said to Catriona on one such occasion, 'I really do swear that when we move to Aikwood Tower there will be no more lame ducks.'

But Dolma, my sweet Dolma, whose family had fled from Tibet to India with the Dalai Lama, was no problem teenager, and as usual I found that knowing her enriched our own lives. We found courses for her to take at Hawick College, gave her pocket money and helped her with student visas. Over the years that she stayed with us she was much loved by everyone who came into contact with her, and when eventually she returned to her own part of the world, it was with a good command of English, albeit with a strong 'yowe-and-mi' Hawick twang. In 2009, David and Rory went to Tibet. We managed to track Dolma down beforehand, thanks to the wonders of email, and they went to see her and met her family. It was a very emotional reunion.

Just before Christmas 1988, while David was still in London, Rory was watching TV. I had retreated to my bedroom to read. I heard his feet pounding up the stairs: he looked horrified and frightened. He had seen a newsflash. 'There's been an airplane crash in a town in the Borders.' We both thought that it would be one of the low-flying jets that plague the air around the peaceful valleys, but before long it was obvious that this was something much more extensive. Catriona phoned from London, her voice shaky: the crash was in the Borders, were we all right? Did we know where it was, which town had been hit? It was, of course, the bombing of flight Pan Am 103. Lockerbie is so near to us, as the crow flies, that it qualifies as our nearest railway station, although the road journey is long. Some of our neighbours with relatives there were trying to get news: they found themselves up against an impasse, a communications blockage. Though we didn't know the small Dumfriesshire town well, it was essentially very similar to the Border burghs in our own area. It would now always be known for that dreadful night and its aftermath.

David went to the church service in Lockerbie, held soon after, where the Moderator of the Church of Scotland, Professor James Whyte – very recently widowed himself – preached a sermon of sensitivity, comfort and hope; the most powerful one, David said, that he had ever heard. The inch-by-inch search in the forests and fields for identifiable human remains continued, so that grieving families could have something of their loved ones to bury. An arm, a leg, a what? I met a mother later who expressed gratitude to the local woman who had found her daughter's identity tag, miles from Lockerbie. It was too unbearable to contemplate, and it was all happening just two hillsides away. In the end, there were nineteen people of whom there was nothing but dust in a Lockerbie housing scheme. The decision was taken to fill a coffin with that dust, representing those dead individuals, and to give them a symbolic funeral. The relatives, mainly parents from America, were flown across: a group united in grief and bewilderment.

To show respect to them, the occasion was made much of, and among those invited were the party leaders. Paddy Ashdown was unable to go, and asked David to attend, but he too had a commitment that he couldn't avoid. Instead of casting around for a more official substitute, he suggested to me that I might go to represent the party at Dryfesdale Cemetery. So I went: I recall that I was wearing an enveloping black woollen cloak against the January weather, and those in charge of the service put me, not among the political squad, but with the representatives of the uniformed organisations who had played such a heroic part at Lockerbie. I felt unworthy to be with them. Thus I passed that unforgettable, heart-wrenching afternoon both at the cemetery, and at the nearby hotel.

One mother spoke to me about how happy her daughter Amy's last three months had been, travelling throughout Europe, about the wonderful letters she had written home. That seemed to give her some strength; Heaven knows, she would need it. Another had managed to place a large, smiling photo of her daughter, Nicole Boulanger, among the flowers at the grave. She asked me about the lament that had been played – *The Flowers of the Forest* – and I told her about its history, and undertook to send her a recording of it, with a Saltire, for she wanted the Scottish flag as part of her way of remembering her daughter.

I drove back over the lonely winter hills, moved to my depths. My route took me away from other people, away from traffic, for it is a remote road, bleak in the fading light of a January day, that takes you from Lockerbie to Eskdalemuir and then home to Ettrick. But there was the comforting sight of Samye Ling, and I stopped there to see Thom, and to unload some of my distress onto him. He promised me that at the evening service, the community would pray once more for all the dead and for all those who had been bereaved.

Back home, I asked Elspeth Smellie to make a tape of Jean Elliot's lovely words of *The Flowers of the Forest* for the mother who'd requested it. My own feelings about this twentieth-century tragedy had formed verses in my head as well, which I dedicated to her daughter and sent to her along with the items she'd asked for. She never replied, and the thought has always haunted me that my words may have brought her even more heartache than she already had to bear. I hope not.

> I saw your drizzle-dampened photograph,
> Smiling amongst the ranks of formal flowers,
> And all at once the horror of that night
> Distilled into one loss, one grief, one death.
>
> You died amongst our rolling Border hills –
> The same my daughter walked, and rode, and played in:
> They make a nursery fit to shape and mould
> A spirit free as water, swift as air.
>
> But you, west-winging through the Christmas dark,
> Found them no playground but a mortuary:
> Your young life poised for flight to women's years
> Destroyed as wantonly as moorland game.
>
> The men and women of the stricken town
> Receive you reverently into their care.
> Blood-sister to the daughters nurtured here,
> Your shrine is granite, grass and unsought peace.

*September, 2009*

*Over twenty years later, and I am at Dryfesdale Cemetery again. I am setting up a theatre tour and an exhibition in Dumfriesshire; my route takes me through Lockerbie, and I have plenty of time in hand. The graveyard and the memorial are beautifully kept, and there are many small, individual memorials as well as the main one. Again, I am struck by the birth date, 1967, that appears on so many of these, for it is also Catriona's. I think of her crowded and fruitful years since 1988, and want to weep again for the loss of all those years by those whose names are on brass and stone.*

Lockerbie: a waste of life, like war. In the Borders, especially in Selkirk, no waste of life is commemorated more than the ill-conceived battle of Flodden in 1513, and Jean Elliot's words *The Flowers of the Forest* were written for the men of Ettrick Forest who fell under James IV's banner on the Northumbrian hillside. The best description of the battle itself is in Walter Scott's epic poem *Marmion*.

> By this, though deep the evening fell,
> Still rose the battle's deadly swell,
> For Scots, around their King,
> Unbroken, fought in desperate ring.
> Where's now their victor vanward wing,
> Where Huntly, and where Home? –
> Some blast should warn them, not in vain,
> To quit the plunder of the slain,
> And turn the doubtful day again,
> While yet on Flodden side
> Afar, the Royal standard flies,
> And round it toils, and bleeds, and dies,
> Our Caledonian pride!
>
> Tweed's echoes heard the ceaseless plash,
> While many a broken band,
> Disordered, through her currents dash,
> To gain the Scottish land;
> To town and tower, to town and dale,
> To tell red Flodden's dismal tale,
> And raise the universal wail.
> Tradition, legend, tune and song,
> Shall many an age that wail prolong,

> Still from the sire the son shall hear
> Of the stern strife, and carnage drear,
> Of Flodden's fatal field,
> Where shivered was fair Scotland's sword,
> And broken was her spear!

No-one bestrides the Borders literary landscape as Scott does. I had made the decision to build the third Borders Festival around him, and was constructing a programme – and looking for ways to pay for it. There was an additional interest in him for me now, for not only had he been descended from the seventeenth-century Laird of Aikwood, William Scott of Harden, but his last, ailing visit to Ettrick was an excursion to the Tower – and to the 'deep linns' of the river further upstream, at Ettrick Bridge. But my real reason was more practical: I could see that each time such a festival happened, the question would be asked, 'When are you going to "do" Sir Walter Scott?' Better to get it over and done with.

I was perhaps fortunate in my childhood experiences with the Great Unknown, as the anonymous author of *Waverley* was known in his own lifetime. There was a series of illustrated books published before the First World War subtitled *Scott Retold for Boys and Girls*, and copies of them had been given to my mother as school prizes. She had kept them, and as a child I had devoured the heavily-edited stories of *Ivanhoe*, of *The Talisman*, *Kenilworth*, *Redgauntlet* and others. Then, in my teens, films were made of *Ivanhoe* and *Quentin Durward*, starring my screen idol, Robert Taylor. It was from these easy sources that I first sampled Walter Scott, and they made the digestion of a couple of the unabridged novels in school English classes a simpler process than it was for many of my contemporaries. Now I applied myself to find out more about him, and to explore ways of presenting him to a new generation. I borrowed *St Ronan's Well* from the library as holiday reading: I had not expected to be rolling around the caravanette with laughter at its humour.

I approached the well-known writer Allan Massie, an authority on Scott and now living just outside Selkirk, to write a play using the same approach that Frederic Mohr had employed for James Miranda Barry and James Hogg – a solo performance, the actor drawing the audience into the life of the subject. I asked the director who had been so helpful to me during his production of my own play two years previously to come back for this one. Alas, fiercely left-wing and fiercely nationalistic, he was not the person to approach either Allan Massie or Walter Scott with the greatest commitment or sympathy. Furthermore, he was giving up his theatre work, whether voluntarily or involuntarily, and was currently more interested in trying to manage pop bands. But there was a decent fee, and he took it on, and I trusted him. It was a mistake.

One problem was that Allan Massie's text for *The Minstrel and the Shirra* was far too long, and needed a lot of pruning. The director, however, declared as his philosophy that he believed in writers' theatre, and that the director's job was to put on stage exactly what the playwright delivered. This seemed like an excuse for not doing any preparation, and I was uneasy, but handicapped by my own inexperience, and the diffidence that came with it, when dealing with those who had more. A result of the director's approach was that there was considerable difficulty in finding an actor to take on the unwieldy text, and the one who eventually did so, whom I shall call Tudor Bradford, was totally unsuited to play such an icon. Every aspect of the production ran into problems. The artist who had asked if he could design the set turned out to have no idea what was needed for the rough and tumble of one-night-stop touring, and his impractical ideas had to be ditched in favour of a very simple set-up.

The play was due to open the wonderfully refurbished theatre at Bowhill. The vision of converting the old game larder of the big house into a theatre was that of Richard, the Earl of Dalkeith (now the 10th Duke), who had agreed to be the festival's patron. For a few years it had operated in a fairly basic way: now it had been given the treatment by leading theatre architects and turned into a jewel-like, properly equipped auditorium with a tiny but workable stage and 70 comfortable seats. The first performance of *The Minstrel and the Shirra* was to be the grand opening.

It was a disaster. Tudor Bradford dried frequently, and his harsh, modern, urban voice had none of the cadences and musicality which such a performance demands. The only part of the production that was admirable was the exquisite ballad-singing and clarsach-playing of Elspeth Smellie. The play toured for several dispiriting weeks, both in the Borders and further afield. I went with the company to Skye, where we had cold halls and single-figure audiences. I could not bear to stay and swell these. Hearing Scott's and Massie's lines mangled was more than I could stomach, so I would stay in the draughty foyer counting the meagre box-office money, or go in search of fish suppers for the company. When I brought Tudor his wages – in those days, Equity liked them to be handed over weekly in cash – he would open the packet in front of me, count the notes, and then quibble about his allowances. Sometimes I look back on that week in Skye as the worst one of my life; and then I am grateful that it was nothing worse than all these irritations and trivialities that made it so.

But somewhere in *The Minstrel and the Shirra*, I felt sure, there was a play, a good play, which in the hands of a more sympathetic director and actor, could present Scott to a contemporary audience.

The second project was a musical one, about which I had even less knowledge, but this time I got things right. Another clarsach player was the Peeblesshire musician Savourna Stevenson. She had played in a concert at the first Border Festival with her pianist/composer father, Ronald, her actress sister, Gerda, and the violinist, Leonard Friedman. I had been enthralled by the clarsach, then a relatively unusual instrument, ever since I'd first heard Elspeth play it in the village hall, and now I suggested to Savourna, recognised as one of its leading exponents, that she should play at a series of concerts down the Tweed.

'Oh,' she said, 'why don't you apply to the Scottish Arts Council to give the Festival a grant to commission something new from me?' So I did, the Scottish Arts Council obliged, and Savourna got her commission. Together we worked out where the concerts should be, and what shape the new music would take. She would begin with a solo concert in Tweedsmuir Church, as near to the river's source as was practical, where she would play the first movement – a solo – of the new piece, *Tweed Journey*; then at each of the subsequent six concerts, she would be joined by another musician, and they would play the next part, until at Berwick-on-Tweed a seven-piece ensemble would perform it in its entirety.

I had thought of the clarsach purely as a traditional instrument, but Savourna, and her harp-making husband, Mark Norris, were at the cutting edge of developing it electronically, and the musicians that Savourna chose to work with were leading Scottish jazz musicians. Meantime I arranged for the concerts to be played, not in public halls, but in interesting and historic buildings along the river: Neidpath Castle, the Lucy Sanderson Hall in Galashiels, with its murals of the town's textile trade, and Melrose Abbey were some of them. It was regarded as a beacon in the cross-over between traditional and contemporary music, and established Savourna's reputation. She never neglected to acknowledge my part in *Tweed Journey*'s creation, and as I learnt, sometimes bitterly, that rivalry, envy and ingratitude in the arts can be crueller than in politics, I came to value her generosity of spirit all the more.

I commissioned a production based on some of Scott's short stories, and a community production of an adaptation by the playwright Donald Campbell of the novel *St Ronan's Well*, which is not historical, but based in Scott's own time, and set in towns bearing the stamp, but not the names, of Innerleithen and Peebles. It was Donald Campbell who told me that up until the early twentieth century, the main repertoire of Scottish theatre had been adaptations of the Waverley novels. I had seen Campbell's own community play based on *The Heart of Midlothian* a few years before, and it had helped me to tackle the book itself. I regard it as Scott's finest, and can never understand why it has been so shamefully neglected in recent years.

My own creativity had been stirred by the festival of ballads and legends as well. The little storytelling show *The Rowan Tree* was the first one I had actually directed apart from the village hall productions of earlier years. I liked what the small company had done, and they had gone on to give other performances of the show, including one at the festivities surrounding the opening – by David – of the new temple at Samye Ling. But I might have left it at that, except that I had particularly enjoyed working with John Nichol, and I could see in his performances that he was an artist of some considerable potential and quality. He has an extraordinary rapport with an audience, especially in the intimate spaces where the show was being performed; he has an intuitive understanding of character – and above all, he has a true, mellow Scots voice that any long-established actor would envy. During my research for *The Rowan Tree*, I had unearthed a story in the nineteenth-century collection, *Wilson's Tales of the Borders*, called *Willie Wastle's Account of his Wife*, and I had used a part of it in the story cycle. Now I wanted to develop the whole story.

Those with even a passing knowledge of Robert Burns may be familiar with his song, *Willie Wastle*, which he wrote in the Crook Inn at Tweedsmuir. For those who don't, I will summarise it by saying that it consists of five verses of insult about the wife of a (supposedly fictitious) local worthy, each one finishing with the chorus,

> Sic a wife as Willie had,
> I wadnae gie a button for her.

But Willie and his wife Kirsty were based in fact on a real couple. The story in *Wilson's Tales* was Willie's defence of Kirsty. It shows her to be domineering, resistant to all the changes he wants to make on his farm, and the destruction of one of his innovations in a fire leads to a dark suspicion on his part. A family tragedy brings them together, and Willie, now in old age, reflects positively on Kirsty and on their marriage, declaring that he would give 'all my buttons, and all the siller [money] in my pooch for her, into the bargain.'

Written in vibrant, first-person Scots, Willie's tale had jumped out of the old pages at me, and I could see now that it would make a marvellous solo performance, and be a great vehicle for John Nichol. I threaded it through with songs by Burns, and approached two superb local musicians to take part: Hilary Bell, who lives in Yarrow, and whose clear, sweet voice has remarkably clear diction, and Lucy Cowan, a brilliant violinist from Berwickshire, one of a family totally immersed in music. Her mother, Jane Cowan, had studied cello with Pablo Casals, and had gone on to teach Steven Isserlis at her Casals Cello School in London. When the Cowan family fell heir to a large house at Edrom in Berwickshire, they moved there and Jane Cowan ran her cello school in it, attracting musicians from far and wide. Some of these settled in Berwickshire: there was a veritable colony of musicians around Edrom.

Once again, Janice Parker and I comprised the entire production team. Although *Willie Wastle* had no relevance to Scott, I programmed a tour of it during the Borders Festival. But before that, we took it to the Edinburgh Fringe for the last week of August, to the newly-opened venue at the Pleasance. I was forty-nine, a bit long in the tooth for a directorial debut there, and driven by a mixture of optimism, ignorance, and necessity. I had to get the production up and running well ahead of the Edinburgh Festival, and rehearse it in John's holiday time.

The company needed a name. I cast my mind back to its parent production, and chose to call it the Rowan Tree Company. We came back from the Fringe with triumphant reviews for the performances, the whole production and its concept. I had adapted, directed and designed it, and I was proud of what I had done. But I had hidden my name away from any credits. I was nervous that, as the wife of a public figure, this would be seized on, and I wanted the work to stand on its own merits. The Rowan Tree Company would become, in due course, a dominant part of my life.

There was another project in this festival which again laid a solid foundation for the future. An inspirational man called John Haswell had come to live at nearby Lilliesleaf. Since there are several Johns in my story, I will refer to him by his nickname of Hazzy. His especial forte was theatre work with young people. Tall and cadaverous, with hair alternately shaggy or in a close-shaved 'No 1' cut, he reached out to and caught the minds and spirits of teenagers – and especially, perhaps, disaffected ones – in a way which found an immediate response. He never judged them, he trusted them; and imposed, mysteriously, a discipline and a camaraderie that produced from them more than they had known they could achieve. His is an extraordinary alchemical leadership. A sponsorship package from Marks and Spencers allowed Hazzy and me to set up the Borders Youth Theatre, which has flourished from then on. The first thirty-odd recruits were housed over their October holidays at Broadmeadows Youth Hostel, three miles up a track from the Yarrow valley.

Hazzy said to me: 'I want to take a group of a dozen or so of the members to somewhere really atmospheric. An old tower or something. Can you think of anywhere?'

'I own one,' I said, to John's amazement – and also, still, to my own – for earlier that year we had received the feu disposition of Aikwood Tower. No stone had been touched on it; we were still at the paperwork stage.

It was late afternoon, the daylight just beginning to fade on a warm October day, when they came, those young people bubbling with energy and enthusiasm. I told them some of the stories I'd unearthed about the Tower, and opened its door to them. 'Write your names on the plaster,' I said, 'and take as many apples as you like from the trees.' And after they left, I wrote:

> It's a russet day.
> The air hangs between damp and beaded mist.
> A pheasant whirrs from tangled branches,
> And the tower is ripe with her mysteries.
>
> The oak door swings inwards:
> Snaking up the kerry-handed stairs
> Run rubber-soled invaders.
> Unhardened fingers caress old crevices,
> Trace the names in crumbled lime
> Of lover, farmhand, prisoner of war.
> Old chaff lies sterile on the pitted flags,
> A legacy of harvest reaped and threshed
> By long-dead holders of the pencilled names.
> Now other seeds germinate,

And in her many-chambered womb,
The tower feeds the embryos of imagination.

Such a day casts no shadows.
Tower-captivated, the invaders sit,
Cross-legged on cobbles, bielded by stone walls,
Telling new tales of old and unknown times.
They mark the future out before the past
And leave new names scratched on the plaster page.

## 23

# A Benign Wizardry

We had our dream tower now, on unbelievably generous terms. The building at the back of the tower was used as a cattle shed: we had to replace this with a new shed for the tenant farmer's use, and we had to pay the legal fees. For the tower itself, Johnnie Buccleuch made no charge.

Before long we also had our architect. Malcolm Hammond was the junior partner in a Linlithgow firm of architects, well respected for their work on restoration projects. For over a year, all was paperwork – the drawing up of the plans, the applications to Historic Scotland and the Borders Council for approval and for grants. He saw all this process through. We waited, we visited our new acquisition, we brought friends to see it and had picnics in it, we cut down dead trees and sprayed nettles in the garden. For decades the ground around the tower had been used as a run for the cattle, and all that was left was the remains of two espaliered apple trees.

> Dismembering the Eden of dead apple trees,
> On midsummer's day
> I uncovered a sunburst of stone
> Amongst the swineweed fronds.
> What mason's hands, with gnarls and scars
> To match the apple's bark
> Gouged out with careful chisel these worm radials?
> What Aikwood laird instructed him
> In the embellishment of a newborn tower?
> In the midge-laden dusk
> My mind creates the donors
> Of my solstice gift.

A young landscape architect, Louise Wall, had come to live in Ettrick Bridge. 'I've always wanted to design a medieval garden,' she said, and got the reply, 'Now's your opportunity.'

We went to visit other restorations, and learned as much as we could from their owners, who were as generous in sharing their mistakes with us as their successes. But we could not so much as pick a piece of decayed plaster off the walls of our tower without the approval of the Secretary of State for Scotland, through Historic Scotland.

We spent a lot of time within the wood-panelled walls of the Scottish Record Office. I liked the silence of the rooms, the feel of the stiff vellum and the crumbling wax seals encased in ancient chamois leather or modern bubble-wrap. But the information we uncovered relating to Aikwood was scanty, and mostly confirmed what we already knew: that it appeared to have been built some time in the sixteenth century by a family called the Scotts of Aikwood, starting with a Maister Michael Scott; and in the following century it had come into the ownership of William Scott of Harden. He was the ancestor of Sir Walter Scott, and according to legend had led a raid on the Tweedside castle of Elibank, been caught by the powerful laird, Gideon Murray, and forced to choose between being hanged from a convenient tree or marrying the laird's plainest daughter. The story has been the subject of plays, stories and ballads over the centuries: a musical, *Marrying Meg*, opened in New York in 2009. These are extracts from James Hogg's ballad version, *The Fray of Elibank*:

> When Will saw the tether draw over the tree,
> His courage misgaed him, his heart it gaed sair,
> He watched Gideon's face, and he watched his e'e,
> But the devil a scrap of reluctance was there.
>
> He found the last gleam of his hope was a-fading,
> The green braes of Harden nae mair he wad see.
> The coffin was there, that he soon must be laid in;
> His proud heart was humbled, he fell on one knee . . .
>
> That day they were wedded, that night they were bedded,
> And Juden has feasted them gaily and free,
> But oft the bridegroom as he rallied and bladded,
> What faces he made at the big hanging tree . . .
>
> So Willie took Meg to the Forest so fair,
> And they lived a most happy and sociable life.
> The langer he kenned her, he loved her the mair
> For a prudent, a virtuous, and sensible wife.

Not many Border legends had such a happy ending. Sir Walter Scott was descended from that union, and the Harden Scotts remained in possession of Aikwood until after the Second World War, when ownership passed to the Dukes of Buccleuch.

Throughout the seventeenth century, one Sir William Scott after another took his place at Aikwood – three in all. In a fit of romanticism as we trawled through their details, I said to David, 'Perhaps it would be nice for the tower to have a knight in it again.'

It was not an idle remark. When David had retired as leader two years before, Paddy Ashdown had tried to persuade him to accept a knighthood, but he thought that would look like compensation for loss of office. The question had been raised again since. I was the stumbling block: I felt that titles put up barriers, set their holders apart. I remembered my own gaucheness about how to address knights, lords and dukes, and I did not want anyone to have that same embarrassment in communicating with me. I quoted Robert Burns, 'The rank is but the guinea stamp', and the wife of James Hogg, who had written to him on the receipt of the news that a knighthood was in the offing: 'From my own heart I like no such titles . . . It would be an honour for you, but a burden for me.' And I couldn't help remembering a wonderful headline in a local newspaper a few years before. David's erstwhile opponent from the 1970 election, Russell Fairgrieve, had eventually got into Parliament and served for a short time as junior minister in the Scottish Office. When he was reshuffled out of it, he was knighted, and the paper reported, 'It's Sir Russell as Fairgrieve gets the boot.' And a story going the rounds that his wife had berated a shop assistant in Galashiels for using the prefix 'Mrs' instead of 'Lady' was a reminder of the very pretentious side of such baubles if you take them too seriously.

But the idea of Aikwood being home again to a knight was beguiling, and in this mood, I softened. The knighthood was announced in the New Year's Honours list. 'I'm telling everyone that he only did it to keep the wife happy,' mocked Donald Dewar, earning a torrent of unladylike abuse.

Nevertheless, a knighthood deserved a celebration, and we were still cash-rich from the libel settlements and the book advance. We went off to Madeira, which seemed an appropriate place to go to mark such an occasion. I had packed, for David's reading, James Hogg's novel about Aikwood, *The Three Perils of Man.*

'I never realised before how funny Hogg is,' said David, echoing what I had said about Walter Scott during my holiday reading three years previously. As we sat at lunch one day on the terrace of Reid's Hotel, David said, 'Don't look now, but there are people we know over there.'

They were Lord and Lady Polwarth, heads of the Scott of Harden family, which had owned Aikwood for three centuries. They had called in at Madeira on a cruise. Truly, there was no getting away from Aikwood: I detected the benign influence of the wizard, Michael Scott.

Malcolm Hammond had guided us through the paperwork. Now he was anxious to assemble his team. We abandoned the idea of a single contractor, and operated what is called a 'separate trades' project. All the contractors, except for the specialist electrician and the slater, were small firms from Selkirk. They all knew each other well, having worked together over the years. In particular, they had recently collaborated on the restoration of Hillslap Tower outside Galashiels, and Malcolm had seen the quality of their work. 'I then went over to Hillslap Tower,' he wrote in a memo. 'The works carried out there are indeed magnificent, and in mason and joiner work both Bunyan and Grieve have carried out works of a first class nature.'

He was determined to set the same standards for this, his first major project.

Among the first of the team were the mason, David Bunyan, veteran of work on various Historic Scotland buildings; the blacksmith, Robin Scott, namesake of the Aikwood owner whose initials were carved into the 1602 marriage stone, Dennis Henderson, head of the plumbing firm, a stalwart of the Selkirk Rugby Club, and Billy Clapperton the plasterer, uncle of my friend John Nichol. The joiner, Falconer Grieve, was the most reluctant to take on such a commitment. He went to look round the tower, taking his dog and his teenage son, now his apprentice, with him. 'The Steels must be mad,' he said to the latter, after they had made their tour of inspection. The dog had refused to come inside at all. But Malcolm pleaded with Falconer and he eventually agreed to take on the contract.

We would share our lives and our vision with these men over the next two years. They were the master craftsmen: they brought with them their journeymen and their apprentices, and there were several young men who learnt their trade in part at Aikwood. When Malcolm Hammond came down for his fortnightly meetings, he would be amazed at how things had progressed. 'I have other projects with a main contractor,' he said, 'and none of them are going ahead so harmoniously.'

It could probably only have happened in Selkirk. Of all the small burghs in Scotland that were once governed by guilds of skilled tradesmen, I believe it is only in Selkirk that the Incorporation of Hammermen still exists and thrives. At the Common Riding, it elects its own Standard Bearer, who carries its flag first in the procession and casts it in the market place: its members have a place of respect and honour. Nevertheless, there could be rivalries and *amour propre* and minor demarcation disputes among them. As the client on the spot, I found myself acting as an unofficial clerk of works, sorting out small problems as they arose, especially with Gordon Robson, the slater, who, being from Galashiels, was outside the Selkirk fraternity.

On the roof in November 1990, Gordon Robson is up to attic height. It's snowing, and the flakes are coming through the open skylights.

'Couldn't you tack those plastic bags over them?' I ask.

'They're Dave Bunyan's.'

'But they're empty!'

'But they're still his, and he's a terrible man to get roused if you use his things without asking him. And he's not here.'

There's a phone on the site, but Gordon hasn't thought of using it. I do, and with one phone call, the problem is solved.

Graeme and Lynne, who both worked on the restoration, had lived in a caravan over the previous winter while renovating a couple of derelict cottages themselves. Now the caravan was brought to Aikwood to use as a site office.

The scaffolding went up in September 1990. Masonry was re-pointed, door and window lintels were repaired, beams were renewed and the slates on the roof were all stripped off and replaced with old second-hand Scotch slates. Under nineteenth-century brick, we made small, charming discoveries: a tiny inter-mural chamber, a short flight of stairs to a turret. We managed to fit in an extra attic floor that had not been in the original scheme, giving better proportions all round and a fourth bedroom. For the first time, water and electricity came to the old building. My Selkirk friend Pat Neil followed the progress with me. In particular, we cooked together for special occasions, such as the press call when David announced our plans for the restoration.

### PAT NEIL'S TROUT PATE

*¾ lb cooked trout flesh*
*4 oz Philadelphia cream cheese*
*2 oz softened butter*
*2 tablespoons single cream*

*1 tablespoon tomato puree*
*1 tablespoon lemon juice*
*1 tablespoon of whisky (optional)*
*Salt and pepper*

Flake the fish and make sure all the bones are removed. Put into a bowl and add all the other ingredients, mixing them well together as you go. Then use the blender on them. Put into ramekin dishes for serving, or spread on oatcakes and serve like that. This freezes wonderfully, and with this basic recipe of fish flesh, Philadelphia, butter and cream, you can make all kinds of fish pâtés, using variations on the tomato purée and whisky. Serves approximately 10.

Sometimes Pat was well ahead of me in following progress.

'I've just seen your windows in Falconer's workshop,' she said. 'They're beautiful.'

They were, and they are. There were over twenty in the tower itself, including two tiny ones in each of the two turrets, and the great arched one in my kitchen, infilling the space below the bricks so admired by Dr Fawcett. Malcolm had designed them all in such a way that they did not need putty, and the edges on which they closed had a design that kept out draughts. Falconer's execution of them was immaculate, and Robin Scott designed and made catches to allow for the inward-opening system I'd demanded.

In our case, on the upper storeys, the windows opened on a level with the treetops. The window-ledges were oak from trees which my father had felled and cut, and which had been lying at my nephew's farm since his death. How often I wished that he could have seen this project launched and completed.

O, you have made me magic windows,
That open – not on foam,
But on enchanted treetops
Where red squirrels make their home.
They open on the treetops
And align me with the birds:
You made me gates to fairylands:
All I can form are words.

Artistry and craftsmanship went into each element of Aikwood's restoration, pride and commitment from all who were involved, and we took delight in its steady progress. Robin Scott, the blacksmith, added a new expression to my vocabulary – along with all the building-trade terms that also enlarged it. Just before the final completion of a task, he would stand back, view it, and pronounce on whether or not he found it 'eye-sweet'.

And Aikwood was surely eye-sweet. When the scaffolding came down, on a sunny April day, the stones seemed to have acquired a warm glow from the winter ministrations of the father and son stonemasons, David and Andrew. Both of them were fine ex-army pipers, and often practised during the lunch breaks. The garden was beginning to take shape, with a large lawn, borders, a terrace of reclaimed stone, and the beginnings of an orchard. Change was all around.

On the political front, too, things were changing. In November, 1990, I was driving Allan Massie to a meeting with the actor Robert Paterson. We were to have another attempt at *The Minstrel and the Shirra*, Allan re-writing and making massive cuts, Robert playing Scott, and myself directing. In due course it would be seen at the Edinburgh Festival – not the Fringe this time, but as part of the official Festival programme. Frank Dunlop, the most inspiring of Festival Directors when it came to theatre, had decided to have a venue for very small-scale work. As Janice and I waited for the lights to go down in Physicians Hall, we looked at each other. 'What are we doing here? We're supposed to be touring village halls in the Borders.'

In the interval a stranger came up to me. 'A very good production, Lady Steel – but you should have taken the laundry label off the napkin.'

It was a salutary lesson in attention to detail.

But that was all in the future: at this time, we were at the very early stages. Allan had brought me a draft of his new novel, *The Hanging Tree*.

'There's a bit about Aikwood in it,' he said. It was an historical novel, set in the fifteenth century. Thanking him, I reflected on how, in the Border countryside, we cannot escape the past. But the present was to intrude sharply. As we passed the village of Middleton, I said to Allan, 'Hang on a moment, we'll get the 10 am news,' and I switched on the car radio, which was so temperamental as to be frequently inaudible, and which seemed to have an inbuilt tinnitus. This time, however, it did not let me down, and together we listened to the announcer say, 'The Prime Minister has resigned.'

Thus did Allan, once one of the few Scottish writers (and indeed one of a minority of Scots) who admired her, and I, one of the many who loathed her, hear about the fall of Mrs. Thatcher. With anyone else, or on my own, I would have given out a roar that would have sounded right at Murrayfield. Later in the day, at meetings in Glasgow, where it was an inevitable subject that intruded into business, there was a general feeling of jubilation. But for now, all I said was, 'I think I'd better pull in to the side.' An era was over, and I was glad to see it go.

I could see other changes happening, less welcome ones. The popular and big-hearted Tory MP for Kincardine and Deeside, Alick Buchanan-Smith, had died. He was one of the Scottish ministers who had tried to temper Mrs Thatcher's glittering-eyed convictions and her very southern stridency, and to limit the damage she was doing, not just to her cause in Scotland but to Scotland herself. His death caused genuine grief across the political spectrum, but now there was a by-election to be fought in its wake, and the Liberal Democrat candidate, the young and able Nicol Stephen, was lying in second place. Both parties threw in all their resources. I made the journey there twice, the first time with David, and Rory, who had just left school, was embedded there for three weeks.

In the days of the Roxburgh, Selkirk and Peebles by-election, a visiting politician would have been expected to address an evening meeting (or two, or three). The press might come to these, and report on them – but *the questions would be from the voters and the answers from the candidate.* What was happening now – and I had seen this developing, but it was at Kincardine and Deeside that I became fully conscious of the extent and permanence of the change – was that the candidate and the supporting politician gave a morning press conference. *The questions came from the journalists and the answers from the established politician*: it was as though the media were dictating the content and direction of the campaign, as if they had interposed themselves between the candidate and the ordinary voter. And the public, to a certain extent, had only themselves to blame: the fall-off in attendance at public meetings had made these an unprofitable way of using a candidate's time.

I came back to Kincardine and Deeside at the end of the campaign with Rory, to help on polling day. As I went out of the door of Cherrydene, I grabbed a rather lurid and hairy jersey which had been a Christmas present from Dolma. Crossing the constituency boundary into the battleground, my old reiving instincts were aroused by the sight of the Tory posters on fences. Reverting to type, Rory and I removed them and piled them into the boot, and when I reported in at the by-election headquarters, I enquired what should be done with them. Shocked young faces and voices answered my casual question, and I was made aware that I should never have done anything so reprehensible, so irresponsible, as to remove someone else's property. To my question, 'Where's the eve-of-poll meeting?' I was told that this was of secondary importance, and that I would be of more use putting a fifth 'focus leaflet' through selected doors.

I thought of David's traditional eve-of poll meetings in the constituency, the climax of the campaign. Perhaps there were no votes left to be decided by then, but as he made his final speech after fifty or more in three weeks, he would inject a fresh stimulus into his supporters, reminding them what their hard work, their freely given time and their commitment to the sheer unremitting slog of it all – and, for many of them, their dedication to the cause for years, sometimes a lifetime –was all about. And they, responding, would send him into polling day on a wave of optimism. Sometimes there would be a piper, sometimes I would be given flowers; once, as they crowded round the car outside the Roxy Cinema in Kelso, I gasped, 'I feel as if they're seeing us off on our honeymoon.'

There was no such climax for Nicol Stephen, although the campaign had gone swimmingly, and victory was in sight. The meeting, when I ran it to earth, was in a school gymnasium, and half-full at best.

On polling day I did as I was told to do, and after the polls closed went back to the hotel where most of the election workers were based, some dozen miles from where the count was to take place. They poured in, satisfied with a good day's work, and that the seat was won. Then, at some point over the next couple of hours, I realised that a large TV screen had been set up, and that this was where they were going to watch the result declared. Again, I remembered the heady experience of David's emergence into the dark Jedburgh night twenty-five years before; how he had been carried on shoulders down the High Street to the Liberal Club, and how people had sung and cheered and embraced.

The SNP would be outside the count, I knew, with placards and slogans. They would only be celebrating the rise of their candidate from fourth to third place, but it would be their enthusiasm that would fill the TV screens, while the Liberal Democrats sat, drinks in hand, cheering in the vacuum of the hotel. When my pleas to come across to the count fell on mainly deaf ears, half a dozen of us set forth, and stood – or rather jumped up and down – with our yellow diamonds outside the town hall, where I led them in a chant of 'Nicol Stephen, MP!', while Rory cringed with embarrassment.

In a London television studio, David was taking part in the BBC results programme.

'Well, things seem to be going well up there in Kincardine,' said David Dimbleby, who was presenting it. 'I can see a very excited-looking Liberal lady there – I'm sure she has something to celebrate.' The image of a short, bespectacled, bobbing figure in a jersey of large proportions and violent hues swam on to the screen.

'That's no lady,' said David to the nation. 'That's my wife.'

But at least the new MP for Kincardine came out to the cheers of his own supporters.

While the building work was going on smoothly over the summer, I too had been working. Since the start of the year, I had been preparing an ambitious arts project which would take place there in the autumn. This would be my last Borders Festival, for I knew that I would need to give all my energies to the completion of Aikwood. This time, I felt less on my own, as the Festival had recruited the wonderful Liz Smith to work with me. She was already something of a legend in theatre marketing and PR and is now very much the doyenne of that profession. At the time, she had just come to live in the Borders, and was anxious to devote her expertise to a local enterprise. By the end of the festival, I had forged a new and lasting friendship.

Liz is amazingly well-connected in theatre. She was at one time married to the son of the playwright Emlyn Williams, and through the latter got to know his protégés Richard Burton and Elizabeth Taylor: indeed, she is godmother to the latter's daughter. During the run-up to the Festival she was invited to Liz Taylor's sixth wedding; but loyally stayed in the Borders, working with me in the Festival's cramped office in the old prison in Selkirk. My son Graeme, to whom I reported this, was less impressed at Liz's sacrifice than I was: 'I expect she'll get another chance to go to a wedding of Elizabeth Taylor's,' he said, drily.

This particular festival took John Buchan as its main theme. Once again, there was a biographical solo production, and I made a storytelling evening, *Moorland Tales*, for Rowan Tree out of some of Buchan's early short stories, set in upper Tweeddale. I had entrusted the major production, an adaptation of the wonderful novel *Witchwood,* to a theatre company that had been set up for the Scott Festival, and which had continued to produce and tour in the Borders over the last couple of years. The director, Ann Plenderleith, having gratefully accepted my help and taken up my contacts at the start, was now exhibiting hostility towards me, and when I tried to make suggestions about the script and the production – which the Festival was funding – she answered everything with the mantra that, 'I'm a professional, I know what I'm doing,' with the implication that I was neither the one nor had any valid views on the other.

Alas, she did not: the production was a disaster. One reviewer described the set as looking as though it had been assembled by the local playgroup, and the company morale was dreadful. My reservations about the length of the script were totally borne out by the reality, and it had become clear that while as a director she could work reasonably well with an existing script, or with short stories, she could not handle the complexities of a great novel like *Witchwood*. From then on she treated me with even greater enmity, and this went on for years. I would learn that, although the arts, and theatre in particular, is a world that can be highly satisfying in terms of sense of achievement, and in which loyal friends can be made, there is also far more rivalry, small-mindedness and envy than in the political arena.

I was busy with two productions of my own for this festival: as well as compiling and directing *Moorland Tales*, with John Nichol, Lucy Cowan, Hilary Bell and a newcomer, Maureen Lawrie, I wanted to use our half-restored tower as a venue during the festival.

The exquisite son-et-lumière at Azay-le-Rideau had lodged in my mind. I could not replicate that at Aikwood, but I could use it as a basis, an inspiration. The tales connected with Aikwood could be told in a promenade theatre performance: to be specific, the tales of Michael Scott, the reputed Border wizard. I had realised early on that there were in fact two men of that name: the one to whom the lands of Aikwood had been first granted, and whom I considered to have probably been its sixteenth-century builder, Maister Michael Scott, and his namesake, so often associated with the tower in legend, the medieval scholar of the twelfth and thirteenth centuries.

This earlier Michael Scott was a major and influential figure in the development of learning in the Middle Ages. He certainly came from Scotland, but he found his place in Europe rather than in his homeland, becoming a noted scholar in Paris and Bologna before ending up in Palermo in Sicily, at the court of the Holy Roman Emperor. Here he found employment as tutor to the future Frederick II, 'the world's wonder', founder of early universities and patron of the arts and of architecture. It must have been an extraordinarily satisfying period for both of them, and Michael also found time to pursue his own researches and to write. When

Frederick, at the age of fourteen, married a twenty-four-year-old widow, his tutor's marriage gift was his own *Treatise on Human Physiognomy*.

From Palermo, Michael travelled to the Spanish city of Toledo, where a new school of translation had been set up. Here, his main work was the translation of the writings of Aristotle, the original Greek versions of which had, over the centuries, been lost. But Arabic versions existed, with commentaries by Islamic scholars, and mastering this language, Michael Scott embarked on the translation of Aristotle's works into Latin, thus making them available for western students of philosophy. He argued, too, for the adoption of the Arabic decimal numerology that we use today, instead of the cumbersome duodecimal system bequeathed by the Romans.

His work did not stop short at translation, and on his return to the Imperial Court he produced original works on astronomy, alchemy, astrology, mathematics and medicine, which are held today in the Bodleian Library in Oxford and the Bibliothèque Nationale in Paris. His *Secrets of Nature* was a standard medieval textbook. And he practised the sciences about which he wrote.

A man far ahead of his time, he was regarded with suspicion by the Church, though protected by Frederick's patronage. Such was the aura of suspicion around him that his contemporary, Dante, in his *Inferno*, describes him among those he sees in the seventh circle of hell:

> As on them more direct mine eye ascends,
> Each wondrously seemed to be inclined
> At the neck bone; so that the countenance
> Was from the reins averted; and because
> None might before him look, they were compelled
> To advance, with backwards guile.
> That other, round the loins
> So slender in his shape, was Michael Scot,
> Practised in every sleight of magic wile.

There were legends about this extraordinary Scotsman throughout Europe, most of them involving an element of transformation. And there were also legends about him in the Borders, in particular linking him to Aikwood Tower. How did this come about?

The evidence would seem to point to James Hogg, and through him, to Walter Scott. Hogg's paternal forebears had come from this part of Ettrick, and it seemed to me that they had confused the sixteenth-century Michael Scott of Aikwood with the earlier figure. At any rate, there was a rich seam to be tapped, and like Malcolm Hammond with the restoration of the tower, I assembled my team.

There would be five of us: myself as writer; a director, Alan Caig Wilson; a choreographer, Jane Houston Green; a musician and composer, Chris Achenbach, and – not a conventional theatre designer, but an installation artist – Mark Haddon. The first and last of these were both Borderers; and Jane and Chris had lived and worked in the Borders for years in their respective disciplines. As well as directing, Alan Wilson would act the different manifestations of Michael Scott as both medieval scholar and sixteenth-century builder of Aikwood and their appearance in the legends. Jane would also play the parts of the later Michael's wife and the young Emperor Frederick. Of these four company members, both Alan and Chris were to continue to play a large part in my life and that of Aikwood over the years.

Such a collaborative approach as we were intending was one which appealed to the Scottish Arts Council, and I managed to get funding and sponsorship from them. We met monthly to make progress on the project, always at Aikwood in the site caravan, and in June, Alan, Jane and I went off to Spain, partly to do some research and filming in Toledo, and partly to try to find some Spanish actors who would come across to take part in the eventual production. It was very hot, and we were on a tight budget which our grant dictated. We stayed at a hostel in Madrid and a modest two-star hotel in Toledo. The accommodation was a far cry from the smart city-centre hotel I'd occupied with David on a previous, political visit.

'I say,' said Alan enthusiastically to me after our first night in Toledo, 'This is a pretty smart hotel, isn't it?'

There was a short pause before I replied, 'I hate to tell you, Alan, but I'm slumming it.'

Slumming it by my standards we may have been, but our days in Toledo were inspirational. We paced the old streets and filmed at crack of dawn; we attended the Mozarab mass – a rite that had been unchanged since the days of Michael Scott – in a side-chapel of the great cathedral, and we visited places of worship of Judaism and Islam as well. Toledo found its way into my clutch of most magical cities.

*Maister Michael* was performed during the last week of October, coinciding with a full moon and marvellous weather. The audience came on foot up the drive, which was lit by flares, and in the courtyard were given mugs of mulled wine and wrapped up in grey blankets supplied by HM Prison, Saughton. Thus, they became the guests of the sixteenth-century Michael and his wife as they celebrated the completion of the building of the tower. A misunderstanding between them led Michael to tell his wife about his namesake, and the stories of the legends were woven throughout the two main storylines. As well as our core of professional performers, we had managed to recruit a substantial body of volunteer actors and musicians – and three Catalan actors came from Barcelona to take part. There was a final hiccup with Mark, the visual artist, who wanted the Catalans to appear whitewashed and naked. In my doubts about this I felt decidedly middle-aged, middle-class and non-experimental; it was Alan who defused the situation by pointing out that the actors would simply be too cold. For this was to take place on frosty Scottish October nights.

Like so much of what I conceived and carried out in theatre projects during those years, the performance was able to go ahead with a minimum of red tape. As I remember such touches as unprotected tea-lights on each step of the stairs up to the first floor, and the blazing fire in the Great Hall, I realise that *Maister Michael* was very much of its time – the time before the present swingeing health and safety restrictions. I don't believe it could be put on now.

As the actors and musicians departed after the last performance, and the shades of the ghosts that they had created faded, Mark Haddon left a more substantial legacy in alchemical symbols drawn in charcoal all over the plaster of the ground-floor walls. It took Lynne and Grame six coats of paint to obliterate them. Nevertheless, if Aikwood had needed to be exorcised of ghosts, I felt that this had been truly done, although we have always ascribed strange coincidences in our home to the benign magic of Michael Scott. And we called our black cat after him.

The completion, or near-completion, of the restoration had taken on a momentum of its own. One decision had been put off at every fortnightly meeting with Malcolm Hammond. It was whether the original front door should be replaced or repaired. At the conclusion of every site meeting, Malcolm and I could be found in deep conversation with the master joiner, Falconer Grieve, debating this important matter. Each week we would conclude: let's decide on it next time. Eventually, it came to the crunch. We decided on the door's restoration, much to the disappointment of the oldest joiner on the team, who had been looking forward to making a new door.

For me, the kitchen would be crucial, and every square inch of it was planned as a team effort between Malcolm, Falconer and myself. It would become the hub of the tower, and over the years I would surprise myself by the ease with which I was able to prepare meals for up to eighty people. We now planned to move in, not in October, but in July 1992, and we were looking forward to the celebration of a family event in June.

First, though, David and I gave a feast for the men. Pat Neil and I, the cooks, were the only women at it. Trestle-tables and benches were brought into the Great Hall, and we cooked two huge legs of lamb in the new Aga. I had had a scroll prepared, with the names and trades of all those who had worked on the project over the last couple of years. Now they all signed it, and we processed up to the top of the stairs where the new stone capping for the newel lay beside its place. In the cavity we placed the scroll, David's final election address and a few of my poems. Each master brought a symbol of his craft: for example, Falconer Grieve, the joiner, had made a miniature plane, with a curl of wood sneaking out from its blade; Robin Scott brought a nail; the electrician, a light bulb, and they were all sealed up below a coping stone.

Then it was down to the Great Hall to the feast, to the Bunyans playing the pipes, and the apprentice plumber, Kenny Pearce, that year's Hammermen's Standard Bearer, leading the singing of 'Up wi' the Souters of Selkirk.'

There was a late start on the site the following day. In the Cross Keys at Ettrick Bridge that evening, a neighbour said to me, 'I hear that was some party you had last night'. New legends were already beginning.

*June 1992*

> It's high and hot midsummer,
> And the tower bursts into bloom,
> Not just with old moss-roses,
> With bugle, thrift and broom,
> Not just with lady's mantle,
> And columbine's many shades,
> But a bride all gowned in ivory,
> And lapis-blue clad maids.

The tower is all but completed, and it is our beloved daughter Catriona's wedding day. She walks from her childhood home on her father's arm towards the small kirk where she was baptised, and went to Sunday school;

before her, the Aikwood masons play their pipes. At the church, Chris Achenbach plays the organ, and her groom awaits: he and his family have spent the week in the warm hospitality of the Maxwell Stuarts, mother and daughter, at that most lovely of Scottish historic houses, Traquair.

'I can't think of anything more romantic than my bridegroom coming over the hills from Traquair to claim me,' I say to my daughter, but Rajiv Bhatia has come a much longer way to his original meeting with Catriona at the London hotel where they both worked. He is from Delhi, and Flora Maxwell Stuart had been my companion in a voyage of discovery to India to meet his family after he and Catriona had become engaged.

'I do envy you,' said Flora, 'having a different culture coming into the family.'

My father-in-law, robed in his gown as doctor of divinity, performs the ceremony, and among the hymns are two from our own marriage in Dunblane Cathedral thirty years before. Unlike that great medieval building, the small church is packed tightly, for it takes just over a hundred of a congregation. The jewelled colours of saris flash among the kilts outside, there is kissing and congratulating, and everyone moves off to Aikwood, the bridal couple in a handsome, open vintage Rolls-Royce: a happy handselling if ever there was one. Champagne flows, as do red and white wine, and a roasting pig forms the centrepiece of the wedding feast. It's just as well, I reflect, that the bridegroom is a Hindu and not a Muslim. Relatives, friends from the village, from politics, from our university days, wander around the nascent garden and into the rooms of the tower, white-painted, unfurnished and full of potential for happy living. The sun shines, and we all feel blessed.

If it was a good handselling for Aikwood, it was also a satisfying farewell to Cherrydene. We had moved there when I was pregnant with Graeme, and it had been a wonderful house in which to raise a family. None of my children had had to undergo the moves that both David and I had experienced during our childhoods: they knew, as neither of us did, where their roots lay. After 1966, David had fought every election campaign from there, and much political trafficking had gone on within its low-ceilinged rooms. Only a few months before the wedding, he had once again returned to Cherrydene from the count electing him as a Member of Parliament for the Borders constituency of Tweeddale, Ettrick and Lauderdale. It would be the last time that he stood for the House of Commons.

I was more sure than he was that this ought to be his final election. Now he was a knight, about to move into a miniature castle; a seasoned campaigner, no longer the Boy David of the first elections. He had been party leader, and led the party into a new, stronger existence. If he was not old in terms of years, he had a substantial record of parliamentary and political achievement, more than any other post-war Liberal. But it seemed to me that while he had been blazing trails, the local party had grown old and tired, with little fresh infusion of enthusiasts in recent years.

Closer to these things than he was, I saw the problems that the local party was facing and that it needed to be re-energised. Perhaps it was time to make changes, and perhaps I had to articulate this. I had never tried to influence David. Over the move to the Borders, over taking up the Abortion Bill, over the leadership, the Alliance and the merger, I had respected his decisions, and backed him all the way. But now I felt quite strongly that this should be his last election, that this wonderful, satisfying part of life had run its course. On the eve of the poll, we met near the A68 almost by chance (it was still before the widespread use of mobile phones) and went down a side road, where we looked together at the magnificent Leaderfoot bridge near Melrose and took photos of each other, on our last day's campaigning together in the Borders.

In the afternoon of polling day, for the first time in ten elections, we met up in the early evening and visited the remaining polling stations together. As ten o'clock came near, it turned dark and we were unable to find the last, tiny outpost. It was the only time we ever missed visiting each and every polling place.

On the way home we listened to the results of the exit polls on the car radio. They forecast a win for the Tories under John Major. We thought they must have got it wrong. Catriona phoned excitedly to tell us that Neil Kinnock had booked rooms at the hotel where she worked in London, to rest there before sallying forth to claim the victor's crown.

At the count at Galashiels Academy we went into a side room to watch the main election results roll in on TV. There was still no doubt in our minds that Labour, under Neil Kinnock, would win it, or that, in Scotland, many Tory heads would roll. We watched in disbelief and disappointment as ministers such as Michael Forsyth and Ian Lang held on to their slender margins in Stirling and Galloway. Kincardine and Deeside swung back to the Tories. Throughout Britain, Labour failed to make the breakthrough that had been anticipated, and the Conservatives, under John Major, were back in government for another parliament. David's own majority went down. He had been the oldest candidate on the ballot paper; he no longer had the glamour of being party leader and he was definitely now seen as an establishment figure by many in the Borders, who did not remember the passionate, eloquent Boy David. My resolve that this should be his last election hardened.

We had been so sure that the time for a Scottish parliament was coming. The ground had been well prepared over the preceding five years, and we had been part of the process. I had been one of those on the group appointed by the Campaign for a Scottish Assembly, which in 1988 had produced the document called *A Claim of Right for Scotland*, asserting the right of the Scottish people to determine their own form of government. The following year, in a simple, moving ceremony at the Church of Scotland's Assembly Hall, the Claim itself was signed by 58 of Scotland's 72 MPs, all but one of its MEPs, the heads of 59 out of the 65 local authorities, and representatives of the other political parties, churches and trade unions.

These signatories had formed the Scottish Constitutional Convention. David was appointed co-convener of it: as with the European movement and many other of his causes over the years, it brought together political parties to work together in a common cause, although in this case only Labour and the Liberal Democrats. The Tories of course were bitterly opposed to the Convention's very existence, and the SNP opted out soon after it was established. This was probably just as well: the entrenched hostility between them and Scottish Labour would have meant a barrier to progress. The work that had already been achieved by the time of the election was considerable. The Convention had expected to be able to present a blueprint for a Scottish Parliament – the word 'Assembly' was no longer used – to an incoming Labour government. Now, despite there being even fewer Scottish Tory MPs, there would be no way forward.

In that classroom at Galashiels Academy, I doubted whether I would see a Scottish Parliament in my lifetime.

# 24
# First Years at Aikwood

Although we moved into Aikwood in the summer of 1992, three months ahead of schedule, we had not sold Cherrydene. Anyone who, like us, was trying to sell property at the nadir of the market then, will remember what a desperate time it was. We had not, of course, managed to keep the costs of the restoration within budget, and now we needed the money from Cherrydene as well. It went on the market in May, and I showed a few people round, convinced that one of them would love it as much as we had, and leap at the chance of buying it. No-one offered. By the autumn, interest had dropped off entirely and the house looked deserted and sad.

Just before the end of the year, an offer came in from people who had seen it back in those balmy May days. It was two-thirds of what we had originally asked for, but we accepted gladly. The hand-over date, in mid-January, coincided with a trip to China by David. I was grateful for the friends who came with me up into the attics as I cleared out twenty-six years' worth of family memorabilia, as the snow drifted in through undiscovered cracks between the slates. The day came when the final items were packed into my car – the last thing was Catriona's dolls' house and its contents – and I walked through each room, reliving memories good and bad. Then, for the last time, I locked the door and went down to the river, looking at the birch trees that had been planted for our silver wedding and stopping at the grave of Hamlet, our old horse. I drove to Jedburgh where Denbeigh Kirkpatrick took me out for lunch and I handed the key over to him.

Those first years in the tower were especially joyous. Friends from all over came to see us in our new surroundings, and wrote rapturously in our visitors' book in both prose and poetry, in English, Scots, French, Danish and many other languages. We were proud of what we had achieved, and not shy of letting it be seen. We welcomed specialist architects, photographers, journalists, groups from interested organisations – and, of course, politicians, including the maverick Tory Nicky Fairbairn who had his own tower in Fife – except that he called it a castle.* Jim Callaghan, now an octogenarian, was among them; so too was the new Labour leader, John Smith. He was an old friend from university days, and I had been on an arts delegation to Russia led by his wife Elizabeth. We all had much in common, and shared experiences over many long years meant that we counted them as good friends. Both David and John were nervous lest such a visit might be construed wrongly, and it was all fixed up with great discretion. Then the Smiths lost our directions to Aikwood, and had to go into Selkirk to ask where it was – so much for secrecy!

Malcolm Hammond entered the tower for various architectural awards, and we finished up with no fewer than five, including the Europa Nostra. We marked them with more feasts for the tradesmen, which became an annual event for several years. There always seemed to be an excuse for celebration. I remembered the words of another tower-restorer, in the north-east of Scotland, whom we had visited during our summer of idea-gathering. 'I think it's important to have a lot of parties. You have to compensate the building for all its years of silence.'

It was a principle that we adopted, and as well as our own parties, we loaned Aikwood for fundraising events: there were Burns and Hogg suppers, Valentine's evenings (complete with the balcony scene from *Romeo and Juliet* performed by members of the Borders Youth Theatre) and summer jazz nights; we celebrated Hallowe'en, Candlemas and Christmas. Friends and family were married at Aikwood, and for a few years I ran a small and (as usual) unprofitable wedding business.

Arts activities continued, though never on the scale of *Maister Michael*. I collaborated with Chris Achenbach on two short chamber operas based on ballads of the Ettrick Valley, a project we had begun under the auspices of the Scottish Chamber Orchestra when they had held a 'sang school' in the Ettrick valley. The first of these was based on a long ballad, *Whaup of the Rede*, by Will Ogilvie, set mainly at Kirkhope Tower. It told the story of how the reiver Wat of Harden returned from a raid to Northumberland, having mistakenly brought a baby wrapped up in the stolen goods. He called the child 'Whaup' after his curlew-like cry, and his long-suffering wife raised the child along with her own son Will, but the young men were very different. A quarrel took place over a girl they both admired. Whaup's origins were thrown in his face, and when he

---

*'What's the difference between a tower and a castle?' I was asked once, and replied, 'It depends on the degree of pretentiousness of the owner.'

was turned out he went in search of his roots. When he was turned out of Kirkhope, all ended in reconciliation and happiness.

The second chamber opera was based on Hogg's version of the much better known *Muckle-Mou'd Meg* story. My libretto for both of the operas had demanded, as well as four or five main parts, a male voice chorus. It is a sound that I like very much, and Chris scored the chorus in such a way that it could be tackled by good amateurs. The operas were performed at two different concerts by Scottish Chamber Orchestra musicians and singers, with the local chorus. I had hand-picked men in Selkirk with good singing voices, and after the operas, they continued to meet regularly at Aikwood under Chris's direction, taking part in other concerts and even the Traquair Beer Festival. They specialised in the songs of James Hogg, and on a couple of occasions, as the Maistersingers of Aikwood, performed in the Edinburgh Fringe. For Hogg was back in my life, to take up residence at Aikwood along with us.

Some years before, I had taken part in the TV programme *Weir's Way*, part of a walking series which on this occasion had explored the Ettrick and Yarrow valleys, and had taken the Ettrick Shepherd as its theme. I was not walking, but was interviewed about James Hogg. In the course of discussions, the producer remarked that it was a pity that there was nowhere in the Borders that you could visit to find the whole story of James Hogg. There was his statue, overlooking St Mary's Loch, a monument at his birthplace and his gravestone in Ettrick. There were a couple of items on show at Bowhill, and a small display case in the museum in Selkirk.

So the idea was born in my mind that James Hogg deserved a permanent exhibition in the Ettrick Valley, and that the ground floor of the building adjacent to Aikwood Tower would be an ideal place to house it. I set up a small charitable company; Ian Brown, the council's museums curator, agreed to chair it, and I set about looking for loans of memorabilia and books. As news of my plans got around, gifts too came in – a curling stone, a pair of spectacles, a plaid and fishing gear, all once belonging to the Ettrick Shepherd. My nephew Iain Black worked on the design of boards and cases, and these were made once again by Falconer Grieve, thus ensuring that there was harmony between the exhibition and its surroundings. Janice Parker worked closely with me on lots of the final, practical aspects and it opened in early 1994.

For almost a decade my summers were taken up with manning it three afternoons a week. We hosted a Hogg conference, the regular Rowan Tree performers built up a repertoire of Hogg's works, and a stream of interesting people came through the doors. Alas, when the Canadian writer Alice Munro came in search of her distant relative, it was one of the times that the exhibition wasn't open, and Janice's husband, Robert Beaton, a fellow countryman of Munro's, who was 'tower-sitting', turned away the writer for whom he had such an admiration, only realising later why she had looked familiar .

There was a second space, and here I ran temporary art exhibitions, mainly of local artists, and sometimes, in the garden, we had sculptures on show.

Among the visitors over the years were several who claimed descent from Hogg. Although he had had five children, only one of them had in turn provided descendants – and these were all in New Zealand. I was in touch with them, and they contributed items to the exhibition. Some of them called in to see what I had done in memory of their ancestor. But both James and Hogg had been quite common names in the valleys, and I often had to disabuse those who claimed direct kinship but who may at best have been progeny of distant cousins. Then, one day, a South African came who also claimed descent. He was on honeymoon, having come to Scotland for the wedding itself. He was full of joy and enthusiasm at seeing the exhibition, and he bought a copy of Hogg's last book, the *Lay Sermons*, to give to the minister who had performed the marriage ceremony. For once, I did not like to spoil his notion that he was related to Hogg. I would never see him again, why upset things for him?

Next year, I was on a plane between Victoria Falls and Harare. My neighbour began chatting to me, and established that I was from Scotland. 'Where exactly are you from?' he asked.

'I live near a small town called Selkirk,' I replied.

He looked at me carefully. 'Aren't you the woman who works at the James Hogg exhibition?' he asked. It was last year's bridegroom. Truly, the spirit of Michael Scott was in the air with us.

During these years I started riding again. I returned to it when John Wilson, a young friend from Ettrick Bridge, was appointed Selkirk's Royal Burgh Standard Bearer. For the last ten years or so, as I attended the Common Riding on foot, I had longed to be out there on the hills with the horses again; but I was badly overweight, out of practice, and our faithful old Hamlet had died. I realised, however, that if I did not follow the Standard Bearer on this particular year, 'John Wilson's year', I never would do so again. With Rory and Catriona, I joined the cavalcade and survived the experience well enough to ride at Lauder Common Riding a couple of months later.

I saw the next two years' common ridings on foot, as Rory, carried away by John's example, had applied to be one of the Standard Bearer's attendants – in effect serving an apprenticeship for the post itself, in another decade or so. I was happy to watch from among the foot-followers and dreamed of seeing my youngest son carrying the flag in the years around the millennium. It never happened: work and other interests took him to London instead.

On my own next outing round the Selkirk marches, I had a horse I couldn't control, became badly frightened and had a nasty fall. Greatly shaken and fearful after it, I had no option but to remount. Rory galloped past. 'I hope you've got your horse under control now,' he said from his eminence as a marshal. Catriona was too mortified to do more than help me back into the saddle. Then Vicky Davidson came to my aid with a lead rope, and I suffered the humiliation of coming sedately in at the Toll under her control. How long had it been since I galloped up that incline, flanked by a child to right and left, both on leading reins?

I relinquished my beastly horse to the hirer with relief, tottered in and out of the Provost's reception, and then we repaired to Pat and Lindsay Neil's for the Common Riding lunch. The pain at the base of my spine was unbearable, and Lindsay gave me a couple of whiskies and a painkiller. Then a decision was reached that I really should go to accident and emergency at the Borders General Hospital. An ambulance was summoned and I was taken off there and X-rayed. The young antipodean doctor told me that I hadn't broken anything, but that it might be a good thing if I stayed there for a couple of days. I protested that I was planning to go to the Common Riding Ball that night – which I did, on crutches.

My family declared that my riding days were past – especially the rough and tumble of the Common Ridings. The only dissenting voice was Graeme's partner, Lynne, and when Falconer Grieve recommended the horse that he had hired, on the basis that she was really too quiet for him but would do me very nicely, it was Lynne who came with me to the small yard near Hawick to try their horses. They were truly wonderful, big, steady hunters, and with Lynne and Catriona I was to enjoy riding for many more years. When the stable owner gave up, we took on two of the horses ourselves, and one of them, Clever Clogs is still with the family, ridden by my grandsons.

While I rediscovered equestrian delights, David had developed a new passion of his own. He had always loved old classic cars, and had bought them over the years in preference to new models. A friend asked him to go on the Monte Carlo Classic Rally in an old borrowed Ford. Neither of them had any idea about the rules of such competitions, and neither had any time to do real preparation for it. But they did finish, and David was caught in the enthusiasm of a new interest.

His close companion on these ventures was our friend Andre Tammes, who was part of the old university circle. They took part in rallies run under the name, 'Claret and Classics', run by the eccentric polymath Roger Deeley. Andre's wife, Astrid Silins, and I would fly out to join them at the finish, and the four of us would spend a few days together. Then the men set their sights further afield, to Morocco. As we gathered over the Tammes/Silins dinner table to make plans, one of the husbands said, and it must have been in a patronising voice: 'You can come and cheer us over the finishing line.'

Astrid and I looked at each other, and I am not sure in which order we said the following: 'Thanks very much. We'll do our own thing. We'll . . .'

There was a pause, and then the other of us came out with: 'We'll go camel trekking in the Sahara!'

And so we did, setting out from Zagora, where a signpost says, 'Timbuctu 72 days'. There were the two of us and a camel driver, all three in the flowing robes and 'cherche' headdress of the Tuareg tribesmen. My camel, Misoud, seemed devoid of all the vices one expects from her breed, and was sweet-natured and even cuddly. Astrid's and my experience was only a few days, but during it, we reached the rippling 'seas of sand' of the true desert, camped under the stars, and on one unforgettable occasion, rode as the sun set in the west and a full moon rose in the east. Astrid and I burst into song: 'We three kings of Orient are!'

Inspired by Mungo Park, I wrote a poem, resting my notebook on Misoud's hump as a writing desk:

> Oh, the desert floor's a pitiless path
>     Of rock and sand and heat,
> And our shadows are short in the noonday sun
>     As they mark our camel's feet.
> And I think, as the orb of the scorching sun
>     Beats on each kerchief'd head,
> Will I ever again see Yarrow's braes
>     Or the green haughs of the Tweed?

> There are golden pillars that spiral up
>> In a frenzied saraband,
> And the sun shimmers hot on the rippling waves
>> Of the limitless sea of sand.
> But I dream of the morning mists that rise
>> Where Yarrow runs quietly down,
> And the russet leaves of Ettrick's woods
>> That dance to autumn's tune.

Lucy Cowan and John Nichol set it to music when I came home: to hear my words sung, not just spoken, was an additional bonus.

With the Tories under John Major back in power, self-government in Scotland was firmly on the back-burner, although the Constitutional Convention continued its work. But in another part of the world, things were moving swiftly, and the dream that so many had for the ending of apartheid, and for majority rule in South Africa, was being realised. When the first democratic elections took place in 1994, David was asked to go out there, as head of a team of observers, to witness the queues of people waiting patiently in the hot sun for the chance to cast their first votes.

We had been invited to a party at South African House on the day after the election. It was, I think, the only time that I took up an invitation to an event in London that had come to both of us without David. I travelled down to it, not expecting to know anyone there, but simply to be a part of that jubilant, historic time. The events in South Africa were broadcast on a big screen as they happened, drinks were dispensed, we were handed protea flowers, and the crowd jostled and shouted, 'Viva Mandela!' John Smith, the Labour leader and our good friend, arrived to share the celebrations and the chant turned to 'Viva John Smith!'

Back in Selkirk the following day, still high on adrenalin and still waving my protea, I was in the front office of the *Southern Reporter* when one of the reporters broke the news of John Smith's death. I was aghast, both personally and politically, for I am among those who believe that at that time, the Labour Party lost not only a great leader, it also began to lose its soul. As with the loss of all good friends, John left a personal vacuum in our lives as well.

When you come into politics very young, as we did, you have many friends of an older generation. John Bannerman had been the first of these icons of our youth to die. In recent years we had lost both Jo Grimond and Laura, who died within a couple of months of each other.

At their memorial service in London, Moira Shearer had read Robert Burns' lovely poem of steadfast love, *John Anderson, My Jo*, and it had never seemed more appropriate. In the Borders, Will Stewart and Andrew Haddon had both gone, and we missed their sagacity and their stories. Even John Mackintosh, whom we missed badly, had been a few years our senior; but John Smith was the first tree to be felled of our generation, our age-group, of those who had been students together before playing a part on the national scene.

In Peebles, a group was convened with the title 'Under One Roof' to press for an arts centre in the town. I was asked to be its honorary president, and agreed eagerly. As well as stirring up interest, formulating a plan as to how the centre might run, and lobbying, the group was also fundraising. The result, in time, was the establishment of the Eastgate Theatre and Arts Centre. One of the leaders of 'Under One Roof' was Richard Nisbet, a remarkable man who had gone from Peebles to train at drama school in the south of England, but who had then decided that he simply did not want the uncertainty of an actor's life. So he came back to his home town, found a job in one of its leading shops, and put his skills and his time into the local drama club and a myriad of other theatre projects there. I had come to know him through *Maister Michael*, when he had gathered a team from Peebles to take part. Now he said to me: 'Catherine Maxwell Stuart has offered us Traquair for a fundraiser for 'Under One Roof'. Do you have any ideas?'

Without a moment's hesitation, I replied, 'Yes – a promenade performance of *A Midsummer Night's Dream* – and look no further for a director!'

For years, I had thought that the Maxwell Stuarts' lovely home would be the ideal setting for Shakespeare productions. They had hosted promenade performances before, mainly of children's plays, and I was amazed that no one had ever thought of asking if an outdoor Shakespeare could be staged there. Richard Nisbet immediately put the idea to Catherine and Flora Maxwell Stuart, and we worked on the production together. He made most of the arrangements for assembling the cast, and his contacts meant particularly that a lot of local children were involved. I edited the text radically, the mortals were all costumed in modern dress and the mechanicals were given occupations that could have been found amongst the craftworkers at Traquair.

Puck's mother obviously felt that I was taking too many risks, as I placed her son on a wall whose coping stones were a bit crumbly.

Worse was to follow. The teenage quartet of lovers came to Aikwood for a weekend's workshop and Puck was to join them for the final session.

'Judy, could we try out the fire escape?' Demetrius asked. It was a breeches buoy. He slipped it around him, climbed out of the window, and when he was about ten feet down, the cord became entangled on its reel, and he was stuck there. Helena was still sorting this out when Puck and his mother arrived, to be met with the sight of Demetrius dangling out of a fourth-storey window.

'We're just rehearsing *Rapunzel*,' I improvised; but her opinion of my fitness to be in charge of young people was no doubt diminished even further.

'Never act with children and animals,' they say, but I conscripted Lynne to take a walk-on part, with two flat-coated retrievers, for the hunting scene. I had also loaned various items of David's shooting gear, which were worn by different actors, thus throwing his own dog, Lucy, into a state of great confusion. But the production was a hit. Richard and I reprised it the following year and then I left him to it. *Shakespeare at Traquair* has continued over the years with different plays, and is now a regular item on the Borders events calendar. Those who run it always make sure that there are children involved. I can think of no better introduction to Shakespeare than to take part in his plays around the enchanted grounds and house of Traquair.

*Old Year's Night, 1995*

*Our Hogmanays have acquired a triennial pattern: one year in Edinburgh at the Sheas' house in Ramsay Gardens, overlooking the crowds gathered on Princes Street and the spectacular fireworks display at the Castle, and in company of some of the 'wrinklies' group as well as the Sheas' Edinburgh friends. One year in three, we stay on our own at Aikwood, but we don't have guests. I make up a plate of ham sandwiches with mustard, David chooses his best bottle of wine, and thus armed, we retreat to our bed and switch the TV on. And in the third year, we go out to Languedoc in France to sample the Hacketts' hospitality and conversation.*

*That is where we are now, gathered around their dining table in company with some of their children and friends from London. My neighbour asks me, as one does, what my children do. My reply leaves him speechless, for I say, in a matter-of-fact way, as though I was describing a career in a profession or in business or in academia, 'My eldest son is in Friarton Open Prison for growing cannabis.'*

Graeme and Lynne had both been arrested in the summer of 1995. I was well aware that Graeme had been using the drug for years, my early suspicions being confirmed by Vicky Davidson when she said to me while we were still at Cherrydene: 'I think you should be careful what Graeme is smoking when there are press in the house.' I recognised the smell, which David did not. Through my theatre contacts, I was in a world where there was fairly common use of cannabis: once, at a post-production party at Cherrydene, a joint had done the rounds, only David and I abstaining. But at least I knew what it was: he thought it was simply a cigarette. He found it very difficult to take my worries over Graeme seriously, and our son's arrest came as a much bigger shock to him than it did to me.

It was Rory who came to tell us what had happened. The way the police, following a tip-off, had behaved at the arrest was contemptible. A veritable army of them stormed the remote cottage and Graeme and Lynne were taken away to different police stations where they were humiliated in unnecessary ways. They were not allowed to phone a friend during the ensuing twenty-four hours to see to the welfare of the dogs shut up in the house. I was more angry than shocked when I heard about what they had been put through.

Some months passed before the case came to court, during which time proceedings were dropped against Lynne, and Graeme agreed to plead guilty to a lesser charge than the original one. Eventually he had to face the pleading diet, and, three weeks later, was sentenced, not in the local Sheriff Court but at the High Court in Edinburgh, where the judge was an old acquaintance of ours, the younger Lord Cameron. Poor man, he did not realise until he read the background reports for the case that the person in the dock was the son of old acquaintances.

We had thought that community service or a suspended sentence would be the outcome. But the Scottish Secretary of the time, Michael Forsyth, was pursuing a very hardline policy against recreational drugs. This had filtered down to the courts, and just recently, a woman advocate had been sent to prison for the same offence. Graeme had grown the plants for his own and his friends' use, but he was a passionate advocate of the legalisation of cannabis, and had been quite provocative and anti-authority over the years. Perhaps that was why his arrest had been accompanied by such an uncalled for posse of police, and why, at the station, they had subjected him to such verbal abuse and humiliation.

He did not want us to come with him to the High Court in Edinburgh when he appeared for sentence. We all knew that there would be a lot of interest from the press – there already had been – and he was adamant that we should be spared that. On that day I had been out, and came back to four messages on my answerphone that I listened to before learning what the sentence was. The first three were from our oldest friends, commiserating – but not saying what precisely the judge had decreed. It was the fourth one from a journalist that broke the news: 'Have you got any comment on your son's nine-month prison sentence?'

Lynne came to us, shattered. Friends rallied round; people from the distant past offered their support. Flora Maxwell Stuart was especially supportive. One lawyer friend spoke of his relief that Graeme was taken immediately to Friarton Open Prison in Perth, rather than staying even overnight in Saughton. He did not have to spell out what might have happened there to a good-looking young man, the son of a public figure.

The press had a field day. Some behaved very badly, tramping over Graeme and Lynne's garden and leaving her no privacy. But the local *Border Telegraph* did something I shall always remember with gratitude: they made nothing of the fact that Graeme was the MP's son, but simply ran the headline and story, 'Stow Man Jailed for Growing Cannabis'. Whatever depths the tabloids may sink to, there is still decency and loyalty in local newspapers.

Graeme would not let us come to see him at Friarton. 'I just don't want you to think of me in this place. We're diminished, depersonalised. I don't want you to see me like that. And it will only be for four and a half months. I won't be stupid.'

David's father said, 'Well, I can go and see him. I'm a minister of religion,' and David realised that he too did not need Graeme to ask for a pass for him. 'I'm his Member of Parliament,' he said, 'as well as his father.' And they both went, whether Graeme liked it or not. In fact he was moved and encouraged by their visits.

My friend Thom McCarthy rang up, appalled. He had grown cannabis in his time; and was very much in a 'There but for the grace of God go I' frame of mind. 'What can I do?' he asked.

'Just write to him,' I said. 'Just write newsy letters about everyday life.' Afterwards, I found that Thom had written to him even more than I had.

Early in the new year, with full remission as he had promised, Graeme came out of prison, and conducted a dignified press conference on his own, restating his belief that cannabis should be legalised. Then he came to Aikwood with Lynne, and we talked about the future. Not long afterwards, Thom asked us to Samye Ling, where those who had been in retreat for three years, three months, three weeks and three days, were due to emerge from their cells. Thom, Astrid Silins, Janice Parker and

I – who had all been present when the retreat began – sat on a bench with Graeme outside Eskdalemuir village hall, to see the procession, led by a pair of Tibetan trumpeters pass from the cells to the temple. 'It's a bit like waiting for the Standard Bearer to come in at the Toll,' I remarked to Graeme, and he agreed.

They had all been changed by their experience. So had Graeme by his; above all by the support he had been shown by friends and family. Both he and Lynne found jobs that involved training in gardening: his days of voluntary unemployment were over, and my own relationship with him, which still suffered from the choice I had made ten years before when I had put Billy's interests before his, was at last healed.

Part of the future that Graeme now saw for himself was that, after a decade of living together, he and Lynne decided to get married. And so there was another midsummer family wedding at Aikwood. In this case, the wedding itself took place in the Great Hall with the bridegroom's grandfather officiating, and Lynne allowed me to make her wedding dress. At night the summer solstice was marked with a bonfire in the centre of the lawn. I had done the catering.

## FLICK DUFF'S RECIPE FOR CHICKEN IN HONEY MUSTARD SAUCE

*1 cooked chicken, approx 4 lb*
*8 fl oz olive oil*
*1 tablespoon grainy mustard*
*2 tablespoons honey*
*1 tablespoon white wine vinegar*
*Juice and grated rind of a lemon*
*1 tablespoon chopped fresh thyme*
*Salt and pepper (optional)*

Remove the chicken from the bones and cut or tear it into small pieces. Mix all the other ingredients together – I use a blender for this – and put the chicken pieces into it. It is best if this is done while the chicken is still warm. Leave it overnight and serve on an ashet. (*Serves 10.*)

A few years later, one of Ian Rankin's Inspector Rebus novels contained a description of how Rebus's arch rival, Alistair Flower (known as The Weed) was moved from St Leonard's Police Station to take charge of the one in Galashiels, where he endeared himself greatly to those above him in rank by arresting the local MP's son for growing cannabis.

## 25

# *Bowing Out, Bowing In*

1997: Election year again. We were grandparents now, Catriona and Rajiv's daughter India becoming the first of the new generation of Steels. It was back to Kirkhope church again with her great-grandfather to baptise her, and then to Aikwood for a new kind of celebration, the welcoming of a new life. At Catriona's own christening, my father had produced a lilac tree to plant in her honour: a West African custom, he said, for girls only. For India, we planted a rowan tree near the door of the tower – it had appeared on the set of at least two productions by the Rowan Tree Company.

The constituency boundary had been changed again, drawing in the Midlothian town of Penicuik, and this finally convinced David that he should not stand again. 'I just haven't the energy to break in new ground,' he confessed.

The local party chose an immensely tall young man, Michael Moore, to succeed him. I took him around various constituency functions and introduced him to people: sometimes there was confusion. 'This is David's successor,' I said to two horse-dealers of my acquaintance in the beer tent at the Yarrow Show. One was with a new second wife, the other with a bidey-in forty years his junior. The former looked up at Michael, assessed him, and said to me: 'I didn't know you and David had split up.'

As sops to Scottish opinion, the Tory Secretary of State, Michael Forsyth, had decided on two gimmicks. One was the return of the Stone of Destiny – the Coronation Stone – to Scotland, seven centuries after it had been removed from Arbroath Abbey by Edward I, and almost forty-five years since a group of nationalist Glasgow students had temporarily repatriated it. His other token innovation was that the Scottish Grand Committee should have meetings in Scotland as well as at Westminster. Before devolution, this was the body that, technically, was supposed to see Scottish Bills through the Westminster system. It comprised all the Scottish MPs, and when the numbers of them had been more evenly distributed between Tory and Labour members, English MPs who had displeased the party whips would be appointed to make the balance the same as that in the House of Commons. But now, with so few Tories from Scotland, it was impossible for it to function in this way, and it was now really just a talking shop. Most of the Scottish meetings were in the old Royal High School in Edinburgh, the building which had been planned for the use of the Scottish Assembly in 1979. But the Grand Committee also met in other parts of the country, including Selkirk.

At the time, the issue of fees for music tuition in schools was high on the domestic agenda. Selkirk High School had an enviable reputation for its music and a fine band. I thought that this meeting of the Scottish Grand Committee – which was, in its way, quite historic – might be an occasion to highlight the question of music fees and bring it to national attention – to stage a kind of musical protest. After discussions with the school and the police the band took up its place outside the hall, and when the Secretary of State arrived, broke into a rousing rendition of 'Rule, Britannia'. Michael Forsyth admitted later that he had been astounded by the choice. It just shows, I suppose, that musicians do not see political implications in the same way as parliamentarians do – or perhaps the music teachers were sending out a message more subtle than Michael Forsyth or I could understand. Next morning, the broadcast of 'Yesterday in Parliament', reporting the proceedings of the Grand Committee, began with the sounds of Selkirk High School's band.

Inside the hall, the Labour MPs were bristling with pre-election tension. The change in the seat boundary had meant that they now saw this as one they could challenge, and there was no doubt that they had a powerful candidate in Keith Geddes. Born in Galashiels, educated in Selkirk and now leader of Edinburgh City Council, he was a formidable opponent for the untried Michael Moore. And the Labour MPs who had come to the Borders for the Scottish Grand Committee made the most of their opportunities to sing his praises.

We were now going to events with the bittersweet thought, 'This is the last time, in this particular way'. One of David's final engagements as an MP included me as well: it was a lunch, not a supper, in honour of Robert Burns at the local primary school in Innerleithen. As the children performed the rites of a full-blown Burns Supper, we both felt a profound sadness that all of this was coming to an end. On the eve of the election itself, I gave a talk to a women's organisation in Peebles about our years at Westminster, and tears choked me as I quoted Lady John Scott's poem *Ettrick*. Its second verse seemed now more appropriate to us than its first:

When we next rade down Ettrick
The day was dying, the wild birds calling,
The wind was sighing, the leaves were falling,
And silent and weary, but closer thegither
We urged our steeds through the faded heather,
When we next rade down Ettrick.

As David's days in the House of Commons drew to their close, I went up and down to London, using my travel warrants as never before. I may have missed his maiden speech, but I heard his final one: it was on overseas aid. But it was Graeme and Lynne who heard him give the vote of thanks to the Speaker which were the final words of that parliament, and who were with him when he left the green benches for the final time. It was right that he was leaving, but it was hard for him as well.

Back in the Borders, we threw ourselves into the fray in support of Michael Moore. Peter Hellyer came back from the Middle East as usual, and other helpers took up residence at Aikwood. There was no doubt that the addition of Penicuik to the constituency had shifted the political landscape, and it was strange to find that the Tories were no longer the main opposition. My friend Flora Maxwell Stuart, who had always tacitly supported David, rediscovered her original Labour convictions, enthused both by Tony Blair's New Labour and by the changed local situation. We met at an exhibition opening within the venerable walls of Neidpath Castle. 'Our man's going to win,' crowed Flora gleefully. 'He's the bookies' favourite.'

This was serious! I phoned Clement Freud, who knew more about betting than anyone else I was acquainted with, and told him the story. He explained to me how much money would need to be laid on Michael to turn the odds. It seemed an awful lot, far more than our usual flutter on elections. 'Is he a certainty?' asked Clement. I knew that if I said yes, he would add a substantial bet as well, and although not being one hundred per cent sure – how can one ever be? – assured him that Michael would undoubtedly win, and then, with some difficulty, went off to find a local bookie to make my own bet. The odds duly turned, but my part in this did not go undetected.

The glory days of the candidates' election meetings were long past. In their place had come all-party hustings, organised by churches, special-interest groups such as senior citizens, and civic groups. The National Farmers Union had always held rumbustious and forthright meetings at an auction mart, where the candidates would be rigorously questioned.

David was always in a state of high nervous tension before them: he had never felt himself adequate on agricultural policy ever since, as a young candidate, he had been asked how much a bushel of wheat would cost under a Liberal government.

I suppose that the organisers of these new meetings thought that they would be like *Question Time* or *Any Questions*, but lacking a chairman with the style of a Dimbleby, they are usually pallid affairs, with answering time strictly rationed, and no space to develop policies and arguments. The questions, written down and pre-selected, rarely contain the unexpected, as they once did. Even now, I can recall a question during my far-off council campaign in Sighthill: What would I do about the rabbit menace? The old type of meeting had provided a hard apprenticeship for a tyro politician, one that fewer and fewer members of today's House of Commons will have experienced.

But the old style of campaigning was going in other ways. Michael Moore was horrified when the local Tories rang up to warn him that Lady Steel and her son had been spotted bundling a Tory poster into a white van with a Rowan Tree Company logo on its side. They wouldn't make a public issue of it, they said, but the Lib Dems should be aware if such a thing happened again, they would go straight to the press. Graeme took to spray-painting the huge, expensive Tory billboards that deface the Border countryside during elections. Michael's constituency chairman, Ian Jenkins, was a very law-abiding teacher of English. What mortified him the most was that Graeme's efforts at graffiti were riddled with spelling errors, for example 'Torries Out'. What would people think of the teaching of spelling in Border schools? David's absence, as he campaigned nationally, allowed his wife and son to get completely out of hand now that they were no longer related to the candidate.

Election day came and we went to vote. It was a strange feeling, putting my cross against another name than David's. Then David went off to London to spend election night in various TV studios, as he has done ever since: we have never again spent election night together. I miss him terribly at those times. I busied myself with the usual tasks of polling day, visiting remote polling stations on Michael's behalf. As the time moved towards ten o'clock, some of the young election workers who had been my houseguests for the last three weeks gathered at Aikwood. 'Have you ever seen the ballot boxes closed up?' I asked. 'Come on, then. Let's go down to Selkirk.' We went to the station where David and I had cast our votes earlier in the day. There we watched as the tin ballot boxes were sealed up with sealing wax melted by a candle. 'You may never see that again,' I said, and I was right. Nowadays, it's all plastic ballot boxes and plastic seals.

We went home to Aikwood to watch the election results, and the first – wins by young Labour women in previously Tory-held seats – seemed to mark a change in the British body politic in more ways than one. As the night wore on, and the scale of the Labour victory in the country dawned on us, we wondered with some trepidation what was happening at our own count. Twice or thrice, nervous phone calls came to us, and I would pass the news on to David in the London TV studio. But at the end of the day, Michael Moore came through successfully, and the Liberal Democrat standard in Tweedale, Ettrick and Lauderdale (with the addition of Penicuik!), had passed into other, younger hands.

In London, Tony Blair appointed Donald Dewar as Secretary of State for Scotland, and in the Queen's speech, it was announced that there would be a referendum and then legislation on a parliament for Scotland – John Smith's 'unfinished business'.

It was no surprise to anyone, I think, when it was announced that David would be made a peer. I found this less difficult than the knighthood had been: there was a purpose in it, to enable him to keep a place in the body politic. I had managed to make my own title almost invisible locally, where the latest development evoked the query to me in one shop, 'Does that make you a lady, then?'

He set about choosing a name. Discussions took place with that erudite and esoteric gentleman, the Lord Lyon, King of Arms. Aikwood had to be in it, of course – I suggested ditching the Steel altogether, but got short shrift for that. 'I wouldn't feel comfortable, changing my name altogether.' Hmm, I thought, I can't remember a conversation like this when we got married, and I gave up the name MacGregor.

Heraldry is in fact a fascinating art, or science – I am not sure which. A peer can either have a territorial name – Aikwood would have done – or, if you use your original surname, you need to be 'of' a place. Usually it's where someone has their home, but a former MP often takes the place-name of a former constituency – especially so if it has been won in a famous by-election. Roy Jenkins chose to be Lord Jenkins of Hillhead, Shirley Williams, Lady Williams of Crosby. David could hardly have been 'of Roxburgh, Selkirk and Peebles, Tweeddale, Ettrick and Lauderdale' – and in any case all these fine and ringing names already had occupants, so to speak – the Duke of Roxburghe, the Marquis of Tweeddale, the Earl of Selkirk, Viscount Lauderdale, Lord Napier and

Ettrick. The name of our home would do us very nicely. For some reason, the Lord Lyon insisted on yet another layer of place-name, and David became Baron Steel of Aikwood in Ettrick Forest in the Scottish Borders. It seemed very romantic, although I have never discovered whether it has made me a baroness, a peeress, or just plain lady.

This followed a bizarre episode in my life. Since I was a child, I have struggled with my self-image: spectacles, shape and flat, difficult hair. My weight – and I have never been sylph-like – had piled on during pregnancies and never shifted. The odd diet never came to anything – I love my food and wine too much – and apart from riding, I have never taken much exercise. A couple of experiments with contact lenses were abandoned, and no hairdresser ever seemed to get my hair looking good, natural and easy to keep. I felt uncomfortable on display, as it were, and photographs were agonising, both to pose for and to look at. At the time of the 1987 smear, an especially bad photograph of me had been published, emphasising the frowziness of the wife from whom David surely wanted to escape.

Two things happened simultaneously. In Selkirk Post Office, I met an old schoolfriend of Catriona's. 'I didn't recognise you!' I said, and she replied, 'It's all the weight I've lost at Scottish Slimmers.' She enthused about their methods. Then a friend, Jean Grieve, who had done battle much more valiantly than I, over the years, against the same enemy, persuaded me to go with her for mutual support.

Over seven months I shed over five stone; I got the contact lenses, Jean became my hairdresser, and my appearance changed so radically that I too was unrecognised. We went to stay with our friends from the 1981 visit to China, Simon and Rina Tanlaw, at their house over the county border in Eskdalemuir for a shooting weekend, and their young son treated me with distinct unfriendliness. After we left, he said to his mother, 'What happened to the first Lady Steel?' adding, I am glad to say, 'I liked *her*.' His mother had watched my exit from the car on our arrival: 'My God, David's brought another woman! What shall we do, Simon?'

At a function in Edinburgh, my transmogrification was not only commented on, it was taken up by the press. Suddenly I became the subject of photoshoots and interviews, and I couldn't help wishing that I'd been able to get similar coverage for the arts projects I'd worked on.

Still, for that brief period of my life, for the first time, I felt elegant and even beautiful. Over the years the pounds and the spectacles came back, but when David took his seat in the House of Lords I felt good about myself in a way I never had during all his years in the Commons.

It was a couple of months into the new parliament before this ceremony took place: it was high summer, and even David's elderly father managed to come to it. We discovered that while there are specific seating areas in the chamber of the Lords for spouses, unmarried daughters, married daughters, eldest sons and younger sons, and the wives of elder sons, there are no seating arrangements whatever for fathers. The hereditary system still rules: fathers are not supposed to be there to see their sons introduced. They are meant to be dead.

Legislation is now being brought forward to turn the House of Lords into an elected chamber. But the hurly burly of elections is not for everyone, especially those with specialist knowledge, and those whose political experience has been honed in the Commons have surely proved themselves at the hustings over and over again. The Lords gives a forum for 'elders' to discuss the affairs of state and the examination of bills in a less partisan way, and also with greater specific knowledge. My personal proposal for its reform is for there to be electoral colleges within the professional bodies of, for example, scientists, medical people, technicians, artists, trade unions and teachers, all of which could hold their own internal elections for nominees to the Lords. But I have never heard that solution put forward with any passion. My fear is that, while political anoraks like me love voting, not everyone does, and ballot-fatigue may set in.

As for the strange Gilbert-and-Sullivan-type robes, the antiquated rituals, are they harmless or harmful in the overall state of things? I am a lover of the old, the historic; I like old buildings, old cities, dead poets, customs that have gone on for a long time and which evolve very gradually. I am not the person to make a judgement. I simply enjoy the pageantry, though with a slightly sardonic eye.

And I was certainly going to enjoy this occasion to the full. I celebrated lunch and then tea in the House of Lords with my newly ennobled husband, with our family and with his political friends, and went off to the airport carrying an armful of lilies, feeling very glamorous indeed. The weekend of Selkirk Common Riding was coming up, and there was much to do before I could get into the saddle and ride the marches behind that year's Standard Bearer.

*June 1997*

Mounted on my kind, solid Cleveland Bay mare, Chit Chat, and in company with a few hundred others, I pass along the streets lined with crowds, ready to cross the Ettrick and head up to the hills. Ahead of us are the bands and the flags that are carried on foot with their followers, a unique and stirring sight. David is among them, following the flag of the three-hundred-year-old Selkirk Merchant Company, founded to support the ill-fated Darien Scheme: in this gathering, neither knighthood nor peerage will add to or subtract from the man his fellow members know. And immediately in front of us, the riders, the Standard Bearer of the Royal Burgh of Selkirk carries the flag that had been handed down through the generations, ready to maintain the ritual of leading us around the old boundaries of the common lands, and of casting the flag in memory of those who had fallen in a battle nearly five hundred years before. It will be the greatest day of his life so far, and will probably remain so. Another old, historic tradition, with a slow evolution, but rather more democratic than those of the House of Lords.

While we are still in the town, a voice calls out to me from the crowd: 'Here, what do we call you now?'

I rein in Chit Chat and turn towards the place where the shout has come from, remembering the week's events in London with some pride. 'I'm the Lady Steel of Aikwood,' I say.

The voice comes back, dismissively: 'Ach, get away with it, you're just Judy.' And that is how it should be.

Less than a month later, I was on my way to South Africa. This was not as a politician's wife, but as a theatre director. John Nichol had written a biographical play about Mungo Park, the eighteenth century explorer of the interior of West Africa. Park, who was a favourite son of Selkirk and a real hero to John, was born four miles from the town at the farm of Foulshiels in the Yarrow Valley. He had gone to school in Selkirk, and after his first explorations brought him fame, he returned to the Borders and married his childhood sweetheart, the daughter of the Selkirk doctor to whom he had been apprenticed. A chestnut tree planted by him still stands beside the site of the house where she lived. John Nichol had planted one of its conkers as a boy: when it outgrew its container many years on, he gave it to us to plant in the Aikwood garden.

Mungo Park was a good man to have as a hero, and a good subject for a play. He was not, like David Livingstone, a missionary: he was an explorer pure and simple, dedicated to opening up and mapping the unknown lands beyond the coastal settlements of West Africa. Above all, there was the mystery of the Niger: Where did it rise? Did it flow to the east or to the west? Where did it terminate? Tales had been brought to the ears of Europeans by Arab traders: but no white man had set eyes on it, although a couple had perished in the attempt. In 1795, Park, backed by the philanthropic Africa Society, set off into the interior with only a couple of African guides. He had already stayed for some months in the Gambia, preparing himself by becoming fluent in the local languages and trying to learn as much as he could about the customs of the Africans.

He was marked out from other British explorers in Africa by the way he immersed himself in these, and respected all the tribes he encountered. His approach probably saved him, for he disappeared for twenty months and was given up for dead before arriving back in the Gambia. He had encountered dreadful hardships, mostly at the hands of a Moorish tribe who took him prisoner and abused him. He managed to escape, with his horse but without his companions. From then on he was on his own, suffering from heat, thirst, hunger and fever – probably malaria – and time after time he had to draw on his last reserves of endurance to remain alive. Amazingly, he managed to preserve the notes he had made, stuffed into his hat, and in time he used these to write a book about his adventures. It was this that John Nichol used as the basis for his play, threaded through with Park's love story, and the conflicts that tore at him in the run-up to his second, fatal expedition ten years later. I directed John and Hilary Bell in it, with the Ghanaian musician Gift Amu Logotse, and we toured it around our usual village hall circuit in the Borders, as well as taking it to the Edinburgh Fringe.

We were invited to go to the South African National Arts Festival in Grahamstown – or, to be more precise, to its Fringe. The invitation came from Nicholas Ellenbogen who ran a venue there, where his own company, Theatre for Africa, performed several shows at each festival. He had had a disappointing experience previously with some Scottish storytellers who had gone there at his invitation, but he liked what we were doing, and he liked the story of Mungo Park. Now, John, Hilary and I, with Lucy Cowan substituting for Amu and Vicky Davidson as stage manager, were on our way to Grahamstown, despite the rather downbeat comment from one local worthy: 'Why on earth are you going to South Africa? Mungo Park didn't get anywhere near it.'

For Vicky, a true Africaphile, the excitement was as much in getting a flavour of the new South Africa as anything else, as it was for me. Grahamstown is hardly typical: it is a white middle-class University town where you can walk everywhere, and without any of the crime levels of Johannesburg. But the Festival, of which the town's permanent residents were justly proud, had managed to remain fiercely free of censorship during the years of apartheid, and much of the theatre was theatre of protest. Some, of course, made its way overseas: David and I had been in the audience at the Traverse on the opening night of *Woza Albert,* the brilliant satire by the Market Theatre of Johannesburg. It was in the week that the South African communist and anti-apartheid campaigner, Ruth First, whom David had known, had been assassinated. The performance was dedicated to her, and at its conclusion the audience rose as one, cheering and crying.

Nick Ellenbogen's Theatre for Africa drew on environmental issues rather than overtly political ones. He recruited his actors from several countries, hoping that in time they would return to their homelands and start their own companies. The vitality of the young men infected us, and an extraordinary rapport grew up between this very physical company and the five of us, who were presenting much more orally-based work. In the student hostel where we were staying, impromptu music sessions knew no boundaries, as Lucy Cowan's fiddle and Hilary Bell's guitar bridged continents and cultures. A very serious trio of black American women with a very pretentious show, trying to find their roots and sisterhood, failed entirely to make the same connections.

Theatre in South Africa was at that stage having to re-invent itself after its old role as a voice for protest. But it was still visceral. The Market Theatre's production of *Ubu Roi and the Truth Commission* consisted mainly of evidence from those harrowing hearings that followed the end of apartheid. Another one-man play, *White Men with Guns,* explored the feeling of lack of self-worth of a white South African soldier, now that he was being told that 'All I have fought for, all my life, is evil.' They were issues that made political theatre in Britain seem pallid by comparison.

Not everything was so politically charged. I was intrigued to see that a story we had followed in Scotland during the year had made its way onstage in a community production, *Mumbo Jumbo.* A South African tribal chief had travelled to Dornoch in the Highlands to try to recover the skull of his ancestor, brought back to Britain as a trophy in a previous century. The production promised to feature the sacrifice of a chicken, so it was not for the queasy. Hilary Bell, temporarily a vegetarian because of what she saw as cruelty in the farmyard, came along in a state of high agitation. When we got into the auditorium, it seemed more likely that the audience might be the sacrifices. We were seated on haybales: the lighting was by naked candles, stuck into the bales on iron spikes. I spotted the chicken in a supermarket trolley, awaiting its entrance. The doomed fowl was paraded aloft around the audience and even the farm-bred Vicky became apprehensive. As the action built up, the sacrificial scene was enacted. There was a convergence of actors, the flash of a knife, a flying of feathers. The actors drew back. The lifeless body was very obviously not the same bird that had been there a minute earlier: its rigid body said that it had met its end some time before, and well out of sight.

Our run ended with full houses and the audience on their feet. David, who had been asked to give a lecture in Durban, arrived in the country before the end of the Festival. Then, while the performers returned to Britain, he, Vicky and I travelled along the Garden Route to Capetown, going riding in the forest on Western saddles and taking an evening sail into the sunset. *En route*, we had agreed to meet up with our friends from Theatre for Africa, to say a final farewell as they gave a performance in a seaside town. When we reached it, we could find no posters, no leaflets, and staff in the information office were totally stumped. At last the reason dawned: 'Try the township!' And indeed, that was where we found them.

In Capetown we made contact with David's South African friends, white politicians who had supported the struggle against apartheid. Among them was the indomitable Helen Suzman, who for many lonely years had been the only opposition voice in the all-white parliament. Age had not tempered her fire, and she was as passionate and feisty now as she had ever been when she was upholding the rights of Africans and taking up the plight of Nelson Mandela and his fellow-prisoners on Robben Island.

I found a delight in South Africa's landscapes and peoples that had eluded me in David's beloved Kenya. Another aspect of the rainbow nation which appealed to me was its cuisine.

## BOBOTIE

*4 oz dried apricots, soaked overnight in brandy or sherry*
*2 oz butter*
*1 finely chopped onion*
*2 cloves garlic, crushed with salt*
*2 tablespoons tomato puree*
*2 lbs minced shoulder of lamb*
*1 tablespoon curry powder*
*2 oz toasted chopped almonds*
*salt and pepper*
*half a pint of double cream*

*2 eggs*
*1 extra egg yolk*

Drain the apricots, reserving the liquid. Chop them coarsely. Melt the butter and cook the onion and garlic till golden. Mix the tomato puree and the reserved alcohol into the lamb mince and season well. Mix the curry powder into the mince. Add to the onions and cook over a gentle heat, stirring from time to time, for about 30 minutes. Fold in the apricots and the almonds and turn into a 3 pint casserole dish. Beat the eggs and egg yolk, add the cream and pour over the mince.

Put the dish into a bain-marie filled with hot water and cook in a moderate oven for 30 minutes.

Serve with yellow rice – simply add turmeric to the rice while you are cooking it – and chutney, chopped bananas and tomatoes.

Now was the time to try to discover my family's past. For years, David had been even more fascinated by the mystery of my grandfather's end than I had been. We struck off across country from Capetown, towards Kwa-Zulu Natal and Ladysmith. Despite the investigations of our friend Peter Soal, Helen Suzman's brother-in-arms and the MP for Johannesburg, we had not been able to uncover any record of the date or place of the decease of William MacGregor. But I had the name of the village near the de Jegers' farm, copied down from Marguerite's birth certificate, and we planned to find that as well as Ladysmith.

David did one of his heroic drives, about three hundred miles across stunning countryside. As night fell, we tried to find an overnight stop, and eventually tracked down a bed-and-breakfast in a village near Blomfontein. 'How many people live in your village?' we asked. 'Six hundred and fifty-four whites,' they replied: the black Africans did not seem to exist for them. After the headiness of Grahamstown, celebrating the new rainbow democracy in music, theatre and visual arts, and the company of liberal whites, who had taken part in the anti-apartheid struggle in Capetown, we received this information like a bucket of cold, polluted water.

We found the village of Wauchope (a name from the Borders) – a run-down, nondescript group of shabby buildings dotted around dusty roads. A nowhere, in the vast sunlands of this great country, a world away from the smart coastal towns of the Garden Route, and Capetown's contemporary architecture. A place, it would seem, barely in the present, and where nothing much had happened in the past. But the latter assumption was wrong: we spotted a monument, and went to examine it. It commemorates the covenant made by the Dutch settlers after the decisive battle of Blood River against the Zulus:

> *Here we stand, before the Holy God of heaven and earth, to make Him a vow that, if He will protect us and deliver our enemies into our hands, we will observe the day and date each year as a day of thanks, like a Sabbath . . . and that we will also tell our children to join with us in commemorating this day, also for coming generations . . .*

It is one of the smaller, but significant things to the credit of Nelson Mandela's government that the 'Day of the Covenant' on 16 December, so long celebrated by the Boer community, became the 'Day of Reconciliation', and continues to be a national holiday.

We did not find the farm, or any trace of the de Jegers, but in Ladysmith we had the address, supplied by Peter Soal, of the secretary of the Ladysmith Historical Society.

She turned out to be an elderly, sprightly lady. She took us up on a hill and described to us vividly the layout of the siege of Ladysmith, nearly a hundred years ago. She pointed out the spot where a prominent citizen was killed by a shot from the besieging army, and took us to the oldest building in the town. It was the Railway Club: the social club – or drinking den – for employees of the railway, and it was over a hundred years old.

'I expect,' I said, 'that my grandfather spent a lot of time in here.'

'So did my late husband,' she replied drily.

Ladysmith has a statue of Gandhi, celebrating the fact that he had lived here. It depicts him in the moment of his death, his hand upraised in blessing. With pride, our guide told us how those who subscribed for the statue also had to outwit the apartheid regime to arrange for its importing and erection.

With a thrill, I realised that Gandhi's time in Ladysmith was when my grandparents lived there. Our visit to Kwa-Zulu Natal was the nearest I got to those long-ago, formative years in my family history, but I left the rainbow nation, then so full of hope and promise, with its spell cast over me. A theatre tour to Canada later in the year was tame by comparison, at any rate for me.

We came back to a run on the Edinburgh Fringe of *Fishtales*, one of the Rowan Tree shows that I'd produced for South Africa, and to the referendum on a Scottish parliament. In 1979, this had come after the passage of the Enabling Act; now, sensibly, it would precede it. On the last night of the Edinburgh Festival, I changed my plans to stay overnight and accepted a lift home to Aikwood from a Selkirk friend. So it was I, not David, who woke up to the telephone at 5 a.m. A phone call at that hour could only be bad news, and I had an immediate chill of worry for my children and my sisters. But this was a journalist. I protested at the time of the call, but he said, 'Princess Diana's been killed.' *Killed*! My immediate thought was that this had been the work of a terrorist or an obsessed gunman, until the journalist told me of the dreadful scene played out in the Paris tunnel before the paparazzi.

I went to London for the funeral. David was deputy to Roy Jenkins as leader of the Liberal Democrat peers at the time, and Roy, of course, was offered two seats in Westminster Abbey. 'I just don't think I could stand the circus of it,' Roy said, and offered them to his deputy. I had found that week of high public emotion very strange, and could not relate to it. But I had never felt as sympathetic as most people towards the princess; I had, for example, been appalled by the famous TV interview in which I saw her as mincing and manipulative. Afterwards I was taken aback by the wave of affection and admiration that had swept along in its wake many women I respected.

David had been easily charmed by her, when she lit his cigar after a dinner given by the Speaker, George Thomas. Two men among my circle of friends knew her quite well. Michael Shea, of course, was one: although initially he found her charming, his attitude to her became very ambivalent during the separation and divorce proceedings. Always loyal and discreet, years after he had moved on from service in the royal household, he would occasionally, to very close friends like ourselves, let his irritation at her inconsistencies show. I remember him saying in exasperation, 'She said she didn't *want* to keep the Royal Highness title – and when the Palace said OK, we'll remove it, she made a fuss and went to the press!' He also challenged her claims that the Palace had given her no support in the early days of learning her new role.

George Reid, on the other hand, knew her later, when she was a single woman, through her work with the Red Cross during the time he worked for that organisation in Geneva. He respected her. 'She was a real professional in her attitude,' he said, and maybe he got near to the core of Diana, who I suspect will remain a conundrum as much as Mary,

Queen of Scots throughout the ages. She was, in Tony Blair's stomach-turning words, 'The People's Princess'; more to the point, she was also a professional one, and she played her role superbly.

Now there was the tragedy of this violent, needless death – a seatbelt would probably have saved her. The antagonism it unleashed towards the Royal Family was ugly and frightening, and to my mind, undeserved. I was baffled by it all. It was in this frame of mind that, at the last minute, I travelled south and walked with David from the House of Lords to Westminster Abbey, through those silent crowds holding roses, hearts and placards, in mourning for the young woman whom they only knew through the media.

The great stillness of the Abbey enveloped us as we walked down its length; then came the wonderful music and the solemn words of the service. We could see the small bereaved boys beside their father. Diana's brother, Earl Spencer, took his place in the pulpit. He started his eulogy of his sister with bitter references to the endless pursuit of her by the paparazzi; he seemed to end it with the same bitterness towards the family of which she had been a part. Inwardly, I thought: 'This is not appropriate', but I had misjudged the public mood. Through the Abbey came the sounds of clapping and of cheering outside. I thought sadly back to the sunny July day when we had been at St Paul's Cathedral as the teenager in a huge, crushed wedding dress had made her vows to the man she should never have married, and remembered how, as they concluded those pledges, the joyful cheers of that day's crowds had also invaded the stone walls.

# 26
# 'There Shall Be a Scottish Parliament'

Between the death of Diana, Princess of Wales, and her funeral, there was virtually no coverage of any other news. Years later, I saw a TV programme about a tornado that had happened in England during that week: nothing was heard about it at the time, except by those intimately involved. Scottish politicians had called a halt to campaigning in the referendum; nevertheless, just over 60% of the population turned out to vote on 11 September. Some of the arguments that had been used against the 'yes' case in 1979 no longer existed, thanks to the work of the Constitutional Convention over a seven-year period. One was the very real fear in the rural areas that the new legislature would be totally dominated by the west of Scotland Labour mafia, as would undoubtedly have happened in 'first-past-the-post' elections. The adoption in the Convention's blueprint of a form of proportional representation – the Additional Member System, used successfully in Germany since 1945 – managed to allay that fear. Unfortunately, it was not thought necessary to bar dual candidature between constituencies and the list. This was never abused in Germany, but it has been, grossly so, in Scotland, by all the main parties.

Another old argument had, bizarrely, been eradicated by the Tories, the great opponents of devolution. It had been claimed that if a devolved national body came about, with two tiers of local government, the regions and the districts, Scottish voters would simply be asked to cast too many votes. Eager to break up the Labour monolith that was Strathclyde Regional Council, the Conservatives had abolished the two-tier system of local government – and demolished one of their stated objections to devolution.

So much had changed in eighteen years since the last referendum; in the minds of most Scots, the argument had long been won. For a while, the bitter tribal differences between Labour and the SNP were set aside, and Donald Dewar and Alex Salmond stood together on the same 'Yes' platform with Jim Wallace, leader of the Scottish Lib Dems.

We watched the results of the referendum come in at the soulless but efficient Scottish Conference Centre in Edinburgh. There was no fudge this time: there were three votes in favour of devolution for every one against. Even the ridiculously small tax-varying power proposed in the second question had received a substantial majority.

The Constitutional Convention had prepared the ground well in Labour's years of opposition, when co-operation with the Liberal Democrats had been useful to them. Useful, too, had been the almost unanimous support of the local authorities and the churches. Perhaps opposition is the best time to prepare for constitutional change, when such cross-party agreements are more attractive than they are to a party with a sweeping majority. Civil servants must have been working on the potential legislation on the basis of the convention's conclusions, for it was only a matter of six months before Donald Dewar rose in the Commons to introduce the Scotland Bill.

David took an active part in its passage through the House of Lords. In the Westminster village there is no tighter group – outside Old Etonians – than the enclave of Scottish politicians, especially those of a similar generation. There were plenty of weel-kent faces on the red benches, and during the passage of the Scotland Act, David was continually sparring with his old colleague, later his adversary, John MacKay, now Lord MacKay of Ardbrecknish.

As the bill went through Parliament, Donald Dewar also put his mind to where the Scottish legislature would sit, and to the construction of the building. Deals with the Church of Scotland and with Edinburgh City Council ensured temporary premises. The Scottish parliament would be housed in the Church's little-used Assembly Hall on the Mound, and would be served by the offices of the old Lothian Regional Council on nearby George IV Bridge – surely one of the ugliest and most inappropriate buildings that the sixties produced in Edinburgh, with the dishonourable exception of the University's appalling desecration of George Square. (It has since been demolished and replaced with a much better building). But these were not permanent arrangements, and Donald put in train the events that were to cast such a shadow over the parliament's early years, and over our lives.

In retrospect – and indeed, even at the time – there was a strong argument that he should have done things differently, and at least waited until the parliament was up and running and could make its own decisions. But I believe that he was afraid such a decision would be put off and put off, that the wrangling over site, architect and design would be interminable, that there would always be arguments for higher spending priorities, and that the parliament would never move out of its temporary home. David believed passionately that the new parliament should have a new and iconic building. As Secretary of State for Scotland, he could kick-start the process to the extent that it would be irreversible by the time the parliament met. He even short-circuited things by having a closed competition for designs, limited to half a dozen invited and highly-regarded architects, rather than an open one, which would have meant a much lengthier run-up period. Every move he made was bound to have its detractors, so he decided and acted as he thought best. And although not a vain man, he had confidence in his own aesthetic judgement.

What I cannot forgive, however, is the ridiculously theoretical price tag that was put on the erection of the parliament building. It was a factor that came back to haunt, again and again, those who were left to carry out the building that Donald commissioned.

The shortlist of design ideas was sent round Scotland to public halls for people to inspect and pass comment, and when they came to the Borders I went along to see them. There was no doubt that Miralles's concept was the most interesting, and above all it had a lightness which contrasted with the rather dense, monolithic edifices that the other architects had deemed necessary for such a constricted space. There was one in particular that puzzled me. For some time I stood studying it, then realised what was wrong, and called over an attendant.

'Excuse me,' I said, 'but I think you've got part of this one upside down.'

Would David be a candidate for the new parliament? He had campaigned and worked over the years to bring it into being; perhaps it was the honourable thing to work in it as well. But he was enjoying the new-found comparative freedom of the House of Lords, the ability to take off on a car rally from London to Capetown in January and February. 'The drive of a lifetime', it was called, and for him and Andre Tammes, it was just that. Our weekends, for the first time in our married life, were free to spend as we wanted.

Our generation was now reaching its sixties, a milestone which, as ever among our old group of friends, we set out to celebrate. But there were breaches in the circle. Cancer was killing Robin Crichton's wife Trish, and, in the south of France, Norman Hackett was coming to terms with the stroke that had robbed him of movement on his right side. It had come upon him on a business trip to the USA, in the week before his much-heralded and intricately-planned 60th birthday party. 'It's cancelled,' Maggi told us, and their London friends made other arrangements for the weekend. The Scots guests – Astrid, the Sheas, and Bill and Sue MacArthur and ourselves, determined not to waste our tickets, went out to France anyway. It was a surreal few days as we awaited the arrival of our stricken host, and for news of the death we were expecting daily from Scotland, but it was a time that drew us even closer together. A week later, we gathered again, for Trish's funeral. Robin's fabled eccentricity made his wife's funeral so personal and moving that even her grieving father said it was a day of beauty and joy rather than of sorrow. Robin had made her coffin, Malcolm Morgan, another of our group, acted as undertaker, a friend from the village officiated at the funeral service which was held in their film studio, her daughter read a poem she had written for Trish, Sue read Norman Hackett's tribute, and I read a poem that Trish herself had chosen.

At the last, Trish was carried to her grave in a small wood near their house by relays of broad shoulders from the village, and finally by the old friends of so many years. As they approached the graveside, a robin flew out.

The following week we met again, in the Playfair Library of the Old College, where we had first encountered each other all those years before. But this was a joyous occasion, looking firmly to the future: the marriage of the MacArthurs' son, Liam. Nearly ten years later, Liam would become the Liberal Democrat MSP for Orkney. Who would have thought of such a thing during Jo Grimond's rectorial?

Not long after this, as we sat around a table for six, with Astrid Silins, Andre Tammes and Michael and Mona Shea, and talked about our mortality, Michael Shea said, 'Of course, statistically speaking, at least one of us will be dead in five years.' With the advent of the grim reaper and his associates on the one hand, and the pleasures of a carefree third age on the other, was sixty the time to be embracing such a challenge as the new Scottish Parliament?

And what about me? I had always said, when questioned about possible political candidature, that the only legislature I wanted to be in did not yet exist. Now it did. I decided to apply to be a candidate, and hard on my heels was Catriona, who saw the parliament as a place for young blood, and who was flexing her own political muscles.

Then something happened that made me draw back. It was a newspaper article about how the three of us had all been approved as candidates.

An MSP's putative pay was multiplied by three, and the conclusion of the piece was how cash-rich the Steel family were likely to be, thanks to the new parliament. The fact that a married daughter's earnings do not normally count as income for her parents was beside the point; nor did the tone of the article allow for the possibility that money might not be our motivation. It came like a bucket of cold water to any aspirations I might have had. I could not allow the contribution that David could make to become muddled by me. I took the idea no further, and Catriona's second pregnancy put her ambitions on hold for several years. But at the last minute the party asked me to allow my name to go forward on the South of Scotland list, so I had the satisfaction of seeing my name on the ballot paper for the first elections of the Scottish parliament.

David was talked about as a potential Speaker, or Presiding Officer, to give the position its uninspiring new name. Wary as ever, he gave nothing away. 'I have to be approved as a candidate first, then selected,' he said, 'and then get elected.'

There was no shortcut, even for a former party leader: he would have to go before a vetting panel like everyone else. He applied to be a candidate on the Lothians party list: it was expected that one Liberal Democrat MSP only would be elected for this, so he had to come top of it, in a vote of all members. There would be a hustings for all the list candidates. Meantime, we again toiled up and down the A7, going to party functions, getting to know people in the different branches in the Lothian area. The choice of placings was no pushover, as there were several other contenders on the list who had put in years of service in Edinburgh, who were well-liked and respected and who felt that they deserved priority. For the first time, I did telephone canvassing among party members – and discovered to my surprise that those on the other end of the line were not annoyed and resentful when approached in this way. We took nothing for granted, and David had to earn his place at the top of the Lib Dem list for the Lothians.

For once, I kept a full diary of the election, for the simple and unedifying reason that I had a newspaper contract to do so. For once, therefore, it didn't peter out around the beginning of week two.

*6th April*
So this is the off. I am not proud of the beginning of the first day. David had to get up at 6 a.m. to drive up to the party press conference. I promised myself and him that I would be up then too, to make him coffee and a bacon roll and see him off. In the event I turned over and went back

to sleep. I did however make the gesture of turning the radio from the Radio 4 *Today* programme to *Good Morning Scotland*.

I spent the day catching up on my mail, which includes my own consent form for the South of Scotland list. Why, so late in the day, did I volunteer to go on it, in such a lowly place, when I withdrew from the heat of the Party hustings? Anyway, my name is signed and witnessed and in a humble way I am a participant as well as an observer.

### 7th April

On the A7 at Newtongrange, there is a poster site on an old building. At the last Westminster election it was hired by the Tories, and their posters of Tony Blair with devil's eyes and of the mangy lion appeared in sequence. This time, I see it is again in use – a picture of Britain split asunder with the slogan, 'Divorce is a messy business'. Or is it expensive? Anyway, like the one I passed in Gala, which actually had the SNP slogan with a negative message about tax, it does not even bear the name of the party that has paid for the space in order to solicit votes. I *think* it is the Labour Party's, but it might just as easily be the Tories.

My meeting in Edinburgh is for the year 2000 *Thrie Estaits* project.★ Slightly depressing news from David Watt of NMEX (National Millenium Experience Co), but we make the decision to hold the press conference to announce the project during the week after the elections, to maximise impact.

### 8th April

The manifesto launch has had good coverage, especially Jim Wallace's remarks about finding common ground. *The Times* and the *Herald* have good photos, and the *Scotsman* says he has had a good day. I should order at least one tabloid for the campaign. The Tories have produced a horrendous advert with Salmond looking like La La the Teletubby.

David gets a phone call from Ken Wollack of the Democrats' office in Washington, wanting to know about the Malawian elections. David explains that he is slightly out of touch with what is happening in Malawi, because he is a candidate in the Scottish ones. Wallack does not know that they are taking place.

### 9th April

The post is late; I suppose Chris Renton (the postie) is busy canvassing for his seat on the council *en route*. The effect of the Holyrood elections

★ See p.339.

on the local ones will be interesting. With everyone banging on about the second vote, I wonder how many people realise that in fact they're going to get three on 6th May. My sister Joan says she's going to vote three different ways as a genuine floating voter. One thing is sure: most people in the valleys who vote for Chris – and I expect he'll get in again – won't do so because of SNP policies, nor because he makes any impact in the Council, but because he delivers their mail and is good at turning up at functions up and down the valleys.

David tells me that he sat next to an active and informed Tory last night at dinner who believes they will get ten seats at most, and none first-past-the-post. Hope she's right. An invitation comes from Elizabeth Smith inviting us to a dinner at Valvona & Crolla's on 7th May. Now *that* sounds fun, if any of us can keep awake.

*11th April*
David watched the inter-leader programme last night and felt Jim [Wallace] had come out of it very well. I was disappointed therefore when the papers didn't give him quite the same five-star rating, reserving that instead for McLetchie. They (the papers) are full of Salmond's uncertain start and the potential ceremony. The fantastic result of the Welsh rugby victory over England comes through, giving us the Five Nations Championship. If I was Pete Irvine I would book the Scottish XV for that opening procession *now*.

I spent the morning at the Floors Castle wedding show hoping to get some more bookings for the wedding venture. 'Why aren't you staying all afternoon?' asks Catriona. I mumble an uncertain reply, and then, in the evening, realise the reason. It was Ian Jenkins' adoption meeting as candidate for Tweeddale, Ettrick and Lauderdale – I missed it. I feel terrible. I regard myself as a fairy godmother at adoption meetings, having spoken at them for Archy Kirkwood's, Ming Campbell's and Mike Moore's successive, successful Westminster elections.

*12th April*
David returns from Edinburgh and West Lothian. Amongst other things he has been to see the final models of the parliament building in the new museum. He is much less happy than he has been with the early ones: he says the building will be terribly massive in relation to the delicacy of Holyrood. For my part, I think there is a real mistake in the flat roofs. Every building in Scotland in the sixties with a flat roof has had problems, and a lot of them have had to have pitched roofs added. They just won't

do for our climate. Oh, dear, what a pity it was that there was no open competition for the building. Of course it would all have taken longer, of course it probably wouldn't have been ready till the second term – but what was the need to hurry over the building, when the institution has taken to long to achieve? Poor old Donald, even if he doesn't like what Miralles has developed so far, he can hardly say so.

### 13th April

David has had to go to London and asks me to watch the SNP party political broadcast for him. I had to leave the Labour one in mid-watch last night, it was so dreadful. Total negativity – the same approach as their adverts. All Nat-knocking and not a word about what a Labour administration would actually *do*. Their own people must be pretty disillusioned – I know some who are. There is an appalled letter from Michael MacKenzie's wife, Helen, in the *Herald*. What has actually *happened*? Have the big parties handed over completely to advertising firms? What became of the togetherness of the referendum campaign, the promise of a new politics? The SNP broadcast, though definitely Brigadoonish, is cheerful, upbeat, has a nice theme of people marching together in gathering droves towards – where? Alex Salmond's visage fades in and out. The knocking of Labour is done subtly, with membership cards etc., being consigned to wastepaper baskets over folk music. There is rather a lot of folk singing, for that matter, in convivial atmospheres. It may not be a substitute for a rational appeal to the voters, but it's better than the Labour party's approach.

### 15th April

This is a worrying story. The BBC wanted David to take part in a programme on education. He said no, Nicol Stephen should do it as he is the party spokesman. The producer didn't want to use Nicol, and tried to heavy David, via the party, into taking part. David stood firm – education is not one of his fields of expertise, and it is Nicol's. Anyway he felt that Nicol should get the exposure, as he is a constituency candidate in a seat we expect to win. (He did very well on an all-party TV panel the other night.) The producer, apparently, has some animus against Nicol and refused to use him, so instead they are doing a programme about the Private Finance Initiative and using Ross Finnie. For BBC Scotland to censor who appears on the basis of personal likes and dislikes is troubling.

*16th April*

I have a group of art-lovers from Manchester at Aikwood, *en route* to a couple of days in Edinburgh. I welcome them outside with a firm statement about what an exciting point of Scotland's history this is, before the main talk and performance, which I try to cut; last time David told me I had been wittering. I give them some stories from Scottish history, as well as the story of the tower. Hilary [Hilary Bell, the singer] is in good voice, and they are a responsive audience. One couple is Scots; they lobby Hilary and me about the awfulness of 'Flower of Scotland'. Our candidates for the Scottish national anthem are either Burns' 'A Man's a Man' or Hogg's 'Both Sides the Tweed'. God knows what we'll get stuck with.

David takes time off to go to Glenvarigill in Selkirk to look at the new Suzuki jeep. There was a time – the length of his Commons career in fact – when he would never have even looked at a foreign car. At the showroom he finds himself pursued by Bill Chisholm of the *Scotsman* and Allan Massie, freelance *extraordinaire*. David McLetchie is trying to make some publicity for the Tories outside Viasystems, which is next to Glenvarigill. Nothing much is happening, so they (Bill and Allan) try to involve David to create a news story. They are out of luck. He is too wily an old fish to give McLetchie *gratis* publicity.

*17th April*

David goes to do a walkabout in Selkirk with Mike Moore and Ian Jenkins. The SNP and the Tories are also in the Square: John Mitchell of the SNP unusually pally, and full of the *Scotsman* speculation about a Lib Dem-SNP coalition. Not very likely, but it's good to see him less snarly than usual – the new politics must be having its effect. David has a lovely time, people full of memories of elections past; then goes off to more campaigning, this time in Dalkeith, and then a cross-party meeting for the World Development Association. Then back to Selkirk to record a Radio 4 broadcast.

I spent the morning delivering leaflets round Selkirk. Talk about being set on a hill: every house seemed to have steps up to it. Amazing how you always discover new things when electioneering; I mean houses you hadn't realised existed before. One woman makes approving remarks at the sight of Mike (Moore)'s image on the leaflet. I wait for her to say, 'I always vote for him'. What is nice about Selkirk is the extent to which you still find people leave their house-doors open: standing open, not just unlocked. Inside one open door I find a pile of Tory leaflets, obviously ready to be delivered by the occupant. I help myself to one. I meet Allan Massie in the Square. 'Are you looking for an election?' I ask him. 'No, the bus to Hawick to go to the Sevens,' he replies. 'What about you, are you looking for one?' I boast of my prowess with leaflets. He imagines that I would rather be doing the garden. 'Certainly not,' I say, 'I'd rather deliver election leaflets any day.' He cannot understand that there is enjoyment to be had in electioneering.

Nevertheless, it is exhausting. The morning knocks me out for the afternoon. I am not as young as I was in the heady days of racing around Roxburgh, Selkirk and Peebles.

*19th April*

This election, which I have longed for and indeed campaigned for ever since I was nine, is proving a terrible let-down. Of course, it is over-shadowed by Kosovo, the awfulness of what is happening there – death, suffering, expulsion, loss – all this puts arguments about our education, our health service, our housing, into perspective. Perhaps we should all abandon the election effort and go out to help sort clothing at the Kwik-Fit centres. Maybe we should look at the more sedate elections that take place, say, in the Scandinavian countries. Where there is PR, and more parties, are there likely to be more muted arguments than in the colossus-type politics of first-past-the-post Britain? Or is it because the effort and the years of actually getting the parliament at all mean the whole election is an anti-climax? Or is it because of the dreadful, visionless steamroller-ing of Labour's election machine?

*20th April*

On a trip to Edinburgh, I count two SNP posters in windows and one Labour one. There is one car parked in George Street with a Tory sticker. My own one for Ian Jenkins is the only sign of activity for the Lib Dems. I have lunch with Elspeth Campbell, who is brimming with enthusiasm. The Clifton Terrace office is full of enthusiastic young people and the constituency returns are good, especially from East Fife.

The *Scotsman* regional round up for the Borders says, 'The smart money is on Ian Jenkins', but the National Opinion Poll in the *Daily Mail*, giving a nationwide sweep, awards the seat to Labour. They immediately make capital out of it for the local papers, and what is really irritating is that the locals are not reporting what a prat the Labour candidate made of himself over the Private Finance Initiative. I think with affection of Duncan Brack and his flow of press releases at the last election.

*21st April*

I spend the afternoon leafletting in Galashiels. Ann McPartlin, whose house is full of the Gala leaflets, says, 'I just love it. I come alive at elections. I just love working as part of the team. We spent all Sunday folding and labelling 35,000 election addresses and it was great. Then one of my friends the next day said, "What a waste, no one will read them anyway".' She is half-angry, half-philosophical. Ann doesn't just come out at elections, though. She beavers away at coffee mornings and focus groups, delivering and taking petitions round. And she is *not* manic, as some party enthusiasts are. But is she a declining breed? All the parties rely more and more on 'the professionals', the young lowly-paid rather than the genuine volunteers.

The second Labour party broadcast was infinitely better than the first. Did they plan it like that, or did they change tack?

*22nd April*

Every morning brings sheaves of circulars for David. As a list candidate, I have only received one, an invitation from Safeways to visit a store and arrange a photo-opportunity, but *not* to canvass. Such is the lowly status of a halfway-down-the-list candidate. David's envelopes contain glossy publications from all manner of organisations: medical, educational, social, artistic, environmental, commercial. The most sensible one has been from a mental health organisation which stated, 'We expect you are inundated with such communications and are confining everything we want to say to you to an A4 sheet.' The thing is that the larger and glossier the enclosures, the less inclined one is to read them; and the stronger the doubts about how wisely the organisation are spending their existing resources. In the olden days, the 60s and 70s elections, ordinary people turned up at public meetings to voice their concerns and advocate the causes dear to their hearts. Now they buy lottery tickets and the lottery gives grants to worthy organisations who pay for designers and advertising people to produce expensive leaflets.

*23rd April*

The papers are full of the SNP's tumble in the opinion polls. Salmond appears to be emulating John Major and his soapbox in 1992, by 'taking the message to the people' – in his case, by abandoning press conferences. Do I feel sorry for Salmond? I am inhibited from this by the memory of his cockiness over the years and his behaviour towards Jim Wallace during the referendum campaign.

In the late afternoon I am actually canvassed – the last time was when the late Len Thomson stood in our ward. Morris Manson, our candidate, has called on every house in the valley today. He may not have much of a chance, being a relative newcomer to the area standing against at least two weel kent faces, but he's putting up a bonny fight.

### 23rd April

A heavy TV day for David, who is yo-yoing to and from London. The final programme is recorded from Stirling. He phones after it, 'I'm just driving down the ramparts'. He gets back in time to catch the second half. There is a constituency profile of Ochil where I was born (Dollar) and where I went to school latterly (Bridge of Allan). Our old friend George Reid was reckoned to be a cert for it for the SNP; now it looks more dodgy. To my astonishment, I find that the Labour candidate is Richard Simpson – when I ran the Freshers' conference at Edinburgh 38 years ago – imagine that! – I conscripted him to speak in the Freshers' debate. Truly, Scotland is a village as well as a nation.

### 24th April

I had meant to go on the trail with David today, but by mistake committed myself to an 11 a.m. meeting with a couple who are getting married here in the autumn. So instead I find myself doing an afternoon's leafletting round the Kingsknowe/Abbotsview part of Gala, a small private housing estate built in the 1980s. Since it's Saturday there are lots of people outside, gardening and car-washing etc., so although it's not a proper marked canvass I get a certain amount of reaction, pretty positive on the whole. The interesting thing is the extent to which people *do* seem to have got the hang of the second vote. One man says, 'I'll vote for Ian Jenkins on the constituency vote – I like being represented by a Liberal Democrat – but for other reasons I'll be voting SNP on the list.' Now, I've no idea what his reasons might be, because the important thing was that he was voting for Ian, and it was better to consolidate that one than badger him about the second. But anyway, though I wish he wasn't voting that way on the peach form, I like the idea that he is thinking through *how* he uses the list vote.

I discover something interesting about my own attitude to electioneering: I prefer going out on my own.

### 25th April

A day off. We drive to Eskdalemuir for lunch with our old friends, Simon and Rina Tanlaw. They have a house party of their London friends, interested but not very well informed about the Scottish elections. However, I find one alleged descendant of the Marquis of Montrose, another of the Rev. James Renwick and a Buchan devotee (though he hasn't read *Witchwood*) so we lose ourselves in the niceties of seventeenth-century Scottish politics and politicians. The Killing Times, they called them. I suppose the atmosphere was not unlike Kosovo today. There is something to be said for boring old democracy.

### 26th April

What does an aspiring MSP do on an evening off? Go down to hear the hustings for the local council, of course.

It was arranged by the Selkirk Community Council in the Victoria Hall, which is huge, and has tricky acoustics. I don't know how many of the audience of 75 heard more than three of the candidates out of the nine on the stage, but we certainly didn't. They were depressingly all male, though at least only one would have been older than us. There was some real old-fashioned savaging of the council, especially from some older questioners. What was the main topic of the evening? Not education, not roads, not social services, but *litter*. Into this fascinating topic I hurled myself, with a question about the green cone composting experiment. Unfortunately there was still discussion going on about the previous question when I rose to my feet with this vital contribution, and I had to be put down by the chairman, thus causing the usual embarrassment to David.

### 28th April

The hustings meeting for the constituency was arranged by the *Southern Reporter*. I managed to get the time wrong, and missed the first half hour. It was, by today's standards, well attended – about 150-plus in the audience. Jobs were the main *genuine* issue from genuine Jock Public questioners, as opposed to interventions from committed party members. Education does not really feature as an issue in the Borders, for the simple reason that the schools are pretty good on the whole.

As well as the constituency candidates, there is a front row of list independents or top-of-the-list candidates who get a chance to have their say. Of these, Keith Geddes is disappointing, John Ross Scott for us is clear and incisive; Phil Gallie of course is just part of a Tory comedy duo with John Campbell, the constituency candidate. 'We won't co-operate with anybody!' is their slogan. Well, I suppose it has taken their party a long time to accept home rule. Their march towards the acceptance of P.R., and coalition politics is still going on. Marion Coyne of the Green Party is quite excellent and the malodorous John Hein makes rather too many interventions, including one very personal attack on David. I shout 'Disgraceful!' Actually, I shout, 'Bloody disgraceful!'*

The three serious constituency candidates show a variety in style. You could say that Ian Jenkins and George McGregor, for Labour, represent the new politics that we hope may emerge at Holyrood. They are consensual, respectful of each other's policies, do not score points. Ian is perhaps a shade too emollient. McGregor, a real New Labour man, says daringly at one point, 'What I am going to say now is just my own view.' He gathers his breath. 'I'm not on message here, it's not party policy,' – wait for it, folks – '*I believe in lowering the voting age to 16!*' Mrs Creech (Mrs Screech, she gets called, with some justification) comes from the hardline fundamentalist wing of the SNP. She talks for too long, and is often arrogant and irrelevant. But she has pizzazz.

*29th April*

My fifty-ninth birthday, which begins in my daughter's Edinburgh flat. I breakfast with my infant grand-daughter, Caledonia Laxmi. Catriona cooks me a spicy Valvona and Crolla's sausage, and then David and I go to the party press conference. He presides over Archy Kirkwood and Charles Kennedy; the former issues a very worthy statement about bed-blocking in the NHS. It seems a little flat to me, and there are few press. They are only interested in gimmicks and conflict. Then down on the bus to Selkirk, where it is an incredibly beautiful day. I discover later that the Borders is the hottest place in the UK. I spend most of the day with my daughter-in-law and grandson: she does my garden and I work on my exhibition *Four Generations of Girlhood*, that is due to open at the weekend. I had expected to spend the evening on my own, waiting for David to return from *Words with Wark,* but during the day a barbecue evolves. The skies are full of planes preparing military manoeuvres, including Hercules troop carriers. Are they preparing for the ground forces to go into Yugoslavia? Despite the menace behind the dramatic shapes they carve in the sky, a beautiful evening in the company of family and good friends. A good way to enter the last year of my fifties, which have been the most creative and happy decade of my life.

*John Hein had been one of those opposed to the merger with the SDP in 1988. He stood as a 'real' Liberal at every Westminster election in the Borders up until 2010.

*30th April*

Another election, or rather selection. The last Friday in April means only one thing: appointment night for Selkirk Common Riding. This year it will be special for us. The Royal Burgh Standard Bearer is our friend Russell Grieve, whose family firm were the joiners on the Aikwood restoration. He has waited eleven years for this, since he was first an attendant to the Standard Bearer of 1988. To be honest, I should think he's waited for twice that time, since he first rode the marches as a five-year-old.

I go down to the town to see him emerge, radiant, from the Town Hall, borne aloft on a ceremonial chair by his predecessors and successors-in-waiting. We follow the silver band along the street for the introductory concert in the larger Victoria Hall. It is packed, and Russell is cheered to the echo on his appearance. He has never spoken in public before: he does it with promising style. His manner is that of a man whose hour has come. Provost Jim Newlands's oratory outshines every candidate at both the council and parliamentary hustings meetings I went to earlier in the week. One thing is certain: it will be a great Common Riding, in this year of the new Scotland, whatever happens in the polls next week.

*1st May*

My son's contribution to the election campaign is getting the posters on the lamp-posts throughout the constituency. The Borders Council does not allow them up till the last week. The SNP are quickest off the mark with this, but Graeme is hard on their heels. His priority is Melrose, for it is the weekend of the Sevens. I meet him there, cheering alternately for the South African teams and Gala, in a condition that precludes any further postering today.

Ian Jenkins is at the Sevens; and so at least are some of the others. I bump into both the Labour and Tory candidates, with mini-entourages. As the latter moves on, the Labour team and I indulge in a little consensual new politics – in other words, slagging off the Tory and SNP representatives in no uncertain way. We also agree that it is *bad form* for one of the Tory team to sport a party rosette at the Sevens.

Returning home, I find that the roundabout at Tweedbank, which earlier on had sprouted a nice crop of variegated posters, is now defoliated. I suspect the Tories, who never got anything up there earlier.

*2nd May*

Morris Manson, our Selkirk chairman (and council candidate) phones me after the Sunday constituency meeting. Postering and leafletting still required, the latter especially in Gala.

*3rd May*

Postering in the morning, leafletting in Mossilee ward in Gala in the afternoon. Our council candidate there wrote in his leaflet that the party would lower taxation. This was spotted after they'd been bundled up into streets along with Ian Jenkins' consituency leaflet, so everything had to be dismantled and the candidate told he must produce a leaflet that didn't go against party policy. He has not reappeared with the new ones, so Ann McPartlin is running up against time for the Holyrood leaflets. It's a lovely day, and because of the public holiday people are out and about in their gardens. I get a good response, apart from a Newfoundland dog and a bad-tempered couple with a Volvo full of children. But where are the posters of yesteryear, that used to adorn so many windows?

The last house on my list is the very highest house in Galashiels. The late Willie Pate, farmer of Mossilee, one of the quartet who persuaded David to come down to the Borders as candidate thirty-five years ago, lived in this house. Looking across to Ladhope and Buckholm Hills, and the Eildons, I give thanks to him and his colleagues for bringing us here.

*4th May*

To Edinburgh with David last night for a rally, Clarissa Dickson-Wright in the chair. Monday night unpopular with the party workers, who want to be out leafletting; Riccarton outside Edinburgh is plain daft as a venue. Apparently it's good for the cameras. What about the punters? However, there is a reasonable turnout. David calls Clarissa our answer to Sean Connery. She responds: 'He's got better legs – I'm just a fat cook who lives in Scotland and pays her taxes.'

In the morning, breakfast TV for David at the National Galleries. He is the token male on the panel, the others being Margo MacDonald and a sonsy, gallus lass whom we take to be the Labour representative, and a willowy blonde whom we identify as the Tory. We are wrong: they are cast against type. Margo has a good line as they trot out politically correct mantras about how good it will be to have so many women at Holyrood: 'Not if they're dumplings'. David couldn't have got away with such a home truth.

Then on to the party press conference, moved to COSLA to accommodate the foreign press who are now beginning to arrive; and a sheltered housing coffee morning in Corstorphine. Here again is politics as I know and love it – real questions from real people, none of the stage fighting that the media encourages.

*5th May*

I work at the exhibition in the afternoon. A 94-year-old friend of my late parents comes to see me. She has already voted – for us, she says, and compains bitterly about the length of the second ballot paper. Peter Scott of the Famous Grouse House phones – I say I can't think about the Fringe till after the weekend. He did not know David was standing.

I go to Peebles to chair Ian Jenkins' meeting. Thirty of the faithful in an ante-room in the Drill Hall. Ian's answers are too long, but he gives the best explanation of the AMS system that I've heard. I remember the days when the main hall, in which a dog-handling class is taking place, was filled to the gunnels with folk and we came in with a piper. David says I have got to stop this nostalgia, elections are different now. Maybe, but they're *not* better.

*6th–7th May*

So the day has come. It was in the 1950 election that I was given a leaflet, in High Wycombe of all places, by a Liberal worker, which contained the phrase, 'The Liberals are in favour of parliaments for Scotland and Wales.' So began, for me, a commitment that has taken my life on such a fantastic, multifaceted journey.

I dress carefully. On polling day, I am always reminded of a sentence in John Buchan's story, *Politics and the Mayfly*: 'It behoves a man to be weel-dressed on siccan an occasion as voting.' For this occasion, I want to wear something that had belonged to my father, who encouraged that early interest in politics. All I can think of that we have are his old anorak, which does not fulfil Buchan's radical ploughman's criteria, and his long-johns, last used by David at Russian state funerals. If I ask him where they are, he will think my eccentricity has gone too far. Then, in the dawn light, I remember a jacket of his, the tweed of which was woven by my mother. So a bit of both of them, who never lived to see the parliament they supported, comes with me to the polling booth.

I actually feel sick with excitement when I go to vote. It seems such a wonderful thing to be able to do; so many people have struggled in the past for that right – the nineteenth-century reformers; the women suffragettes; now, those of us for whom Scottish Home Rule has been the major political article of their creed. It is the issue on which I first supported the Liberal party, nearly fifty years ago; the issue on which

I joined it after speeches by John Bannerman and Russell Johnston. It was one of the sustaining links in our friendship with John Mackintosh, whose name should be remembered today along with John Smith's.

I mark my local government paper first, then the constituency one; and then, finally, that most historic one of all – The List. I am glad my name is on it, no matter how lowly its place.

After voting, we came home. I sat down at the computer to write up the events of the morning before faxing it off to the *Sunday Times*. Hardly were four lines written before there was a power cut. Was this an omen? Were the lights going out all over Scotland? Would the last person to leave snuff out the candle? We'd be away all Friday. No: someone had cut through a cable. The power was back on before two, so I got things finished and off we went to Edinburgh, calling in at the Tweeddale, Ettrick and Lauderdale offices on the way up. Given the dismal press coverage and poll ratings of the last few days, and the lack of sparkle to the local campaign, our mood was sombre.

Catriona came with us to the Edinburgh count at the vast Meadowbank stadium. I remembered the intimacy of Jedburgh Town Hall, where David's first counts were; and then Selkirk's Victoria Hall and later Galashiels Academy (I never liked that, but I did at least get the returning officer to put up Beautiful Borders posters for the TV cameras). Meadowbank has nae style. Furthermore, it has nae efficiency. None of the tellers seem to know what they are doing. Jeremy Purvis seems to know more about the rules of procedure than the returning officer. There are three halls: Pentlands, Central and North Edinburgh and Leith in one; South and East Edinburgh and Musselburgh in another, and West Edinburgh on its own in the third.

The results began to come in: David had either phone or radio permanently at his ear. In the canteen we watch an unimpressive man from Hamilton become the first Member of a Scottish Parliament for nearly 300 years. He makes an acceptance speech that is devoid of style and constructed of parrotted clichés. 'We've held Gordon,' says David. Then the rumour comes that Nicol Stephen has taken South Aberdeen. Things *must* be going better than the pundits had prognosticated.

They are. As the Lothian results emerge, our percentages are marginally up. In West and Midlothian, the second vote is another two percentage notches. It looks good. Jim's share of the tiny Orcadian vote is an indecent 67%. Wisely, his returning officer announces the list vote first.

In the Meadowbank halls, the counts drag on and on as Glasgow churns out results. We hold seats that were thought to be vulnerable:

Argyll, Caithness, Ross and Cromarty. Then comes our own Tweeddale, Ettrick and Lauderdale – Ian Jenkins has actually *increased* the majority. I cannot believe it. Well, I can, it's all due to the slump in the Labour vote after the Keith Geddes peak. But well done, Ian. Mrs Screech has only just squeaked into second place. Oh, good faithful Liberals of the Borders! Ewan Robson, too, holds Roxburgh and Berwick comfortably.

The SNP are not gaining seats. We hear with some sadness that George Reid had just failed in Ochil; he's in, anyway, second on the SNP list, but I feel his heart was set on representing Ochil. The ghastly Phil Gallie just fails to recapture his old Ayr seat. I experience a mixture of reactions: one, the Tories aren't winning any first-past-the-post and it would be nice if it stayed that way. However, this means (1) he will now lord it all over the South of Scotland and (2) Keith Geddes hasn't got a top-up seat, and he *deserved* to be there.

It is impossible to make much head or tail of what is happening on the Lothian lists at this stage – the verification – though all the parties make an attempt at a rough tally. One thing becomes clear in some areas – the Greens are making a strong showing. In Central, Andy Myles polls a respectable 16%, but the list vote's a percentage point down. On the other hand, Mike Pringle, just behind the SNP's popular, larger-than-life Margo, achieves 23–24%. In his declaration speech he excoriates the organisation of the count, a statement that needed to be made. The place *looks* such a mess, too. At one point I take a bag for used votes and begin collecting Irn Bru empties from the chaotic tables.

The rumour that Nicol Steven has won South Aberdeen is confirmed. Inside the hall, the drama focuses on Pentlands. Will McLetchie win? Even worse, do we *want* McLetchie to win, so that it will increase our chances of list seats? My old gut instincts have not yet caught up with the niceties of PR. It looks close; then, Labour's Mike Gibb slips ahead in the piles of lilac papers. Ian Gibson is squeezed to 11%. We don't get any list figures from Pentlands at this stage.

Throughout the count I am going on David's calculation that to get a seat on the list we will need 13% of the vote. Now maths was never my strong point, and I struggle with the attempt to reconcile the high South Edinburgh vote with the low Mid and West Lothian ones. But the tide in the West Edinburgh count is now flowing strongly for Margaret Smith, and surely we will get a strong list vote there.

Mike Pringle, still hoping for a second list seat, wants to ask for a recount on the list vote in South Edinburgh. I think he wants to do it partly because he is so angry at the inefficiency of the count. As a discussion goes on between him, Jeremy and the returning officer, the rumour of this gets to the tellers. They pack up and go home.

In fact, there is only one list count still to be done: West Edinburgh. Catriona and I go through to Hall 3, where a solitary counter punches figures from a tally list into a calculator. He is so tired and frazzled that mistakes seem almost inevitable. We stand over him. We are not sure that we should be doing this – I think we were in an area restricted to officials. But we are both wearing our Ola Gorrie House of Commons brooches, which has an unexpected result: we are taken for officials, and have been able to wander at will throughout the night.

Margaret Smith had 36% of the first-past-the-post votes in West Edinburgh. On the showing of this sample, we are nowhere near that. There is a huge SNP total, and the Greens are at 4,000 to our 5,000. Catriona takes down our exact total on a bit of tissue and we go back to the main hall where she commandeers a calculator: 13%. It looks as though the Greens will get the seventh seat (we have all, notionally, awarded three each to the Tories and SNP). Marion Coyle of the Greens says excitedly, 'We think we've got a seat.' 'Yes,' I say, 'but it's at our expense.' They are genuinely sad for us, but, 'We need it more,' they say. At 6 a.m. the returning officer abandons the whole exercise until 1 p.m.

Jeremy, rule-book in hand, insists that we must have the up-to-date figures and leaves John Barrett to collect them while we go, grey-faced in the grey haar, towards the new day, leaving Catriona to look after her children. I am reminded of emerging from the count at dawn in Jedburgh in 1970, in the old Roxburgh, Selkirk and Peebles days, when David scraped back ahead of Russell Fairgrieve with a majority of 570. But at least then we knew the result as we left.

At Clifton Terrace, John Barrett arrives with the figures. The de Hont formula by which method the top-up seats are calculated, is much more sophisticated than David's crude percentage calculation. John and Willie Rennie feed in the figures, and add a West Edinburgh scenario that is so pessimistic that it has no possible reality. Even using these, their calculations give seats to both the Greens *and* us. It is the Tories who are losing out.

Still haggard, but slightly more relaxed, we stagger through the morning, including Jim Wallace's triumphant return to the capital. Amazingly, the sun comes out.

Then back to Meadowbank, where the council elections are being counted. A whole different atmosphere obtains. Catriona resurfaces with Caledonia in her back-carrier. The list count is in Hall 7. I am greeted by Annie Dana, fourth on the SNP list and loser to Malcolm Chisholm in North Edinburgh and Leith. 'There are four people after three seats,' she says authoritatively, 'Lord James, David, me and Robin Harper.' This is a new scenario, the possibility of four SNP seats. I panic again. Then reason of a sort asserts itself, and I realise it is only Annie's conviction that she would get in that is bringing her to this conclusion. And she has worked so hard for it.

But it is still nip and tuck until the last minute, at any rate in our minds. Then, sixteen hours after the ballot-boxes were sealed up in the polling stations, comes the declaration. David will indeed take his seat in the first Scottish Parliament since 1707, along with James Douglas-Hamilton, Margo MacDonald, David McLetchie – and Robin Harper, the Green list candidate whose party fought such a good, imaginative campaign on no money, but lots of vigour and passion. His acceptance speech is emotional: all we Steels are affected.

Back at Catriona's, David sleeps for an hour or so and I write and dictate my last *Sunday Times* piece. Then I sleep and he goes off to do interviews. Rajiv takes us off to Elizabeth Smith's party at Valvona and Crolla's.

It was mainly a Labour Party celebration, and Robin Cook and Gordon Brown were there with the new MSPs, but we were with a few Liberals and several non-party people were included. Valvona and Crolla's delicatessen is, in its way, an Edinburgh legend, and the combed ceilings, informal setting and the good, unpretentious Italian food of its restaurant seemed to create the right atmosphere for this exhausted gathering. When Donald Dewar, hero of the hour, soon to be the first First Minister, arrived, we all rose spontaneously to applaud him. He looked bashful, but his words, as always, were apt for the occasion, including teasing Gordon Brown for 'working the tables'.

But he was not yet sworn in as First Minister, and over the weekend there was hard bargaining to be done between the Labour and Lib Dem negotiating teams before a coalition agreement could be struck. The appointment of the Presiding Officer was not, and could not, be a part of that negotiation: but in time we learned that there would be no Labour nominee for the position. However, someone with parliamentary experience would be required.

*12 May, 1999*

I am sitting on the wooden benches of the gallery in the Assembly Hall, between the journalist and critic Joyce McMillan and Catriona, who is suckling her baby, Caledonia. Beyond her is Michael Shea. In the past

I have seen my father-in-law preside here as Moderator of the General Assembly of the Church of Scotland, often regarded over the centuries as a substitute for Scotland's Parliament and speaking with an authoritative voice on domestic and foreign policy issues, including its steadfast support for the coming of this day. Here, from time to time, we have been guests of the Queen's Lord High Commissioner at that gathering. Here, Margaret Thatcher made her ill-judged 'Sermon on the Mound', widening the divide between her and the people of Scotland. Here, during more than one Edinburgh Festival, I have seen the great spectacle of Sir David Lyndsay's sixteenth-century *Satire of the Three Estates*. Now the Estates – the Scottish Parliament – is back. The old, uncomfortable, dark benches of the Assembly Hall are stripped out, replaced by blue chairs and blond wooden desks, complete with state-of-the-art technology.

It has been decided, somewhere along the line, that proceedings should be opened by the oldest MSP elected. By a happy coincidence, this is Winnie Ewing, one of the best-known public faces among their number: the firebrand young winner of the Hamilton by-election over thirty years before, veteran of the House of Commons and of the European Parliament, and holder of the affectionate nickname there, 'Madame Ecosse'. As she speaks the historic words recalling the parliament 'That had been adjourned on 28th March 1707,' I reflect on the perfection of the casting.

David's nomination as Presiding Officer did not go unopposed. When the Scotland Bill was passed, our good friend George Reid had come back from Geneva, where he had been working for the International Red Cross. He had been on the cross-party committee preparing some of the procedures and protocols for the new institution, and had been elected on the SNP list in Central Scotland. He was certainly well-qualified for the post. He, too, hated the title 'Presiding Officer' and had tried, unsuccessfully, to instate the old word 'Preses'. Obviously, his party were keen to put forward such a powerful candidate, and I believe it was only his friendship with David that was making him prevaricate. It was only as I walked up the Lawnmarket to the Assembly Hall on that afternoon, that my old friend from Borders Festival days, Lloyd Quinan, now also elected under the SNP banner, confirmed to me that there would be a contest. The new parliament was well ahead of Westminster: the vote was to be the only one of its proceedings to be held under a secret ballot, thus ensuring that no Presiding Officer could ever hold a personal grudge or a favour.

The two of them, not only of the same age but of the same height, and with similarly greying hair, stood in front of Winnie Ewing as she announced the result in favour of David. I reflected that their friendship probably spanned more years than any other in that chamber.

At the end of the proceedings of that first afternoon, with David in the chair, we repaired almost next door to the Sheas' hospitable house in Ramsay Gardens. George, sworn in as one of his deputies, was with us as we toasted the parliament, and looked forward to its official opening on 1 July. But this day was its real rebirth.

David emerged from his first briefing meeting with the civil servants appointed to be his advisers. The role of the Presiding Officer was, in many ways, more extensive than that of the Speaker of the Commons. He and the whips – in Scottish parliament-speak, business managers – from the different parties, would meet as the 'parliamentary bureau', responsible for the planning of the business, a procedure that in the Commons is the prerogative of the governing party, and in particular the Leader of the House. He would also chair the parliament's Corporate Body – and among its responsibilities was the completion of the new Miralles building.

Within a matter of weeks it was realised that the brief that the architect had been given for the number of people to be accommodated in the building was grossly underestimated, and far more would need to be squeezed into the restricted space of the Holyrood site. For Miralles, used to producing plans which were always greeted enthusiastically by Donald Dewar, it was a hard turn-around to work with that most difficult of clients – a committee. For David, it was the start of a nightmare that would haunt his whole time in office.

As 1 July approached, the fledgling parliament came under attack from the press – trivial attacks, but enough to take the shine off the sense of anticipation. The Scottish press had been to the fore in arguing the case for devolution over decades: now the niggling and the negative stories started. They foretold that the day would be a damp squib, a let-down – and that the responsibility for the flop would be that of the Presiding Officer. It was discouraging for all those so full of ambition to create the new body that had been the dream of so many for so long. There were journalists we knew and respected who were very unhappy at what was happening. Worryingly, one of them warned me, 'You should know, there's deliberate briefing against David – and it's coming from someone close to Donald.' I have never believed that Donald knew about this. I can only assume that because this person wanted nothing negative to touch the First Minister, he deflected all criticisms onto the other figurehead of the parliament, the Presiding Officer. But the result was we would never know where the next negative story would come from. There was one, about a medal that had been commissioned for each of the new MSPs. 'Steel spends £ — on medals for MSPs who've done nothing yet,' was one such story – the medallions, which were actually a nice gesture and could have been portrayed as such, had been commissioned by Donald while he was still Secretary of State for Scotland.

Until the Kirking of the Parliament service in St Giles on the Wednesday evening, I was feeling downbeat and undermined. Then, the glorious music, the visual pleasure of seeing the clerics in their colourful robes, the prayers and readings and, above all, the sermon of Gilleasbuig Macmillan dispelled the mean-mindedness and carping that was threatening to blight the whole occasion. Democracy, he reminded us, is a two-way process which makes demands on ordinary people as well as elected representatives. Thursday was to prove that it was his judgement of the public mood that rang true, as joyful crowds thronged the streets, thrilling to every moment of the spectacle and history in the making. That was all to come: in the meantime, I left St Giles cleansed and uplifted.

You can't plan anything in a Scottish summer without knowing that it may well be a meteorological wash-out. But the day of the official opening of the parliament was as luminous and sunny as could have been wished. Outside the old Parliament House there were bands and a choir. Inside, the MSPs gathered, marking the ending there of the old sang nearly three hundred years before. Then, behind banners, they walked, rather than marched, some with their children, in a semi-formal way, for the short distance up the Lawnmarket to their temporary premises. Inside, I sat with my sons in the crowded galleries; David's father was with Gilleasbuig MacMillan in another part. Behind us was Sean Connery; in pride of place was Betty Boothroyd, Speaker of the House of Commons. Absent, at the last minute, was Tony Blair. Maybe he was exercising tact: he would have been strangely out of place. But Scotland's politicians from both houses at Westminster, and from Brussels, were there in force, and so was civic Scotland. Catriona and my niece, Kirsty MacGregor, chose to spend the day with their families among the crowds.

From Holyrood Palace, the Queen, the Duke of Edinburgh and Prince Charles came up the crowded Royal Mile in a carriage with a mounted escort. They came into the chamber, preceded by the crown of Scotland itself, to a fanfare composed for the occasion. David spoke;

the Queen spoke in reply and officially presented the mace, with the first words of the Scotland Act, 'There shall be a Scottish Parliament,' and the aspirational virtues 'Wisdom – Justice – Compassion – Integrity' embossed on its silver. Then came the folk singer from Fife, Sheena Wellington, with Burns's great song, 'A Man's a Man for A' That'. The previous night, at the Secretary of State's dinner, I had buttonholed as many MSPs as possible and suggested that they joined in the singing of the last verse, and had cornered the business managers of each party. 'Bring it up at your meeting before the opening,' I urged them, 'and enourage them to join in.' They did so, tremulously at first, and then with growing confidence, and it was at that point that many eyes filled with tears, even on the press benches. For many, it was the emotional high point of the morning.

It was a perfect day. After the ceremony there were bands, a parade of 1,500 young people – a school chosen from every constituency – and a fly-past of Concorde and the Red Arrows. The windows of the buildings lining the Royal Mile were open and watchers at most of them. The Queen, with her husband and son, watched from a platform outside the Assembly Hall with Donald and David; they were the only ones with seats. In the debate about the trappings of the monarchy, it is often asserted that the more informal style of Scandinavian sovereigns is a better one for our day and age if the British monarchy is to survive. And it has occurred to me that, when the Queen is in Scotland, and especially on that day, it is very much a relationship on the Scandinavian model that we see between monarch and people.

Above all, it was a family occasion, with people bringing even very small children, saltires clutched in their hands, to be a part of history. In the afternoon and evening, there was music and dancing in Princes Street Gardens, fireworks bursting from the Scott Monument and aerialist musicians high above the National Galleries. There was a glorious feeling of optimism and hope.

We spent the summer in Edinburgh and the Borders; there was ongoing work at the parliament even while it was on recess, and I brought a Rowan Tree show to the Fringe and then took it on tour. *War and Glaur*, which John Nichol had devised, was not actually a play but a collection of poetry and song of the First World War, put together in such a way that it created a narrative. It was a good showcase for his acting and for Hilary's singing, especially when she ended the performance with a passionate rendering of Eric Bogle's *No Man's Land*, with its haunting chorus,

> Did they beat the drum slowly,
> Did they play the pipes lowly,
> Did the rifles fire o'er you as they lowered you down?
> Did the bugles sound *The Last Post* in chorus,
> Did the pipes play *The Flowers of the Forest*?

It was done on such a tight budget that when we toured, we couldn't afford to hire a van, and the set was transported in our horse trailer, towed by the antique Austin Gypsy in which David had driven to Capetown.

By the time the parliament's October break came, I was as ready as David for our holiday. We set out by car – not, this time, in the Gypsy – for a week in the artists' town of Collioure in the south of France, not far from the Spanish border, *en route* to a few days with the Hacketts. While with them, we discovered that the prices of properties in the Languedoc were still remarkably reasonable. David had acquired a couple of modest directorships and we had some money saved: although we had toyed with the idea of a state-of-the-art caravanette, it seemed that it would be more prudent to invest in a holiday house. We went away home with this in our thoughts.

Meantime, there was the question of Edinburgh accommodation for the Presiding Officer. In the late 1980s, we had bought a studio flat at St Leonard's Crag in a development of the old James Clark School on the edge of Queen's Park. Rory had occupied it during his university years. But then we had sold it to my friend Janice Parker and her husband Robert Beaton. To begin with, during the parliament, we would stay overnight when we had to in Catriona's spare room, an arrangement that had the advantage of costing the taxpayer nothing. But it could not be a long-term solution. The parliamentary authorities had been looking for accommodation for the Presiding Officer. Every time they did so, there would be an outcry about its address and its cost. The transparency and accountability of the new parliament and its doings was not an illusion, and at that time there were more press accredited to it per parliamentarian than in any other legislature – and that for one whose remit only covered domestic affairs.

So I was deputed to look for a flat within reasonable distance of the chamber and the offices, which meant, practically speaking, in the Old Town. It was a depressing business: the market for rented accommodation was buoyant at the time, there was little that appealed, and everything was snapped up quickly. In desperation at the negativity of the press, I once said to David, 'I've a good mind to try and get you a flat in Dumbiedykes.* That might shut the press up about your posh-ness.' One such flat came up during the Festival, and I emerged from the daily performance of *War and Glaur*, flagged down a taxi and gave the driver the address. We fell into conversation, and the taxi-driver was very forceful that such an address would not do for a 'nice educated lady' like me. When, in response to his questioning, I admitted to being the wife of an MSP, he asked me which one. I told him. He fell into a paean of praise for David, and a rant against the press for the way they were treating him. I was soothed by him, thinking that perhaps there were many more like him out there who were not taken in by the parodies that I read with raw hurt day after day.

And, when I saw the padlocked, iron-grilled shop-fronts and the boarded-up windows in Dumbiedykes, I had to agree with my driver that, for all its proximity to the new parliament, perhaps it wasn't for us.

Some time later, an estate agent gave me the keys of a flat which was conveniently near to the Assembly Hall, one floor up a common stair. When I tried the door, the keys refused to work. I opened the letter box and peered through. There was a nice sanded floor, a contrast from the swirly carpets that had adorned most of the flats that I'd visited in my search. On that basis, I agreed to take it. It was a dreadful mistake, and for six months the first Presiding Officer of the Scottish Parliament had, as his Edinburgh *pied à terre*, a tiny student flat with a futon rather than a sofa in the sitting room, and a bedroom whose window faced, a couple of feet away, on to the wall of the next-door house, and was approached through a less-than-salubrious common stair.

Before the lease came to its end, we had bought back into St Leonard's Crag, acquiring a bright one-bedroomed flat with schoolroom high windows and stunning views. The partial mortgage interest, which David did indeed claim as part of his expenses, cost considerably less than the rent of the squalid flat in the Upper Bow. We still have it, and use it regularly.

*A problem housing estate near the site of the new parliament building.

## 27
# The Millennium

> The year 1900 had an almost mystical appeal for me; I could
> hardly wait for it. 'Nineteen hundred, nineteen hundred,' I
> would chant to myself in rapture; and as the old century drew
> to its close, I began to wonder if I would live to see its successor
> . . . I had been ill and was acquainted with the idea of death;
> but much more was the fear of missing something infinitely
> more precious – the dawn of a Golden Age. For that was what
> I believed the coming century would be.

So says Leo Colston, the schoolboy narrator of L.P. Hartley's novel *The
Go-Between*. And I too harboured such expectations of the year 2000.

Ever since I was a child, even when it was decades away, I'd looked
forward to the year 2000. It seemed a privilege to be able to witness
such a unique, pivotal point in time – it would coincide with my sixtieth birthday, and even though, in my childish thoughts, it seemed that
would be a great age, I was likely still to be alive. Now it was here.
Would it be a new age of peace and prosperity? It was impossible not to
have such hopes.

In a conversation on the 95 bus between Selkirk and Edinburgh with
two elderly ladies that I knew, I was asked what I expected from the millennium. My answer was that I had been influenced in looking forward
to it by the Christmas carol *It Came upon a Midnight Clear*, which contains
the verses:

> But with the woes of sin and strife
> The world has suffered long,
> Beneath the angel strains have rolled
> Two thousand years of wrong;
> And man, at war with man, hears not
> The love-song which they bring;
> O. hush the noise, ye men of strife,
> And hear the angels' song.

For lo! The days are hastening on
By prophet bards foretold,
When with the ever-circling years
Comes round the Age of Gold,
And peace shall over all the earth
Its ancient splendours fling,
And the whole world give back the song
Which now the angels sing.

This had led on, in my mind, to lines from John Milton's 'Ode on the Morning of Christ's Nativity', three verses of which I had learnt in the singing class when I was ten or eleven:

Time will run back and fetch the age of gold . . .
Yea, Truth and Justice then
Will down return to men
Orbed in a rainbow, and like glories wearing,
Mercy will sit between
Clothed in Celestial sheen . . .

I told my travelling companions that these lines, from the carol and from the poem, informed what were my hazy, aspirational visions as to what might happen – a new order of peace and understanding. I looked forward to the dawn of the millennium with expectation and optimism.

Turning down official invitations, and a more tempting one to join a party at the Sheas in Edinburgh, we had a family gathering at Aikwood – our children, David's father and brother, the relevant in-laws, and the two MPs who had succeeded him in the Border seats, Archy Kirkwood with Ro, and Michael Moore.

'Last this of the century, last that of the century,' I kept saying to myself at the end of the last week of 1999. My last shopping trip to Selkirk came. As I wrote the likely-to-run-out-of items on my list, the very basic nature of them struck me: oatmeal, oil, butter, salt, flour, kindling. A thousand, two thousand years ago, these same items would have been used in the kitchen. That they were what I happened to need at that time – it could equally easily have been washing-up liquid, tinned tomatoes or cat-food, or frozen prawns – gave me a good feeling of continuity with the past.

At the end of that final day of December, I found I had forgotten to buy salt, so asked Catriona to bring some down from Edinburgh. That was the very last thing that came into my kitchen in the twentieth century. Over the previous weekend I had watched the video of *Gandhi,* in which one of the most moving sequences is the Salt March. The Indians were not allowed to make their own salt, on which the British Raj levied a tax. Gandhi led an ever-swelling company of protestors to the sea where they made salt, courted imprisonment and changed history. That this staple, vital commodity was brought to me by the Indian part of my family was all the more appropriate.

Thus, in our own house, and with our family, we passed into the third millennium. Next day, New Year's Day, our friends came. Joanna Lees from the USA was our first foot. Among our old university group, Robin Crichton was absent. He had married my good friend Flora Maxwell Stuart at Traquair on Old Year's Night. At sunset four generations of Steels planted an oak tree. Perhaps it will last into the next century.

The millennium spurred me to do other things that I had been putting aside. I commissioned the sculptor, Chris Hall, to make a carving out of a dead apple tree in our orchard. He had carved John Smith's gravestone at Iona Abbey. Ten years ago, I'd given him wood from its neighbour, and had later bought the figures he had carved from it. Alas, my idea of a sculpture *in situ*, while it produced a stunning piece which we called 'Millennium Man', turned out to be temporary, for the carving rotted away in a couple of years.

I bought our burial plot in the churchyard at Ettrick Bridge. About eighteen months ago we had decided we should look ahead and do this. We were sent a copy of the map and had a long family suppertime discussion about it with our children, including the rival merits of burial and cremation. Since then we had done nothing further, but then I found myself in Galashiels with a half hour to spare, so I went off to the Council offices to discuss the purchase of a family lair.

'I could book it for you provisionally,' said the helpful girl in charge of such matters, although she obviously found my forward planning unusual.

'No, no, we'll need it sometime, make it definite,' I said. So there it is, the Steel plot, ready for us in the fullness of time, among so many friends and neighbours from our years at Cherrydene. I felt a certain sense of satisfaction at having faced up to the atavism of such a transaction. In Japan, people go so far as to commission their tombstones – or perhaps one should say, monuments – in their own lifetime. I asked Chris Hall whether he had ever had such a request. Once, he said; but then the person concerned had changed his mind.

And yet, why not? Death, like taxation, is inescapable, and to have some plans made when you are hale and healthy takes the burden off those you love at a time when they are vulnerable. After all, insurance for such an eventuality has been with us for a long time. Pre-purchase of burial plots and even of memorials seems to me to be a reasonable provision, though I would not go so far as the redoubtable wife of Willie Wastle. In the story of his courtship, he is assured by his future mother-in-law that his beloved has a 'kistful of her ain spinning and bleaching that will provide for you . . . even after you are deid.' Willie comments: 'I didna like the idea o' sic a premature providing of winding sheets.'

At Easter, basing ourselves with the Hacketts, we went out to France to look for a holiday home. They had already done research for us with local estate agents: 'Not *too* near us,' they said, and the search was concentrated around Clermont l'Herault and Pezenas in the Languedoc, in hilltop villages surrounded by vineyards on the plains below, and with a backdrop of scrub – box, broom, lavender and rosemary – on the hills behind.

David arrived later than I did, having come straight from the second debate on the future of the parliament building at Holyrood. It had been especially dispiriting. He had decided that he should not chair this debate, but speak from the floor instead: it was the only time he did so. By now, ten months on from the previous debate, the figures were showing an alarming spiral from the £109 million estimated at that time. The main problems at this stage were, firstly, that now that the parliament was up and running, the amount of space that was needed had increased considerably from that catered for in the original plan; and secondly that the only historic building on the site, Queensberry House, had been found to be structurally unsound: its demolition was even considered. These were the major problems at this stage; but almost everything seemed to throw up another one. For example, the chamber, for which the specification had clearly been for a horseshoe shape, turned out to be a much flatter design, and had to be re-drawn.

This debate had been a crucial one: the costs had now escalated to £195 million and there was heavy pressure from the SNP and the Tories – and some Lib Dems – to abandon the whole project. The vote to go ahead had been a close one. The problems of the building never left David, and weighed him down: the idea of a bolt-hole in France was one to look forward to.

Maggi Hackett and I had already spent a couple of days visiting possible houses with a local (English) estate agent, and drawing up a shortleet.

We narrowed the candidates down to two: a tiny 'maison cocotte' as the particulars described it (I called it a vertical caravan), and a larger one, in another village, with a feature that particularly attracted David – a sun terrace. But the latter needed quite a lot of improvement, whereas the 'maison cocotte' had been a letting holiday home, and we would be able to take it over with furniture, crockery and cutlery. After deciding, with Rory ('I'm here to represent the next generation'), to offer for the larger house, David changed his mind after a night made sleepless by worries about the Holyrood building.

'I can't face another building that needs anything done to it,' he said as I awoke, 'We'll go for the maison cocotte.' So we purchased our vertical caravan, which turned out to be the perfect antidote to the huge, crushing project back in Scotland. We bought it in my name, and the press never learned about it. From then on, we and our children have used the *petite maison*, as we called it, and its successor, on a regular basis throughout the years.

At home, my sixtieth birthday came with a 'round' birthday ball (a Danish expression to describe significant birthdays) at Aikwood. Eighty guests squeezed in, and again I did all the cooking for it. Remembering my teenage wallflower days, I decided that each dance was to be a 'ladies' choice'. The accordionist Ian Lowthian composed a Scottish dance tune in my honour, and Karen Ingram who 'called' the dances at the ball, choreographed a new reel. I felt I was becoming a senior citizen with quite a flourish. I applied for my bus pass, I went at long last to have my hearing tested. And I followed the Hawick Cornet on the Mosspaul ride-out, opened that year for the first time to women.

Until a few years before, the ridcouts leading up to Hawick Common Riding had been an all-male preserve. Then a challenge came from four brave women who braved the jeers of the men – and women – of Hawick, and four years previously they had joined in one of the rideouts. Legal cases came and went, all the way to the European court, and Hawick got a bad press nationally and internationally. In 1997, women were allowed on two of the rides, and Lynne and I had ridden at the second one. As we came back into Hawick, booing for the women riders mixed with the traditional cheers for the Cornet, and my daughter-in-law and I held hands together and wept with emotion. Now the most daunting ride of them all, to Mosspaul on the Dumfriesshire border, was opened up to women as well. I determined to be one of them.

As the time drew nearer I got more and more apprehensive. Lynne was still feeding baby Hannah, and decided to give it a miss. Then Chit

Chat, the horse I usually rode, went lame, so I had the perfect opportunity to duck out, but by this time I'd started riding my other horse
and realised that what everyone said about her was true – she was even
better-mannered than my normal mount. She was indeed Clever Clogs
by name and by nature.

'Who's going to look after you?' asked concerned friends.

'My horse,' I replied.

'Do you think there'll be any other women?' To which my answer
was, '*Masses* of them,' because I knew of at least three who were going.
And then every single man I know who is a Mosstrooper – bar one – told
me what a hard ride it was. The exception was Archy Kirkwood.

My better half took the day off to drive the horse-box to Hawick,
bring the picnic and generally support me, resplendent in his own
Mosstroopers' badge and tie, earned all those years before as a young parliamentary candidate. By the time I was tightening Clever Clogs' girth,
my fingers were shaking. I tried reminding myself of the big rides I'd
done in the past – Coldstream to Flodden, Kelso to Yetholm, Jedburgh
to Redeswire right on the border. But those rides were over thirty years
ago – and I had come back from Redeswire with a blistered bottom. I
thought of more recent ones – at Duns, the year the principal had been
a woman, and Caverslee three years ago, behind the Hawick Cornet.

'What am I afraid of?' I asked myself: 'Having an accident that leaves
me badly injured – making a fool of myself and letting down the sisterhood – not completing the ride – or another raw posterior?' In real
terms, only the first mattered.

'The first field's the worst,' I'd been told. 'There are usually lots of spills
– it takes a sudden dip in the middle.' It passed without incident. Then we
were out on the hills, and the lines of John Buchan's ballad about a mare
that goes hell for leather over the moors kept ringing in my head:

> Like winter rain across the plain
> In hurrying gust they ride;
> Like a bolt from God they scour the sod,
> And never a moment bide.
>
> They scatter through crowds of fighting men,
> Din and clatter and blaze;
> And they are out on the bent again,
> And off on the mountain ways.

A fearful man was Gideon Scott,
With terror was he ta'en;
And he strove to leap from the flying mare,
But ever he strove in vain.

For swifter still the black mare flew,
And stranger was the way,
And the night grew black as the mouth of a pit,
And wild as the Judgement Day.

But it was never like that, although on a couple of occasions at Selkirk
Common Riding, I have ridden hired horses that would have answered
to the description. Now, however, my own mare went as steadily as she
does around the forest tracks near home.

I encountered the Selkirk Standard Bearer, Steven Squance. We had
never got on: he and Rory had clashed when they were both attendants
to Steven's predecessor in the early nineties. He was an ardent Tory, and
always made sly little partisan digs when we encountered each other.
Recently, however, he had come out as gay, causing much tittle-tattle
among the older generations in Selkirk. I thought it was brave of him:
even now, in the third millennium, the small-town minds of the Borders – as in small towns elsewhere, no doubt – found it hard to come
to terms with such a part of everyday life, and I told him how much his
openness had raised him in my estimation. He countered by congratulating me on this present escapade, and we sealed a truce there on the
moors.

I met up with a neighbour from Cherrydene days. Jayne Tait had
been best friend to both Catriona and Graeme, and has probably completed more rides at Border Common ridings than anyone else, male or
female. She certainly wasn't going to miss this one.

'When do you think we get to the scary bits?' we asked each other.
We were still asking when we got to Mosspaul, where the cavalcade
stops at the inn for two hours. 'Perhaps they're on the way back.' I
made discreet enquiries of an ex-Cornet, who assured me that the return
journey was much faster – 'The horses know they're on their way home.'
But Clever Clogs went her own canny way again, and I found a grey
horse that matched her in temperament and stride. Its rider was also a
first-timer, only a couple of years younger than me; he too felt that time
was running out for new challenges, and was determined to make the
most of it. I felt a glorious sense of achievement, especially comparing the

sorry state David had been in at the end of the same ride when we were in our twenties with my present sense of well-being.

A couple of weeks later, David was the chief guest at Hawick Common Riding, and I wore my new badge with pride. I helped him to craft his speech for the occasion, including a joke about 'the days when my wife knew her place – which was holding my horse.' It went down well with his all-male hearers.

We had a millennium grandchild, Persia Shanti Judith Bhatia, who shared her baptismal weekend with her great-grandfather's ninetieth birthday. She was born at home in Edinburgh, but before the end of the year the Bhatia family had moved back to the Borders, to the outskirts of Peebles. They called their new-build home Kiltane, after my parents' wooden house in Dunblane. I knew I was very fortunate to have both my 'breeding pairs' of the next generation so close at hand, merely forty minutes' drive away, and to be able to watch and take part in the growing up of India, David, Caledonia, Hannah and Persia – and in due course, James and Rio.

The year 2000 was a year for all kinds of initiatives – one of them, in which I became involved, was a production of Sir David Lyndsay's *The Thrie Estaites*. Written in the sixteenth century, it is a savage and timeless satire on the corruption within the Catholic church. In Lyndsay's time, it was performed before that great upholder of Catholicism, the Queen Regent Mary of Guise; then it had lain dormant until the text was rediscovered, and revived as a play for the Edinburgh Festival of 1948, directed by Tyrone Guthrie, in the Assembly Hall on the Mound. There had been later productions there as well; but otherwise it was not staged apart from student performances. It demands a huge cast, and after the iconic staging in the Assembly Hall, that seemed to be its natural home: it was as if no other venue for it would suffice.

I had been drawn into this millennium project by John Carnegie, a director whose work I had admired in the past, especially his small-scale productions of Frederic Mohr solo plays, which had had such an influence on me. This was no small-scale project, however. John's strategy was three-fold: first, to stage it at the venue where it had first been performed, at Castlehill in Cupar (now, conveniently, a council car park), secondly, to mix professional and amateur performers, and thirdly – and most important – to commission a new translation of David Lyndsay's old Scots into a modern Scots text by the writer Alan Spence. I became chairman of the company set up to run the project. It was the most ambitious one I had been involved in since the days of the Borders Festival, and there were many setbacks along the way. I admired John Carnegie's tenacity in bringing it to fruition, and taking that great piece of work out of the sixteenth century and into the twenty-first.

In Selkirk, too, there was a new event for the millennium: this one was thought up by the Borders Tourist Board, which, since the advent of VisitScotland, no longer exists. The idea was to promote the Borders in terms of literary tourism, and as part of this, to start a pre-Christmas Fair in Selkirk under the name of 'Scott's Selkirk'. It would take the town back to the early part of the nineteenth century, when Sir Walter Scott had been the sheriff there and presided over the courtroom that now houses a small museum.

There was a groundswell of enthusiasm. John Nichol wrote short dramas based on some of the more bizarre of Scott's cases, to be re-enacted in his court house, and reprised his persona of Mungo Park; actors were hired to play Scott and Hogg; the local bands played throughout the weekend and there was a great procession re-enacting the 'False Alarm' of 1804. This was the occasion when it was thought that Napoleon's troops had landed; beacons blazed throughout the Borders and the local home guard, set up by Scott, rallied and marched to Dalkeith, where it was discovered that it was all – well, a false alarm, and that the first blazing beacon had in fact been a charcoal-burner's fire. Scott himself describes the event with great vividness and humour in *The Antiquary*. There were street entertainers and stalls, and the local shops threw themselves into the event, opening up for the whole weekend and dressing their windows with great imagination. There was a great hiring of, and making of, reasonable approximations of the costumes of that time. There was plenty of scope for the Maria Rankin part of me.

I joined the committee enthusiastically and stayed on it for several years, and for the first time I became a performer. I found that I could improvise a character, and maintain it, on the streets, and enjoyed becoming that disreputable old lady, Maggie Steenson, widow of Wandering Willie, the blind fiddler from *Redgauntlet*, peddling ribbons and bewailing the loss of Willie. ('He was found deid in a ditch like a cadger's pownie, just as I aye said he wad be.') When a ghost walk was instituted, I was prevailed on to play a ghost in that as well.

In June of 2000, we returned to our *maison cocotte* for the wedding of the Hacketts' eldest son, Piers. Not long after we came back, there was worse news concerning the Holyrood project when Enric Miralles, the architect, died from a brain tumour that had been diagnosed earlier in the year. This was indeed an unexpected blow to the whole project. Donald Dewar had been ill, too, over that summer with a heart condition, but seemed to have recovered and was back in harness when I met him at a dinner in Edinburgh Castle. He was gentler than his usual abrasive self, and was deeply touched by the way his children had come to support him and taken charge of him during his illness. He seemed to have recovered well.

In the October break, we were on our way back to France again. David was already in London, where I was to join him. My plane was diverted to Southampton: when we landed I phoned him to say what had happened, and that I would be getting a train to the city. His voice on the phone was shocked and stricken.

'Donald's dying,' he said. 'He slipped on the steps outside Bute House this afternoon, and fell and knocked his head. He's haemorrhaging, and the doctors can't do anything to save him. They're just keeping him going until his children get there.'

It was a night of terrible grief. Their friendship stretched back to when they had gone together to Russia as students forty years before; now, when they met regularly and privately as First Minister and Presiding Officer – without any civil servants, to the disapproval of the latter – they could talk without reserve and in confidence about the teething problems of the parliament. Their casual friendship over the decades had become very close over the last year. As for me, I remembered that night so long ago in the Edinburgh Union when he and John Smith had enraptured us all with their wit; and the many occasions over the decades, intimate as well as official, that we had all shared, right up to that last meeting in the grandeur of Edinburgh Castle.

David went back to Edinburgh the next morning, persuading me to continue to France. Donald was dead by the time he got there. He recalled parliament and the stunned MSPs gathered to pay their tribute to the man who, more than any other, had brought the legislature into existence. 'It'll be broadcast on the internet,' said David. I went to the Post Office in Clermont l'Herault, and switched on their machine. All I could get was a still picture of the entire body of MSPs standing in silence to honour Donald Dewar. It was surreal in the extreme to be there in that busy French market town, its citizens bustling around me, and to watch that image of shared sorrow back home.

The funeral was in Glasgow Cathedral. As the coffin, a single red rose lying on it, passed down the aisle after the service, the musicians Phil Cunningham and Aly Bain played 'A Man's a Man for A' That'.

It was only sixteen months since Sheena Wellington had sung it at the Parliament's opening. We piled into buses taking us to the Kelvingrove Art Gallery for tea and sandwiches – unbelievably, there was no whisky – sitting behind Gordon and Sarah Brown. Beside them, Henry MacLeish hovered, paying court, and I thought, 'Already the jockeying for the succession has begun.'

In retrospect, I think that Donald Dewar's death was when the glow and hope that had surrounded the new millennium began to fade, and the next year was a bad one on all fronts – local, international, and personal. From early in 2001 the countryside shut down as foot and mouth disease raged over parts, first of England and then of Scotland. It seemed ironic that the first Scottish outbreaks were confirmed in Lockerbie in Dumfriesshire. But even in the Ettrick and Yarrow valleys, farmers suffered the loss of their stock. There were two in particular, whose beasts had shared transport with others going to Longtown market and then on to the Carlisle abattoir. When they got to the abattoir, they found it closed, so the sheep were brought home again. But once Longtown had been identified as a source of infection, even those sheep that had briefly come off the lorry there were condemned – and so were all the others back at their home farms.

Each night, on the local news programme, Border Television would give the roll-call of the most recently infected farms in Cumbria, Dumfriesshire, Northumberland and elsewhere in the region. In the Scottish parliament, the familiar rich voice of Ross Finnie announced the slaughter necessary to try to contain the disease. It spread to some farms in Roxburghshire, though no further, but in swathes of countryside the only stock left in the fields were horses. There was a dreadful feeling of siege, of depression, of shutting down, and the pyres of blazing carcases were like scenes from a medieval depiction of Armageddon. The following year, I wrote a play about it, and gave the female protagonist this speech:

> 'There were two kinds of farmers at that time. There were those who could handle none of it, who turned the whole process over to the soldiers, the slaughtermen, the vets. Went into their farmhouses, drew the curtains, turned the TV up full blast to drown out the shots. God knows when they came out again.
>
> Then there were those like my uncle who wanted to do everything himself for his beasts, right up to the end. Everything bar the slaughtering . . .

Didn't take them long to bring the sheep down from the hills. Five hundred years they'd grazed there, Uncle Dod used to say . . .

Twenty-four hours it took them from confirmation to completing the slaughter. Another twenty-four to dispose of them . . .

When it was all ready my uncle lit the pyre himself. He said that he had held the cord at his father's graveside, and at his mother's, and that his beasts deserved respect just the same.

He came inside once the flames took hold. It was when the bodies started exploding – that was when my stalwart, stubborn Uncle Dod could take no more. He came inside, but the glow and the smell and the sounds seeped through the doors, the windows, down the lums it seemed, through every draught crack of the farmhouse. Just as the shots had done.'

As well as the effect on the farming community, the foot and mouth epidemic had its implications in the Border towns. Social life more or less shut down. The most obvious manifestation of this was when the various Common Ridings were curtailed: in Selkirk, only four horsemen rode the marches – a dreadfully appropriate number which gave me the name for my play, *The Four Horsemen*. No Royal Burgh Standard Bearer was appointed, something that had only happened previously in wartime, and the flag was cast by the ex-standard bearer of twenty-five years previously. In Hawick, the marches were walked, not ridden, some months after the usual date. In Melrose and Peebles, the respective principals led followers on bicycles, a compromise that I found faintly ludicrous, but which had so much support in Melrose that it was continued in later years.

Only in Lauder, at the beginning of August, had restrictions been lifted for long enough for the Common Riding to take place as usual. I was among a much smaller contingent of riders than usual. There is a cup awarded at Lauder Common Riding to the oldest rider: for the last dozen years or more it had been won by a splendid man, ex-Cornet William Johnston. His family had persuaded him that, at eighty-two, he should retire, and as I cast my eye around the other riders I realised that his successor might very well be me. Thus did I win the only cup for riding I had in my entire life – for being old. I surrendered it the following year.

Two months later, I was sitting at my computer when the phone rang. It was John Carnegie. 'Sorry to drag you away from the television but I need to update you about a meeting I've just had about the publication of the *Thrie Estaites* script,' he said. I responded huffily that I didn't watch TV during the day.

'Haven't you heard?' he asked.

And thus I heard the news that was to break any romantic ideas about an age of gold, about truth and justice and mercy returning in the third millennium. The men who hijacked the planes that flew into New York's Twin Towers and into the Pentagon, and the fourth one, brought down by its courageous passengers, turned the world turned upside down.

To begin with, I still had a sense of disbelief. Two days after the tragedies, I stopped reading the newspapers in any depth: normally I devour two or three a day. A barrier seemed to come up, shutting me off from absorbing the frightful images, with their extra impact as still photographs rather than on the TV screen.

Like many others, I wept – not just on hearing and reading those heartbreaking final messages of love from those who died, but on hearing British bands and orchestras play *The Star Spangled Banner* in tribute, and on those many occasions we may think are special to ourselves but which have undoubtedly been shared worldwide.

I thought about how the American people had had, until now, a kind of innocence, though it could equally be described as isolationism. 'Why do they hate us?' was the hurt, pathetic query. Most had not known what some of the wiser among them had understood – that America's disastrous Middle East policy had built up a huge, crippling bank account of resentment. Now that innocence had gone for good – that self-confident belief that American values are universally accepted as admirable, as well as the belief in America's impregnability.

Then came a personal shock, and it seemed as though the curse of the Holyrood building on those involved with it had struck again. A routine medical examination gave a suspiciously high reading for the PSA in David's blood, and he was diagnosed with early prostate cancer.

It felt unreal. He had no obvious symptoms: it came completely out of the blue. We were lucky that his brother Michael, by this time Professor of Medical Science at St Andrews University, is an authority on cancer, and was able to add his advice to that of our own GP and the specialist at the Western General Hospital in Edinburgh. He told David about a new treatment, brachytherapy, which involved less disruption than other treatments – but not everyone was suitable for it.

What David really worried about was the time that he would need to take off if surgery or a long course of chemotherapy or radiotherapy was required. In the establishment of the Scottish parliament there was no provision to cover for the illness of the Presiding Officer by the temporary assumption of the office by the deputy, nor for the appointment of an extra, temporary, deputy.

To see if he could have the brachytherapy, he had to undergo some uncomfortable hormonal treatment first, but at the end of it, he was deemed an unsuitable candidate for the treatment. That was the only time his optimism dipped. 'You know I always like to be a pioneer,' he said, in disappointment, but that was left to others in this particular case, and he would have to go through radiotherapy for several weeks in the New Year. On a more positive note, he also found that there was a prostate cancer support group in the Borders, some members of which he already knew. One of them, Ian Mitchell, a local newspaper photographer, gave him constant support throughout the whole period. Sadly, Ian died when his own cancer reappeared years later.

All through this time, there was the endless worry and pressure about the building as well as the day-to-day business of the parliament. There was no question of convenient private treatment: our commitment to the NHS has included a deliberate choice not to have any private health insurance.

There was no point in trying to be discreet about the cancer, but the NHS were extremely helpful, and he managed to have the radiotherapy sessions arranged so that they interfered as little as possible with his duties as Presiding Officer. They finished just before the February week's break, and, rather against my better judgement, we went off to the *maison cocotte* for a recuperative week. While we were there, we saw a larger house for sale a couple of doors away. It needed a lot of renovation, but we decided to buy it, and to sell our tiny house. The DIY the new place required would keep our holidays occupied for several years, it would accommodate the children and grandchildren more comfortably and it seemed a positive act to take, a defiance of the cancer. This time we bought the house in the children's names, so that, as owners, they would escape the complicated horrors of French inheritance laws.

# 28

# *Live Theatre, Dead Writers*

Throughout this time I was still running the Hogg exhibition at Aikwood, but our lives had changed. With David in Scotland most of the time, we wanted to reclaim our home for ourselves and our family – including the burgeoning troop of grandchildren. I was proud of the exhibition – it was simple and well-designed and gave out just enough information for visitors to absorb. It compared very favourably with other exhibitions we had seen devoted to the life and work of single writers – the Rupert Brooke exhibition near Cambridge, for example. I began to look for another home for it.

Obviously, it would be best if James Hogg stayed in the Ettrick Valley. Once again, the Buccleuchs came to my aid, finding space for it in the public courtyard area at Bowhill, and responsibility for it was transferred to the Buccleuch Heritage Trust. The company that had run the exhibition up till now was wound up, and this raised the question: what should now happen to the Rowan Tree Company, which had also come under its umbrella?

I had thought that this would be quite a straightforward matter, and that the board would decide that the theatre company should continue. But I was in for a shock. At a meeting when neither David nor Liz Smith were present, it was decided that Rowan Tree should also be wound up. The main voices in favour of this were Gordon Webster (Hilary Bell's husband) and also Catriona. None of my children have ever liked my theatre work, resenting the time spent on it for no pecuniary reward, seeing only the stresses it has brought me and not understanding the soaring satisfactions. I had been in a downbeat frame of mind and no doubt this influenced my daughter, but I was taken aback by the decision, not realising that there were other agendas behind it. There was a period when it looked as though this would be the end of Rowan Tree, but the situation galvanised me, and with the support of Liz Smith and Janice Parker – and David – I asked the board to look at it again. This time I was better prepared, and Rowan Tree Theatre Company was set up as an entity in its own right, with Liz as chairman of the new board of directors.

However, there were more underlying problems than I had realised. My interest in Walter Scott had been fanned by my involvement with the Scott's Selkirk weekend, and I had decided on a production of *Wandering Willie's Tale*. It's a self-contained short story in the novel *Redgauntlet*, written entirely in Scots vernacular. In it, the blind fiddler Willie Steenson tells the story of how his grandfather, the piper Steenie, goes to hell and back for a rent receipt. I could see that it would make an ideal performance piece for John Nichol; but the instruments that it called for were the fiddle and the pipes, and I could find no way of working Hilary and her guitars into it. I simply did not realise how much she resented this, nor that it would be the beginning of the end of the way we had operated for over ten years.

It is not easy to keep building a repertoire around two specific performers, and the fact that they both had many other calls on their time now meant less and less was available for rehearsals. John and Hilary were happy to reprise *War and Glaur* year on year in early November, and to devise, along with Lucy Cowan and Alan Caig Wilson and myself, shows built around the repertoire – sometimes little-known – of Robert Burns, at Bowhill in late January. Of new work there was almost nothing. The cracks sometimes showed; and those on the new board who had a wider experience in theatre than the relative cosiness of the Borders could see them only too clearly.

I began to rely a lot on our young stage manager, Matthew Burgess. He had come through the ranks of the Borders Youth Theatre, where he had been given a sound grounding in both acting and stage management by John Haswell. He was one of those rebellious and disaffected young people whose lives were turned round by Hazzy. From time to time I could find acting parts for him in Rowan Tree productions, but it was as a stage manager that I especially valued him.

At that point he couldn't drive, so I had to go out with every show. For *Wandering Willie's Tale*, we simply used the first of my Berlingo Citroens as a touring van, everything including lighting either carefully stowed in its interior or strapped onto the roof bars. It was a particularly happy production, both on the tour and during its run at the Fringe, but I had decided to give up directing after a bad experience with *The Four Horsemen* during this same time, which had dented my self confidence. From now on, my role would be mainly that of producer.

To coincide with the move of the Hogg exhibition to Bowhill, I was keen to initiate a production of Hogg's *Confessions of a Justified Sinner*. It is a work which is regarded as one of the most significant Scottish novels of all time: there had been theatre treatments of it over the years, and indeed an opera in the 1970s. Some years before, Steve Owen, the actor who had played the anti-hero Wringham in the TAG production, had, at my behest, made a short solo version of it for the Hogg festival and the Fringe. I still had the script. I thought that it was a role well suited to Matthew Burgess, and that he deserved such an opportunity after his years of support and commitment to Rowan Tree. During the Edinburgh Festival, I arranged to see John Carnegie and, as we walked up Johnston Terrace under the shadow of the castle, I put my idea to him, and asked him to come and direct it.

John had just come back from Kraków, and as always was greatly inspired by the theatre he had seen there. He had already been thinking that *Confessions* was a book from which he could create strong theatre, so my approach to him was timely. But he wanted to write his own script, for two actors, not one. And he insisted on nearly four weeks' rehearsal time. It was agreed that at the outset we would plan only for three performances at Bowhill, then decide whether or not to try it at the Fringe.

John Carnegie proved to be a hard taskmaster, who knew exactly what he wanted from the beginning and was determined to achieve it. His preparation was meticulous, and his production standards are particularly high. Once he had established this level for Rowan Tree, there could be no slippage. The production had wonderful reviews, and one of the actors, Alan Steele, was nominated by *The Stage* as best actor in the Fringe. Once again, though, Hilary Bell and John Nichol felt sidelined. They decided that they had no place now in Rowan Tree, and set up a company of their own. For most of the board this came as a relief, but for me it was painful. There were unspoken conflicts about ownership of costumes, props, scripts and productions, and in the end I felt that I had to consult a lawyer to see just where I stood. 'I feel as though I'm in the middle of a divorce,' I said to David, as he unfalteringly supported me.

After the success of *Confessions,* I thought that this time we would surely get a Scottish Arts Council grant for a tour, but once again we failed, both for this and for the next planned production, another play written and directed by Carnegie, this time using Robert Louis Stevenson's *Weir of Hermiston* as its source. Carnegie has a good principle in his approach, which is that you should not think in terms of an *adaptation* of a novel, but of creating theatre which *acknowledges* the novel as its source.

The attempts to find public funding were sapping. I was fortunate in having two good private sponsors, the Buccleuch Group and Stobo Castle Health Spa, but I believed that we were producing work that was worthy of public support from the Scottish Arts Council. We were the only company that was regularly producing work focusing on Scottish culture, language and literature; and one of very few based, and touring intensively, in rural Scotland. But we were turned down again and again for project funding to develop or tour, in favour of more 'interesting' or 'cutting edge' proposals. We were not alone. Another small company in the North East was recently knocked back because their Equal Opportunities policy was not 'specific' enough.

Occasionally we would be lucky with a small lottery application or with another sponsorship approach, and the Arts Development Department of the Scottish Borders Council was always as helpful as it could be within the limits of its own financial parameters. But the repeated rejection of applications for substantial assistance meant anxiety and stress about the finances of every project I undertook. Sometimes, too, it led to me modifying a project in order to fit the guidelines of a fund. This was something I did for the tour of *Confessions*. Baulked by the SAC, I looked for other sources of sponsorship and applied to the European 'Leader+' fund for money to pay fees and wages. To make it eligible, I had to insert a 'new' element into the project.

'School performances?' I asked the helpful person who administered the applications in the Borders.

'Not really enough.'

I pondered. 'A back-to-back tour of another production?'

'Yes, that might do.'

And on that basis, I applied for funding to partner the darkness of *Confessions* with a new production of a play from years back that I'd directed with some success, an adaptation of a comic story by James Hogg, *The Love Adventures of Mr George Cochrane*. Going back on the vow I'd made to myself and my family, I prepared to direct it again. The application went through easily, and from then on things went awry.

Realising that my tour plans would not work and that some dates would need to be cancelled, I totally lost confidence in my ability as a director, and crumbled like a digestive biscuit. I obsessed about such things as the welfare of Matthew's cat, and the problem (which wasn't as great as I thought it was) of the construction of a sound-proof box which John Carnegie had specified for the tour of *Confessions*. Coming to my rescue, Liz Smith, who was working at the Glasgow Citizens at the time, used all her contacts and found a young director there, Carter Ferguson, who agreed to come to direct at short notice from Glasgow.

Just beyond Peebles, his car gave up on him. He phoned me on his mobile. 'I'll get my son-in-law to come and help you,' I said, for Catriona and Rajiv's house was only a few hundred yards from where he was stranded. He may have been surprised by the emergence of a distinguished-looking Indian from the Peeblesshire darkness, but it was when he was on his way to Aikwood, rescued by David, that his experience became totally surreal. As they drove together through the hills and valleys to which he was so unaccustomed, he thought he recognised the voice of his driver. He looked sideways. He recognised the face. Then they drew up at a five-storey high tower: Aikwood. He must have thought he was in some supernatural Border myth. All Liz had given him was the name, Judy Steel. She had said nothing about medieval towers or well-known politicians. No wonder: there was a madwoman somewhere in there.

It is a kind of madness, depression. In the blackest despair for years, I kept myself to myself, shut away two floors up at Aikwood, while, around me, others – the Rowan Tree board, the actors and others recruited for the two productions – picked up the pieces and brought the work to fruition. Peter Soal's daughter Kate, arriving in Edinburgh from South Africa like a *dea ex machina,* came and took the reins of running Aikwood into her willing and inexperienced hands.

From then on, Rowan Tree has gone from strength to strength, through productions of John Carnegie's *Hermiston*, my own *The Journey of Jeannie Deans*, derived from Walter Scott's *Heart of Midlothian*, which played, *inter alia*, at the festival of politics at Holyrood in Miralles' debating chamber, and through a year of 21st birthday celebrations. These comprised three tours of four plays, all with different directors, an exhibition and a playwriting competition – and, of course, a party. None of the plays were new, but all of them were worthy of a new production. The last one was Stephen MacDonald's beautiful play about the friendship between the great First World War poets Wilfred Owen and Siegfried Sassoon, forged at Craiglockhart Hospital for Nervous Diseases. This was directed by John Haswell: his two most faithful acolytes of many years before, Matthew Burgess and Oliver Bisset, played the poets.

Neil Cooper, theatre critic of the *Herald*, wrote:

> It's a quietly exquisite affair, in which Matthew Burgess's Owen
> moves from literary groupie to be the creative co-dependent

of Oliver Bisset's Sassoon. As they skirt around each other, their passions occasionally spill into something physical. Awash with implied stiff-upper-lip homoeroticism, there's something unspoken here . . .

When the Rowan Tree tour of *Not about Heroes* goes to the site of Craiglockhart Hospital itself this weekend, it will be a poetic gesture of some magnitude.

And it was, and there were more good things to come for Rowan Tree. I was asked in an interview, on the day that I was writing this, what advice I would give to anyone starting a rural theatre company. I realise that I have had some advantages: top of these are generous sponsors who have believed in our work, and committed actors and directors who respond to our core philosophy. Another advantage is having the use of the theatre at Bowhill as a production base and for rehearsals, as is having Aikwood as free convivial theatre lodgings.

My years as an MP's wife had given me access to people in different communities throughout the Borders, and I built on this during the years of the Borders Festivals. So it was easier to make approaches to possible promoters in village halls, and my reasonably high profile meant that I could introduce myself easily. If, in time, I have earned the right to be known for the work I have done, I am not blind to how I was able to establish it. It compensated for the reverse snobbery which I found initially in some circles, and which I suspect has contributed to my lack of success in prising grants from the Scottish Arts Council.

But in the end my advice was threefold: know and respect your audiences, look after your actors, stage managers and creative team, and make sure that your product has integrity and quality. It is not easy to make theatre in rural Scotland, but it can be done.

## 29

# High Rank and (mrs) Gladys Prickle

The first cycle of the Scottish Parliament was drawing to its close. David had always said that he would only serve for that period. It had not been an easy time – the deaths of Donald Dewar and the architect Enric Moralles, the continuing nightmare of the new building, and the resignation in disgrace of Henry McLeish as Scotland's second First Minister were all unforeseen.

'What is the most influential element in politics?' the young American President, Jack Kennedy, had asked the experienced British Prime Minister Harold Macmillan.

'Events, dear boy, events,' was his reply, and there could have been none other.

It was the first time since the early years of our marriage that David and I had seen each other week in and week out. There were official engagements throughout the week and frequently at the weekends, but I was often able to go with him. Being a list MSP, there was no constituency work for David; as the Presiding Officer he had had to cut his ties with the party in Scotland. Until then, he had not realised how much he had gained from the companionship of his colleagues. He felt, for example, that he could not have a *tête à tête* dinner with his old House of Commons colleague Jim Wallace, or his position would have been suspect. ('Cosying up to the Lib Dems' would have been the reaction of Labour, SNP and the press if they had been spotted, and a conspiracy no doubt invented.)

With the death of Donald Dewar, the only old friend he had in the parliament was George Reid. It was a lonely time in some ways, and there was some personal hostility to him. In the Borders, however, there were long memories of the Boy David, of over thirty years of representation and service, and the restoration of Aikwood was seen as the bringing back to life of a part of architectural and cultural history.

Jack McConnell, the third First Minister, calculated that the average age of the MSPs in that first parliament was about 41 or 42. That meant that David had become an MP before they were even at primary school – as McConnell put it, his political courage over the years was not always remembered by this younger generation of Scottish politicians.

It was true that they (and the Scottish press, of whom there were so many accredited to the new parliament that they were having to spin stories from straw, and who were on the lookout for anything they could embroider) seemed to know nothing of his radicalism and his pioneering work during his years in the Commons. They simply saw him as an establishment figure – one, moreover, with a couple of titles and a 'castle'. Nor did they credit him with a sense of humour. On a visit to a National Trust property, we had seen merchandise bearing coronets and the legends 'His Lordship' and 'Her Ladyship'. As a joke, we had bought a pair of socks for David and an apron for me. One day, while he was having lunch at the Hub, the Edinburgh Festival's café next door to the Assembly Hall, he was aware that his neighbour at the adjacent table was staring at the socks. The following day, a story appeared to the effect that the Presiding Officer was so puffed up with his own importance that he had socks with coronets on them.

I found it all hard to thole.

We celebrated our ruby wedding during that time, but it was low-key. My sisters Joan and Fay had both lost their greatly-loved husbands in the six months before their own similar anniversaries, and I felt more than a little superstitious about it, especially after the cancer scare. So we booked in with the children and grandchildren for a family weekend at Crieff Hydro, and finished off the weekend by going back to Dunblane Cathedral for Sunday morning service and then being treated to lunch by the children. Within a month we did indeed hold a wedding anniversary party at Aikwood, but not for ourselves – it was the 400th year since the marriage of Robert Scott and Elspeth Murray, whose initials and date adorn the marriage stone in the Tower.

'Wear something glamorous from the last four centuries – or what you got married in' – were the dress instructions, and invitees were those who over the years had been a part of the tower's renaissance: Malcolm Hammond, the architect, Falconer Grieve, the joiner, Denbeigh Kirkpatrick, who as our lawyer had completed the transaction, Andrew and Anna Polwarth, the present-day heads of the Scotts of Harden, those who had been involved with the Hogg exhibition, and artists and musicians who had brought life back to the tower's walls. About fifty of us sat down to celebrate at long tables: once again, I managed to produce the meal myself from the Aikwood kitchen.

David's father had moved from his sheltered house to the residential part of a Church of Scotland complex in the Grange area of Edinburgh, where he was well looked after. But he was losing touch with everyday life: he had had to give up his car, and now even fishing had lost its eternal joy for him. Since his 90th birthday, there had been a downward spiral of his capacities, and when, in November of 2002, he went into hospital with a chest infection, he died there peacefully. At his funeral, in St Michael's Church in Linlithgow, his last parish, the coffin was adorned with a single wreath of thistles, bird-of-paradise flowers – to represent Scotland and Kenya – and lilies. Having commissioned it from the same Selkirk florist who had made Catriona's wedding bouquets, I felt there was an extra element to it that I couldn't put my finger on, that I hadn't asked for. Then I realised: it was like the crown of thorns. One of my father-in-law's great projects at St Michael's had been the restoration of a crown above the church's tower, and the artist, who had also worked on Coventry Cathedral, had taken Christ's crown of thorns as his inspiration.

His grandsons carried his coffin down the aisle, and his granddaughters processed with them. Our two eldest grandchildren, aged five and four, came as well: I hope they will remember it. I was once told that the reason for having small children as attendants at a wedding is so that they will be able to talk about it when they are old, and when all the other participants are no more. Graeme once told me he had bitterly resented the fact that we did not take him and Catriona, then aged eight and nine, to my own mother's funeral, and I believe, now, that if children are old enough to understand, they are old enough to share, and should be allowed to say their own goodbye.

David was going out to their beloved Kenya the following week, and he took half of his father's ashes with him. In Kenya, it is not the custom to scatter ashes, but to inter them, so at that time they were simply received there. He and his brother Ian, with the latter's son, Tim, their sister, Felicity, and her husband, Ken Geddes and Graeme, returned some time later for their burial at the Scots mission station in Kikuyu. At Easter, the family reconvened at St Michael's and scattered the remaining half in the churchyard.

Just after his father's death, a letter came to David with the Royal insignia, inviting him to be the Queen's Lord High Commissioner at the General Assembly the following year.

'I wish he'd known,' he said, and I was reminded of the day of his first election, when the news of his grandfather's death came. Later, at that post-funeral tea, which was as celebratory of David's election as it was a wake, his grandmother told the gathering that there had been an MP in the family before: the Labour MP James Brown, in the 1920s and 30s. She was even prouder, however, of the fact that he had also been Lord High Commissioner to the General Assembly, the first commoner to hold the office. At the time, I did not really understand what the Lord High Commissioner was, but I learned over the years, especially when, in 1974, David's father held the office of Moderator of the General Assembly. But I suspect that there are still many Scots, including churchgoers, to whom it is a cloudy mystery.

The office is one of the oldest ones in Scotland. The person appointed – and there have been a few women – becomes the sovereign's personal representative for the week of the General Assembly. Indeed, I have heard it described as the personal embodiment of the sovereign, although the status of Regent is probably a better approximation. It dates from 1580, although for the first hundred years there were only sporadic appointments. From 1690, however, the office has been in place continuously, uninterrupted even by the great wars of the twentieth century. In *The Heart of Midlothian*, Walter Scott describes it thus:

> We are now under the necessity of returning to Edinburgh, where the General Assembly was now sitting. It is well known, that some Scottish nobleman is usually deputed as High Commissioner to represent the person of the King in this convocation; that he has allowances for the purpose of maintaining a certain outward show and solemnity, and supporting the hospitality of the representative of Majesty. Whoever is distinguished by rank or office, in or near the capital, usually attend the morning levees of the Lord Commissioner, and walk with him in procession to the place where the Assembly meets.

The morning levees and the foot procession to the Assembly have long since gone. The list of appointees up till that of James Brown are indeed those of Scottish hereditary noblemen, but over recent years it has more and more become the habit to appoint those of more humble origins, on the basis of their public service. Willie Ross, one of the great Secretaries of State for Scotland, had been one of these, and so had his fellow cabinet minister, Peggy Herbison. From time to time, a member of the Royal family attends in that capacity, and twice during her reign, including in 2002, the Queen has attended in person.

By the time her invitation to David came, I was properly *au fait* with the General Assembly and the different offices attached to it. We had been the guests at Holyrood of more than one Lord High Commissioner, and I knew the formality and the splendour surrounding the incumbent. We had been caught out on the first occasion of an overnight stay by a habit of David's that I find irritatng: he always collects freebies from hotels, be they miniature soaps, shampoos, body lotions or sewing kits. I have not bought a bar of soap for decades. On our arrival at the Palace, the cases were unpacked for us, and neatly arranged on the dressing table was a long line of soaps, shampoos and every other little gimmick given away by a variety of hotels.

To be hosts in a royal palace was a daunting prospect. We would live in Holyrood House for a week, where we would be treated, liter-ally, as royalty, each of us addressed as 'Your Grace', the pre-Union Scots title of the sovereign, and where we would be expected to enter-tain continuously. We would have a 'household', headed by the Purse Bearer whose existence had been such a mystery to me all those years ago during my legal apprenticeship. (The purse is really more of a cross between a handbag and a briefcase: it is not passed down, but each Purse Bearer has his own one made and embroidered.) There would be three *aides-de-camp*, one from each of the three military services, and I would be expected to appoint up to three ladies-in-waiting: they would ensure the smooth running of each day's events, and look after the guests to the Palace.

What a scenario! Both Catriona and Lynne were too tied with young children to be my ladies-in-waiting, and in the event I decided to make do with only two: Janice Parker and my niece Kirsty MacGregor. Jan-ice and I had worked together over the years on so many projects, and I knew I could depend on her utterly; as well as being a close friend, she was also a superb stage manager, and that, I felt, was what was needed. Kirsty would provide glamour and style in bucketloads. And, unlike the days when she was four-years-old, and my mother had banned her as one of my bridesmaids on the grounds that she was too naughty, she could be relied on now not to do a handstand in church. David, meantime, had to choose a chaplain, and his father's successor both at St Andrew's Nairobi and at St Michael's, Ian Paterson, seemed the appropriate choice.

I was warned by the Purse Bearer that hats would loom large during the week. This caused some problems. For Catriona's marriage a decade ago, I had bought a very plain but beautiful straw hat in Jenners. It cost so much that I vowed it would have to last me for the rest of my life, and during that time I had more or less managed to keep to this, with the odd supplement from the charity shops in South Clerk Street in Edinburgh or in Selkirk. For Holyrood, more was expected: to be exact, a different hat every day. In the end, I managed with only three new hats (one of which was a mistake) – the others were borrowed. Janice did much of her shopping in TK Maxx and our favourite charity shops, while Kirsty found a top milliner, Yvette Jelks, who generously supplied several. I raided my cupboards for some of the lovely clothes from Jersey given to me over the years by the Dinshaws, and despite my reluctance to spend money on clothes, steeled myself to do so.

All this flurry of preparation was going on as the elections came up for the Scottish parliament. I went to the final sitting of the first parliament on 27 March. With his usual sense of what was appropriate to the occasion, David called Winnie Ewing, who had been the first person to speak when the parliament was convened, to ask the final question; then, with George Reid in the chair, there came tributes. Not for the first time during the lifetime of that first cycle of the Scottish parliament, I felt choked with emotion.

Because he was still Presiding Officer, David wasn't able to campaign during the election that followed, but I was. There was also going to be a tight fight for the parliamentary seat: this time our young candidate, Jeremy Purvis, David's last House of Commons assistant, was head to head with the SNP.

The fact that the Labour party had taken on board the need for proportional representation during the discussions of the Scottish Constitutional Convention, and had afterwards enshrined it in the Scotland Act, was a great triumph for the Lib Dems. The Additional Member System worked well in Germany, where the 'list' MPs did not interfere in the business of constituency MPs, so what happened here was not foreseen. Some candidates who had stood in constituencies had also, in a belt and braces operation, been on the regional lists. Indeed, the Tories insisted that all their list candidates also fought a constituency.

What this meant was that the winning constituency candidate found that his or her defeated rivals were still around after the election, as list

MSPs. In some cases, instead of being representatives of their party over the wider regional area, they concentrated on the seat that they had just lost, and planned to fight it again. What happened in the Borders seat was one of the worst examples of this, when a list MSP set up rival surgeries, issued a stream of press releases describing herself as 'the local MSP' and sailed close to the wind in many ways. The mild-mannered Ian Jenkins, who was the Lib Dem constituency MSP, was demoralised by her, and did not stand again. Jeremy Purvis was a tougher politician altogether, but he was not well-known. He would have to earn every vote.

For the first time, I was also actively engaged in the elections for the Borders Council. Catriona, enraged by the lack of action by her council-lor over some matter dear to her heart, had decided to stand: so had Vicky Davidson, in the ward that covers the Ettrick and Yarrow valleys. I spent the eve of poll going round Peebles with Catriona, putting out last minute leaflets and posters. As we stopped at a lamp post, an SNP placard was within easy reach. We looked at each other.

'Come on,' said my daughter. 'It's tradition.'

'It should really be a Tory one,' I said.

'There aren't any.'

So we put the SNP poster in the boot of the car, and replaced it with a Lib Dem one.

Apart from voting – and, on the list, I voted Green, a curiously liber-ating act – David and I spent the day and night of the election babysitting, and Catriona came in with the dawn. Jeremy had retained the seat, the SNP candidate had thrown a wobbly and demanded a recount, and Catriona herself had caused a bit of a diversion by behaving much as I had done at Kincardine and Deeside. In the morning we went with her for the count for the Borders Council. Both she and Vicky Davidson were returned with substantial majorities – they were a new breed altogether among the ranks of mainly rather self-satisfied and post-middle-aged men who had made up most of the Council previously.

After years of having an intimate view of the machinations of the House of Commons, and, more recently, the Scottish parliament, the political landscape I have been closest to since then has been that of the Scottish Borders Council. There must be a lesson here about shrinking horizons, but I am not sure what it is.

Before David said goodbye to the Scottish parliament, however, there was one final duty. He had to oversee the swearing in of members and the election of his successor. It was something of a rainbow parliament: seven Greens had been elected, including Chris Ballance from the south of

Scotland, and six of Tommy Sheridan's Scottish Socialist Party. Tommy Sheridan had courted expulsion from the parliamentary chamber on a regular basis over the past four years: David had managed to deny him the satisfaction. Now, his new colleagues managed to hijack the proceedings by stunts such as holding up a hand with a biro-ed message on it in the case of one of them, and another singing, rather badly, the Burns song 'A Man's a Man' that had provided such an emotional high point when the parliament was opened.

George Reid was elected as the second Presiding Officer: we foresaw that he would have a tricky time with this rowdy element. But he would have the satisfaction of seeing the opening of the new building, and the parliament settled into its permanent home. A difficult but fulfilling period in our lives was over.

The small girl in the bus queue in High Wycombe, fifty years earlier, who had been inspired by the concept of a Scottish parliament, had seen her wish come true; and if she was never going to be Scotland's first woman Prime Minister, she had at least been near to the heart of it. She certainly could not have visualised the week at Holyrood during the General Assembly.

Holyroodhouse: home of the Scottish kings since the fourteenth century, its present building begun under James V under the influence of his French queens, where Mary, Queen of Scots held court and where her devoted musician and secretary, the Italian David Rizzio, was murdered in front of her eyes by jealous Lords, and from which she escaped, seven months pregnant, to gallop to Dunbar and safety. Holyrood, finished by Charles II, the last king to be crowned in Scotland, and where his namesake, Bonnie Prince Charlie, held a premature victory ball after entering Edinburgh in triumph in 1745.

Now, we were to be within these history-laden walls for a week, the inheritors of all that history, and the representatives of today's monarch.

On James Brown's appointment as Lord High Commissioner, his wife had been asked by a neighbour, 'Kathleen, won't you get an awful shock if you meet the ghost of Mary, Queen of Scots?'

'Not half as big a shock as she'll get to see me!' was Mrs Brown's unperturbed reply.

The official car came to meet us at our flat in the not-very-fashionable area of St Leonard's. Janice waited with us: the car, when it arrived, flew the royal standard and had no registration plates. It was not far to the Palace, and as we arrived, the fountain in the forecourt was playing, and so was a military band. The staff were lined up to greet us: there was bowing and curtseying and we were taken off to our suite, past banks of flowers and through the historic rooms hung with tapestries and portraits.

The first overnight visitors were due to arrive, and at night there was a reception at which the keys of the city of Edinburgh would be handed over by the Lord Provost to the Lord High Commissioner in a symbolic ceremony. It was less difficult than I had thought to step into the role, so perfectly did all the supporting cast play their parts, and so conditioning are the surroundings of the Palace itself. It demands a certain formality, and we were kept well away from any casual interaction with our guests, even those who were old friends, except in the privacy of our suite.

As I have said, I had expected my niece Kirsty to provide glamour, and certainly she had assembled an array of hats that was sensational. What I hadn't expected was that she would also provide a love interest. One of our first overnight guests was our friend Denbeigh Kirkpatrick, now a widower. A romance began between them that night that developed into a deep love, lasting until his sudden death three years later. They had both been at many of our family gatherings before, from the time that Denbeigh was an usher at our wedding, and Kirsty was a four-year-old too naughty to be a bridesmaid, but they had never noticed each other. Now, when they did, there was an initial problem: Kirsty was not allowed to leave the Palace. She had to ask me for leave to absent herself to go on their first date. She then got locked out – something that my generation might have encountered in our student days, but a very anachronistic occurrence for a forty-year-old divorcee in the twenty-first century.

It was a fourteen-hour day, beginning with morning prayers in the drawing room next to our suite. Then there was breakfast, while a band played outside in the courtyard. The foot procession described by Walter Scott, and the horse-drawn carriage landau occupied by James Brown MP, and his predecessors and successors, had given way to a limousine and a couple of people-carriers, and where once the entourage had the traffic stopped for it, we now went in by a way that caused the least inconvenience to other vehicles, under police motor-cycle escorts.

Each morning was spent at the Assembly itself, with all its austere formality. The hymns and psalms at it are sung unaccompanied, and I recalled my first visit, the year that my father-in-law was Moderator. All the commissioners, ministers and elders, were men then, and the sound of the Old Hundredth psalm, 'All People That on Earth Do Dwell', issuing from all those male throats, was enough to make the hair bristle on the back on my neck. Flora Maxwell Stuart, a devout Catholic, confessed herself unexpectedly moved by the Protestant communion when she joined us.

There were various rituals, including a roll-call of those ministers who had died since the last assembly – David's father's name among them – and of those who had been called to the ministry, including our own splendid new parish minister in the valleys, Samuel Siroky. ('Why must Samuel *always* dress down?' despaired David. But Samuel was well-supported in his sartorial statement by his wife Esther when they came to the Palace for lunch: complementing her husband's casual dress, she was shod in Doc Martens.)

But the main business of the Assembly is its debates, and the standard of speeches is very high indeed. For centuries, until the restoration of the Scottish parliament, the General Assembly had been the nearest there was to a democratic voice for the people of Scotland. This was especially so in regard to one of its committees, the Church and Nation Committee, which delivers pronouncements on contemporary issues. It had been in the vanguard of many of the causes we had espoused over the years – Scottish self-government, abortion law reform, opposition to apartheid in South Africa. More recently, the Moderator had delivered a gentle rebuke to Mrs Thatcher when she had addressed the Assembly in her infamous 'Sermon on the Mound', by giving her a copy of the Church's report into urban poverty. I don't expect that she read it.

We would spend the morning listening to the debates at the Assembly, and then go back to the Palace, where our lunch guests would have arrived. They would assemble for drinks, then line up and we would come in and pass down the line, greeting them, while they bowed and curtseyed and called us 'Your Grace'. It was hard to keep a straight face. We were free to invite plenty of our own friends to stay during the week, but there were niceties to be observed: leading churchmen and politicians, and holders of some of the hereditary posts, had also to be invited. We had been encouraged to lighten the formality somewhat, but this didn't always go down with the latter category. A countess complained that my ladies-in-waiting didn't curtsey deeply enough – she herself would bob so low that her backside almost bumped on the floor.

After lunch, the overnight guests would depart and we would go on a visit with one of the aides-de-camp and one of the ladies-in-waiting. This might be to a church and an associated project, or to a hospital or a school or university. We went to Linlithgow, with all its associations for David, to the Rudolf Steiner community for special needs adults at Garvald, which we already knew well, and to Colinton Church where Kirsty had been baptised, and where she found a plaque commemorating her grandfather. Another day it was a centre for the homeless, and one afternoon we went by helicopter to the RAF base at Leuchars. It was a week as full of interest and variety as an election, and almost as hard work, for as in that situation, you are giving out all the time to the people you are meeting – and you are learning. By the time we returned to base each day, full of admiration for the royals who are committed by birth to take on this work unremittingly, week after week and year after year, the next overnight guests would have been greeted, given tea, and be in their rooms getting ready for the evening's formal dinner. The same pre-prandial presentations took place, and then we would preside over a table of candles, gleaming silver and banked flowers, the host and hostess in Holyrood Palace.

We brought one or two small innovations with us: usually, there was a military band at the Saturday garden party: we managed to have the Selkirk Silver Band invited to play instead. The main guests for the garden party are the commissioners, but we were also encouraged to ask as many other people as we wanted, and as we went round, it seemed as though half of Selkirk and the Ettrick Valley was there. We were able to say thank you for all the years of acceptance, tolerance, support and loyalty over the years.

Instead of a Highland piper to play at the end of dinner, deafening the diners over their coffee, we asked Dave Bunyan, who had been the master mason at Aikwood and who had played at Catriona's wedding, and his pupil Colin Turnbull, who had played in Rowan Tree's production of *Wandering Willie's Tale* a couple of years before, to play the sweet-toned small Border pipes. Many of the guests had never heard them before. I had been enthusiastic about them ever since I had first heard them some years earlier, and had persuaded Dave to take them up. He in turn had encouraged Colin.

There would sometimes be a more formal short concert after the meal, and at one of these my cousin Edith Budge sang. For our silver wedding party in the village hall in Ettrick Bridge, fifteen years previously, we had booked a local jazz band.

'I'm going to sing for you as your present,' Edith said, and we had absolutely no idea what she would be like. When she got to her feet and belted out, 'Won't You Come Home, Bill Bailey?' the whole place erupted with enthusiasm. She's a big lady, Edith, even bigger than me, and her voice comes not from her throat but from way, way down: it has all the quality and colour of a truly great jazz singer. If you closed your eyes, you could believe her to be a black American. From that evening in Kirkhope village hall onwards, in her fifties and sixties, Edith had built a career and name for herself in the Edinburgh jazz scene, and had enlivened many an occasion at Aikwood; now she was making Holyrood's tapestries and portraits resound.

We also tried to modify the sleeping arrangements. Believe it or not, guests are provided not just with a double bedroom but a 'dressing room' with a single bed. When Malcolm Rifkind, as Secretary of State for Scotland, was staying at Holyrood, his wife Edith was asked by staff, 'And will the Secretary of State be joining you for tea in bed in the morning?' We tried to free up these single rooms for single people, and it worked while we were there, but I gather that the old Victorian sleeping customs have found their way back.

After the last session of the Assembly, there is a line-up of those attending down the steps of the Assembly Hall and into the courtyard with its statue of John Knox. As the Lord High Commissioner exits for the last time, he is 'clapped out' – this was something completely new to me. Outside, the official car was waiting, with no royal standard and with normal registration plates, to take us back to Holyrood, where the fountain had stopped. We were no longer 'Your Grace', and the last night became a family party. The adventure was over: but we went back to enjoy this wonderful privilege for a second year. And by that time, we were able to look out at Enric Miralles' building, completed if not yet occupied.

One morning in 2006 I was down in Selkirk and stopped to have coffee at a café called The Jaggy Thistle. Our post had arrived while I was out, and David had dealt with it. He had left one letter propped up on the kitchen table. Again, it had the royal imprimatur at the head: it was about another kind of thistle. The Order of the Thistle, to be exact: Scotland's order of chivalry, limited to only sixteen holders at any one time, and in the personal gift of the monarch, untrammelled by politicians or committees.

'Even I'm impressed,' I said to David.

We were now introduced into a very esoteric world indeed. I knew little about the Order of the Thistle, although I knew several of its knights, and Johnnie Buccleuch was its chancellor. He phoned me the day before the announcement was made public and invited me to share a kitchen lunch with him and Jane at Bowhill, while he filled me in on some of the background details. As coffee came, they asked me for some gossip about local worthies. 'I don't really move in the same circles as you do,' I said, but a moment later remembered to tell them about the marriage break-up, a good few years before, of a very self-important local couple.

'But I think he's got a bidey-in now,' I added.

'A *what?*' chorused the Duke and Duchess of Buccleuch.

So I explained, adding, 'I did tell you I move in different circles.'

There are a few lines in Scott's epic poem *Marmion*, which describe King James IV in prayer at St Michael's church in Linlithgow during the time leading up to the battle of Flodden:

> In Katherine's aisle the monarch knelt,
> With sack-cloth shirt, and iron belt,
> And eyes with sorrow streaming;
> Around him in their stalls of state
> The Thistle's Knight-Companions sat,
> Their banners o'er them beaming.

The last three lines are purely from Scott's vivid imagination, for the Order does not go back as far as those days. It was founded in 1687 by King James VII of Scots (and II of England). In a wonderfully illustrated book about the stalls of the Thistle Chapel, Charles Burnett describes the background: '[The Order of the Thistle] was created as a political tool to enhance the Scottish heritage of the English-based Stewart Royal family . . . at a period when the Sovereign sought to re-introduce the Roman Catholic faith.'

Alas for King James VII, this policy ended in his abdication and flight; and the original knights never met in the chapel he had created specially for them at Holyrood. For two centuries, the Order was run from London, and although Queen Victoria, in her enthusiasm for all things Scots, revived interest in the Order, and tried to make a spiritual home for it by creating a purpose-built chapel, it was not until 1911 that this was actually completed. Accessed from, but independent of, St Giles Cathedral, the Thistle Chapel was designed by the great Scottish architect R.S. Lorimer, and created by Scottish craftsmen from Scottish materials. It is one of Edinburgh's lesser-known jewels, with its banners, its crests and its enamelled plates bearing the coats of arms of the knights. I had seen photos of the Knights processing for the annual St Andrews Day service, clad in their bottle-green velvet mantles, gold collars and floppy hats: that was as far as my knowledge went. If I had been diffident about the knighthood of 1991, I was bowled over by this.

But some Selkirk folk took it in a more matter of fact manner. 'Does that mean you're Mrs. Prickle now?' asked someone, after it was announced. I pounced on the name. I had felt that in my role as a cook, I needed an avatar: now I had one. I added a Christian name, and these days, especially when Aikwood is full of theatre people, it's (mrs) Gladys Prickle who labours over the Aga; and it's her name that goes on my jars of jellies and chutneys.

David's appointment came together with that of the former Labour MP, now Lord (George) Robertson of Port Ellen. Although many of their predecessors as Knights of the Thistle had served as Tory MPs, I can only find one Liberal and two Labour politicians before them. Like the Lords High Commissioner, the appointees until recently came from the ranks of the hereditary aristocracy, with very occasionally a self-made man among them; but most of those in recent years have been life peers, and several have come from academia or the law. Outside the Royal family there was only one Lady of the Thistle, Marion Kerr-Fraser.

A Knight of the Thistle is required to have all the heraldic trappings: a banner, a motto, a crest. A flat-coat retriever was David's first suggestion for the latter: I poured cold water on it. Then he tried out a peacock, because we had one at the time. The Lord Lyon was not enthusiastic: 'It has connotations of self-aggrandisement,' he said.

We were stumped. Then one day Janice Parker called us from her mobile: 'I'm just walking past Appleyard's [the Jaguar dealer in Edinburgh], and I've thought of just the right thing for David's crest. What about a leaping Jaguar?' It was a perfect suggestion.

Next was the motto. I suggested that we took a line from 'A Man's a Man', and he settled for the last line of the first verse:

> Is there for honest poverty
> That hings his head, an a' that?
> The coward slave, we pass him by –
> We dare be poor for a' that!
> For a' that, an a' that,
> Our toils obscure, an a' that,
> The rank is but the guinea's stamp,
> The man's the gowd for a' that.

Translated into Latin, it read *Vir Tamen Aurum Est*. It was a reminder not just of the day of the opening of the Scottish parliament, and not just of the great-hearted Robert Burns himself, but of those who had given him the first and greatest of all his honours, by electing him as their MP.

'You can have supporters [the figures that prop up a heraldic shield] – but they're extra,' the Lord Lyon told David: so he chose a Masai warrior to hold up one side of the shield, and a Border reiver for the other. And so we sailed on towards the day of the installation. The Queen invited us to a private lunch at Holyrood, where she gave David the insignia of the Order. We had learned somewhere of a tradition that the Lord High Commissioner should make a gift to the Queen as a thank you for staying at her palace during the week of the General Assembly. I had begun a tapestry cushion there, and decided that this was a good occasion to hand it over. She seemed genuinely pleased that it was home-made.

The solemn ceremony in St Giles installing the two new knights came and went. The usual legions of Steel family and friends had made ours a lengthy invitation list. Graeme and Lynne and the children were, as usual, rather late, and found places at the back of the church. Lynne, not a great monarchist, was bowled over when the Queen caught Hannah's eye, and gave her a lovely smile.

Next day, we had a celebration at Aikwood, the food now by courtesy of (mrs) Gladys Prickle. The dress code was 'hats', and I wore the old straw hat that our mother had brought back from Sierra Leone, which had later been her and my father's shared gardening hat.

My sister Joan was unimpressed by all the flummery, and by the final design of the coat of arms, now displayed on the wall. 'What a lot of nonsense,' she said. 'I don't know what our father would have thought. He always admired the Soviet Union; he was practically a communist. Still,' she relented, 'Granny MacGregor would have enjoyed it.'

There is nothing like friends and family to keep your feet on the ground.

## 30

# The Granny with the Jaguar Tattoo

At the party celebrating both the 70th birthday of my dear brother-in-law Jimmy, my sister Fay's husband, and the 40th birthday of Joan's daughter, Kirsty, David said to the former: 'Three score years and ten, Jimmy. Every day is a bonus now.' Within two days he had died peacefully and unexpectedly in his sleep. David agonised over his careless words, as if they had been a curse.

When the same anniversary rolled around for my sister Alison, we, her siblings, were faced with a dilemma. What do you give someone whose world has dwindled down to a ward of fellow psychiatric patients, whose possessions are stored in a locker? She was so physically frail by now that we could no longer even take her out for lunch, as we had done when she was no longer able to come and spend a few days with one or other of us. Our sisterly meetings would be in a private room at the hospital, and would not last long. Forced conversation would run out of steam rapidly – she was not interested in our activities or those of our children, and we found it difficult to work up any lengthy chat about conditions in the ward. She was well and truly institutionalised. We always left the hospital with a great feeling of sadness and hopelessness, which must have been worse for Joan and Fay who remembered the beloved little blonde sister of pre-war days. Yet sometimes she would startle me with a remark that came from that clever young girl, such as when she looked out of the window at Liff's beautifully landscaped grounds and said, irritated with herself, 'I wish I could remember the Latin name for the monkey-puzzle tree.'

Eventually I hit on the idea of marking the birthday by offering her a concert from one of my musician friends, and she showed quite a spark of enthusiasm about it. We discussed instruments, and at her request I hired a cellist. He and I arrived in Dundee on the birthday. I had asked whether she wanted to share her concert with other patients, but the answer was a very definite 'no', so there were just Alison, Fay, the cellist and me in the visitors' room as we settled down to listen. 'More Bach,' she kept saying to him, 'more Bach.'

The four MacGregor sisters met again just before Christmas 2003, when we talked to her, as the hospital had asked, about her deteriorating health. We looked forward with some dread to a painful, drawn-out end for her in the coming year; but instead, she died suddenly between Christmas and New Year. It was only then that we found out how faithful her church had been to her. Unlike the rest of us, she was a member of the Episcopal Church, not the Church of Scotland. The rector had visited her regularly over the years to give her communion – the last time, only the day before she died.

Our mourning was less for Alison's death than for her life; for all that bright promise never fulfilled.

I would like to say that our own lives settled down to a more tranquil course, but they still seemed full of things to do. Now that David's term in the Scottish parliament was complete, he travelled up and down to the House of Lords most weeks. He also involved himself again with African politics – a thankless task, I often thought; but the continent drew him back again and again as surely as it had exercised its pull on Mungo Park.

*March, 2006*

It's Sunday morning, a week or two after Charles Kennedy has been forced out of office as leader of the Lib Dems, and our good friend and contemporary Menzies Campbell is the front-runner to succeed him. David feels that Charles has been badly treated by his colleagues, and is angry with them. However, this is a day when such resentments are dissolved by the beauty of the Border countryside. David and I are driving up the ten miles or so to Ettrick Kirk, where James Hogg is buried. All around us is peace and tranquillity: in many ways, it is the same countryside and way of life that Hogg knew. To complement the rural idyll, the *Archers* omnibus edition is on the radio. I like the church services up at Ettrick: they are timed to allow me this Sunday morning ritual, even though I often find the lives of the Ambridge folk less dramatic than those of the people who live in the Ettrick Valley. And they're certainly more predictable than mine.

'It's thirty years since you stood as leader,' I ruminate. 'What energy we had then! I can't believe that Ming wants to take on the leadership at our age.' We both thought that he was making a mistake, that he should have taken the same course as Jo Grimond had in the wake of the Jeremy

Thorpe scandal. Jo had agreed to become interim party leader for a few months until things calmed down and the leadership ballot among party members was put into place. In 1976, Jo had welcomed the handover to the next generation, and for the rest of his life played the Grand Elder Statesman to great effect, not forgetting to exercise his irrepressible mischief from time to time. But Jo had already served his time as leader of the party; Ming hadn't, and now he had the opportunity to make a contribution to British politics from that position before his distinguished career in the House of Commons came to a close. Respect for him was running particularly high after his principled stand against the Iraq invasion, a time when the Lib Dems spoke for so many of their fellow citizens who were disturbed and disgusted by Blair's supine compliance with George W. Bush's foreign policy. Ming's voice in opposition to the war had been consistent and strong, despite the fact that he was receiving treatment for cancer throughout the crucial time.

So to aspire to the leadership of the party, even at the age of sixty-five, was both an understandable decision and also a very human one. Ming could not have foreseen either the disaster of his first Prime Minister's question time, nor the viciousness with which the media – and especially the cartoonists – used his elderly appearance as the butt of their ridicule. It was an episode in collective hounding by the press which was disgraceful even by their standards: if he had been black or female, they would never have dared such licence.

Increasingly, Ming's speeches at conferences and meetings, full of wisdom and principle, went unreported; journalists would persuade some hapless Lib Dem to comment on the leader's advancing years, and that would be the story. It was a dreadful indictment of the way the media operate today, and it must have been very hard for Ming to come up against such cruelty. Throughout his life, sporting, legal and political, he had earned nothing but plaudits and golden reports: now, his message was being totally obscured by the perceived image of him as the messenger. When, in autumn 2007, the new Prime Minister, Gordon Brown, decided against calling an election, Ming realised that another eighteen months of this battering would do neither him nor the party justice.

I had come down to London for a couple of days with David, and was in the taxi from Euston to the flat he shares with Atul Vahder on the south embankment of the Thames, when he called to tell me the news of Ming's abrupt resignation. We were grieved for our friend, but we had both thought that he had been ill-advised to take on the leadership in the first place.

One of the reasons for my sojourn south at that time was to attend a fundraising Diwali dinner for an Indian charity in the Mansion House. Ming was scheduled to attend it with us, but was not now coming. I was aware of a certain amount of flaffing around with place settings in my area of the table, but thought little about it, save that such a last minute kerfuffle was typically Indian. The place-card next to me bore the name, 'Mr George Chatterjee', and I wondered whether my dark-haired, rather saturnine neighbour, who joined the table slightly late, was a successful Indian businessman or film star, because these seemed to be the two main categories of guest.

'We've never met,' said Mr Chatterjee, 'because David and I weren't in the House together.'

I was so far removed from Westminster politics that I couldn't even think what house he was talking about. He tried again. 'I'm your leader,' he said. I was still stuck in the world of Bollywood movies. What on earth did he mean?

Eventually he spelled it out, as for a total political novice. 'I'm Vince Cable. I'm the deputy leader of the Lib Dems in the Commons. And now that Ming's resigned, I'm the acting leader.'

I cringed and crawled, and then I asked him if he would stand in the coming leadership election. No, he said, for two reasons. One was that, if elected, he would undoubtedly come in for the same press ridicule as Ming had, for being older and for being bald. His message would be swamped, as Ming's had been, by the ageism of the media. But also, he said, he couldn't afford it. 'It costs a lot of money to run a leadership election. Chris Huhne made money before he came into the Commons, and Nick Clegg's got rich backers. I have neither.'

I am sure that thirty years previously, when David and John Pardoe stood against each other, this was not an issue.

But Vince Cable's acting leadership did wonders for the party, and it owes him a lot for the way he repaired the leaky vessel at that time, and made it seaworthy for its new captain from the younger generation, Nick Clegg.

We now had a respite from politics. We discovered cruises. Michael Shea had for several years been a guest lecturer on cruise ships, and now, with typical generosity, he recommended his friends to the cruise companies as potential lecturers. Robin Crichton's venture into giving talks about Santa Claus on a Christmas cruise – he had made a film and written a book about this gentleman – was not a success: he and Flora hated their Caribbean expedition. 'It was obviously full of people whose family couldn't stand the thought of Christmas with them, and had packed them off on a ship instead,' they reported. I took some persuading about trying it out, and agreed only when a Baltic cruise to Stockholm, Helsinki, St Petersburg and my beloved Copenhagen was offered. On the voyage my prejudices were all swept away, although we never took to it in quite the same way as Michael and Mona, who at times seemed never to be on dry land. Michael was in great demand as an amusing raconteur about his life in the Diplomatic Service, in the Royal Household, and as a successful novelist. David spoke about his life in politics, about his great car journey from London to Capetown, and together we gave a poetry reading. On one cruise I also gave a talk about Mungo Park.

It was a real gift that Michael gave us; nothing can compare with the sights you see by ship. Perhaps the most memorable was the Easter Island Moai sculptures, rearing their stone faces away from the ocean; but I remember, too, getting up early, as the captain had suggested, to experience sailing past the archipelago of islands on the approach to Stockholm in the clear air of a Baltic dawn.

Our own seventieth birthdays were on the horizon. David had three parties for his: one in London, a formal dinner with no speeches in the village hall, and then a lunch for the younger generations of friends and family at Aikwood. My cooking alter ego, (mrs) Gladys Prickle, ducked out of the cooking on these occasions: she was beginning to feel her age. Rolf Jelnes came from Denmark, Andre Tammes from Australia, Sandy and Gina Mountford from Canada, David's schoolfriend Jim Archer from Kenya, and Norman and Maggi Hackett from France. The journey of the Hacketts was more challenging than Andre's, for Norman was by now badly incapacitated and only mobile when using a wheelchair. Immediately after the celebrations, we set off with our friends from Galashiels, David and Daphne Pratt, for a classic car rally in Spain.

As I flicked through the cruise brochure in 2008, I spotted a round-Africa cruise early in the following year. It called at Freetown, in Sierra Leone, one of those parts of West Africa where my parents had lived, but none of their daughters had set foot. 'Let's go on it,' I said. We decided to stay on the ship until it had called at Réunion, in the Indian Ocean, which our son in law Rajiv told us was the most beautiful place he had ever seen. This meant a five-week cruise, calling at such places as Sao Tome, Togoland, Ghana, Cameroon, Mozambique, Namibia, Capetown and Durban, as well as islands off the African coast, before we left the ship in Mombasa. As it turned out, it was really too long, and the latter part of it was dogged by monsoons, pirates and riots on Madagascar. We zig-zagged back and forth across the Indian Ocean, and never did see Réunion, Mauritius or Madagascar. We were more than glad to get home, but it had been a wonderful experience all told: and towards the end of it, I had come to a major decision about our future.

We knew that Aikwood was not a sensible home for septuagenarians. We had been interested in a proposed development of flats in Selkirk, but they seemed to be stuck, with nothing happening other than the demolition of the church on whose footprint they were to be built. But I felt that we had to give ourselves a date to move in a year or so. We had had twenty joyous years at Aikwood; we did not want our time there to end in inconvenience and frustration. David's cancer, and a recent fall I had had which resulted in a broken ankle, had shown us how difficult life would be there if one or other of us was incapacitated. At some sad day in the future, one of us will be on our own: Aikwood was not the place for that. Catriona in particular was keen for us to downsize; she foresaw that, as the only daughter, she would undoubtedly bear the brunt of caring for us in the future.

Somehow the cruise brought me to face this reality, and to decide that we must make this change in the next year or so. On our return, we had confirmation of what I had suspected from the emails from Rory and Vicki, whom we had left in charge of Aikwood and our very elderly and ailing cat. 'If the cat dies on your watch, you're out of the will,' I warned, but also gave my usual instructions: 'Don't bury her yourself – wrap her in muslin and put her in the freezer.'

The cat was a magic cat. She was the sleek black product of a misalliance between Pat Neil's pedigree Tonkinese female and a Selkirk tom, and I first saw her, and her siblings, in their birthplace of Pat's laundry cupboard when they were a week old. She came to us in our last year at Cherrydene, when she kept turning up mysteriously at Aikwood from time to time during the restoration, no doubt having slipped, unnoticed, into a car. When we moved in, she immediately took possession, so much so that I renamed her Michael Scott, after the wizard.

Encouraging emails from the happy couple in the tower suddenly stopped mentioning the cat, and sure enough, there was a little muslin-wrapped corpse in the freezer when we returned. She had to be given a state funeral.

I'd already arranged that my other children and all the grandchildren would come for Sunday lunch and a catch-up, so I scheduled the funeral for that afternoon. Pat and Lindsay Neil, who had bred her, were also invited, as were Robert Beaton, Janice Parker and Matthew Burgess, all of whom had acted as tower- and cat-sitters in their time and who loved her dearly.

After lunch, we wanted to tell Graeme and Catriona about our decision to leave Aikwood, so the grandchildren were sent out to dig the grave in the garden with a strict injunction against interrupting the adults. After some time a note was slipped under the door. 'Emergency. The spade has broken in half. Help. SOS. Please.'

Graeme, the most practical of our children, went out to help them. I found a nice basket tray to fit her little corpse, attached ribbons to each corner, edged the muslin with ivy leaves, and made up a snowdrop posy. 'She's definitely having a Muslim funeral,' said Graeme, and I thought, well, that's quite appropriate, because the original thirteenth-century wizard Michael Scott was an Islamic scholar among his other skills.

The grandchildren threw themselves into the funeral arrangements with such enthusiasm that they forgot to be sad about the cat. My Stow grandchildren, having been through the deaths of three ponies and two dogs, were definitely the leaders, with the pet-less Peebles family lagging behind, though not without suggestions. 'Granny, can we sing the national anthem?' asked Caledonia, impressed with the solemnity of the occasion.

The five adult mourners arrived. Janice had just flown in from Romania, and brought with her special funeral bread from that country. 'Smacks a bit of sin-eating,' I commented, 'and the cat was definitely without sin.' Though maybe some wee sleekit cow'rin tim'rous beasties would disagree.

We stood in the orchard at the grave. I explained to the children about lowering coffins into the ground and asked for volunteers to hold the ribbons with me. The Stow contingent, used to the more substantial funeral obsequies of ponies and dogs, stepped forward as one, and down into the earth went pussy.

I gave a little oration, heckled, it must be said, by David, Graeme and Lindsay Neil. Pat Neil read a lovely poem by an eighth-century Irish monk about his cat, and young David recited a silly little jingle that I used to amuse them with when they were tiny:

> Rat-tat-tat,
> Who is that,
> Only Grandma's pussy cat.

In the tradition of Highland funerals, we filled in the grave there and then. A decision was made to abandon the national anthem, and we trooped back to the kitchen for the Romanian funeral bread.

Any further discussions about our future would have to be postponed, for I came back to a full scale crisis with the new Rowan Tree production, rehearsals for which had just started. *The Lasses, O,* was our contribution to the 'Year of Homecoming', envisaged originally by the Lib-Lab Scottish government to celebrate the 250th anniversary of the birth of Robert Burns, and taken over with a vengeance by the SNP following their election in 2007. Gerda Stevenson had approached the company with a proposal that seemed to fit in perfectly with the aims of the Homecoming. Some years before she had produced, on radio, a series of five schools programmes, each featuring one of Burns' songs and using it as the theme of a story illustrating different aspects of his life. The stories were by the writer Janet Paisley, and they were told from the viewpoint of five women: the midwife who delivered him on a stormy January morning; the elderly relative who helped to bring him up, and who told the young boy tales which sparked his imagination; his mother-in-law who despised him and thwarted his marriage to Jean Armour; the daughter of a smuggler whom he arrested during his days as an exciseman, and, finally, the young neighbour who helped to nurse him when he was dying.

Now Gerda asked if Rowan Tree would take on the project of turning this into theatre, with herself playing all the women and her colleague, Gerry Mulgrew of Communicado, directing. Music would play a large part; she herself would want to take the artistic lead on this. It was a dream project, which needless to say had been turned down by the Scottish Arts Council when it had been put up by Communicado. Now, as I struggled to raise the funding for a production, it was also knocked back by the Homecoming organisation.

Once again, sponsorship and the Borders Council allowed the project to go ahead; but I came back to find that Gerry was ill and had had to resign from directing. There had also, ominously, been emails from Gerda to the ship indicating that all was not well between her and the writer. There had already been a clash over the title: Janet had settled on *The Lasses, O.* It was not a 'play' in the conventional sense, but theatre created from music and stories.

I will not go into the depressing details of what happened, but by the following week we had a new director, the wonderfully calm and even-tempered John Bett, and Janet Paisley had agreed that, given the shortened rehearsal time, we could go ahead with only four stories, not five. She had no sooner agreed to this than she obviously regretted it, and while she had to stick to the agreement for this tour, she would not give us permission to remount this near-perfect production unless we added in the smuggler's daughter again. All this went swirling around in the background, and was terribly difficult for Gerda, but within the rehearsal room, all was creative and positive as she and the three brilliant young musicians, Lilias Kinsman Blake, Rachel Newton and Seylan Baxter, laboured under John Bett's direction to breathe life into Janet Paisley's words and give voice and richly textured music to Burns' immortal songs.

*The Lasses, O* was an instant success. It benefited from the loss of the fifth monologue, which would have made it too long. Schoolchildren loved it as much as adult audiences, and Gerda's performance earned her a nomination for the Critics Awards for Theatre in Scotland as best actress. The musicians carried off the award for best use of music and sound. It was a long journey from the start of Rowan Tree, with a tree tied on to the back of our elderly caravanette as Carol Wightman and John Nichol brought that first cycle of songs and stories to village halls, to *The Lasses, O* and the CATS awards.

We could have taken the production anywhere in Scotland and any-where in the world. But Janet Paisley was intransigent: unless we added the fifth story, it was going nowhere. So it didn't. It was a terrible waste.

Rowan Tree had a second Homecoming project in the autumn, to tie in with the Scott gathering at Bowhill. Allan Massie rewrote *The Minstrel and the Shirra*. I had always felt that the title was incomprehensible to anyone outside Selkirk, whose citizens alone knew that 'Shirra' was 'Sheriff', and some of whom believed that his office as lawman in the burgh was at least as important as his literary output. After the 1991–2 production, Allan had written a novel using much of the same material, *The Ragged Lion*. This title, and new material from the novel, informed the new script, and the actor Crawford Logan – Gerda Stevenson's radio 'husband' in the Paul Temple series – came down to the Borders to play Scott. The casting could not have been bettered, and Crawford Logan's beautiful voice made each performance a treat.

And this time, the production has a future.

The designer on both of these productions was Jessica Brettle. As she leaned over her cutting table one day, a tattoo appeared on the gap of flesh between her trousers and her top.

'That's beautiful!' I said, and then a flash of inspiration came to me: 'That's what I'll do for my seventieth birthday.' I swore Jess to secrecy.

And the night before my birthday, I kept my appointment at the Selkirk tattoo parlour. I had asked the owner to tattoo a jaguar, David's heraldic crest, onto my shoulder. I cannot say that the knight himself was overjoyed at this example of my fidelity. 'Surely it's a transfer!' was his immediate reaction, and I am not sure that he really approves of it, but my teenage granddaughter India thinks it's really cool.

During the year we had been saddened to watch Michael Shea's decline. At first it showed itself by difficulty in ending sentences, then in forming them at all. He grew more and more reliant on Mona: they were inseparable in any case, but now there was an added necessity for such closeness. Despite a hip operation, she still managed to care for him in their house in Ramsay Gardens, which has almost as many stairs as Aikwood. She was worn out, but she went on valiantly supporting him and looking after him, and even managed to take him on a visit to America to see their daughter Katriona and her twins, their longed-for grandchildren. Their other daughter lives in Australia. Once again, I reflected how fortunate I was to have my family close by: now Rory and his fiancée, Vicki Fox, had made the move from London to Edinburgh as well.

Bill MacArthur hosted his own 70th birthday party in October. Mona brought Michael, a shadow of the debonair young student we'd all known, the witty and sociable man-about-town of later years, the amusing raconteur who entertained audiences on cruises worldwide. I felt honoured that Bill had placed me next to our old friend. Words were now difficult, but I held his hand a lot before he grew restless and Mona took him home. Within 48 hours of the party he died suddenly, and we all gathered again at Warriston crematorium with the many, many others whose lives he had touched, to say goodbye.

Only a few weeks later, the Steel and MacGregor families made a joyful expedition to St Michael's Church in Linlithgow, for Rory's wedding to Vicki. It was held there for a series of reasons, but to our side of the family it could not have been a better place, redolent with so many memories. Rory had borne his grandfather's coffin down that long aisle along with his brother and cousins seven years before: now he led his lovely bride. Completing full family circles is very satisfying: this made one of them; another was to come.

In the summer of 2009, the MPs' expenses scandal broke, and the reputation of politicians was at a nadir. I became dreadfully saddened by it all. I was also aware that many of the incidents related in this book could well have been meat for the pack-dogs of the modern media – and yet they all had come about with an innocence that now seemed to be lost.

We never bought property in London, but when we did so in Edinburgh, the cost of the mortgage interest was less than the rent of the tiny flat David had occupied for six months. We did not think of the flat as an increasing asset, but as somewhere we could call our own and have some privacy. All the zest seemed to have been bled out of political life; although Catriona, when she was persuaded to stand in the Dumfriesshire, Clydesdale and Tweeddale seat, the sole Tory seat in Scotland, seemed to bring back a little of the mood in which her father had first laid siege to Roxburgh, Selkirk and Peebles.

Michael Moore was now under siege in Berwickshire, Roxburgh and Selkirk. The Tory candidate who had stood against him at the last election, John Lamont, subsequently stood for Holyrood, and had unexpectedly won the seat of Roxburgh and Berwick from us at the last election. Now, the Borders seat was the top Tory target in Scotland, and they were pouring money into winning it as though there was no tomorrow. Lamont's position as an MSP ensured a constant stream of publicity in the local media. Letter after letter from him streamed through targeted doors, until a website was set up, *No! I don't want another letter from John Lamont.*

On the eve of the election, I met David McLetchie, former leader of the Scottish Tories, at an event in Edinburgh. My main contribution this time, I said, would be taking meals on wheels to Peebles to feed the family of the candidate for Dumfriesshire, Clydesdale and Tweeddale. He was scornful, with that special Tory brand of arrogance.

'You'd be better minding your own backyard,' he said. 'We're expecting to take Berwickshire, Roxburgh and Selkirk. John Lamont's very much loved in the Borders, you know.'

'I've no doubt he is – by the Tories,' I returned, 'Just as Mike Moore's very much loved by the Lib Dems.'

But his certainty made me more uneasy, and I divided my time between both constituencies, while David yo-yoed between broadcasting studios and winnable seats, or those of the Lib Dems that were under threat. He did, however, return to the grassroots with a vengeance, leafleting the whole of the village of Lillesleaf on his own.

Peter Hellyer arrived from the Middle East to give Catriona few days of his time at the start of the campaign. He threw himself into the fray with his usual gusto and efficiency, but after canvassing well-known streets, reported apathy at best, and sometimes hostility towards politics and politicians as a whole.

The first party leaders' debate took place when Peter had returned to Abu Dhabi, so he never saw the sudden shift in mood towards interest and even enthusiasm. All at once the election came alive, and it remained so. The weather helped, of course – there's nothing nicer than putting out election leaflets in the sunshine, nothing worse than doing it in cold, wet conditions. I'm not a great walker, but give me a sheaf of election literature and a council house estate and I'll trot round as happy as Larry.

I rediscovered the delights of Burnfoot, the largest council estate in Hawick. Although I was really delivering leaflets, I also made some contact with electors, in between getting my fingers nipped by one dog and another attempting, with loud baying, to break a door down to attack me. I had recruited Rolf Jelnes, across in Scotland for my birthday celebrations, to expand his knowledge of Scottish life.

A woman said to me, 'Are you something to do with the MP?'

I admitted to it.

'There's some information I want.'

'I'll try to help you. What is it?'

'How can I vote BNP?'

'You can't,' I said, 'there's no BNP candidate on the ballot paper.' Before I turned away, I added, 'But if you want to vote BNP, I wouldn't even *consider* voting Lib Dem. UKIP's your nearest.'

I *will not* scrounge for votes, any more than when, in the wafer-thin election of 1970, I told a voter, 'If those are your views, David wouldn't want your vote anyway.'

At the last house, we encountered the SNP candidate with a wonderful, feisty couple of voters, a retired bus driver with a zimmer and his wife, a woman near my age with long blonde dyed hair. Paul Wheelhouse, the candidate, and I engaged in debate with them, both of us determined to be the last on the doorstep, while the SNP agent and Rolf watched, the latter amused by the *pas de deux* between us.

My party was a supper at my old haunt, the Cross Keys in Ettrick Bridge. I had on the dress I wore for the similar celebrations ten years ago, the christening shawl knitted in the 1960s by my poor dead sister Alison, and the bracelet that my mother gave me which is made from her father's watch chain. Among its charms is the disc of New Zealand gold dust which Fay brought me back from her first visit there, so there was something to link me with all those who were at Devon Lodge in Dollar on the day of my birth seventy years ago. My Swarkowski tiara got a rare outing, and with it on my head I was neither (mrs) Gladys Prickle (cook and thespian landlady), nor Maria Rankin (costume designer and maker), nor Maxie Austin (transport manager and chauffeuse), nor Wilde MacGregor (occasional poet, sometime political blogger and potential future author of historical bodice-rippers). For this evening, I was definitely the Lady Steel of Aikwood.

There could have been no better place to have the party than the Cross Keys, so much a part of my life during the Cherrydene years. We were crammed into the dining room of the pub – 28 of us, divided almost equally between friends and family, is more or less the complete limit of the room's capacity. The hubbub of noise never stopped.

Despite my plea for 'no presents', there was a healthy pile of them. The cake was the top half of the one that my sister-in-law Judith made for David's 70th two years ago – her finely detailed decorations of his coat of arms, motto and crest (the same that now appears on my shoulder) were still in pristine condition, and the cake itself had matured well. Bill Goodburn proposed my health in a wonderful McGonagall-like poem composed by the absent Ann, originally for my 60th birthday and now added to for the 70th. First, though, he marked 'absent friends', and I thought especially of Fay, in New Zealand recovering from a bad car crash, and of Denbeigh Kirkpatrick and Michael Shea, who had shared so many similar occasions with us and will never do so again. Bill had undertaken the same duty at my 21st birthday party in the Beehive Inn in the Grassmarket. I warned him that he was down in my instructions for my funeral oration, if he survives me – Denbeigh, the alternative, was now out of the running.

'But I read a nice poem for him at his funeral,' I said.

'Would you do one for me, if I go first? One of your own?' asked Bill, who had had a triple-heart-bypass operation about eighteen months ago. I retrieved 'Michael Scott's Benediction' from my *Aikwood Cycle* out of my memory bank, and we settled on that.

> Have I lived here before?
> Perhaps. Perhaps we all have,
> Who can tell?
> All we can do is hazard hopeful guesses,
> And let our minds go questioning afar,
> And not to fear what we don't understand,

And make our own creations:
As we have.

I gave my reply to McGonagall/Goodburn from my scrappy notes. I
realised, while compiling them, how the friends gathered there that night
had each played, not one, but several parts in my life's history. I gave
thanks to them, and to all my family who were with me that night, but
by mistake I left one person out – David!

It was time to go home and leave the room to the pub regulars who
were crammed into the rest of the accommodation. I showed the tattoo
to selected friends from the valley as we went out. Some took photos,
and all of them had a good laugh.

But the evening's festivities were not finished. My Tory poster
improvement kit needed to be tested. Rolf drove Janice and me over the
hill to Ashkirk where I made the first sortie to one of the huge billboards.

### TORY POSTER IMPROVEMENT PACK
### CONTENTS:

1. 2 pieces of yellow card with blutack.
2. 1 roll of white sticky tape.
3. 1 roll of blue sticky tape.
4. 12-inch ruler.
5. Small pair of scissors.

### STEP-BY-STEP INSTRUCTIONS FOR IMPROVEMENT

*1. Cut one 12-inch length of white tape and leave it loosely attached
to one side of the ruler. Tuck cut edge left on roll of tape under about
1/8 inch to make it easier to pull off the next length, when you
should trim off the doubled edge before measuring.*

*2. Cut two 4-inch lengths of blue tape and attach loosely to the other
side.*

*3. Drive to poster site.*

*4. Park your car and stick the yellow cards over your number plates
(optional).*

*5. Approach poster, peel off white tape carefully and stick it across the
letter 'O' just above the mid-way point.*

*6. Stick blue tape just above and below white tape, on right hand
side of the 'O'. THE WORD 'LAMONT' WILL NOW
READ 'LAMENT'.*

7. *Return to car.*

8. *Remove yellow card from number plate, if used.*

9. *Drive on to next Tory poster and repeat the manoeuvre.*

With only a few hiccups, our mission was accomplished, and we returned to Aikwood, to David and to the log fire and wine in the Great Hall. I reflected that being seventy allowed much leeway for eccentricity!

# Epilogue

When we had thought about an inevitable move from Aikwood, we first had to make a decision about where we would move to. It would be either Peebles or Selkirk. Peebles, as well as having many friends, four of our grandchildren (and their parents), the Eastgate Theatre and nearness to Edinburgh, obviously had many attractions. Selkirk only has the first of these, but it had been our market town during the Cherrydene years, our children had been to the high school there, and since the move to Aikwood we had found ourselves more and more integrated into the town.

Catriona and Rajiv would have liked us to come to Peebles, but in the end it was our daughter who made the decision for us, when she made the comment: 'In Selkirk, you'll always be David and Judy. Anywhere else, you're likely to be called Lord and Lady Steel, or Sir David.'

She was right. It's not wise to transplant old trees: they don't flourish.

When we had seen the plans for a block of flats to be built on the site of an old church, next to the magnificent building of Selkirk Sheriff Court, almost in the town centre, and with views over the surrounding country, it seemed an ideal location. We were keen on what we saw of the plans, which were very much of the Prince Charles' school of architecture at the front, but had large windows to the back with views to the hills. Amazingly, for Selkirk, there was no opposition to the granting of planning permission. The flats were on the small side, and so we put our names down for two adjoining ones, despite the fact that Catriona had warned us about problems the Council planning department had previously had with the developers.

The months and years dragged on, and although eventually the church was pulled down, nothing else was happening on the site. That had suited us very well while the move from Aikwood was a distant possibility, but now we had made up our minds that it should be within the next couple of years. Still, a penthouse flat with a lift in it, in the new development, was very much what we had in mind: maybe we would have to rent somewhere in the meantime, until they were built.

Then, towards the end of 2009, I spotted that a flat in the Victorian mansion on the other side of the Sheriff Court was for sale. 'Let's go and look at the views,' I said. 'They'll be almost the same as the new flats will have.'

We arranged to meet the lawyers and went up the rather unprepossessing stair, testimony to a cut-price 1960–70s conversion. The front door opened and we were met with a flood of light. The lawyer led us into the living room.

'There's something in here that you'll want to ask a question about,' he said.

I didn't have to. The feature was a fireplace with a window above it. I had only seen one like this before: it had been in my teenage home outside Dunblane, now demolished in favour of a luxury bungalow. I was delighted at this reminder.

'I know what we're meant to ask,' I said. 'We're meant to ask: where does the chimney go? And the answer is, it takes two right-angled bends.'

The decor in the flat was terrible, but the views were indeed magnificent. All four main rooms were of a decent size, all had the same fireplace-and-window feature, and off one of them there was a funny little turret. The flat had an attractive eccentricity to it. I noticed that David had become very thoughtful.

On the way home, he said, 'What did you think of it?' and I knew he was not talking about the views.

'I think,' I said, 'that we could be very comfortable and happy there together, and that, in time, one of us wouldn't rattle around in it too much.'

We had had another Cherrydene moment. We bought the flat, and found out that the house had been built for the Selkirk historian Thomas Craig Brown. And it is another restoration job.

Meantime, Rory had come to us with the proposition that he and Vicki should buy Aikwood from us and run it as a small conference centre/exclusive-use let/wedding venue. We hope that this will come about, although, as with the flat in Selkirk, there's a lot of work to be done.

*May 2010*

The election has come and gone. In Scotland, there's a two percent swing to Labour – brought about, I believe, from my doorstep experiences, partly as a reaction to the hounding of Gordon Brown by the media, a blood-sport that does not go down well among his fellow Scots. Not a single seat changes hands. In Berwickshire, Roxburgh and Selkirk, Michael Moore's majority is exactly the same as before, despite the vastly superior Tory money and manpower. Catriona has increased the Lib

Dem vote in Dumfriesshire, Clydesdale and Tweeddale, and has won every ballot box in the last-named, but she has failed to overtake Labour in second place, However, her feisty, old-fashioned campaign has rattled the local Tories badly, and left them spiteful and venomous towards her. Within a couple of months those who are on the Borders Council – in a coalition administration with the Liberals – gang up with the Independent and SNP councillors to remove her from her position as portfolio holder for education. She is shaken by the vindictiveness and the timing of their attack, but she is made of tough stuff.

Nationally, however, we have to learn to think of the Tories as comrades and not as the enemy. The events unfold for us amid the surreal, beautiful surroundings of the Buccleuchs' Northamptonshire home, Boughton, 'The English Versailles'. I am there to attend a meeting at which the two Buccleuch Trusts – the Buccleuch Heritage Trust, of which I've been a trustee for about twenty years, and the Living Landscape Trust, based down here at Boughton – are to be merged into one. They will become the Buccleuch Living Heritage Trust, which will have the responsibility for the educational and public aspects of four magnificent houses: Boughton itself, and, in Scotland, Drumlanrig in Dumfriesshire, Dalkeith Palace outside Edinburgh, and Bowhill, neighbouring us in Ettrick Forest.

The 10th Duke and Duchess, Richard and Elizabeth, have turned the meeting into a house party to coincide with one of the schools' open days at Boughton. They are reinstating the old water system at Boughton from eighteenth-century plans, but not forgetting to commission a magnificent twenty-first-century feature by the landscape architect Kim Wilkie. Richard shows us the glories of this part of his inheritance: and over the couple of days that we are there, while his daughter teases him gently that he is like 'a tour guide on speed', news of party negotiations filters through to us via David's mobile phone and the TV news bulletins. Eventually it is confirmed that the Tories and Lib Dems have formed a coalition government at Westminster, and Nick Clegg is Deputy Prime Minister. David's call to his party to 'Go back to your constituencies and prepare for government' was nearly three decades premature, and our coalition partners are not the expected ones: but, as with self-government for Scotland, as with democracy in South Africa, it has happened. The Lib Dems are in government.

The Lord and Lady Steel of Aikwood hold a dinner in their home which has seen so many political gatherings over the last twenty years. The guests are Archy and Ro Kirkwood, now the Lord and Lady Kirkwood of Kirkhope, the MSPs Jeremy Purvis and Jim Hume, the councillors and Scottish Parliament aspirants Vicky Davidson and our daughter Catriona Bhatia – and the Secretary of State for Scotland, the MP for the Borders, Michael Moore. All of them, not just Catriona, are David's political inheritors.

I had been apprehensive about reaching my three-score years and ten. In January of 2010, I was prevented from going to France to work on this memoir by the snow, and became trapped in Aikwood for two or three weeks. Writing in a mainly unused room (it's the one that we think might be the haunted 'Jingler's Room') at a table which had belonged to Granny MacGregor, and on which, as a teenager, I'd done my school homework, I wrestled with memories, some of which had been consigned to the basement of my emotions. Attacked by cabin fever and Seasonal Affective Disorder, I went into one of my downward spirals.

Then, in an early foray to Selkirk, I encountered a familiar face at the petrol station. Michael was Billy's elder brother; I had first known him through his appearances before the Childrens' Panel. His road to adulthood had been a rough one, but he became a frequent visitor to his brother at Cherrydene, and when he went to London to make a fresh start, we saw something of him then. He acted as chauffeur when he drove us to the wedding of Prince Andrew and Fergie. For the last few years he'd been living in Selkirk, and we'd met up with him at the last Common Riding. Now, he greeted me enthusiastically, but I was in no mood to respond, and to his questions about what I was doing currently, gave very negative replies, blaming the approaching anniversary.

Two days later, I found tucked into my windscreen an envelope with the following letter: I reproduce it with Michael's permission, with his own idiosyncratic grammar and spelling.

*Hi Judy*

*It was nice seeing you again at the garage in Selkirk. But I felt you didn't want to speak . . .*

*It sadden me to hear from you to say your "70" and was giving up everything. The woman that gave me inspiration in horse riding, Painting, and life in genarl.*

*I'm so in your debt.*

*But when I seen your sad little face the other day it got me thinking off all the things I done with David and yourself. And to me they are very special and good times.*

*Judy I know I'm not the best person to take advice of. But you have still got so much to give.*

*When you speak about the Arts there's so much energy there. And so many ideals.*

*Rememebr when you took me to that opening night in London I can't remember the artist name but you spoke with so much energy I could have listened to you all night explaining the works.*

*I miss all that but we all have to take the good out off life. And learn from it.*

*At the end of the day Judy when you strip life down only the memories are left. And all my memories with the Steel family were great. And yourself: 70 is still young its how you feel inside.*

*I do hope you can understand my letter Judy I just had to sit down and write it.*

*Lots of hugs*
*Forever in your debt*
*Mike*

Now I will be forever in Michael's debt, for the heart and sustenance that his letter gave me, and for its lesson in how the arts fulfil a yearning in the human soul in a way that is universal. And for his challenge: that every decade brings its opportunities.

There are new skills to learn: I have started, for the first time in my life, to go to a choir. I, who was always derided as being tone-deaf, and who can't really read music, but who has always loved singing in company, am now getting a kick out of singing in parts. I think I am an alto, but I am not quite sure. It is the kind of choir that is set up for enjoyment, not for high art.

I am determined to fulfil an ambition originally scheduled for my too-busy sixties, which is to learn to ride side-saddle. Now that Clever Clogs and I are both rather arthritic, I may buy a Highland pony, like the first, much-loved pony of my teens.

A few weeks ago, for the first time in my life, I saw an otter, scampering along the verge of the Ettrick road. There are many sights and experiences to look forward to, as well as much to look back on.

# INDEX